CW00734718

# PEOPLE, MANAGEMENT AND ORGANIZATIONS

## ANNA SUTTON

macmillan international HIGHER EDUCATION

palgrave

© Anna Sutton 2018

All rights reserved. No reproduction, copy or transmission of this
publication may be made without written permission.

No portion of this publication may be reproduced, copied or transmitted save with
written permission or in accordance with the provisions of the Copyright, Designs and
Patents Act 1988, or under the terms of any licence permitting limited copying issued by
the Copyright Licensing Agency, Saffron House, 6–10 Kirby Street, London EC1N 8TS.

Any person who does any unauthorized act in relation to this publication may be liable
to criminal prosecution and civil claims for damages.

The author has asserted her right to be identified as the author of this work in
accordance with the Copyright, Designs and Patents Act 1988.

First published 2018 by
PALGRAVE

Palgrave in the UK is an imprint of Macmillan Publishers Limited, registered in
England, company number 785998, of 4 Crinan Street, London, N1 9XW.

Palgrave® and Macmillan® are registered trademarks in the United States, the
United Kingdom, Europe and other countries.

ISBN 978–1–137–60504–7 paperback

This book is printed on paper suitable for recycling and made from fully managed and
sustained forest sources. Logging, pulping and manufacturing processes are expected
to conform to the environmental regulations of the country of origin.

A catalogue record for this book is available from the British Library.

A catalog record for this book is available from the Library of Congress.

Printed and bound in Great Britain by Bell and Bain Ltd, Glasgow

# DEDICATION

To my OB/HRM colleagues and friends at Manchester Metropolitan University,
especially Sarah, Andrew and David. Teaching with you has been a privilege:
your enthusiasm for your subjects and genuine concern for students'
learning and growth are a continuing source of encouragement.

# BRIEF CONTENTS

# CONTENTS

# 4 PART 4: SUSTAINING ORGANIZATIONAL EFFECTIVENESS 220

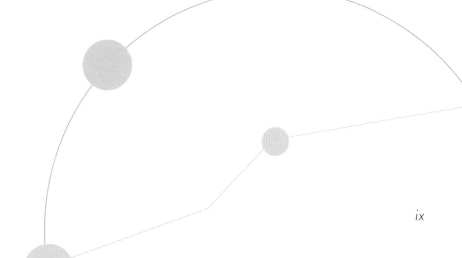

# LIST OF FIGURES AND TABLES

## Figures

## Tables

# ABOUT THE AUTHOR

Anna Sutton is a Senior Lecturer at the University of Waikato, specializing in the application of psychology to understanding and improving work and workplaces. She was previously a Senior Lecturer in the Business School at Manchester Metropolitan University, leading modules in Organizational Behaviour and Human Resource Management for undergraduate and postgraduate students. Prior to this, she lectured in occupational psychology at Leeds Metropolitan University on the BSc (Hons) Psychology programmes.

With experience working in HR, Anna is also a Chartered Psychologist, Associate Fellow of the British Psychological Society and Fellow of the Higher Education Academy. Her consultancy work involves using personality psychology to encourage individuals and teams to develop self-awareness, improve communication and enhance their teamworking. Anna's research and publications centre on the role of personality at work and particularly how the development of self-awareness can impact on our work lives and well-being. In addition, she has engaged in research projects that explore teaching-related issues, such as students' understanding of plagiarism and the research–teaching link at universities. She is also the author of *Work Psychology in Action* (Palgrave, 2015).

Julian Perkins

# ABOUT THIS BOOK

Human Resource Management (HRM) and Organizational Behaviour (OB) are closely allied topics, both concerned with how people behave at work and the best ways to manage for individual and organizational success. Yet, they are often studied entirely independently, meaning that, at best, we may find ourselves repeating topics from slightly different angles or, at worst, we simply miss out on all the ways the two subjects can inform one another. Instead, I believe that we can truly benefit from seeing how the insights and applications from both subjects can be combined, which is what this book does. It takes an integrative approach, drawing on HRM and OB to provide you, as future managers or HR practitioners, with a solid, detailed understanding of how to apply your knowledge to managing people at work. In addition, I've endeavoured to put the 'human' at the centre of Human Resource Management and consider organizations as groups of people providing a humane and balanced view of the business world.

## ORGANIZATION OF THE BOOK

This book is organized in such a way that if you read from beginning to end you will be guided through the concepts and issues in a logical pattern: from past to future and from individual to organizational level, as illustrated in Figure I. It is always helpful when learning a new topic to be able to see how it is immediately relevant or useful to us. So, we start with issues that are directly relevant to each of us as employees, such as selection procedures and our relationships with our managers or subordinates, and then move on to consider the wider issues of organizational effectiveness and sustainability.

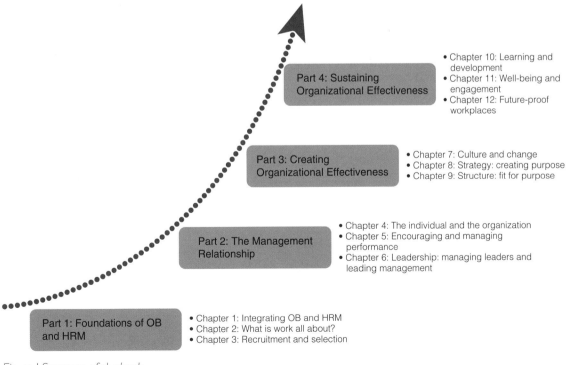

*Figure I Structure of the book*

The book is divided into four parts, each of which has an introduction to the main themes of the chapters it contains and is concluded by a case study to illustrate and explore the key issues.

## Part 1: Foundations of OB and HRM

Chapter 1 begins with a discussion of the history and background of OB and HRM to provide the context for current theories and applications covered later in the book. We move on to consider the wider issue of what work is all about in Chapter 2. It is important to clarify these basic concepts early on: for example, if we do not have a clear grasp of what 'work' actually is and why people might want to do it, how can we evaluate different motivational theories for ways to encourage employees to work harder? Chapter 3 introduces the essential elements of recruitment and selection – the basic tasks an organization has to complete in order to bring employees in.

Case study: Care workers

## Part 2: The management relationship

Once employees are in place within the organization, the next important consideration is the central role of the management relationship. In Chapter 4, we start by looking at the role of contracts, communication and trust in building that relationship and then, in Chapter 5, move on to consider how performance at work can be encouraged and managed. Part 2 ends with a detailed discussion of leadership in Chapter 6, which provides a bridge to considering wider organizational issues, such as strategy and structure, in Part 3.

Case study: Social CEOs

## Part 3: Creating organizational effectiveness

The discussions of ways of managing individual effectiveness in Parts 1 and 2 lead us quite naturally into considerations of organizational-level issues that can determine success and failure. We start with Chapter 7 on culture and change, looking at how culture can be a source of opportunity and challenge for the organization. Chapter 8 considers the critical role of strategy, engaging with discussions over how HR and organizational strategies can be aligned. Finally, Chapter 9 brings Part 3 together with an evaluation of the role of structure in helping to make the organization fit for its purpose.

Case study: From startup to scaleup: Tala

## Part 4: Sustaining organizational effectiveness

In Part 4, we turn to the future, looking at ways we can ensure the organization survives. Chapter 10 considers the essential role of individual and organizational learning and development. Chapter 11 makes the case for employee engagement and well-being as being an essential component of long-term sustained success. Chapter 12 draws the book to a close by considering the wider issue of how we define organizational success and the role of research in helping us to create future-proof workplaces.

Case study: The end of the circus?

Alongside this structured organization, throughout the book you will also find links between the chapters: this is important to help you understand the subject as an integrated whole rather than as isolated topics. For example, the role of pay or financial reward at work is considered in Chapter 2 (the meaning of work), Chapter 5 (motivation) and Chapter 6 (CEO pay and leadership).

Finally, at the end of the book you will find the Glossary, which provides brief, clear definitions of the technical terms and main theories used throughout the book.

# CHAPTER FEATURES AND ACTIVITIES

There are many different features and activities in this book, which are designed to help you learn the material and see its relevance to your practice as a manager or HR professional. The activities focus on application and developing transferrable skills, all within an international context that reflects our current working environment.

## INTERNATIONAL PERSPECTIVE

In our increasingly globalized business world, it is important to be aware of cultural and national differences. Careful consideration of these differences is an important element in determining the success or failure of management initiatives or HR programmes. We can also gain new perspectives on our work and organizations by seeing how things are done in other countries. In this book, there are many international examples embedded in the text and there are also specific activities, extended discussions or case studies that are based in different countries.

## APPLICATION AS AN ESSENTIAL

The *application* of subject-specific knowledge to the real world of work is often the most useful element of university study and, simultaneously, the most challenging. So, in this book, I have developed a range of features to help you apply and use the theories we cover. From short case studies to activities exploring the range of resources on the web, to discussions of HRM and OB topics in the news, each chapter makes the link from theory to practice that bit easier.

| Chapter | Applications | Weighing the Evidence | Web Explorer | In the News |
|---------|--------------|----------------------|--------------|-------------|
| **1** Integrating OB and HRM | 1. Why study OB? 2. Humans or resources? 3. Analytical HRM 4. Measuring performance | Are happy workers productive? | Professional bodies and reflective practice | HRM principles and national governments |
| **2** What is work all about? | 1. What is work? 2. More pay, less work? 3. The centrality of work 4. Emotional labour | We all just want an easy life | Attracting volunteers | Unconditional basic income |
| **3** Recruitment and selection | 1. PEST analysis for workforce planning 2. Writing a competency-based job description 3. Personality at work | Racial and sex differences in intellectual ability | Migrant or expat? | Ageist selection? |
| **4** The individual and the organization | 1. The psychological contract 2. Trust at work 3. Communicating difficult messages 4. Informal networks and rumour | High commitment HR practices | Workers vs management | Uber and the gig economy |
| **5** Encouraging and managing performance | 1. Hiring motivated people 2. Job crafting 3. Flexible and voluntary benefits | Does performance management deliver? | Total rewards | Instant performance feedback |

| Chapter | Applications | Weighing the Evidence | Web Explorer | In the News |
|---|---|---|---|---|
| **6** Leadership: managing leaders and leading management | 1. Should all managers be leaders? 2. Leading in a new context 3. Managing leaders | Leadership is inherently moral | How to be a good leader | Volkswagen cheats emissions tests |
| **7** Culture and change | 1. Future changes 2. Communicating change 3. Action research in action | Can we plan change? | Espoused values | Organizational culture clash |
| **8** Strategy: creating purpose | 1. Thinking differently 2. SWOT analysis 3. Developing HR strategy | Strategy as practice | How unique are HR strategies? | SHRM failure? |
| **9** Structure: fit for purpose | 1. HR professionals 2. Strategic design? 3. Developing participation in NGOs | Bureaucratic or bureaupathic? | Organizational charts | Self-managed organizations |
| **10** Learning and development | 1. Using rewards to change behaviour 2. Does personality affect how we learn? 3. Managing your own CPD | Are learning organizations real? | E-learning | Project ECHO |
| **11** Well-being and engagement | 1. Preventing workplace violence 2. International H&S 3. Work friends | Well-being is good for business | EAPs | Technology and workaholism |
| **12** Future-proof workplaces | 1. HR information systems 2. Research implications 3. Greening HRM | A shareholder view in the public sector? | Inspirational management talks | Paid parental leave |

# DEVELOPING TRANSFERRABLE SKILLS

Transferrable skills are increasingly essential in managing our own careers. It is no longer enough when seeking employment to be able to demonstrate university-level expert subject knowledge. Instead, employers are looking for people who can hit the ground running and have a range of practical skills. In addition, organizations expect their managers and employees to stay up to date with current practice and emerging trends. This book is designed to help you to do just this: in each chapter, there is a detailed activity for developing a specific transferrable skill. You develop the skill within the context of that chapter's topic but are given guidance on how to practise it and use it in new situations. You may find it helpful to collect your work and reflections on these activities into a portfolio, which you can draw on when preparing for selection or promotion events. The list of these skills is given below.

| Chapter | Transferrable skill |
|---|---|
| 1. Integrating OB and HRM | Identifying underlying assumptions |
| 2. What is work all about? | Critical thinking |
| 3. Recruitment and selection | Interview skills |
| 4. The individual and the organization | Negotiation |
| 5. Encouraging and managing performance | Holding a performance conversation |
| 6. Leadership: managing leaders and leading management | Leading a group |
| 7. Culture and change | Dealing with change |
| 8. Strategy: creating purpose | Scenario planning |
| 9. Structure: fit for purpose | Analysing organizational function |
| 10. Learning and development | Designing a training programme |
| 11. Well-being and engagement | Enhancing engagement |
| 12. Future-proof workplaces | Reading original research |

# INSIGHTS FROM PRACTICE

One of the exciting features of this textbook is Practice Insights: a range of video interviews with practitioners, managers, consultants and others, each associated with a specific chapter. In the videos, the interviewees talk about their experience with the topic of that chapter, as well as give some insight into their career paths to help illustrate the variety of careers that are available to students in this area.

| Chapter | Interviewee job title | Topic of video | Country |
|---|---|---|---|
| 1. | Jennifer Dootson: Part-time HRM student and HR Business Partner | Studying HRM and OB | UK |
| 2. | Carrie McKenzie: Voluntary Services Manager at a large hospital | Managing volunteers | UK |
| 3. | Kirsten Henderson: Recruitment Consultant | International recruitment | New Zealand |
| 4. | Mark Harcourt: Professor of Strategy and HRM | Employment relationship | New Zealand |
| 5. | Roger Longden: Performance Management Consultant | Advances in performance management | UK |
| 6. | Claudia Nario: Leadership Development Consultant | Leadership development | Spain |
| 7. | Rebecca Lencho: HR Manager | Managing culture and change | USA |
| 8. | Kris DeLano: Corporate HR Director | Organizational and HR strategy | USA |
| 9. | Darren Cook: Director of a film company | Networks and informal organizational structures | UK |
| 10. | Paul Walsh: Learning and Development Specialist | Learning and training at work | UK |
| 11. | Ginger Chen: Senior HR Manager | Employee engagement | Taiwan |
| 12. | Lara Montefiori: Head of Psychology at a game-based assessment company | Gamification and using research | UK |

# ONLINE RESOURCES

There are further resources and activities to support your learning available on the companion website, including video introductions to each chapter and multiple choice questions to test your understanding, as well as the Practice Insights videos related to each chapter. See Online resources on p.xx for further details.

# TOUR OF THE BOOK

Every chapter has a range of interactive activities and the majority are designed in such a way that you can work through them alone or in a study group.

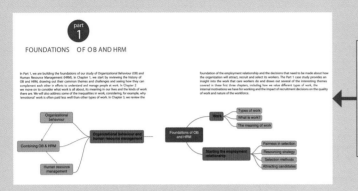

## PART AND CHAPTER MIND MAPS
A diagrammatic overview of the topics covered and how they all link together. These can also be a useful revision aid.

## APPLICATIONS
Case studies, work scenarios and questions to help you apply what you have learnt to real-life situations.

 Applications: **What is work?**

Write a list of everything you did yesterday. Now go through each item and mark it as 'work' or 'not work'.

Compare your list to a colleague's or friend's. What kinds of things do each of you view as work? Consider issues such as whether the activity has to be paid and whether studying or household tasks like grocery shopping and cleaning count as work. Where you have similarities or differences in your definitions of work, explore your reasons. What does this tell you about your underlying beliefs of what work is?

 **Video overview**

 Go online to www.macmillanihe.com/sutton-people to access a video of Anna Sutton introducing the chapter's main themes.

 Web Explorer: **Workers vs management**

It is common for workplace disputes to be couched in terms of workers versus management and for trade unions to be thought of as fighting *for* workers *against* management. But what of the actual managers? They are employees of the organization just as much as non-managerial workers and they too may find that their interests do not coincide perfectly with those of the organization. Are they able to join a union to have collective representation? In fact, several unions do include managers in their membership alongside other professionals, and

- Pro
  and
Read t
these

- Wh
  go a
- Hov
  mer
- Wh

## VIDEO OVERVIEW
An introduction to the main chapter topics and themes from Anna Sutton, the author.

## WEB EXPLORER
Suggest ways to explore online content related to the chapter and encourage wider discussion and application of chapter concepts.

## WEIGHING THE EVIDENCE
Focus on a key debate related to the topic of the chapter and examine different viewpoints and research findings, providing an up-to-date evidence-based conclusion.

 Weighing the Evidence: **Are happy work**

It is a commonly held belief that we work better when we are happier in our jobs. Much of the current emphasis on well-being at work or promoting job satisfaction rests on an unspoken assumption that if we can help people feel more positive at work, they will be more productive. But how true is this? It is a question that has long interested both HRM and OB researchers and there are hundreds of studies investigating the link between job satisfaction and performance.

A significant review of this published research has given us a fairly definitive answer: there is a correlation of about 0.3 between job satisfaction and performance (Judge et al., 2001). While not very large, this is a significant association and the relationship is stronger for more complex jobs than it is for simpler jobs. However, one of the difficulties in understanding this relationship

is
goe
sect
per
us v
vice

rese
that
up
atti
In a
out
was
effe
reve
it d
imp

## IN THE NEWS
Reflect on OB and HRM issues that have hit the news around the world, which help to illustrate the content of the chapter and stimulate discussion.

 In the News: **Unconditional basic income**

At first glance, unconditional basic income (UBI) sounds like a utopian and unrealistic idea: pay everyone enough to meet their basic costs of living, regardless of their other income, employment status or any other factor. It is an idea that dates back centuries but has recently been making the news all over again. Switzerland held a referendum on introducing UBI in June 2016 and the majority (77%) rejected it. But Finland and some Dutch cities are starting to experiment with it by stopping the means-testing of benefits payments, essentially giving claimants a basic amount of money each

with having a variety of c 2016). It is gaining po particularly Silicon Vall suggesting it is a way to increasingly automated With estimates suggesti and a third of all jobs in be automated within 20 suggested that UBI is th future.

**For discussion**

 Transferrable Skills: **Holding a performance conversation**

As we've seen, conversations about performance at work are among the most important tasks a manager can have, yet are also often avoided. In this activity, you will practise your skills at doing this. It is inspired by advice given by ACAS (the Advisory, Conciliation and Arbitration Service), an organization focused on improving workplace relations and with many years' experience in dealing with difficult conversations. More details can be found at www.acas.org.uk/index. aspx?articleid=3799.

There are three practical steps you can take to make difficult conversations a little easier:

addressing poor perform impact on the organiza lower the morale of oth

2. Prepare: This involves ga you need and planning h problem. Start by estab evidence is there of t What were the emplo they made aware of t what you know abou there extenuating fact problem? Finally, che

## TRANSFERRABLE SKILLS
Offer a guided activity to help you develop a key practical skill that will enhance your employability as well as help you in your wider university studies.

## END OF CHAPTER SUMMARIES
Recap key ideas and topics discussed in the chapter.

 Practice Insights: Rebecca Lencho

Rebecca Lencho is a Human Resources Manager at Rockline Industries, an American manufacturing company with five sites in the USA as well as locations in the UK and China. She is based at the Springdale, Arkansas site. In the video she talks about the range of tasks she undertakes as a general HR manager as well as sharing insights into managing culture and change within her organization.

Go online to www.macmillanihe.com/sutton-people to access the interview with Rebecca.

## PRACTICE INSIGHTS
Video interviews with practitioners, managers, consultants and academics, shedding light on the application of OB and HRM in the real world.

## SUMMARY
We started this chapter by looking at organizational culture as the context in which change happens and a subject of change management itself. We then moved on to consider the current trends that

 FURTHER READING

- The psychological contract is a rich area of research and this paper provides a good basis for understanding its basic tenets; Rousseau, D. M. (2001) 'Schema, promise and mutuality: the building blocks of the psychological contract', *Journal of Occupational and Organizational Psychology*, 74(4), pp. 511–41.

- To find out more about the relationship between trust and performance, see Brown, S. Gray, D., McHardy, J. and Taylor, K. (2014) 'Employee trust and workplace performance', *Journal of Economic Behavior and Organization*, 116(8284), pp. 361–78.

- This website provides lots of data on trade union membership that you can use to find out about different countries. It allows you to construct your own graphs: https://stats.oecd.org/Index. aspx?DataSetCode=UN_DEN.

## FURTHER READING
Curated selection of three to four key additional texts or papers to take your studies a step further beyond the content of the chapter.

## REVIEW QUESTIONS
1. What is the psychological contract and why is it an important element in understanding the employment relationship?

2. Why might an organization wish to increase employee feedback and how could it go about doing this?

3. Evaluate the role of collective representation in the modern workplace: to what extent does HRM promote an individually based rather than collective employment relationship?

## REVIEW QUESTIONS
Test your knowledge and understanding of the chapter and can be used as practice essay questions in revision.

## ONLINE RESOURCES
Access to video interviews and introductions, plus a range of additional resources to support teaching and learning.

ONLINE RESOURCES
Go online to www.macmillanihe.com/sutton-people to access a MCQ quiz for this chapter and for further resources to support your learning.

# ONLINE RESOURCES

To complement the print book there are a number of supporting and additional materials provided online, through the companion website www.macmillanihe.com/sutton-people.

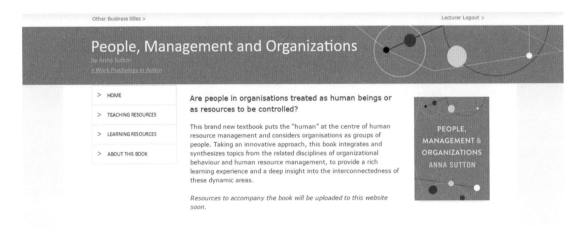

## LEARNING MATERIALS

For students, these include:

• Self-test multiple choice question quiz to check your understanding of each chapter.

• Author video chapter introductions outlining the key issues discussed in each chapter

• Practice Insights videos, featuring the following interviewees:

**Jennifer Dootson**
Part-time HRM student and HR Business Partner at d-Wise, UK

Carrie McKenzie
Voluntary Services Manager, Sheffield Teaching Hospital, UK

**Kirsten Henderson**
Recruitment Consultant, Jo Fisher Executive, New Zealand

**Mark Harcourt**
Professor of Strategy and HRM, University of Waikato, New Zealand

**Roger Longden**
Performance Management Consultant, There be Giants, UK

**Claudia Nario**
Leadership Development Consultant, Center for Creative Leadership, Spain

**Rebecca Lencho**
HR Manager, Rockline Industries, USA

**Kris DeLano**
Corporate HR Director, Rockline Industries, USA

**Darren Cook**
Director, Scruffy Bear Pictures, UK

**Paul Walsh**
Learning and Development Specialist, Manchester Metropolitan University, UK

**Ginger Chen**
Senior HR Manager, Cigna, Taiwan

**Lara Montefiori**
Head of Psychology, Arctic Shores, UK

## TEACHING MATERIALS

For lecturers, the following resources are available to support course delivery and assessment:

- An Instructor's manual containing:
  - Suggested timetables and pathways through the book for different student groups
  - Lecture and seminar content suggestions
  - Guidance for in-text exercises
- Lecture slides to form the basis of lecture presentations; editable for your own needs
- A Testbank of multiple choice questions and answers that can be used in assessments.

# NOTE TO LECTURERS

Thank you for adopting this textbook for your course. I hope that you will find it useful as a basis for your lecturing, enabling students to see how OB and HRM complement each other in the study of how work and people are organized and managed. Rather than keep OB and HRM separate throughout the book, viewing everything independently from two angles, I have worked to combine them so that each topic is addressed in a unified way, providing students with understanding and applications that would not be otherwise available.

## ORGANIZATION OF THE BOOK

Integrating two distinct fields of study such as HRM and OB can be very rewarding in the way it provides unique insights for learners but also presents distinct challenges in how to cover the material. In developing this concise textbook, I have necessarily had to make choices about what to include and what to leave out. My guiding principle has been to maintain a focus on current utility and application, rather than try and give a detailed review of historical theories and models. I have aimed to provide students with a sophisticated theoretical understanding of the subject that leads naturally into evidence-based application. So, I do not claim that this book will cover everything of interest and value in OB and HRM (and my apologies if your favourite topic is missing), but, rather, that it provides a unified discussion of the essentials of the two fields in a way that will help students to understand the underlying principles and apply them to their own work lives.

## ALTERNATIVE PATHWAYS THROUGH THE BOOK

HRM and OB are wide-ranging topics with many different applications at work, so it may be that a different pathway through this book will suit your course or students better than simply working through from Chapter 1 to 12. Here are some suggested alternative pathways to suit different needs, using different 'blocks' of chapters that you can mix and match to create your course. For example:

*Pathway 1*

1. Macro to micro path

2. Focus on employees

3. Understanding the context

*Pathway 2*

1. Understanding the context

2. Employee life-cycle

3. A focus on leadership

---

*Macro to micro*

Although the book is structured so that we start with the individual and move up to the organizational level, an alternative approach is to start with the bigger picture issues such as strategy and how to manage change and then move down to the individual-level topics of performance management, recruitment and so on. This approach may be more suitable for students studying higher level management (including MBA) who wish to look more closely at how HRM integrates with organization-level strategies and directions, emphasizing the role of leaders in doing this:

* Chapter 8: Strategy: creating purpose
* Chapter 9: Structure: fit for purpose
* Chapter 7: Culture and change
* Chapter 6: Leadership: managing leaders and leading management
* Chapter 5: Encouraging and managing performance
* Chapter 4: The individual and the organization

| | |
|---|---|
| *Employee life-cycle*<br><br>If the focus of your course is more on the tasks HR carries out on a day-to-day basis and how the function interacts with employees at different stages of their career, this pathway may be more appropriate. It moves through a basic employee life-cycle, from attraction and selection through to performance, development and longer term engagement:<br><br>• Chapter 3: Recruitment and selection<br>• Chapter 4: The individual and the organization<br>• Chapter 5: Encouraging and managing performance<br>• Chapter 10: Learning and development<br>• Chapter 11: Well-being and engagement | |
| *A focus on change*<br><br>One of the most challenging issues managers have to deal with in the modern workplace is change. This pathway focuses on the chapters that are most relevant to change management. It covers models of change and the role of culture, how to embed learning and development within the organization, recognizing future trends, and how best to lead people and organizations:<br><br>• Chapter 7: Culture and change<br>• Chapter 10: Learning and development<br>• Chapter 12: Future-proof workplaces<br>• Chapter 6: Leadership: managing leaders and leading management | *Understanding the context*<br><br>This block emphasizes the importance of understanding the context within which HR and management activities take place in order to develop a critical understanding of key theories. It would work well as an introduction to the rest of the course or as a concluding section that allows students to use these key contextual factors to re-evaluate and expand their understanding of the preceding issues:<br><br>• Chapter 1: Integrating OB and HRM<br>• Chapter 2: What is work all about?<br>• Chapter 12: Future-proof workplaces |
| *A focus on employees*<br><br>This block focuses on the key issues of selecting, developing and engaging employees to create flexible, sustainable organizations that will survive into the future:<br><br>• Chapter 3: Recruitment and selection<br>• Chapter 10: Learning and development<br>• Chapter 11: Well-being and engagement<br>• Chapter 12: Future-proof workplaces | *A focus on leadership*<br><br>The role of leaders as creators of organizational direction and purpose can be explored in this block, which starts with the leadership chapter and the central importance of strategy and then moves on to consider the broader issues of organizational structure, culture and change:<br><br>• Chapter 6: Leadership: managing leaders and leading management<br>• Chapter 8: Strategy: creating purpose<br>• Chapter 7: Culture and change<br>• Chapter 9: Structure: fit for purpose |

# TEACHING MATERIALS

Because I believe the best way to learn an applied subject is to work through the implications and applications, there are a variety of pedagogical features in this book designed to help students do just that. I have developed them so that they are integral parts of the text, not just attractive 'add-ons', and have constructed them in a way that should make them easy to adapt for seminar or tutorial work with students. You may find the Instructor's manual, available on the companion website, helpful here for suggestions on how you can use different activities in the book with your students. The manual is designed to help with the delivery of a course based around this textbook and includes:

• Suggested timetables and pathways through the book for different student groups

• Lecture and seminar content suggestions.

In addition, on the companion website you will be able to gain access to lecture slides for every chapter to support your teaching and a Testbank of multiple choice questions. See Online resources on p. xx for further details.

## A NOTE ABOUT EMPLOYABILITY

One of the recurring themes in this book, and an issue of increasing importance in university study, is the development of transferrable skills and I have included an extended activity in each chapter that will help students to develop their own skills. Not only do these activities help to illustrate the applicability of the chapter content to students' own work lives, but they will also enable students to see concrete ways they can evidence their own skill development. If employability is a key element of your own course, you could encourage students to use these activities to develop a portfolio of their skill development.

I wish you all the best in your teaching and would welcome any suggestions or feedback you have about the book that would help to improve the next edition. Please contact me via the email address on the companion website.

# ACKNOWLEDGEMENTS

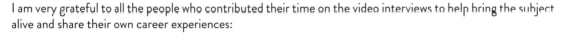

I am very grateful to all the people who contributed their time on the video interviews to help bring the subject alive and share their own career experiences:

| | |
|---|---|
| Jennifer Dootson | Paul Walsh |
| Carrie McKenzie | Kris DeLano |
| Kirsten Henderson | Darren Cook |
| Mark Harcourt | Ginger Chen |
| Roger Longden | Rebecca Lencho |
| Claudia Nario | Lara Montefiori |

My sincere thanks also to the anonymous reviewers who provided detailed and considered feedback at various stages of this project. Your input was invaluable in strengthening and improving the book.

Thanks to my family: as usual, you have been incredibly supportive and enthusiastic about my work on this book. Thanks to Kate for insisting on celebrating each milestone with me, to Mum and Dad for the practical help and contagious parental sense of pride in what I do, and to Julian for the unflagging support and continuous stream of small treats to keep me going.

Finally, I am deeply grateful to the team at Palgrave: Ursula Gavin and Niki Jayatunga, who have supported and inspired me in the writing of this book; the design team for producing such an attractive and creative layout; and all those working behind the scenes to bring this book to fruition. Thanks also to Maggie Lythgoe for the patient copy-editing and corrections of my sometimes idiosyncratic grammar.

# FOUNDATIONS OF OB AND HRM

In Part 1, we are building the foundations of our study of Organizational Behaviour (OB) and Human Resource Management (HRM). In Chapter 1, we start by reviewing the history of OB and HRM, drawing out their common themes and challenges and seeing how they can complement each other in efforts to understand and manage people at work. In Chapter 2 we move on to consider what work is all about, its meaning in our lives and the kinds of work there are. We will also address some of the inequalities in work, considering, for example, why 'emotional' work is often paid less well than other types of work. In Chapter 3, we review the

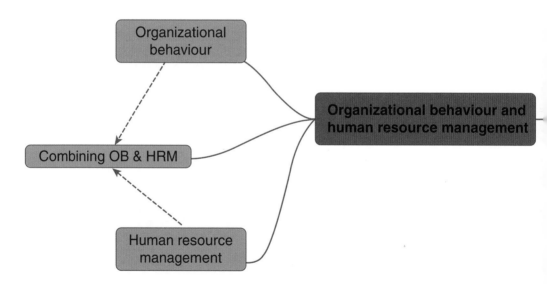

foundation of the employment relationship and the decisions that need to be made about how the organization will attract, recruit and select its workers. The Part 1 case study provides an insight into the work that care workers do and draws out several of the interesting themes covered in these first three chapters, including how we value different types of work, the internal motivations we have for working and the impact of recruitment decisions on the quality of work and nature of the workforce.

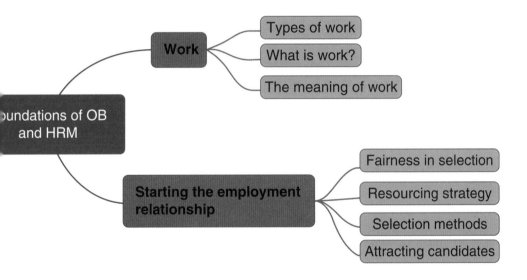

# 1 INTEGRATING OB AND HRM

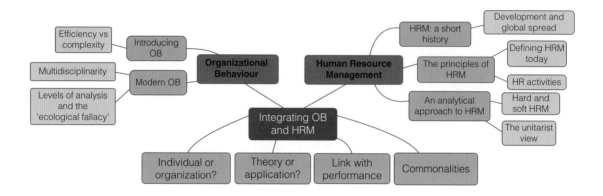

## INTRODUCTION

This introductory chapter sets the scene for the rest of the book. We will see how different approaches to Organizational Behaviour (OB) and Human Resource Management (HRM) have, at their root, basic assumptions about what these fields of study are for. Are people in organizations to be treated as individual human beings or as resources to be controlled? We will see that both OB and HRM have grappled with this question in different ways.

We start with a short history of both subjects: it is important to have an understanding of how current thoughts and models have their foundations in the concerns and approaches of the past. Seeing the development of both disciplines in this way will help us to identify parallels and differences between OB and HRM. It will also allow us to gain an insight into how theoretical frameworks can often be limited by the assumptions we have about how businesses should function, a question we will return to in the final chapter after we have worked through all the topics in the book. We conclude this introductory chapter by discussing how the integration of insights from OB and HRM can help us to address some major challenges in our study of people, management and organizations.

*Getty Images*

## LEARNING FEATURES

Applications: Why study OB?

Applications: Humans or resources?

Applications: Analytical HRM

Applications: Measuring performance

Weighing the Evidence: Are happy workers productive?

Web Explorer: Professional bodies and reflective practice

In the News: HRM principles and national governments

Transferrable Skills: Identifying underlying assumptions

Practice Insights: Jennifer Dootson

 ## Video overview

Julian Perkins

Go online to www.macmillanihe.com/sutton-people to access a video of Anna Sutton introducing the chapter's main themes.

# ORGANIZATIONAL BEHAVIOUR

*Organizational Behaviour (OB)* is the study of how people behave in organizations and how the organizations themselves behave. As an applied field of study, OB is not just an attempt to understand *what* is happening in organizations, but also *why* it happens and how we can develop models to manage or change certain behaviours. OB is also a multidisciplinary field: with the emphasis on how

useful a theory or model is to the real world of management, OB draws on a wide range of academic disciplines. There is no doubting that this makes OB a very broad subject. Ultimately, it could encompass any topic that affects behaviour *in* or *of* organizations. But, by exploring how OB has developed and some of the main drivers behind this development, we can gain a clearer overview of the subject.

# Introducing OB

The study of management and how people behave in organizations has a long history. Perhaps the beginnings of OB as a topic of study can be traced back to the emergence of **scientific management**, which was an attempt to apply scientific principles to the study of work, seeking the most efficient way to organize jobs and workplaces.

## Efficiency vs complexity

One of the earliest writers in this area was Max Weber (1864–1920) who was, among other things, a sociologist. He wrote several books and essays in the early 1900s about capitalism, Protestant Christianity and their effects on society and the way we work, including possibly his most famous work, *The Protestant Ethic and the Spirit of Capitalism*. Weber was very influential in what has now evolved into OB. He suggested that **bureaucracy** was the most efficient and rational way to organize modern workplaces, although he acknowledged that bureaucracy in the real world would rarely match up to his 'ideal' type. As part of this, he made some recommendations to organizations that seem so obvious to us now it is hard to imagine how groundbreaking they were at the time. Here are some of the things he proposed that an organization provide to employees in order to work efficiently (Waters and Waters, 2015):

- selection of job applicants on the basis of relevant qualifications

- a permanent place to work (e.g. office)

- a career structure with promotion decided by superiors

- fixed salary or wages

- pension.

Try to imagine for a moment what a job would be like that did not have those things. While you can probably think of unusual jobs for which these are not the norm, the majority of modern jobs take these principles for granted.

Working around the same time as Weber, Frederick Taylor (1856–1915) promoted a scientific approach to management. He said that the 'principal object of management should be to secure the maximum prosperity for the employer, coupled with the maximum prosperity for each employee' (Taylor, 1911, p. 9). However, he also had a slightly pessimistic view of people's approach to work, suggesting that we have a tendency towards working at a 'slow, easy gait' and therefore the role of management should be to try and increase workers' productivity. He suggested that this could be done using his five principles of scientific management:

1. The manager should organize the work and do all the 'thinking'. The worker should 'just work'.

2. The manager should precisely define how the worker should do the work, using **scientific methods**.

3. The best person should be selected for each job.

4. Workers should be trained properly.

5. Workers' performance should be monitored.

Taylor's focus was on efficiency but the downside of this approach was that it could deskill workers, removing autonomy and increasing boredom. This was because one of the simplest ways to increase efficiency was a **division of labour**, which broke down tasks into small components and gave each small part to one worker to repeat over and over. It also suggested that there was 'one best way' to organize work and underplayed the role of human factors. Mary Parker Follett (1868–1933), another early management theorist, addressed this issue by recommending that organizations try to address employees' human needs. Instead of seeing interpersonal relations as a source of inefficiencies, Follett (1924) looked at how they could best be managed to promote organizational effectiveness. For example, she described how good management of conflict – by moving from coercive to participative ways of managing workers – could result in higher quality outcomes.

A turning point in OB came with the **Hawthorne studies** (1929–32) conducted by Elton Mayo and colleagues. Originally an attempt to apply scientific management principles to identify the most productive physical environment for workers, the researchers concluded that social relationships and informal group dynamics had a much greater impact on productivity than changes to lighting levels and so on (Mayo, 2003). This paved the way for many theorists to begin to examine motivation at work, with the focus being on the inter- and intra-individual aspects of work behaviour. Rather than recommending a 'one best way', OB began to develop as an academic discipline addressing the multi-level complexity of human behaviour at work.

The Weighing the Evidence box examines the commonly held assumption that more satisfied workers are more productive.

 Weighing the Evidence: **Are happy workers productive?**

It is a commonly held belief that we work better when we are happier in our jobs. Much of the current emphasis on **well-being** at work or promoting **job satisfaction** rests on an unspoken assumption that if we can help people feel more positive at work, they will be more productive. But how true is this? It is a question that has long interested both HRM and OB researchers and there are hundreds of studies investigating the link between job satisfaction and performance.

A significant review of this published research has given us a fairly definitive answer: there is a correlation of about 0.3 between job satisfaction and performance (Judge et al., 2001). While not very large, this is a significant association and the relationship is stronger for more complex jobs than it is for simpler jobs. However, one of the difficulties in understanding this relationship

is knowing in which direction the causality goes. Most studies in this area have been cross-sectional, that is, they measure satisfaction and performance at the same time point, so don't tell us whether performance influences satisfaction or vice versa.

This causal problem is common to much of the research on job attitudes, but there is evidence that attitudes can affect performance levels for up to three years, while performance only affects attitudes for about a year (Winkler et al., 2012). In a review of longitudinal studies (those carried out over an extended period of time), however, it was found that there was a small but significant effect of job satisfaction on performance, while the reverse effect was not found (Riketta, 2008). So, it does seem that higher satisfaction in our work improves our performance.

*Getty Images/Sydney Roberts*

Historically, OB has focused on work behaviour in profit-making organizations (Schneider, 1985), although it has expanded in recent years to include

non-traditional definitions of work, for example voluntary or unpaid work. We will explore this further in Chapter 2 when we consider the meaning of work, but it is worth remembering that much of the early research and theory in OB does limit itself to trying to understand behaviour in traditional paid work.

## Modern OB

This move into addressing the complexity of organizational behaviour led to a profusion of different theories. In the late 1970s and early 80s, Miner (1984) conducted a survey of experts in the field to determine the current state of the emerging science, asking them to nominate the theories they believed were most important. These theories were then rated in terms of their usefulness in applied settings and their scientific *validity*. The findings were not promising: it seemed that very few of the theories were useful *and* valid and, perhaps more worryingly, there was no relationship between how frequently a theory was nominated as 'important' by the subject experts and its rated usefulness or validity. Miner noted that while this might be expected in such a young, emerging science, there was still a need for the development of a more integrative, diverse approach to studying management and organizations.

When Miner carried out a similar piece of research twenty years later, however, there was better news. In this study (Miner, 2003), the importance of the theories was strongly correlated with their scientific validity, and the validity of the theories also correlated with their usefulness in practical applications. It seemed that organizational behaviour was developing into a field with a growing consensus among experts that there is an established, well-supported foundation of useful and valid theories. Those theories often have their roots in a variety of other disciplines.

### Multidisciplinarity of OB

As we saw at the beginning of this section, OB is the study of how people behave in organizations. It incorporates individual-level behaviour (e.g. individual work motivation), through group behaviour (e.g. team dynamics) right up to organizational-level aspects (e.g. how to structure organizations). In trying to understand and predict how people behave in organizations, OB draws on several different areas of study at these different levels (Schneider, 1985), including:

- **Psychology:** the study of human and animal behaviour, psychology contributes an understanding of learning, personality, motivation and job **attitudes**, to name but a few. The emphasis in psychology is on understanding the individual and, particularly in social psychology, how we behave in groups.

- **Sociology:** the study of our social relationships and how we relate to our society and culture. Some of the important contributions made to OB from sociology include an understanding of organizational change, **communication**, power and conflict.

- **Management studies:** beginning with a search for the 'one best way' to manage workers in scientific management and developing a greater understanding of the impact that human relations have on our behaviour at work, this field of study is all about how we can improve management.

Other contributing disciplines include political science and economics (Heath and Sitkin, 2001). Political science seeks to understand and explain political behaviour in the widest sense, that is, not limited to governmental politics but an appreciation of the role that power and influence play in our day-to-day working lives. And, of course, there is the contribution that economics makes: understanding the factors that influence income and wealth, and, more recently, well-being.

Drawing as it does on so many different disciplines, OB sometimes walks a difficult line between the underlying assumptions of these fields. For example, management studies have typically focused on ensuring an organization's effectiveness or survival, while psychology and sociology are more concerned with the human element and focus on the employees (Schneider, 1985). Traditionally, psychology has been the largest single contributor to the field and many OB theorists today still have psychological backgrounds (Miner, 2003). This has, perhaps unsurprisingly, led to a focus on individual and group behaviour and less of an emphasis on the higher level organizational issues that contribute to predicting and understanding behaviour at work. Several OB researchers (e.g. Heath and Sitkin, 2001) have called for a renewed emphasis on the organizational aspects of OB, pointing out that it is only by doing this that OB can be properly distinguished from the other fields of study which contribute to it.

## Levels of analysis and the 'ecological fallacy'

The **ecological fallacy** is a fault in reasoning made when we assume something about an individual based on something we know about a group. This happens when we do not keep it clear which level of analysis we are using for a particular piece of research or theory. For example, there are research studies that have found differences between men's and women's leadership styles (Eagly et al., 2003). At the group level, these studies give some clear conclusions. We can say that, on average, women tend to use a more transformational leadership style than men (see Chapter 6 for further discussion of leadership styles). However, where it might become a fallacy is if we were to take this finding about group differences and conclude that a specific departmental manager we know, who is a woman, is therefore a transformational leader. In this case, we have taken some information that is true at the group (average) level and assumed it is true at the individual level.

This ecological fallacy is a particular challenge for OB because we are considering such a broad range of issues when we are trying to predict organizational behaviour: right from the individual's current state of mind, through to the dynamics of the team that person is in, the context of a particular organizational culture and even the present economic *climate*. We cannot assume that just because we have a good understanding of what influences teams to work more effectively, we will be able to predict how well a particular individual will function within that team. So, bear this in mind when you are learning: there are very few, if any, definitive answers to the key questions in OB. It is a wide-ranging, ambitious discipline, and while that can make studying OB occasionally frustrating, it is also what makes it interesting.

 Applications: **Why study OB?**

Schneider (1985) contrasted OB with other business disciplines like marketing, finance, accounting and economics by saying that the latter shared a 'common language of dollars', while OB speaks a 'foreign language of motivation, leadership, job satisfaction' and so on.

» To what extent do you think this distinction still holds true?

» Why do you personally want to study OB? What do you hope to find out?

# HUMAN RESOURCE MANAGEMENT

**Human Resource Management (HRM)** differs from Organizational Behaviour (OB) in that it is both a field of study and a profession. In fact, for many authors, defining the field of HRM is simply a case of identifying all the activities (such as selection, pay and benefits) and roles (from administrative assistance through to director) associated with human resources in work organizations. This is the source of the great diversity in HRM: the goals of HRM vary depending on the strategic choices made in individual organizations and the wider environment or industry context in which they are embedded.

## HRM: a short history

In the industrialized West in the late 1800s, functions that we now consider part of HRM were typically carried out by supervisors. Tasks such as hiring, firing and **training** were simply a part of the supervisor's role. Things started to change with the introduction of two different types of roles in these industrialized organizations. First, from the 1890s onwards, was the creation of employment offices: specialized administrative offices to deal with employment-related matters such as payroll and employee records. Concurrently, as a result of an increasing concern for employee welfare, there was a move to provide employees with better conditions and extra amenities, such as medical care, employee housing and libraries. 'Welfare officers' were employed to administer these new developments.

In line with these developing concerns about how to manage employees, scientific management was born. As we saw earlier, one of the most influential among those seeking a more rigorous approach to management was Frederick Taylor, who promoted the idea that a scientific approach to management would lead to more effective selection of employees, better supervision and, perhaps most attractively to organizational leaders, increased efficiency and reductions in costs.

These two concerns of employment management/administration and welfare became combined into *personnel management*, although this term was most common in the USA and only later adopted by other countries. These two functions are still at the heart of modern HRM and perhaps help to explain the sometimes paradoxical goals that HRM attempts to meet: organizational efficiency and cost-effectiveness versus employee welfare. Interestingly, welfare officers were predominantly women and this gender dominance continues into today's HRM.

However, the emerging personnel management in the USA took a battering during the Great Depression. There was an increase in union membership and collective bargaining that came to a peak in the 1950s and personnel departments at this time were typically concerned with two main tasks: industrial relations and personnel. These departments did not generally have high status and were not involved in strategic-level decisions.

## Development and global spread of HRM

HRM as we recognize it today emerged in the 1980s, when influential academics put forward a model of HRM that distinguished it from traditional personnel management or industrial relations. The Harvard model of HRM (Beer et al., 1984) was one of the first of these and it emphasized employees as an asset to the organization rather than a cost, and HRM as having a key role in strategic and business decisions rather than being a side-lined administrative department. Instead of seeing employees and managers as engaged in a constant struggle, HRM was portrayed as a way of bringing about unity in the organization, proactively engaging all employees to work towards organizationally important outcomes. The model illustrated in Figure 1.1 shows how HRM choices, such as the reward or work systems, influence HRM-relevant outcomes, such as employee commitment and cost-effectiveness, and then how these outcomes in turn influence long-term consequences like organizational effectiveness. This is set in the context of various stakeholder interests (from employee groups to government) and also takes account of the array of situational factors that can influence, and be influenced by, HRM policy and consequences. From this model, it is clear that HRM was being promoted as a wide-reaching field with important influences on the organization as a whole.

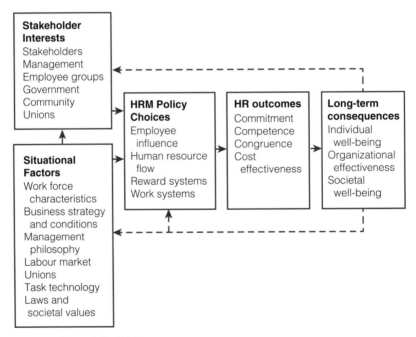

*Figure 1.1 Map of the HRM territory*

Source: Beer, M., Spector, B., Lawrence, P. R. and Mills, D. Q. (1984) *Managing Human Assets: The Groundbreaking Harvard Business School Program*, p. 16. New York: Free Press. Reprinted with permission from the authors.

From the USA, HRM started to spread across the globe. Why was an approach developed in the USA so appealing to an international audience? David Guest (1987) suggested that HRM's popularity was based on five factors, ranging from its focus on competitive advantage to its ability to deal effectively with workforce-related changes such as an increasingly educated and demanding workforce:

1. Proponents of HRM argued that more effective people management and organizational structure would lead to competitive advantage. This meant that, in an increasingly competitive global environment, HRM was being proposed as an essential part of the organization's success.

2. 'HRM' was practised by those companies that were identified as being particularly 'excellent' in case studies. Organizations wishing to emulate this excellence naturally wanted to adopt the practices that appeared to contribute to those achievements.

3. Personnel management was perceived to have failed and to be too marginal to the organization, whereas HRM was a mainstream activity. Rather than being a side-lined administrative role with little impact on the organization, HRM was a way for people management professionals to take part in the day-to-day running of the organization and have real impact on its future.

4. **Trade unions** and adversarial relationships between 'employees' and 'managers' were declining in influence, leading to the development of the more unitary, cooperative approach to people management that HRM seemed to offer: employees and managers could work together to support organizational success.

5. A more educated and demanding workforce combined with changes in technology that allowed more flexible jobs seemed to require a different form of people management. The new HRM appeared to offer this and could meet the challenges of the emerging and changing workforce.

## The principles of HRM

One of the early critiques of HRM suggested that if it was going to make a real impact, HRM needed to be clearly distinguished from traditional personnel management (Guest, 1987) and that this distinction could be summarized as one of ensuring compliance (personnel management) versus encouraging commitment (HRM) (Guest, 1991). Guest outlined four main dimensions of HRM based on the goals it is trying to achieve:

1. **Integration:** HRM should be integrated into organizational **strategy**, providing a coherent, cohesive set of policies that contribute to that strategy, and recognized as a part of each line manager's job with the goal of encouraging employees to feel part the organization.

2. **Employee commitment:** HRM can develop individual employees' organizational and job commitment, thereby promoting satisfaction, higher job performance and willingness to accept change.

3. **Flexibility:** HRM can contribute to developing organizational flexibility and responsiveness by strengthening trust, commitment and motivation.

4. **Quality:** By ensuring the selection, training and retention of high-quality employees, HRM can contribute to the quality of work.

The value of these principles, developed in a US-centred context, to global HRM is explored in the In the News activity.

Despite some concerns over the applicability of HRM to all organizations, by the early 1990s, Guest (1991) recognized that HRM had become the commonly accepted approach to employment-management relations. Although still cautioning against the ambiguity of the HRM label (which we explore in more detail below), he also recognized it as an 'optimistic' view, working to an ideal of committed, integrated employees sharing common concerns with the whole organization.

A more recent discussion of the goals of HRM provides a simple model for understanding some of the tensions apparent in the reality of HRM as it is practised in organizations today, as well as the historical legacy that still influences the development of theory and practice. Boxall (2007) argues that HRM can be understood as an attempt to manage strategic tensions, as shown in Figure 1.2.

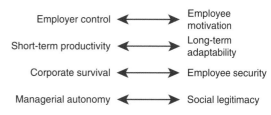

*Figure 1.2 Strategic tensions within HRM*

HRM's mission, therefore, is to contribute to the organization's survival by stabilizing a system of labour management that is cost-effective and socially legitimate. This is a complex task, involving the weighing up of different priorities and the

**In the News: HRM principles and national governments**

Several governments in Middle Eastern countries have initiated programmes to promote the employment of nationals rather than expatriates. These politically led programmes have arisen out of a belief that a dependence on expatriate workers could lead to long-term problems, such as a clash of **values** between local and foreign workers, instability when foreign workers return home and a lack of control over the nation's own affairs. One of the countries that has adopted this policy is the United Arab Emirates (UAE), which has the most disproportionate ratio of nationals to expatriates in the world, with nearly 99% of private sector workers being expatriates (Al-Waqfi and Forstenlechner, 2014). In its vision for 2021, the UAE government embraces **globalization**, while emphasizing the importance of the local workforce in promoting economic progress (Haak-Saheem et al., 2016).

'Emiratization', as UAE's programme to recruit and develop UAE nationals is called, faces significant barriers, including the fact that expatriate workers are often preferred because they are paid less and are easier to control (Al-Waqfi and Forstenlechner,

2014). The government has introduced several initiatives to try and encourage Emiratization, such as restricting the number of work visas or requiring employers to choose between investing in training and development for a UAE national or paying a fee to employ an already trained expatriate (Rees et al., 2007).

Despite these efforts, Emiratization is still facing an uphill struggle. Responding to the Emiratization programme requires a distinctive approach from HR, with an emphasis on training and developing young Emiratis not just in technical skills but also in their ability to work in a competitive, multicultural environment (Moukhallati, 2017).

**For discussion**

» How could the four dimensions of HRM outlined by Guest (1987) be applied to aid Emiratization efforts?

» Can you see any potential sources of tension between these HRM principles and a government programme that promotes national workers?

development of balanced plans to ensure that the organization is making effective use of its resources as well as acting in a way that is in line with societal and legal expectations.

## Defining HRM today

Boxall et al. (2007a) define HRM at its simplest as 'the management of work and people towards desired ends' and make the point that HRM is fundamental to every work organization. The work and the people need to be managed; thus, activities we currently identify as HRM will always exist. There may be arguments about what kind of umbrella term to give to these activities or even who should carry them out – line managers or HR professionals – but the practices themselves are necessary to any organization's survival. In a similar vein, Watson (2010) suggests treating HRM as a general term for employment or labour management rather than as a specific model or paradigm of how employment should be managed.

Perhaps one of the best ways of conceptualizing what HRM is all about is to think of it as centred on managing the employment relationships in an

organization. Boxall et al. (2007a) identify three broad (but overlapping) areas:

1. **Micro HRM:** this includes HRM policy and practice and contains two categories. The first involves issues around managing individuals and small groups, such as recruitment, **training** and **development** and performance management. Similar to the 'individual' level of analysis in OB, this category of policy and practice draws heavily on psychology. The second category draws more on sociological concepts and includes functions around organizing work and **employee voice**.

2. **Strategic HRM (SHRM):** this takes a 'big picture' view and is interested in how the micro HRM activities can be best integrated with each other and how they relate to the wider business context. SHRM takes the view that HR should not be a concern solely of HR practitioners but of all those involved in making strategic decisions. It is closely linked with strategic management and also shares a lot of common ground with general OB concerns.

3. **International HRM:** the main concerns are around how HRM functions in multinational companies. It considers how micro HRM functions can be adapted to individual cultures as well as how HR strategies need to be developed or refined to suit different countries.

In this sense, HRM draws on a range of social sciences in an effort to understand and, particularly, to manage these relationships. In common with other management and business studies, there is also now an increasing emphasis on the role of ethics in managing these relationships. It is no longer good enough, as it might have been claimed in previous generations, for HRM to focus on cost-effectiveness or organizational viability. HRM now can play a leading role in ensuring that organizational goals are met in an ethical manner and that ethical considerations are central to the management of the employment relationship. Ironically, the very term 'human resource' management has led some critics to suggest that HRM has played a role in reducing employees from 'people' to 'things' that can be exploited for the firm's gain. We explore this controversy further in the Applications box and look at the continuing distinction between 'hard' and 'soft' HRM in the section on analytical HRM.

## Applications: Humans or resources?

The term 'Human Resource Management' is somewhat controversial. Particularly in its early days in the 1980s, when HRM was first gaining ground and replacing the term 'personnel management', some people objected to 'HRM' on the grounds that it represented a negative and depersonalized change in how employees were viewed. No longer seen as humans with needs and rights of their own, 'human resources' could be moved around and exploited in a way that would best serve the organization's needs.

However, others have suggested that this name change actually served to raise the importance of employees. By referring to them as 'resources', HRM emphasizes how vital people are to an organization's success. This in turn raises the profile of HRM itself: instead of being a low status, fringe administrative role, human resource management should now be central to the organizational strategy. They argue that no organization will succeed if it destroys its own resources, and investing in developing and retaining those resources will benefit it in the long term.

It seems that the discipline of HRM is now here to stay, but the name still has implications for how we view employees. What do you think about the debate? Write a brief discussion of the advantages and disadvantages of using the term 'human resources'. Or, if you are working in a group, split into two subgroups and debate the issue.

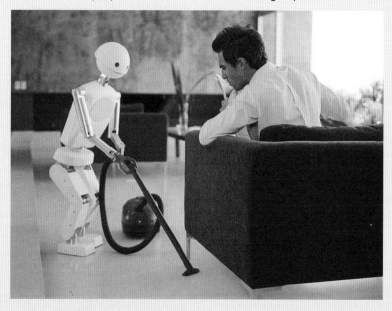

*Getty Images/Javier Pierini*

## HR activities

The management of employment relationships can be conceptualized as a range of different tasks and activities that HRM engages in through the employee's life-cycle with the company. A generic employee life-cycle consists of four main stages:

1. **Recruitment and selection:** ensuring the best employees are recruited and selected, including using the most effective selection methods and ensuring legal compliance. Important issues to consider here are **job design** and specification as well as training for those involved in the selection process.

2. **Induction/joining:** the main HR concerns here are in negotiating the beginning of the employment relationship and ensuring that the new employee quickly moves from 'new starter' to fully productive member of the organization.

3. **Retention:** generally the longest part of the life-cycle, covering a range of HR activities including performance management, employee **engagement**, reward, and training and development.

4. **Separation:** one of the key activities here is succession planning: how can the organization continue to be successful when employees leave?

An important point about HRM is that it is not only HR professionals who are engaged in HRM activities. While many organizations do have a dedicated HR department or function, there are plenty that do not, devolving the HR activities to line managers. In fact, many so-called HR activities, such as developing employee commitment, are responsibilities shared by most managerial staff and could not be achieved without those managers. HR policies may well be developed by a dedicated HR function but they are often enacted by other members of staff. For example, the HR department may design a recruitment and selection policy or procedure but perhaps only play a quality control role in its enactment. Line managers and even peers may conduct interviews and decide on the best applicant, with HR acting in an advisory role only.

## An analytical approach to HRM

If HRM is, as has been suggested above, so focused on the practical tasks of managing employees, what is the point of studying it at university level? Wouldn't HR practitioners be better served by learning on the job than by spending time studying theoretical models and concepts? The answer to this lies in the consideration of HRM as a profession. Professionals need a high level of knowledge of their field as well as the skills to reflect on and continually improve their practice. It is only by developing a depth of understanding of HRM theory that we can raise HR practice above a mindless repetition of 'best practice' examples from organizations that may or may not be similar to our own, to a truly professional practice that can understand current experience in relation to evaluated models. Boxall et al. (2007a) call this *analytical HRM* and suggest that it strives to answer these questions:

- What is management trying to do with people and work, and why?

- How do different models of HRM work and why are some better than others?

- Who is HRM benefitting and how well is it doing this? This question is concerned with the outcomes of HRM and whether they serve employee or employer interests (or perhaps both).

By encouraging an analytical approach to HRM, we can start to identify some of the underlying assumptions in the field and address some of the criticisms that have been levelled at it. We return to this theme at various points in the book, including when we discuss the importance of continuous professional development in Chapter 10 and evidence-based practice in Chapter 12.

 Applications: **Analytical HRM**

With a partner, briefly describe your own experience of HRM. This could be formal work in an HR department or experience of dealing with HR as an employee in a different department or through a selection process. Drawing on this personal experience, consider Boxall et al.'s suggestion about the questions that analytical HRM should be trying to answer: Who do you think HRM benefits and how well is it doing this? How does your experience compare with others in your group? Taking this further, how important do you think it is for HR professionals to have an analytical understanding of their field?

## Hard and soft HRM

Storey (1989) pointed out that because HRM is such a broad term, it includes two quite different approaches to labour management. The 'hard' approach is quantitative, managing the 'human resources' in the same way as other factors and emphasizing the business strategy. In this approach, the value of the resource lies in its scarcity or otherwise and the resources are deployed just as any other business resource would be to meet demand. The 'soft' approach emphasizes human interactions, focusing on communication, leadership and motivation. In this approach, HRM's purpose is to aid the organization in developing employee commitment and motivation, which will lead to high performance. Although both approaches note the necessity of being aligned with business strategy, that link is made more explicit in the hard approach.

The first HRM models included well-being as a key longer term outcome to which HRM could effectively contribute. Yet, this ethic of duty of care towards employees often gets lost in a focus on business priorities, particularly cost savings (Keegan and Francis, 2010). This is another example of an inherent paradox in HRM: the well-being of employees versus the success of the business. The impact of this on how HR professionals view their profession was well illustrated in a study by Keegan and Francis (2010), which noted a distinction between the *business partner* and the *employee-centred* approaches in HRM. The business partner discourse focused on issues of cost, value-adding and business priorities and viewed employees as passive resources to be utilized in whatever fashion best serves the business. In contrast, the employee-centred discourse dealt with issues of **fairness**, welfare and well-being, seeing employees as active agents who were involved in creating their own organizational realities. The HR practitioners who were interviewed for this study reported experiencing the tensions of these two approaches and were generally concerned that their profession was heading down the business-focused route and losing sight of the employee concerns.

These discourses are examples of a continuing discussion in HRM over **'hard'** and **'soft'** approaches.

## The unitarist view

There have been arguments, particularly prevalent in HRM's early days in the 1980s but still relevant today, over whether HRM is a particular style or brand of managing employment relationships or whether it can be used as an umbrella term for all policies, practices and approaches to managing employment. Critics have suggested that HRM is a prescription of how to manage that is focused on a 'unitary' view of organizations: seeing the organization as a single entity with one goal and claiming that employee and organizational interests are one and the same. This approach rests on an underlying assumption that harmoniously working together will be in everyone's best interests. The Transferrable Skills activity will help you to identify this kind of underlying assumption in the field of OB and HRM.

As an example, a **unitarist** view of pay would suggest that it is in the organization and the employees' interests to ensure fair but not excessive pay levels. If staffing costs become too high, the organization will not be able to compete effectively and may even fail, leading to job losses. On the other hand, fair and reasonable pay can be a good way of rewarding or even motivating employees, so if pay levels are low it could have a negative impact on the motivation and performance of individuals and ultimately of the organization itself. Therefore, the argument goes, employee and organizational goals should be the same: competitive but rewarding pay levels.

However, this unitarist approach disregards the idea that employees may have very different goals from employers, and even that different groups of employees may have opposing interests and concerns within the same organization. To continue our example, it may be that individuals or particular groups of employees believe their work is much more essential to the effective performance of

---

 ## Transferrable Skills: Identifying underlying assumptions

Being able to read (or listen) critically is a key skill you will develop through your time at university and will be invaluable to you in your future career. One of the contributing skills to critical thinking is the ability to identify the underlying, often unspoken, assumptions behind an argument. It is important to be able to identify underlying assumptions because they often mean that information is presented in a biased way, with the aim of swaying you in one way or another. Assumptions also limit the ways we look at issues, meaning that we may completely miss a potential solution to a problem simply because we are looking at it in a particular way.

This exercise takes you through some examples to help you develop this skill, enabling you to weigh the evidence for new claims or suggestions and to draw balanced conclusions for yourself. Read this extract and take a moment to consider what the author's underlying assumption might be. That is, what is the author assuming is true without providing evidence for it?

> Although trade unions look after the interests of their members, they also recognise the advantages of working in partnership with employers. This is because a successful, profitable business is good for workers and therefore good for the union and its members.
>
> (nibusinessinfo.co.uk, 2016)

*Example underlying assumption:* In this extract, the author is assuming that a successful business is good for everyone and using that as 'evidence' that trade unions will work in partnership with employers. Do you think this is always true? Can you perhaps think of examples of successful businesses that are not good for the workers?

Now try with a longer piece. This is a blog post titled 'David Smith: Trade unions are outdated' by Tim Smedley (2009). Here, see if you can identify the underlying assumptions of David Smith, who is quoted in the article:

> The traditional conflict role of trade unions is outdated and no longer required in the modern world of work, according to David Smith, the former people director of Asda. The role played by trade unions, he argued, has taken a back seat because of improvements in employment law and the increasing importance of **employer branding**. 'Clearly unions grew out of the fact that the employer was abusing the work relationship – that was about redressing the balance of power. In the modern era, however, there's a legal framework and a competitive framework, all of which are

driving people to be good employers.' The future role of unions, Smith believes, will be as more of an information and advice resource than about 'protecting people in the traditional sense'.

Smith's interest in union issues goes back a long way. A veteran of personnel in the mining industry during the miners' strike, he joined Asda in the mid-1990s to deal with its union issues. Under the tutelage of the infamous Archie Norman and Allan Leighton, Smith's role soon enveloped 'a cultural change programme to take the business forward'. The turnaround of Asda from the verge of bankruptcy to become the UK's second-largest retailer was all done on Smith's watch; as was the supermarket's accolade of the Best Big Company to Work For in the Sunday Times' 2004 list. By 2005, however, the unions came back to bite – depot strikes and a sustained campaign by the GMB posed one of Smith's 'most difficult times'.

Source: Smedley, T. (2009) David Smith: 'Trade unions are outdated', *People Management*. Available at: www2.cipd. co.uk/pm/peoplemanagement/b/weblog/ archive/2013/01/29/david-smith-trade-unions-are-outdated-2009-04.aspx. Extracts reproduced with permission of CIPD.

Now move on to see if you can identify the assumptions of Tim Smedley, the author of the article. What conclusion might the author want you to come to? What words has the author chosen to get his message across? Try comparing the first and last sentences: do they suggest an assumption that is not explicitly stated?

You can practise this skill with any text you are reading – even this one. As far as possible as we go through this book, I will, as the author, try to make it clear to you where the assumptions are in different theorists' models and even in my own writing. But there may well be other assumptions that I don't specifically mention. Becoming aware of them will help you to evaluate the arguments presented here and come to your own, better informed conclusions.

the organization than others' and therefore should be rewarded at a higher level. Or, the **leaders** of the organization may not be interested in long-term success but simply short-term profits, in which case cutting employee pay would be an effective method of achieving this. This reliance on a unitarist view of organizations is a continuing criticism of HRM and one we will return to during the course of this book.

## COMBINING OB AND HRM

Most textbooks treat OB and HRM as separate subjects. This book aims to bring both fields of study together. Why? It is my belief that OB and HRM share a common central concern – that of people at work. As you have hopefully seen through this chapter so far, both subjects are seeking to understand how we behave at work and, perhaps more foundationally, *why*. In addition, OB and HRM are both concerned with how we can apply the knowledge we gain to enhance organizational and individual performance. Both subjects also have a strong thread of concern for employee well-being running through them: researchers and theorists in both areas have traditionally wanted to improve our experience of and at work, seeing work as a positive force rather than simply a feature of society. In addition, the current topic areas of both subjects show considerable overlap: motivation, leadership, selection, performance and so on are all areas of key importance to OB and HRM. In fact, it could be argued that it makes little sense to try and consider OB and HRM separately. To do so would be to miss out on potentially valuable contributions from either discipline.

In this section, we will consider three challenges that OB and HRM share, and explore the ways the two disciplines can contribute to each other in addressing these challenges.

### Challenge 1: Individual or organization?

Both OB and HRM are concerned with how people behave at work and how organizations can be structured or organized in order to promote organizational success and, often, individual well-being. However, where to place the emphasis in trying to achieve this understanding is a common debate. We considered this in an earlier section when we were discussing the 'ecological fallacy' in OB and return to it here because it is a shared challenge for HRM and OB.

For some theorists, it is the people that make the difference in organizations and so we should focus all our efforts on understanding individuals. For example, Schneider (1987, p. 40) claimed that it was the kinds of people in a particular work organization that defined how that organization behaved, saying that: 'the attributes of people, not the nature of the external environment, or organizational technology, or organizational structure, are the fundamental determinants of organizational behaviour'. This was the basis for Schneider's attraction-selection-attrition framework, in which he suggested that people are attracted to, selected for, and stay with organizations they 'fit' with. This 'fit' is simply how similar the people in that organization are to the individual in question. In this model, any organizational effects on behaviour are the result of the people in the organization: the level of analysis that is most important then is the individual employee.

Other theorists emphasize the organizational-level aspects. This has been particularly important for HRM researchers who want to demonstrate the impact of HR practices on organizational performance. Because HR practices are commonly organization-wide, it seems perfectly reasonable to consider HRM issues at an organizational level. Yet, this can lead to problems in understanding HR effects: it is the employee's *experience* of the HR practices that may well be the key to unlocking their impacts on organizational performance (Boselie et al., 2005), and this can only be understood at the individual level.

This challenge has led to calls in both the OB and HRM literature for multi-level models (e.g. Heath and Sitkin, 2001). These are models that try to take account of individual level variables (such as an employee's skills or experience of a particular HR practice) and organizational-level variables (such as organizational strategy or structure) in understanding and predicting outcomes at work. While these models are, by necessity, more complex, they also have the advantage of being more true to life, and research in this direction is providing some promising insights (Clausen and Borg, 2011; Wood et al., 2012). As we progress through this book, we will consider some of these individual/organizational level issues in greater detail, and we will continue to emphasize the importance of evaluating problems at the right level.

## Challenge 2: Theory or application?

One of the persistent challenges in learning about OB and HRM is to strike a balance between theories and practical applications. If we focus on theory, we gain a grounding in the general approaches we can take in managing people at work and develop our ability to do big picture thinking, as well as our awareness of critical issues related to these concepts. This can help to identify and analyse problems more accurately and develop solutions based on solid research that have a good chance of success. Too much emphasis on theory, however, and we can lose sight of the details of how those solutions can actually be applied to specific situations.

It may therefore be tempting to think we should emphasize practical applications. After all, most people who engage in learning about OB and HRM want to do so in order to improve their own management practice, to develop others' or to enhance their own organization's effectiveness. And learning about what specific applications have been successful in the past can help to build a store of experience that can be drawn on to address these issues. But without an understanding of the overarching theories or models, we can fall into the trap of blindly trying to apply 'best practice' from one organization to a situation that is completely dissimilar, or trying something previous research has shown to be ineffective.

This theory/application balance is an ongoing challenge in business education and the relative importance of each side of the balance tends to change over time. In a survey of business school academics, Wren et al. (2007) found that the teaching of HRM and OB had followed roughly opposite patterns in the emphasis on theory or application over a 30-year period. While the majority of courses taught at business schools, including HRM, had an emphasis on theory in the 1970s, then a swing towards application in the 1980s, followed by a swing back to theory, OB teaching did the opposite. In addition, OB and HRM tend to have slightly different theory/application balances, with HRM teaching throughout that time focused more heavily on application than OB. This latter result is

to be expected as HRM, by necessity, includes a consideration of specific HR practices.

The ideal, then, is to combine well-researched and well-founded theory with a clearly developed understanding of practical application. That is what this book aims to do. In addition, by drawing on the stronger theory present in OB and the stronger application in HRM, you will be able to develop your skills in critical awareness and practical application in your future career.

## Challenge 3: Link with performance?

Both the OB and HRM literature rely on an implicit assumption that learning about and understanding these fields better will help to improve work performance, whether of the individual or the organization. Indeed, it could be argued that this is an underlying assumption of all business disciplines. It would be an unusual student who wanted to study a business subject at university but did not expect to be able to use that knowledge to improve their current or future work. So it would seem that demonstrating the impact of different models or approaches on organizational performance is essential. Yet, it is surprisingly difficult.

The first issue we face in trying to demonstrate the effect of a particular practice or theory on performance is how we actually define and measure performance. The Application activity explores this issue in relation to your own performance at university. Boselie et al. (2005) suggested three broad areas of HRM outcomes or performance measures that could be taken into account:

1. **Financial:** including profits, sales and market share of the organization

2. **Organizational:** including productivity or quality measures

3. **HR-related:** including employee attitudes and behaviours.

While the first category, financial measures, is often considered the 'most important' because it demonstrates the impact of HR or OB on the bottom line – the organization's profits and expenses – it is also arguably the furthest removed from the people issues considered by models in these areas. There are so many other variables that can impact on these financial outcomes that it becomes difficult to demonstrate with any certainty that, for example, a particular HR practice has had a positive effect on profit levels. There is a similar issue in the OB literature, although it tends to be even further complicated because OB considers such a large array of different theories, concepts and systems.

## Applications: Measuring performance

One of the challenges in OB and HRM research is how researchers can measure performance. Let's illustrate this difficulty by thinking about your own work as a student. The most obvious measure of a student's performance is the final degree grade. But how else could you (or would you want to) measure the 'success' of your time at university? Make a list of all the different ways you can think of to measure student performance or outcomes. What do you think would be the best or ideal way of measuring your own success as a student?

Image Source/Craig Wetherby CM

Now compare your list to the distinctions that Boselie et al. (2005) drew in how we can measure organizational performance. Can you see any parallels? What do you think is the best way to measure organizational performance?

A definitive review of studies into the HRM–performance link concluded that there was good evidence for HRM having a positive impact on performance (Boselie et al., 2005). However, the same report cautioned that there was so much variability in how the studies were conducted that we could not make a clear statement of the size of this impact or draw definitive conclusions about the HRM–performance relationship. Wall and Wood (2005, p. 453) were more critical in their review and pitched the question as an imaginary court case: an international company is suing a firm of HR consultants because the 'performance-enhancing' practices they were advised to adopt have shown no return on investment. An expert witness (HRM scholar) is called to the stand to testify on the HRM–

performance link. The expert witness concludes that, while the published literature and research generally promotes a link between HRM and performance (often simply assuming it exists), the actual evidence is 'promising but only circumstantial'.

How can this challenge be addressed? Wall and Wood (2005) have three suggestions:

1.  Researchers and practitioners should temper the claims they are making; for example, by noting that an HR practice may be 'associated with' performance rather than claiming it is a 'determinant'.

2.  We should evaluate competing hypotheses more rigorously. Instead of picking a favourite model or hypothesis and sticking to it, we should be aware of alternate hypotheses and evaluate them against each other to see which is most accurate.

3.  We need stronger research designs. For example, measures of the HRM practices and performance should not rely on a single source and longitudinal research designs would help to identify the real effect of HR or OB on performance.

These research issues are not just important for researchers to be aware of, but for managers and HR practitioners too: without a good understanding of where the conclusions come from, you will not know how much you can rely on them.

## What do OB and HRM have in common? Management as a reflective practice

Management is essentially a process of convincing people to work together to meet the aims of the organization; it is a management of relationships rather than 'things'. Human relationships are complex and this means there is often no 'one right answer' to the questions that managers face. However, by developing knowledge of the theories and models in OB and HRM, you can learn to be a better manager. This book will help you to develop your critical thinking skills and become a reflective practitioner: this is someone who does not settle for doing what they have always done, but constantly assesses their practice and learns from it.

 **Web Explorer: Professional bodies and reflective practice**

Look up the professional body for HRM practitioners in your country (there may well be more than one). Explore the relevant website and find out more about it, then compare it to the professional body of another country. What differences and similarities can you identify? For example: What requirements do they have for membership or what different levels of membership are there? Are there also requirements for continuing professional development? Does the institute accredit professional qualifications from other countries?

Here are a few to get you started:

• Australia – Australian Human Resources Institute (AHRI): www.ahri.com.au

• India – Society for Human Resource Management (SHRM): www.shrm.org/india/pages/default.aspx

• South Africa – South African Board for People Practices (SABPP): http://sabpp.co.za and Institute for People Management (IPM): www.ipm.co.za

• UK – Chartered Institute of Personnel and Development (CIPD): www.cipd.co.uk

• USA – Society for Human Resource Management (SHRM): www.shrm.org (with branches all over the world)

Reflective practice is an essential part of becoming an HR professional because it is the basis for identifying what you need to develop or learn and how it will help you. For example, the Chartered Institute of Personnel and Development (CIPD), the professional body for HRM in the UK, recognizes how reflective learning is the foundation for professional practice (www.cipd.co.uk/cpd/reflective-learning.aspx). Have a look at the Web Explorer to explore the HRM professional bodies around the world and the role of reflective practice and continuing professional development in other countries.

Weick introduced the term 'sensemaking' to organizational theory to explore this idea of reflecting on practice and says it is a key competency for managers. Sensemaking can be defined as a process of turning an experience or set of circumstances into something you consciously describe and understand in words (Weick et al., 2005). We tend to do sensemaking retrospectively, that is, looking back over our experiences to make sense of what happened and to provide a rationalization of our current actions. When faced with ambiguity, we 'search for meaning, settle for plausibility and move on' (Weick et al., 2005, p. 419). The authors point out that this sensemaking is where we create meaning and this in turn influences our identities and how we behave. Understanding this process of sensemaking gives us the possibility of influencing the story that is told and the subsequent actions of those involved.

 ### Practice Insights: Jennifer Dootson

Jennifer Dootson is HR Business Partner at d-Wise, a technology and consultancy company providing solutions for the life science and healthcare sector. She is also studying part time for her MSc in HRM at Manchester Metropolitan University. In the video she talks about what attracted her to HR as a career and why she chose to study it at university, sharing some tips on making the most of your studies and finding the right job.

Go online to www.macmillanihe.com/sutton-people to access the interview with Jennifer.

## SUMMARY

In this first chapter, we have defined OB and HRM, seeing how their history is shared but also how they have developed into fields of study in their own right. OB has developed from a concern with efficiency at work to an understanding of the complex, multi-level reality of behaviour in work organizations. HRM has gone through a similar process, from a time when specific HR practices were promoted as the best way to manage people in organizations, to a more nuanced understanding of the various organizational and environmental factors that can affect HR success.

We saw how OB and HRM can complement each other in building our understanding of management and work by discussing three challenges that both face and seeing what the two fields have in common. Throughout this chapter, we have also seen how important a critical or analytical approach is, whether that be in evaluating HR practice or identifying underlying assumptions in OB theories. And that ability to critically evaluate is not just important for learning about this subject area, but is also vital for the development of professional practice: a skill that will be developed throughout this book.

## FURTHER READING

- For a more detailed review of the history of HRM, see Kaufman, B. E. (2007) 'The development of HRM in historical and international perspective', in Boxall et al. (eds) *The Oxford Handbook of Human Resource Management*, pp. 1–19.

- For an evaluation of the HRM–performance link that presents the discussion in terms of evaluating claims in a court case, read Wall, T. D. and Wood, S. J. (2005) 'The romance of human resource management and business performance, and the case for big science', *Human Relations*, 58(4), pp. 429–62.

## REVIEW QUESTIONS

1. Briefly outline the history of the organizational behaviour field and give examples of how its historical roots still influence the theory and practice of management today.

**2.** To what extent do you think that HRM, which originally emerged in the USA, can be said to be globally applicable?

**3.** Why is it worth studying OB and HRM together rather than as separate subjects?

# ONLINE RESOURCES

Go online to www.macmillanihe.com/sutton-people to access a MCQ quiz for this chapter and for further resources to support your learning.

# REFERENCES

Al-Waqfi, M. A. and Forstenlechner, I. (2014) 'Barriers to Emiratization: the role of policy design and institutional environment in determining the effectiveness of Emiratization', *International Journal of Human Resource Management*, 25(2), pp. 167–89. doi: 10.1080/09585192.2013.826913.

Beer, M., Spector, B., Lawrence, P. R. and Mills, D. Q. (1984) *Managing Human Assets: The Groundbreaking Harvard Business School Program*. New York: Free Press.

Boselie, P., Dietz, G. and Boon, C. (2005) 'Commonalities and contradictions in HRM and performance research', *Human Resource Management Journal*, 15(3), pp. 67–94. doi: 10.1111/j.1748-8583.2005.tb00154.x.

Boxall, P. (2007) 'The goals of HRM', in *The Oxford Handbook of Human Resource Management*. Oxford: Oxford University Press.

Boxall, P., Purcell, J. and Wright, P. M. (2007a) 'Human resource management: scope, analysis, and significance', in *The Oxford Handbook of Human Resource Management*. Oxford: Oxford University Press, pp. 1–19.

Boxall, P., Purcell, J. and Wright, P. M. (eds) (2007b) *The Oxford Handbook of Human Resource Management*. Oxford: Oxford University Press.

Clausen, T. and Borg, V. (2011) 'Job demands, job resources and meaning at work', *Journal of Managerial Psychology*, 26(8), pp. 665–81. doi: 10.1108/02683941111181761.

Eagly, A. H., Johannesen-Schmidt, M. C. and van Engen, M. L. (2003) 'Transformational, transactional, and laissez-faire leadership styles: a meta-analysis comparing women and men', *Psychological Bulletin*, 129(4), pp. 569–91.

Follett, M. P. (1924) *Creative Experience*. New York: Longmans, Green and Co.

Guest, D. E. (1987) 'Human resource management and industrial relations', *Journal of Management Studies*, 24(5), pp. 503–21. doi: 10.1111/j.1467-6486.1987.tb00460.x.

Guest, D. E. (1991) 'Personnel management: the end of orthodoxy?', *British Journal of Industrial Relations*, 29(2), pp. 149–75. doi: 10.1111/j.1467-8543.1991.tb00235.x.

Haak-Saheem, W., Festing, M. and Darwish, T. K. (2016) 'International human resource management in the Arab Gulf States: an institutional perspective', *International Journal of Human Resource Management*, pp. 1–29. doi: 10.1080/09585192.2016.1234502.

Heath, C. and Sitkin, S. B. (2001) 'Big-B versus Big-O: What is *organizational* about organizational behavior?', *Journal of Organizational Behavior*, 22(1), pp. 43–58.

Judge, T. A., Thoreson, C. J., Bono, J. E. and Patton, G. K. (2001) 'The job satisfaction-job performance relationship: a qualitative and quantitative review', *Psychological Bulletin*, 127(3), pp. 376–407.

Keegan, A. and Francis, H. (2010) 'Practitioner talk: the changing textscape of HRM and emergence of HR business partnership', *International Journal of Human Resource Management*, 21(6), pp. 873–98. doi: 10.1080/09585191003729341.

Mayo, E. (2003) 'The Hawthorne Experiment Western Electrical Company', in K. Thompson (ed.) *The Human Problems of an Industrial Civilization*. New York: Macmillan.

Miner, J. B. (1984) 'The validity and usefulness of theories in an emerging organizational science', *Academy of Management Review*, 9(2), pp. 296–306. doi: 10.5465/AMR.1984.4277659.

Miner, J. B. (2003) 'The rated importance, scientific validity, and practical usefulness of organizational behavior theories: a quantitative review', *Academy of Management Learning & Education*, 2(3), pp. 250–68. doi: 10.5465/AMLE.2003.10932132.

Moukhallati, D. (2017) 'More young Emiratis warming to the idea of working in private sector', *The National*, 9 April, pp. 1–6.

nibusinessinfo.co.uk (2016) *The role of trade unions and their representatives*. Available at: www.nibusinessinfo.co.uk/content/role-trade-unions-and-their-representatives (Accessed 31 May 2016).

Rees, C. J., Mamman, A. and Braik, A. Bin (2007) 'Emiratization as a strategic HRM change initiative: case study evidence from a UAE petroleum company', *International Journal of Human Resource Management*, 18(1), pp. 33–53. doi: 10.1080/09585190601068268.

Riketta, M. (2008) 'The causal relation between job attitudes and performance: a meta-analysis of panel studies', *Journal of Applied Psychology*, 93(2), pp. 472–81. doi: 10.1037/0021-9010.93.2.472.

Schneider, B. (1985) 'Organizational behavior', *Annual Review of Psychology*, 36, pp. 571–611.

Schneider, B. (1987) 'The people make the place', *Personnel Psychology*, 40(3), pp. 437–53.

Smedley, T. (2009) David Smith: 'Trade unions are outdated', *People Management*. Available at: www2.cipd.co.uk/pm/peoplemanagement/b/weblog/archive/2013/01/29/david-smith-trade-unions-are-outdated-2009-04.aspx (Accessed 31 May 2016).

Storey, J. (1989) *New Perspectives on Human Resource Management*. London: Routledge.

Taylor, F. W. (1911) *The Principles of Scientific Management*. London: Harper & Brothers.

Wall, T. D. and Wood, S. J. (2005) 'The romance of human resource management and business performance, and the case for big science', *Human Relations*, 58(4), pp. 429–62. doi: 10.1177/0018726705055032.

Waters, T. and Waters, D. (eds) (2015) *Weber's Rationalism and Modern Society*. New York: Palgrave Macmillan.

Watson, T. J. (2010) 'Critical social science, pragmatism and the realities of HRM', *International Journal of Human Resource Management*, 21(6), pp. 915–31. doi: 10.1080/09585191003729374.

Weick, K. E., Sutcliffe, K. M. and Obstfeld, D. (2005) 'Organization science and the process of sensemaking', *Organization Science*, 16(4), pp. 409–21. doi: 10.1287/orsc.1050.0133.

Winkler, S., König, C. J. and Kleinmann, M. (2012) 'New insights into an old debate: investigating the temporal sequence of commitment and performance at the business unit level', *Journal of Occupational and Organizational Psychology*, 85(3), pp. 503–22. doi: 10.1111/j.2044-8325.2012.02054.x.

Wood, S., Van Veldhoven, M., Croon, M. and de Menezes, L. M. (2012) 'Enriched job design, high involvement management and organizational performance: the mediating roles of job satisfaction and well-being', *Human Relations*, 65(4), pp. 419–45. doi: 10.1177/0018726711432476.

Wren, D. A., Halbesleben, J. R. B. and Buckley, M. R. (2007) 'The theory-application balance in management pedagogy: a longitudinal update', *Academy of Management Learning and Education*, 6(4), pp. 484–92. doi: 10.5465/AMLE.2007.27694948.

# 2 WHAT IS WORK ALL ABOUT?

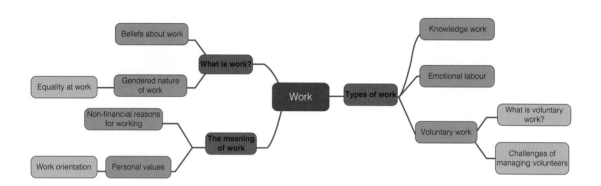

## INTRODUCTION

In this chapter, we continue to lay the foundations for understanding OB and HRM. We start by taking some time to think about what work is all about: how our beliefs around what work *is* affect our own working lives and the management of people at work. We will also see how we can develop a critical approach to the study of work and evaluate the role of pay in work here, as a basis for a more detailed discussion of the role of pay and reward in motivation in Chapter 5.

There are many reasons that people work and in this chapter we will look at financial and non-financial reasons, from personal values to the role of work in the rest of our lives. Finally, we will distinguish between the different types of work involved in the range of jobs available, from knowledge work to emotional labour, before considering the special case of voluntary work. In all of this, the emphasis will be on what we can learn about management and HR in the modern workplace from understanding these fundamental concepts.

*Image Source/David Oxberry*

## LEARNING FEATURES

Applications: What is work?

Applications: More pay, less work?

Applications: The centrality of work

Applications: Emotional labour

Weighing the Evidence: We all just want an easy life

Web Explorer: Attracting volunteers

In the News: Unconditional basic income

Transferrable Skills: Critical thinking

Practice Insights: Carrie McKenzie

 Video overview

*Julian Perkins*

Go online to www.macmillanihe.com/sutton-people to access a video of Anna Sutton introducing the chapter's main themes.

## WHAT IS WORK?

Have you ever stopped to think what you define as work? The Applications activity will help you to explore this concept before we move into formal definitions.

## Applications: **What is work?**

Write a list of everything you did yesterday. Now go through each item and mark it as 'work' or 'not work'.

Compare your list to a colleague's or friend's. What kinds of things do each of you view as work? Consider issues such as whether the activity has to be paid and whether studying or household tasks like grocery shopping and cleaning count as work. Where you have similarities or differences in your definitions of work, explore your reasons. What does this tell you about your underlying beliefs of what work is?

Keith Thomas, a historian who wrote about the development and meaning of work, notes that any definition of work will have to be slightly ambiguous or fuzzy (Thomas, 1999). Dictionary definitions focus on work as an activity that involves effort, which can be mental or physical, carried out to achieve a result or goal. But Thomas goes further to develop a pragmatic definition of work which has three main components:

1. Work is not an end in itself, but is designed to produce or achieve something.

2. Work has an element of obligation or sense of necessity: it is a task that we either set for ourselves or others set for us, something we 'have' to do.

3. Work involves a degree of effort or persistence beyond the simply pleasurable.

But this definition could also apply to many activities that we do for leisure, for example playing sports, baking cakes or playing computer games. Each of those activities aims to produce or achieve something, is a task we have set ourselves, and involves a certain degree of effort. Conversely, it is easy to imagine a day at work in which you did not feel you achieved anything, or a day when you felt you 'worked' hard but that your work was simply enjoyable.

This ambiguity makes it tempting to define work more concisely as the *tasks or activities* we carry out in our paid employment. However, Thomas also points out that this definition will not do either: for much of our history people were not paid for the work they did and even today there is a lot of unpaid work. Williams (2005) reports on a study of 'underground' work: work that is done cash in hand,

that is, not reported for tax purposes. He found that purely financial reasons for engaging in underground work were given in only 30% of the cases. In the remaining 70%, other reasons were mixed in or even dominant. These other reasons could be grouped into two themes:

- **Community-building:** the work helped to build or strengthen a social relationship. In these cases, paying the worker was seen as a form of gift exchange: the worker had done the 'employer' a favour and the 'employer' was returning the favour. Gift exchange is a well-known method for strengthening relationships and this rationale was seen particularly between friends and neighbours.

- **Redistributive:** the work was seen as a way of 'helping people out' or redistributing wealth and favours. This reason was particularly prevalent among relatives. For example, the 'employer' saw the work as a way to give the worker some much-needed money in a way that did not seem like charity. Or the worker did the work for a lower-than-market fee as a way of helping out relatives who were not able to do the work themselves.

*PHOTODISC*

*Work is sometimes seen as a way of 'redistributing' wealth and favours among relatives.*

One of the advantages of looking at these non-mainstream forms of work is that they help us to explore the other elements of work, including why people work and what it means to them. Thomas (1999) gives a further example when he discusses how early male economists refused to acknowledge women's work in the home – cleaning, cooking, looking after children – as 'real' work, but defined it as unproductive activity. The shadow of this prejudice still hangs over us, as, for example, with government initiatives in many countries that aim to get parents 'back into work' and do not recognize childcare and household tasks as valuable work. So, in this chapter, we will consider the gendered nature of work as well as the specific challenges of unpaid voluntary work and the insights we can gain from this broader understanding of what work is. We start by looking at how our beliefs and values influence our view of work.

## Beliefs about work

We saw in Chapter 1 that one of the early theorists who contributed to the development of OB as a discipline was Max Weber. Writing in the 19th and early 20th centuries, one of Weber's major concerns was with how Protestant Christianity and capitalism were entwined, their effects seen particularly strongly in Western Europe and the USA. It may seem strange to consider how religious beliefs influence work, but as major belief systems, the religions of the world have had an undeniable effect on how people in different cultures approach and view their work. Harpaz (1998) notes that religion affects behaviour in work organizations in direct (e.g. religious holidays or observances such as Ramadan) and indirect ways (e.g. individual wishes and activities). The Applications activity uses one of Weber's examples to illustrate how different beliefs can affect our approach to work.

 Applications: **More pay, less work?**

Max Weber used many examples to bring his sociological arguments to life. This one, adapted from his book *The Protestant Ethic and the Spirit of Capitalism* (1930), contrasts the 'spirit of capitalism' with a more traditional view of work. It illustrates how a mismatch between an employer and employee's beliefs can have surprising effects.

In agriculture, harvest time requires the most intensive work effort on the part of the labourers. Let's assume that labourers are paid €100 a day and usually harvest one field in that time. An employer, wishing to encourage the labourers to work harder, decides to introduce **piece-rate pay**. The employer announces that, instead of being paid by the day, labourers will now be paid €200 for each field they harvest. The idea is that this will encourage the labourers to work harder so that they can earn

more money. But instead of an increase in the rate of work, the employer finds that the labourers actually work less! From their point of view, they can now earn just as much as before by doing half the work. 'The opportunity of earning more was less attractive than that of working less' (Weber, 1930, p. 24).

» If you were an employee in this situation, what effect do you think the change in pay schemes would have on you? Discuss with your colleagues and find out if there are any differences among you. Why do you think this is?

» If you were the employer and were faced with labourers who were seemingly unmotivated by the potential to earn extra money, what solutions could you develop?

Weber was interested in why the Industrial Revolution and the rise of capitalism happened in the West. He argued that it was because of the influence of Protestant Christianity in Western countries, which inherently promoted a capitalist approach to work. Protestantism, particularly the branch of it called Calvinism, promoted the idea of work as a moral duty and material success was seen as a sign of God's favour. Unlike Catholics, who could

be assured of going to heaven if they followed the Church's teaching, Protestants felt the need for some outward sign that God favoured them and they were doing the right things. This gave rise to a 'capitalist spirit' that took on a life of its own: the capitalist belief system sees profit as an end in itself and makes a virtue out of pursuing profit.

Interestingly, however, this close relationship between Protestantism and the so-called 'work ethic' is not supported in recent research. Instead, it seems that traditionally Protestant countries now have a *lower* work ethic than other countries. Using information from the World Values Survey, a survey of changing values around the world, Norris and Inglehart (2004) considered three elements of a 'work ethic', or the values people hold about work:

1. **Intrinsic benefits:** work gives us the opportunity to achieve, gain respect or is interesting in itself.

2. **Material rewards:** work provides good pay and holidays, not too much pressure and good security.

3. **Duty:** work is a duty and people who do not work are lazy.

They found that increasing affluence and education as well as the presence of a welfare state (meaning that work was no longer a necessity for living) led to a decrease in the work ethic. And even controlling for these factors, Christian societies (Catholic, Protestant and Orthodox) and Eastern religions (e.g. Buddhism) place significantly less value on work than do Muslim societies. This finding was supported by a study within the USA that compared the work ethic of non-religious, Catholic, Protestant and Muslim people, which also found that Muslims scored higher than all the others on work ethic beliefs (Zulfikar, 2012). Similar to the Protestant beliefs that Weber referred to, the Muslim view of work emphasizes work as a service to God and a way of balancing individual and societal needs (Zulfikar, 2012).

Harpaz (1998), in fact, suggests that all the world religions view work in a positive light and encourage their followers to work hard as an expression of their faith. His research shows that it may be the *degree* of religiosity, that is, how strong someone's religious beliefs are, rather than the specific religion that affects a person's work ethic. There is certainly some indication that this is true for Christians and Jews (Harpaz, 1998; Sharabi, 2012), although there is less evidence that it holds true for Muslims, perhaps because the work ethic is stronger in this group anyway.

## The gendered nature of work

We cannot discuss the meaning of work without referring to the role that gender plays. Stereotypically and traditionally, the man's role in the family is as the 'breadwinner', the main income-generator and provider for the family, while the woman's is as the homemaker. Gender roles are often a source of meaning in people's lives, but the problem arises when 'masculine' work is valued more than 'feminine' work. There is no rational reason that this should be the case; after all, it is hard to justify a view that caring for and bringing up children is less important or valuable than, for example, designing a marketing campaign. Yet, that is often the assumption that many societies have: it is deeply engrained and difficult to change.

An international report on gender inequalities conducted by the International Labour Office (ILO) collected data from 178 different countries and came to the following conclusion (Addati et al., 2016, p. xi), which is worth reading in full:

> Inequality between women and men persists in global labour markets, in respect of opportunities, treatment and outcomes. Over the last two decades, women's significant progress in educational achievements has not translated into a comparable improvement in their position at work. In many regions in the world, in comparison to men, women are more likely to become and remain unemployed, have fewer chances to participate in the labour force and – when they do – often have to accept lower quality jobs. Progress in surmounting these obstacles has been slow and is limited to a few regions across the world. Even in many of those countries where gaps in labour force participation and employment have narrowed and where women are shifting away from contributing family work and moving to the services sector, the quality of women's jobs remains a matter of concern. The unequal distribution of unpaid care and household work between women and men and between families and the society is an important determinant of gender inequalities at work.

Overall, worldwide, the ILO report found that women earn approximately 77% of what men earn and it is estimated that if current trends continue, it will take 70 years for this gap to close. And closing the gap is not something that will happen 'naturally' as economic prosperity increases; some of the countries with the highest per capita levels also have the highest pay gap. It needs explicit affirmative policies, such as setting targets or quotas, to address the problem, as well as education and training programmes to reduce occupational segregation.

Why is the pay gap so resistant to resolution? The ILO report (Addati et al., 2016) suggests that several complex and interrelated factors are at play:

1. Women are often paid less than men for doing the same work because 'women's work' is stereotypically seen as of less value than men's.

2. Women are disproportionally represented in lower paid jobs. It is common for traditionally female occupations, such as caring, to be undervalued and not paid at an equivalent level to traditionally male occupations.

3. Women are also more likely to have unpaid home and childcare responsibilities that restrict the time available for paid work, meaning that the majority of part-time workers are women (57%).

When both paid and unpaid work are taken into account, employed women work longer hours than employed men: 33 minutes more each day in developed countries and over 70 minutes more a day in developing countries. In a year, this adds up to an extra 200 hours in developed countries and 444 hours in developing countries. The Transferrable Skills exercise delves into the issue of gendered work in more detail.

## Transferrable Skills: Critical thinking

Critical thinking is one of the essential skills you will need to engage in knowledge work, which we discuss later in this chapter. It involves being able to think clearly and rationally, to analyse information and weigh it up so that you can come to an informed and justifiable conclusion. It is a very useful skill because it is 'domain general'. This means it is not just a skill you develop in relation to one area of learning but a skill which, if you develop in your study of HRM and OB, you will be able to apply to any new situation or subject you come across.

Having said all this, a word of caution. Critical thinking is not easy! It is a skill you have probably been working on to some degree throughout your education and will continue to develop through this course. On the plus side, however, it *is* a skill you can practise. It involves training yourself to ask open-ended questions. This exercise is an example of how you can do that. Read the following paragraphs and then work through the steps in order. Take your time over it. Critical thinking is not something you should try to rush but spend time in thinking and analysing. Read the following paragraphs and then work through the steps in order:

Saudi Arabia is widely recognised as having some of the most gender restrictive laws and customs of any country in the world. Men and women are segregated in most public spaces and women are not able to have driving licenses. It also has one of the lowest rates of female participation in the workforce (18%) and in an interview with *The Economist* (2016), Muhammad

bin Salman, Saudi Arabia's deputy crown prince, suggested that this was because of women themselves: '[The woman] is not used to working. She needs more time to accustom herself to the idea of work. A large percentage of Saudi women are used to the fact of staying at home. They're not used to being working women. It just takes time.'

Even in countries with greater gender equality, there remains controversy over whether women should have access to all of the same jobs as men. One of the most controversial areas in several Western countries is allowing women in the armed forces to fight on the front lines. Australia and the USA have recently passed laws to allow this. In the UK, Admiral Alan West, a retired Royal Navy officer was quoted by *The Guardian* (2015) as saying he was unsure about 'women in the infantry and the Royal Marines, where they have to actually advance on the enemy, climb into a trench and fight and kill each other … There is no doubt at all that women are very, very brave. We have always been willing to let women die in wars and actually they are very competent, particularly at computer operating – they have longer concentration power than men.'

In other countries, such as Canada, Denmark and Poland, there are no restrictions on which combat units women can be in. Captain Ashley Collette of the

Canadian armed forces was deployed with her platoon of 60 soldiers to the front line in Afghanistan in 2010. After her return, some of her men told her they had initially been wary of her but would now follow her anywhere. Captain Collette says that she thinks it is normal for soldiers to be wary of a new leader, no matter what their gender: 'They always want to feel out your style of leadership.' She wants people to see her as a soldier, rather than a 'woman soldier' and says that the whole debate over whether women can actually take on a combat job is 'null and void … In my experience, there's no reason why a band of brothers cannot be a band of brothers and sisters' (cited in Kremer, 2013).

1.  What emotional reaction do you have to the quotes featured in the paragraphs above? Why do you think you have had that reaction? What is the underlying issue at stake for you?

It is important to be able to identify your own emotional reaction and the reasons behind it because in critical thinking you need to be able to take a clear and rational approach to analysis. This does not mean your emotional reaction is 'wrong' or useless. It can be a valuable guide to understanding some of the important issues in a debate. But you

need to be able to express *why* you feel that way if you are to take it further. So use your answers to these questions to write down a clear and concise summary of the issue as you see it.

2.  Consider the points of view of the three people quoted here. Write a short summary of the issue as each of them sees it.

When thinking critically, you do not only need to understand and analyse your own thoughts and feelings on an issue, but also the points of view of other people so that you can develop the justifications for your argument.

Now we can take it a step further and consider some of the wider implications.

3.  Are there some jobs which women should not do? How about jobs which men should not do?

Explore your reasons for thinking this. What evidence do you have for thinking it? What would it take to change your mind?

Finally, an even further step is to start considering what should be done in the future to deal with this issue.

4.  To what extent do you think governments should intervene by creating and enforcing policies promoting equal access to and treatment at work for men and women?

## Equality at work, positive action and affirmative action

Gender inequality is only one type of discrimination and inequality that exists at work, and people may experience discrimination based on their religion, sexual orientation, ethnicity, disability and so on. Developing equality at work is a long, difficult process and different approaches have been developed to try and address the problem. 'Affirmative action' is the term most commonly used in the USA and refers to actions that are taken to increase the proportion of women or minority ethnic groups in employment, in order to overcome historical discrimination or exclusion.

In South Africa, there has been much work on this in an attempt to redress the problems caused by the historical racial discrimination of apartheid and the legal requirements go further

than in many other countries. Affirmative action in South Africa is an attempt to make workplaces fairer and more representative of the population by ensuring that designated groups, that is, black people, women and people with disabilities, have equal opportunities. It requires employers to take steps to identify and remove barriers that have an adverse impact on these groups, promoting diversity, providing training and skills development and making reasonable accommodation for them to undertake their roles. It also includes the provision of preferential treatment for designated groups, although excludes the use of quotas, which establish fixed targets for representation of designated groups.

Sometimes, affirmative action efforts might include **preferential selection**: where the standards for selection are actually lowered in order to increase the success of a particular group. This is a controversial approach, not just because of its perceived unfairness, but because of the longer term impacts of the process on the individuals who were selected. In fact, research seems to indicate that if we know we have been selected for a task simply because of our gender or race, rather than our ability, we are less successful at it. A study found that women who were told they had been selected as leaders for a team task simply because they were women performed worse on a problem-solving task than women who were told they had been selected for their ability (Brown et al., 2000). Some countries have introduced quotas for certain groups to try and improve equality; for example, Norway, Germany and India have introduced quotas for female board members. In other countries, such as the UK and USA, preferential selection or setting recruitment quotas for specific characteristics (e.g. female or a particular ethnic group) is illegal. Instead, employers are encouraged to take action to compensate for disadvantages a particular group has faced. So, for example, they can encourage underrepresented groups to apply for a job or provide targeted training to potential applicants, but the actual selection must be based on merit.

We will discuss the details of different selection procedures and methods further in Chapter 3. Having seen the impact that our beliefs about work and the value we ascribe to it can have, we now turn to consider what work means to people, that is, its place in our lives.

## THE MEANING OF WORK

The Meaning of Working (MOW) research programme began in 1978 and attempted to discover what working meant to people in different countries and, in subsequent studies, whether these meanings were changing over time. The original studies were conducted in eight different industrialized countries (Belgium, Britain, Germany, Israel, Japan, Netherlands, USA and Yugoslavia) and identified general agreement that the primary reason for working was financial: in order to earn money (Vecchio, 1989). This does not, however, tell us *why* people want the money. It could be to support their family, to fund holidays abroad or a particular lifestyle or status in society. The reasons behind the financial motive can be just as varied as all the other

reasons we work, and it is as important to understand them as it is to recognize that the primary motivation for working is financial.

It is entirely possible, of course, that most people do not think beyond this financial motive when they are asked why they work, but that if it were taken away, they might continue to work for other reasons. For example, many countries have fairly effective welfare systems designed to keep their citizens out of absolute poverty. Some people, it is true, use the system so that they do not have to work even if they are able. But the majority of people still want to work. For some, it may still be an extension of the financial motive in that they want to be able to buy more than just the basics they need to survive: a better lifestyle. And for others, work also provides **intrinsic rewards**. We can enjoy work, get a sense of satisfaction and achievement from it, make friends at work and gain recognition from others. It enables us to contribute to wider society and to meet our own needs and there is evidence that the more sources of meaning we find in our work, the more satisfied we are (Brown et al., 2001). An interesting extension of this idea is explored in the In the News box.

The job demands-resources model (Bakker and Demerouti, 2007), which we discuss in greater detail in Chapter 11, suggests that it is the balance between the demands a job places on us and the resources we have available to us that predicts occupational health outcomes such as **well-being** and **stress** levels. A longitudinal study applied this model to our understanding of work meaning and found some interesting results (Clausen and Borg, 2011). Instead of a clear-cut association between resources and positive outcomes, and demands and negative outcomes, it found that increased job resources (e.g. quality of leadership, team climate) and some job demands (e.g. work pace, emotional demands) predicted increased work meaning. Clausen and Borg interpreted this as evidence that some job demands can present workers with a challenge that they enjoy engaging with. In our consideration of the meaning and purpose of work, we need to bear this important point in mind: many people enjoy the challenge of work and the sense of accomplishment they get from meeting and overcoming challenges. We will look in more detail at motivations and work in Chapter 5, but for now we will turn to consider further the non-financial reasons for working.

## In the News: Unconditional basic income

At first glance, unconditional basic income (UBI) sounds like a utopian and unrealistic idea: pay everyone enough to meet their basic costs of living, regardless of their other income, employment status or any other factor. It is an idea that dates back centuries but has recently been making the news all over again. Switzerland held a referendum on introducing UBI in June 2016 and the majority (77%) rejected it. But Finland and some Dutch cities are starting to experiment with it by stopping the means-testing of benefits payments, essentially giving claimants a basic amount of money each month and allowing them to keep anything extra they make (Boffey, 2015).

The idea behind it is that it will help build stability and therefore increase people's desire to work, as well as reduce the administration costs associated with having a variety of different benefits (Karakas, 2016). It is gaining popularity in the USA too, particularly Silicon Valley, with arguments there suggesting it is a way to bring some equality to an increasingly automated and technological world. With estimates suggesting that between a quarter and a third of all jobs in developed countries could be automated within 20 years, some people have suggested that UBI is the only way to build a fairer future.

### For discussion

» How might our view of work change if each of us was guaranteed a basic income?
» What could be some of the benefits of UBI and some of the potential drawbacks?

## Non-financial reasons for working

If the economic necessity of working were removed, how many of us would continue to work? This is often referred to as the 'lottery' question: If you won the lottery and had enough money to live comfortably, would you continue to work? Using this approach, the MOW study found that the majority of people would continue working even if they no longer needed the money (MOW International Research Team, 1987). So, it seems that although people report their primary reason for working to be financial, when this is removed from the equation, many people would continue to work.

In the 1990s, a research team took this question from the hypothetical to the concrete and asked actual lottery winners in the USA whether they had continued to work (Arvey et al., 2004). They suggested that *work centrality* (defined by the MOW research team as the degree of importance that working has in one's life at any given time) would be a key factor influencing whether lottery winners continued to work. Real lottery winners were more likely to continue working after their win if they won less money and had higher work centrality. Interestingly, the average amount won by those who continued working was $2.59 million dollars and even a $20 million winner is quoted as saying that the 'lottery is just a bonus that came my way, it has

not or will not affect my work habits and goals in life'. Clearly, work means more than just earning money.

In the 1950s, sociologists Nancy Morse and Robert Weiss conducted a seminal study on the *meaning* of work that explored just this issue (Morse and Weiss, 1955). They wanted to find out whether the doomsayers had it right: that increasing industrialization and complexity in work meant that more and more people were seeing their jobs solely as means to earn a living. They surveyed 401 men in full-time employment in the USA and found that 80% of them said they would continue working even if they inherited enough money to live comfortably without working. The type of job was an important factor here though. Of those in traditional working-class jobs, such as trades and service roles, who would continue to work, the majority said they would work in a different job. Those in 'middle-class' jobs, such as managers and professionals, said they would continue in the same job.

When asked for their reasons for continuing with work, about two-thirds of the respondents gave positive reasons such as 'to keep occupied', 'I enjoy the work' or 'it keeps me healthy'. A third gave more negative reasons, including 'without work, I'd feel lost or go crazy'. Morse and Weiss (1955) also found that younger men were more likely to want to continue working than those approaching retirement age (from 90% down to 61%). When they were asked what they would miss if they did stop working, two-fifths said they would lose something important to their well-being and a third said they would miss the social aspects of work.

One of the key findings in the Morse and Weiss study was that satisfaction with work was associated with a desire to continue working. A more recent study investigated this association by conducting interviews and observations to find out the different sources of meaning for individuals with high or low satisfaction (Brown et al., 2001). Several sources of meaning in work were found, including identification with the organization, opportunities for creativity, and maintaining relationships outside work, and these in turn influenced how satisfied the individuals were with their work.

The Morse and Weiss (1955) study was replicated in the 1970s with an even larger sample of men and the majority (72%) still reported they would continue to work even if they did not need the money (Vecchio, 1980). Again, younger men and those in professional or managerial jobs were more likely to want to continue working. Vecchio, while noting that the majority of men wished to continue working, suggested that the results indicated a significant decline in the value and meaning of work, perhaps due to a 'leisure ethic' replacing the traditional 'work ethic' in the USA. This leisure ethic can be summarized as giving an increasing importance and meaning to non-work rather than work activities.

One of the drawbacks of these studies was that they were fairly limited by the sample they used: they only considered men (predominantly white) in full-time employment. In 1950s' America, for example, only 30% of the workforce was made up of women (Toossi, 2002), so the relevance of these findings to today's workforce can be questioned. Interestingly, a recent study in Israel found that the non-financial desire to continue working remained fairly stable at 90% between 1981 and 1993, despite significant economic changes (Harpaz, 2002). These cultural differences provide further evidence that we should be careful about applying findings from one culture or time to another: individual and cultural values play a substantial role in determining the meaning of work to different people.

## The role of personal values

We can gain further insight into the meaning of work by considering what we believe is important in life and how work can help us to attain those goals. Ros et al. (1999) suggest that our work values can be seen as expressions of our basic life values. In this approach, values are the things we believe are important in life and work is meaningful to us when it enables us to pursue those values. Based on a model of personal values supported by significant cross-cultural research, Schwartz and Sagiv (1995) theorize four types of work values corresponding to the four higher order life values:

1. **Intrinsic or self-actualization values** are concerned with the pursuit of **autonomy**, interest, growth and creativity in work.

2. **Extrinsic values** are those concerned with material rewards or security from work.

3. **Social or relational values** are seeking positive social relations with others at work and a sense of contribution to society at large.

4. **Self-enhancement or prestige values** look for influence, authority, achievement and power at work.

Using this model, it is possible to identify how central work is to people in different occupations. The Ros et al. study (1999), for example, compared student teachers and employed teachers. For student teachers, work was seen as central to the achievement of all four of the higher order values, reflecting perhaps an idealized view of how their future careers would contribute to fulfilment in life. For employed teachers, however, while work was important for social and relational values, it was not seen as contributing to self-enhancement. Ros et al. suggest that this difference is due to the teachers' experience of working within the constraints of a school setting. Teachers 'have apparently learnt that work cannot organise and contribute much to pleasure and excitement in life. Nor [is it] a vehicle for achieving much recognition or exercising much power' (Ros et al., 1999, p. 68).

A cross-cultural study of work centrality in middle managers in the USA, Korea and Brazil found that while work was a core life concern in each country, family life was rated as more important by all of them (Kuchinke et al., 2010). In addition, the higher the work centrality rating, the higher the levels of work stress the managers reported, although the aspects of work centrality which were related to stress were different for different groups. These studies provide us with some insight into how the centrality of work can change over the course of our careers, and how managers and HR professionals can take this into account when designing work and reward systems. The Applications box helps you to think about how to apply centrality of work values to your own life.

## Applications: **The centrality of work**

Think about the future career you hope to have and are working towards. Taking each of the four higher order life values (Schwartz and Sagiv, 1995) in turn, evaluate the extent to which you think your future work will give you the opportunity to express those values.

Now see if you can identify someone who is already working in that area and ask them about the reality of working in that job. Does it match your expectations? How do you think you will cope with any differences? See if you can find out how much scope there is to develop your future job in a direction that will more closely match your values.

## Work orientation

**Work orientation** can be defined as the purpose paid work serves in an individual's life, the meaning that an individual finds in work. It is often conceptualized in terms of three different ways we can view our work (Wrzesniewski et al., 1997):

1. **Work as a job:** the focus is on the financial rewards and sees work as a necessity. Work is simply the way to make money and not a source of particular pleasure or enjoyment.

2. **Work as a career:** work is the route to personal success and recognition, and advancement in the organization provides self-esteem.

3. **Work as a calling:** work is seen as fulfilling and socially useful, an end in itself rather than a

means towards external reward as in the previous two views. These people tend to have the highest life and work satisfaction.

While these orientations are not mutually exclusive, an individual's primary orientation has been shown to be related to the level of challenge that they prefer in work (Shea-Van Fossen and Vredenburgh, 2014). Those with a job orientation tend to avoid challenging work, those with primarily a career orientation to their work neither avoid nor prefer challenge and those with a calling orientation prefer to engage in challenging work.

Another way people find meaning in work is considering its role in their future career or in terms of 'reflected glory' when working for a well-known or high-status brand. Brannan et al. (2015), for example, describe an ethnographic study of a call centre and how identifying with the brand of the wider organization helped the call centre workers to find meaning in their otherwise mundane work. While the customer service representatives were realistic about the low level work they were doing, they were pleased to be working for a high-status brand and this helped them to frame their current work in terms of a first step in their future career.

Much of the discussion around the meaning of and reasons for working reveals our underlying assumptions about what people are like. Are people in general lazy and need to be 'convinced' to do work for financial or other extrinsic gain? Or are they intrinsically motivated to work and do a good job even if the financial rewards are not there? We consider this debate in more detail in the Weighing the Evidence box and also in the later section on voluntary work.

## Weighing the Evidence: **We all just want an easy life**

Ever since Frederick Taylor said that workers, if left to their own devices, will prefer to work at an easy pace, a debate has raged in the OB and HRM literature: Do people want challenge in their jobs or does work have to be designed to 'force' them into working harder?

Douglas McGregor (1957) recognized that the traditional management approach had a rather negative view of people. He noted a difference between this traditional view, which he named

'theory X' and a more positive view, which he named 'theory Y'. Theory X assumes that people are, by nature, lazy, lack ambition and prefer to be led, are self-centred and unconcerned with the needs of the wider organization, resistant to change, gullible and not very bright. Managers or researchers working from these assumptions will aim to find ways to coerce or trick people into working towards the organization's goals. But McGregor argued that these characteristics were the *outcome* of current working systems, not the *cause*. Essentially, he said, if you treat people like this, if you restrict and monitor and control them at work, this is what they will become.

On the other hand, if managers start from the assumption that people are *not* passive or resistant to the organization's needs, it becomes the manager's role to recognize and develop the characteristics that are already present in workers: motivation to work, capacity for responsibility, potential for development and a desire to work towards the organization's goals. This is 'theory Y'. It assumes people want to work and that they and the organization will thrive if given the right opportunities.

*Image Source/Milk and Honey*

What does the evidence say? Are people inherently lazy or inherently keen to work? There is certainly very convincing evidence that people inherently want to work: increased challenge can itself be a strong motivator at work (May et al., 2002) and some people can even feel intrinsically driven to work to the point of complete exhaustion (Schaufeli et al., 2008). In addition, there is evidence that the majority of managers themselves believe that most employees are capable of good work and that there is usually a reason if they are underperforming that can be addressed by encouragement, training or removing obstacles (Goodhew et al., 2008). Interestingly, believing employees to be generally lazy (a theory X view) is one of the contributing elements of abusive management (Tepper, 2007).

However, the reason this debate still persists today is that, of course, we cannot issue blanket statements about 'all people'. Studies of **personality** at work demonstrate that while being more conscientious is associated with higher performance, there is a wide range of individual difference and a substantial number of people would be described as lazy, irresponsible or careless at work (e.g. Barrick and Mount, 1991). And there are variations within individuals as well. You have probably had days yourself when you want to take on new responsibilities and days when you would rather not have to keep working hard.

Admittedly, this makes the job of the manager harder. We cannot simply adopt theory X and take a controlling, authoritative approach to making people work. Neither can we adopt theory Y on its own and assume that all workers will be delighted to take responsibility for their own work and development. Instead, a balance needs to be created that will develop the structures to ensure that people having an 'X' day are still productive, while opening up opportunities for those having a 'Y' day to contribute even more to the organization.

## TYPES OF WORK

So far in this chapter we have looked at our beliefs about work, the reasons we work and what it means to the rest of our lives. We now turn to consider different types of work. Here, we are not thinking about the variety of jobs, but the kinds of work we do in those jobs. We focus in this chapter on three types or elements of work: knowledge, emotional and voluntary, and consider how they affect our definitions of what work is and how workers can be best managed. Looking in detail at these different forms of work also helps to expand our consideration of non-financial incentives for work.

# Knowledge work

Peter Drucker first proclaimed the dawn of **'knowledge work'** as early as 1959, describing how workers would generate value by using their minds rather than physical efforts (Wartzman, 2014). He claimed that for most of history, apprentices had learnt their trade by early adulthood and would not need to learn any new knowledge for the rest of their working lives (Drucker, 1992). In contrast, he believed that workers now needed to learn new knowledge every five years or risk becoming obsolete. Particularly important here is the increasing interdisciplinary nature of new developments: innovation in pharmaceuticals, for example, can come from microbiology and genetics. Drucker was so convinced that this was a major change in world history that he claimed we were in the midst of a shift to a **'knowledge society'**, where knowledge would become the primary resource for individuals and organizations. He recognized, however, that knowledge is only useful when it is integrated into a task and so the challenge facing managers would be to utilize employees' knowledge effectively.

Critics of this idea, however, argue that knowledge has always been needed for certain types of work. And indeed, what set expert craftspeople apart from newly minted apprentices was that they had continued to learn and refine their expertise. There are also arguments that much of this so-called 'knowledge work' does not require high skill levels or knowledge, but is often mundane or routine work with a large element of scripting and monitoring. Perhaps part of the attraction of the concept is that many people would like to be recognized as knowledge workers, especially as they often have a good deal of knowledge *about* their work. Blackler (1995) distinguished between five different ways of looking at knowledge in organizations, which we consider in greater detail in Chapter 10. The typology shows us that knowledge exists in many different forms within organizations and is not just the prerogative of 'knowledge workers'. For example, embodied knowledge is knowing 'how' to do something and is often specific to local contexts: an administrative assistant may know how to navigate the bureaucracy of the large organization in which they work in order to ensure timely reimbursement of their team's expenses.

Warhurst and Thompson (2006) called for knowledge work and knowledgeability to be disentangled; that is, recognizing that many people are knowledgeable about their work, but 'knowledge work' has two key characteristics. First, it draws on a body of theoretical knowledge, which must be both specialized and abstract. For example, it is not about knowing the best ways to input data into a computer, but having knowledge of different ways to organize data, the potential uses it can be put to, and even knowledge of how to programme different types of software to manage the data. The second characteristic of knowledge work is that the knowledge is used and applied to create innovation by workers with autonomy. This means that workers who are tightly controlled and monitored (e.g. many call centre operatives are expected to respond to customers from set scripts and are monitored on the basis of call length) cannot be defined as knowledge workers.

It is certainly the case that knowledge work is increasingly important as it is the basis for modern organizations' competitive advantage. It is important, therefore, that both the knowledge workers have *of* their work as well as their ability to work *with* knowledge is managed appropriately for organizations' success. It may well be that effective management of knowledge and knowledge workers requires high levels of emotional labour skills, and we turn to look at this next.

# Emotional labour

The economy is traditionally divided into three broad sectors, primary, secondary and tertiary, as illustrated in Figure 2.1.

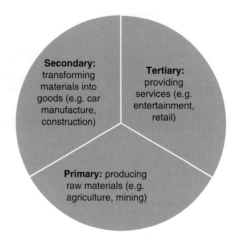

*Figure 2.1 The three economic sectors*

As economies develop, the numbers of people employed in the primary and secondary sectors decrease, with the result that half of the world's working population is now employed in the services sector (Addati et al., 2016) and with this increase in the number of customer-facing roles has come an increase in the importance ascribed to emotional labour. That is, employees are expected to follow particular rules about how and when they display emotion. Doing so involves managing or working with their own or others' emotions. It can be by suppressing what they really feel or displaying specific emotions that are required by their employer (Hochschild, 1979), as well as managing a customer's emotions. This is all part of providing good service to the customer and is explicitly emphasized by organizations wishing to promote good customer service.

But ***emotional labour*** is not all about presenting a friendly, smiling face to the customer. For some jobs, workers might be expected to convey hostility (e.g. bouncers) or sadness and seriousness (e.g. undertaker) (Rafaeli and Sutton, 1987). In fact, many jobs expect us to display different emotions in different situations. A nurse, for example, might be expected to be emotionally neutral in the operating theatre but warm and comforting with patients and families.

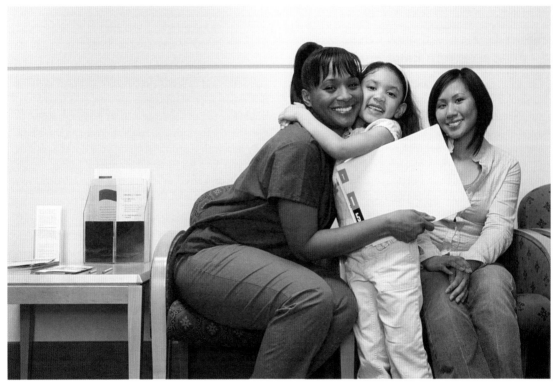

*Image Source*

*Nurses are expected to engage in emotional labour, for example by being warm and comforting with patients.*

The central issue with emotional labour is that the employee has to express emotions they do not necessarily feel, in a way that the customer perceives as authentic. Arlie Hochschild (1979), one of the first writers on emotional labour, noted that we can undertake this effort in two ways, similar to how actors might display emotions. In 'surface acting', we fake the emotion by displaying emotion-appropriate behaviours and expressions. In 'deep acting', we manage our own feelings in such a way that we actually experience the required emotion and so make a genuine display. Some people suggest that this kind of acting is no different from the rest of our lives, that we are always presenting a certain self to others and this is simply an extension of that performance. Others, however, maintain that there is a key difference with emotional labour in that we have little control or discretion over whether we engage in this performance: we are required to do it by the job. This lack of control is recognized as one of the demands in work that can increase stress and negative health outcomes (Bakker and Demerouti, 2007).

Interestingly, deep acting seems to be associated with greater perceived authenticity by customers as well as lower stress for the 'actors', and while both types of acting are related to lower *job satisfaction*, the relationship is stronger for surface acting (Grandey, 2015). Thus it seems that emotional labour certainly places demands on workers but the negative impact might be reduced if workers can engage in deeper acting. Alicia Grandey (2015) suggests this might be due to the payoffs associated

with deep acting: in deep acting, the person actually feels the emotion and so does not experience a sense of dissonance and also receives more positive reactions from customers.

Emotional labour remains poorly recognized or rewarded by organizations, despite being key to their customer relations. It is often left out of skills appraisals, which tend to focus on information processing or technical abilities (Korczynski, 2005). The challenge for HRM, therefore, is to develop a more comprehensive understanding of the types of work that people do and find ways to appropriately reward and develop the necessary skills. The Applications box explores how emotional labour can be recognized and employees trained.

 ## Applications: **Emotional labour**

Go to a coffee shop and take notes on all the examples of emotional labour that you notice the staff are engaging in. This could be anything from a friendly greeting to taking a complaint seriously and treating a customer with respect.

As you make a note of each example, also note down how authentic it felt to you. Which things do they do well? Which elements do you find less authentic or convincing? Emotional labour is only worthwhile for the organization if the customer *feels* that it is convincing: that the employee genuinely feels pleased to be offering the service or genuinely wants to help. No one wants to be served by a barista who gives an obviously fake smile or rolls their eyes as they turn away!

Now imagine you were the manager of this coffee shop. You have received some complaints from customers that the staff seem disinterested and that the atmosphere is a little unpleasant. You know your staff work hard and are concerned that perhaps at busy times they have become so focused on the practical side of ensuring drinks are made

correctly and quickly that they have lost sight of the importance of engaging with the customers. You would like to put together a short training session to give them a few tips and suggestions to improve how they deal with customers. Using your notes as well as what you have learnt about emotional labour, design a half-hour 'refresher' course for your baristas. You will want to consider the following issues:

» What can you do to emphasize to your staff the importance of engaging emotionally with customers? How can you encourage them to see this as just as important to their job as making the coffee correctly?

» What top three things will you focus on in the training?

» How will your staff know when they are doing things well? How will they know if they're not getting it right?

» Is there any further support that you as the manager could implement?

## Voluntary work

Knowledge work and emotional work can be thought of as 'elements' of many different kinds of jobs. **Voluntary work**, on the other hand, provides a dramatic contrast to everyday paid work that can help to illustrate some of the non-financial reasons for working. It is of interest to organizational

behaviourists and HR practitioners for two reasons. First, there is the issue of discretionary effort within formal work organizations. Can employees be encouraged to voluntarily increase their effort in their jobs? Could employers learn from the experiences of managing volunteers or is discretionary effort in paid work an altogether different type of work from volunteering? Second, there is the special case of managing the voluntary workers themselves. How are volunteers similar to or different from employees? Do we need completely different approaches or can they be treated fairly similarly?

## What is voluntary work?

In starting to consider these questions, we need to define what we mean by volunteering. Wilson (2000, p. 215) defines volunteering as 'any activity in which time is given freely to benefit another person, group or cause'. Despite this simple sounding definition, there is an ongoing debate over whether we should define voluntary work based on the volunteer's motives (if someone does this work because they want to help, then that counts as volunteering) or by the actual product of their work (it only counts as volunteering if it results in a 'public good'). If we take this latter, behavioural approach, volunteering could be defined as 'an activity that produces goods or services at below market rate' (p. 216). That is rather a problematic definition though, as it would then mean that organizations who are producing products more cheaply than others could be defined as 'volunteering'.

About 25% of people in the USA do some kind of volunteering (Bureau of Labor Statistics, 2016), with the rate slightly higher for women and slightly lower for men. In the UK, rates are fairly similar, with 27% volunteering regularly and 42% volunteering once a year (Community Life Survey Team, 2015). Australians seem to volunteer more, with their rates being around 36% (Volunteering Australia, 2015). Across the EU, volunteering rates vary considerably but on average are around 22% and there is evidence that they have been gradually rising in recent years (GHK Consulting Ltd, 2010). The United Arab Emirates has a similar level of volunteering, with 21% of people saying they engage in some kind of volunteer work (Charities Aid Foundation, 2016).

Volunteer work has economic and social impacts. Measuring the economic impact can be difficult; estimates show quite a large range from less than 0.1% of GDP in some EU countries up to 5% in others (GHK Consulting Ltd, 2010). The social impacts include:

- **Social inclusion and employment:** volunteering acts to bring social cohesion, improve quality of life for the individual and society, and also provides some people with a path to employment.

- **Education and training:** unemployed people can gain skills and experience in volunteering that can be transferred to their jobs or even 'try out' a job when seeking to decide on a *career path*.

- **Active citizenship:** volunteers are directly involved in developing their local communities. The sports sector in particular relies heavily on volunteers and the contributions that volunteers make here allow many sports clubs to keep membership rates low and increase participation and access.

The EU report on volunteering (GHK Consulting Ltd, 2010) identified two of the main challenges to managing volunteering: how to engage volunteers and the impact of the increased professionalization of the sector on the management of human resources. This was echoed in a survey of volunteer administrators in US hospitals, which identified the biggest challenges facing healthcare volunteer management as including HRM issues such as recruitment, retention and administration (Rogers et al., 2013). In the UK, organizations from the voluntary sector have become increasingly involved in providing publicly funded services and there is some suggestion that this has meant the government has driven the adoption of formal, more sophisticated HRM practices. A study using data from the 2004 Workplace Employment Relations Survey found that voluntary organizations had indeed adopted HR practices that aim to enhance performance, including performance appraisals, training, communication and involvement (Kelliher and Parry, 2011). But HRM practices initially developed in private, profit-focused organizations and then later adapted for publicly funded organizations may not be easily transferred to the voluntary sector. We will therefore now consider some of the specific challenges that HRM faces when dealing with volunteers.

## The challenges of managing volunteers

Voluntary organizations, for example trade unions or charities, increasingly have paid staff to deal with the complexities of management and this may create problems as the paid and voluntary workers within the same organization may have differing expectations of each other and the organization itself (Brosnan and Cuskelly, 2001). Paid workers, for example, may find themselves compared to volunteers who are working for very different reasons or feel that unrealistic demands are being placed on them. On the other hand, volunteers might feel resentful if they think they are expected to do the job of the paid worker. Particularly problematic in voluntary organizations is the general lack of funding. This often keeps wages for employed workers lower than in other sectors, leading to added pressure in recruitment. For example, in a study of social care voluntary organizations in Scotland (Nickson et al., 2007), recruitment was identified as a significant problem due to a tightening labour market, low pay and misconceptions about the voluntary sector (specifically that potential job candidates were unaware that paid work was a possibility or of the range of jobs available). Nickson et al. suggested that a way of enhancing recruitment would be to

emphasize the high job satisfaction that workers had, as well as seeking to attract employees whose values matched the sector, capitalizing on the potential to make a difference in people's lives.

In terms of managing volunteers, just as with general HRM, voluntary organizations face the issues of finding, motivating and training workers. For example, recruiting volunteers is dependent on being able to find people with the appropriate skill set or, if this is not possible, deciding whether to compromise on a less skilled worker. Similarly, the training of volunteers faces similar challenges to training employees, with restricted training budgets and workers perhaps being reluctant to be trained. The Web Explorer activity further explores the challenges of attracting volunteers.

---

 ## Web Explorer: Attracting volunteers

Choose a charity or non-profit organization you are interested in and search its website for ways you could get involved. Answer the following questions:

- To what extent does the website make you feel that the organization would value your help?

- How does the organization pitch itself to potential volunteers? (e.g. Does it say what you can expect in return for your time? Does it offer training? Does it specify particular skills it is looking for?)

- How easy does it make it for you to make initial contact?

Now imagine that this organization is struggling to attract and retain volunteers and has asked for your help. What suggestions would you make to it in terms of its advertising, selection procedures and so on?

If you'd like to take it a step further, why not contact the organization and follow through with volunteering. You could continue your analysis of its processes as well as helping it out.

---

Brosnan and Cuskelly (2001) suggest that managing workers' performance is more difficult in a voluntary context than in paid work because the manager is entirely dependent on persuasion and commitment. Volunteers effectively have a higher bargaining power than employed workers. Managers of volunteers have very little power to bring sanctions to bear on volunteers who are not performing acceptably or to coerce them in any way. In addition, volunteers can simply leave en masse in a way that is highly unlikely in paid organizations. This means that managers of volunteers need to be particularly sensitive to volunteers' feelings and motivations, and it can be even more important than with paid workers to understand the meaning they ascribe to their work. Indeed, Clary and Snyder (1999) note that volunteers often ascribe multiple meanings to

their volunteering and that persuasion should focus on matching the message to these motivations.

Another struggle for managers of volunteers is that, despite the relatively high rates of volunteering, voluntary organizations have a high turnover rate (Wilson, 2000). **Burnout** (physical and mental exhaustion) can be a serious issue, particularly where the voluntary work is risky, such as medical volunteering in war zones. With voluntary organizations often working with limited budgets, there is also the problem of lack of resources. Other predictors of dropout from voluntary work include feeling that one's efforts are not recognized, having a mismatch between skills and projects and a lack of autonomy. You will probably already be recognizing that these issues are not unique to voluntary organizations but can, in fact, affect a wide range of employers. Developing an understanding of how to address these issues in an employment context can help managers of volunteers to reduce the turnover of their staff.

A significant proportion of voluntary work occurs within a sports context (GHK Consulting Ltd, 2010) and a recent study looked at the effect of specific HRM practices on volunteer retention in rugby union clubs in Australia (Cuskelly et al., 2006). Planning (including identifying potential volunteers, succession planning, providing role description and maintaining a database of skills and qualifications) was the most effective practice in terms of contributing to retaining volunteers overall, with training, orientation and support being important for different voluntary positions such as board members and coaches. Cuskelly et al. point out that formal HRM approaches might not fit well with voluntary organizations if they overlook the importance of the relational side of management, but are important in improving or maintaining quality. The emphasis in managing volunteers, then, should be on developing positive relationships with the volunteers while ensuring that the basic organizational details of their roles are clearly articulated.

## Practice Insights: Carrie McKenzie

Carrie McKenzie is the Voluntary Services Manager at Sheffield Teaching Hospitals in the UK. She and her small team coordinate and manage the nearly 600 volunteers who contribute to the hospital, including three therapy dogs. Volunteers provide services ranging from helping patients with their food to running arts and crafts activities. In the video Carrie talks about how everyday management and HR activities can be adapted to volunteer workers.

Go online to www.macmillanihe.com/sutton-people to access the interview with Carrie.

## SUMMARY

In this chapter we have discussed some of the underlying concepts in understanding the world of work. By gaining a good grasp of these concepts and becoming aware of some of their assumptions, we can start to recognize how the structures and practices of the modern workplace have evolved. We started by looking at how our beliefs about what work is can impact on the value we ascribe to different tasks or even whole roles, as well as how it can impact on attempts to motivate people to put more effort into their work. This led into a discussion of the meaning of work and the role of financial and non-financial reasons for working.

To close the chapter, the discussion took in some of the different forms of work, including knowledge work, emotional labour and voluntary work. Building our awareness of these elements of work will help us in the coming chapters to gain a greater understanding of the practical implications of different policies and practices in organizations. Ultimately, it will aid a more informed choice of approach when dealing with the complexities of how and why people work as they do.

## FURTHER READING

- For an overview of statistics about women and work, see www.catalyst.org/knowledge/statistical-overview-women-workforce.

- For a good review of the different theories for understanding voluntary work, see Wilson, J. (2000) 'Volunteering', *Annual Review of Sociology*, 26(1), pp. 215–40.

# REVIEW QUESTIONS

1. How do our beliefs about work influence our understanding of the value of different types of work?

2. Compare and contrast knowledge work and emotional work.

3. Why do people work?

# ONLINE RESOURCES

Go online to www.macmillanihe.com/sutton-people to access a MCQ quiz for this chapter and for further resources to support your learning.

# REFERENCES

Addati, L., Bonnet, F., Ernst, E., Merola, R. and Wan, P. M. J. (2016) *Women at Work: Trends 2016*. Geneva: ILO.

Arvey, R. D., Harpaz, I. and Liao, H. (2004) 'Work centrality and post-award work behavior of lottery winners', *Journal of Psychology*, 138(5), pp. 404–20. doi: 10.3200/JRLP.138.5.404-420.

Bakker, A. B. and Demerouti, E. (2007) 'The job demands-resources model: state of the art', *Journal of Managerial Psychology*, 22(3), pp. 309–28.

Barrick, M. R. and Mount, M. K. (1991) 'The big five personality dimensions and job performance: a meta-analysis', *Personnel Psychology*, 44(1), pp. 1–26.

Blackler, F. (1995) 'Knowledge, knowledge work and organizations: an overview and interpretation', *Organization Studies*, 16(6), pp. 1021–46.

Boffey, D. (2015) 'Dutch city plans to pay citizens a "basic income", and Greens say it could work in the UK', *The Guardian*, 26 December.

Brannan, M. J., Parsons, E. and Priola, V. (2015) 'Brands at work: the search for meaning in mundane work', *Organization Studies*, 36(1), pp. 29–53.

Brosnan, P. and Cuskelly, G. (2001) 'Volunteer workers: on the margin of the industrial relations system?', in *Crossing Borders: Employment, Work, Markets and Social Justice across Time, Dicipline and Place*. Proceedings of the 15th AIRAANZ Conference.

Brown, R. P., Charnsangavej, T., Keough, K. A. et al. (2000) 'Putting the "affirm" into affirmative action: preferential selection and academic performance', *Journal of Personality and Social Psychology*, 79(5), pp. 736–47. doi: 10.1037/0022-3514.79.5.736.

Brown, A., Kitchell, M., O'Neill, T. et al. (2001) 'Identifying meaning and perceived level of satisfaction within the context of work', *Work*, 16(3), pp. 219–26.

Bureau of Labor Statistics (2016) *Volunteering in the United States 2015*. Available at: www.bls.gov/news.release/volun.nr0.htm.

Charities Aid Foundation (2016) *Caf World Giving Index 2016*. Available at: www.cafonline.org/about-us/publications/2016-publications/caf-world-giving-index-2016.

Clary, E. G. and Snyder, M. (1999) 'The motivations to volunteer: theoretical and practical considerations', *Current Directions in Psychological Science*, 8(5), pp. 156–9. doi: 10.1111/1467-8721.00037.

Clausen, T. and Borg, V. (2011) 'Job demands, job resources and meaning at work', *Journal of Managerial Psychology*, 26(8), pp. 665–81. doi: 10.1108/02683941111181761.

Community Life Survey Team (2015) *Community Life Survey 2014–2015: Technical Report*. Available at: www.gov.uk/government/publications/community-life-survey-2014-to-2015-technical-report.

Cuskelly, G., Taylor, T., Hoye, R. and Darcy, S. (2006) 'Volunteer management practices and volunteer retention: a human resource management approach', *Sport Management Review*, 9(2), pp. 141–63.

Drucker, P. F. (1992) 'The new society of organizations', *Harvard Business Review*, 70(5), pp. 95–104.

GHK Consulting Ltd (2010) *Volunteering in the European Union*. Brussels: EAC-EA/DG EAC.

Goodhew, G. W., Cammock, P. A. and Hamilton, R. T. (2008) 'The management of poor performance by front-line managers', *Journal of Management Development*, 27(9), pp. 951–62. doi: 10.1108/02621710810901291.

Grandey, A. A. (2015) 'When "the show must go on": surface acting and deep acting as determinants of emotional exhaustion and peer-rated service delivery', *Academy of Management Journal*, pp. 86–96. doi: 10.2307/30040678.

Harpaz, I. (1998) 'Cross-national comparison of religious conviction and the meaning of work', *Cross-Cultural Research*, 32(2), pp. 143–70. doi: 10.1177/106939719803200202.

Harpaz, I. (2002) 'Expressing a wish to continue or stop working as related to the meaning of work', *European Journal of Work and Organizational Psychology*, 11(2), pp. 177–98.

Hochschild, A. R. (1979) 'Emotion work, feeling rules, and social structure', *American Journal of Sociology*, 85(3), pp. 551–75. doi: 10.1086/227049.

Karakas, C. (2016) *Basic Income: Arguments, Evidence, Prospects*. European Parliament briefing.

Kelliher, C. and Parry, E. (2011) 'Voluntary sector HRM: examining the influence of government', *International Journal of Public Sector Management*, 24(7), pp. 650–61. doi: 10.1108/09513551111172477.

Korczynski, M. (2005) 'Skills in service work: an overview', *Human Resource Management Journal*, 15(2), pp. 3–14. doi: 10.1111/j.1748-8583.2005.tb00143.x.

Kremer, W. (2013) 'Captain Collette: The life of a woman on the front line', *BBC World Service News Magazine*, 23 October. Available at: www.bbc.co.uk/news/magazine-24622762.

Kuchinke, K. P., Cornachione, E. B., Oh, S. Y. and Kang, H.-S. (2010) 'All work and no play? The meaning of work and work stress of mid-level managers in the United States, Brazil, and Korea', *Human Resource Development International*, 13(4), pp. 393–408.

McGregor, D. (1957) 'The human side of enterprise', *The Management Review*, 46(11), pp. 22–8.

May, T. Y. M., Korczynski, M. and Frenkel, S. J. (2002) 'Organizational and occupational commitment: knowledge workers in large corporations', *Journal of Management Studies*, 39(6), pp. 775–801. doi: 10.1111/1467-6486.00311.

Morse, N. C. and Weiss, R. S. (1955) 'The function and meaning of work and the job', *American Sociological Review*, 20(2), pp. 191–8. Available at: www.jstor.org/stable/2088325.

MOW International Research Team (1987) *The Meaning of Working*. London: Academic Press.

Nickson, D., Warhurst, C., Dutton, E. and Hurrell, S. (2007) 'A job to believe in: recruitment in the Scottish voluntary sector', *Human Resource Management Journal*, 18(1), pp. 20–35. doi: 10.1111/j.1748-8583.2007.00056.x.

Norris, P. and Inglehart, R. (2004) 'The Protestant ethic and the spirit of capitalism thesis', in *Sacred and Secular: Religion and Politics Worldwide*. New York: Cambridge University Press.

Rafaeli, A. and Sutton, R. I. (1987) 'Expression of emotion as part of the work role', *Academy of Management Review*, 12(1), pp. 23–37.

Rogers, S. E., Rogers, C. M. and Boyd, K. D. (2013) 'Challenges and opportunities in healthcare volunteer management: insights from volunteer administrators', *Hospital Topics*, 91(2), pp. 43–51. doi: 10.1080/00185868.2013.806012.

Ros, M., Schwartz, S. H. and Surkiss, S. (1999) 'Basic individual values, work values, and the meaning of work', *Applied Psychology: An International Review*, 48(1), pp. 49–71.

Schaufeli, W. B., Taris, T. W. and Van Rhenen, W. (2008) 'Workaholism, burnout, and work engagement: three of a kind or three different kinds of employee well being?', *Applied Psychology*, 57(2), pp. 173–203.

Schwartz, S. H. and Sagiv, L. (1995) 'Identifying culture-specifics in content and structure of values', *Journal of Cross-Cultural Psychology*, 26(1), pp. 92–116.

Sharabi, M. (2012) 'The work and its meaning among Jews and Muslims according to religiosity degree', *International Journal of Social Economics*, 39(11), pp. 824–43. doi: 10.1108/03068291211263880.

Shea-Van Fossen, R. J. and Vredenburgh, D. J. (2014) 'Exploring differences in work's meaning: an investigation of individual attributes associated with work orientations', *Journal of Behavioral & Applied Management*, 15(2), pp. 101–20.

Tepper, B. J. (2007) 'Abusive supervision in work organizations: review, synthesis, and research agenda', *Journal of Management*, 33(3), pp. 261–89. doi: 10.1177/0149206307300812.

*The Economist* (2016) 'Interview with Muhammad bin Salman', *The Economist*, 6 January.

*The Guardian* (2015) 'UK military could allow women in frontline by end of 2016', *The Guardian*, 20 December. Available at: www.theguardian.com/uk-news/2015/dec/20/uk-military-could-allow-women-in-close-combat-roles-by-end-of-2016.

Thomas, K. (1999) *The Oxford Book of Work*. Oxford: Oxford University Press.

Toossi, M. (2002) 'A century of change: the U.S. labor force, 1950–2050', *Monthly Labor Review*, May, pp. 15–28. Available at: www.bls.gov/opub/mlr/2002/05/art2full.pdf.

Vecchio, R. P. (1980) 'The function and meaning of work and the job: Morse and Weiss (1955) revisited', *Academy of Management Journal*, 23(2), pp. 361–7. doi: 10.2307/255439.

Vecchio, R. P. (1989) 'Book reviews: The Meaning of Working, MOW International', *Journal of Organizational Behavior*, 10, pp. 97–100. doi: 10.1179/1465312512Z.00000000045.

Volunteering Australia (2015) *Key Facts and Statistics about Volunteering in Australia*. Available at: www.volunteeringaustralia.org/wp-content/uploads/VA-Key-statistics-about-Australian-volunteering-16-April-20151.pdf

Warhurst, C. and Thompson, P. (2006) 'Mapping knowledge in work: proxies or practices?', *Work, Employment & Society*, 20(4), pp. 787–800. doi: 10.1177/0950017006069815.

Wartzman, R. (2014) 'What Peter Drucker knew about 2020', *Harvard Business Review*, Oct. Available at: https://hbr.org/2014/10/what-peter-drucker-knew-about-2020.

Weber, M. (1930) *The Protestant Ethic and the Spirit of Capitalism*. Trans. P. Talcott and G. Anthony. London: Unwin Hyman.

Williams, C. C. (2005) 'Unraveling the meanings of underground work', *Review of Social Economy*, 63(1), pp. 1–18.

Wilson, J. (2000) 'Volunteering', *Annual Review of Sociology*, 26, pp. 215–40. Available at: www.jstor.org/stable/223443.

Wrzesniewski, A., McCauley, C., Rozin, P. and Schwartz, B. (1997) 'Jobs, careers, and callings: people's relations to their work', *Journal of Research in Personality*, 31(1), pp. 21–33. doi: 10.1006/jrpe.1997.2162.

Zulfikar, Y. F. (2012) 'Do Muslims believe more in Protestant work ethic than Christians? Comparison of people with different religious background living in the US', *Journal of Business Ethics*, 105(4), pp. 489–502. doi: 10.1007/s10551-011-0981-z.

# 3 RECRUITMENT AND SELECTION

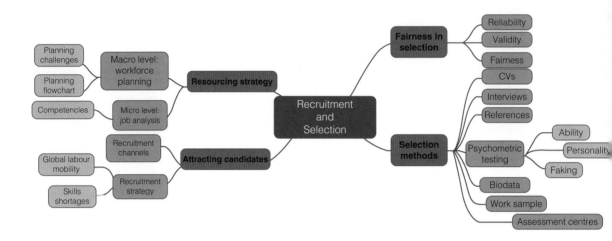

## INTRODUCTION

An organization will only be able to meet its business goals or fulfil its strategic aims if it has the right human resources in place. It is the people who provide the organization with its competitive advantage, whether that is in terms of providing better service than competitors, developing higher quality products or designing new ones. In this chapter we look at how HRM and OB issues play out in the key tasks of recruitment and selection.

HRM and OB perspectives are closely related on many of the issues at stake here, such as the validity, reliability and fairness of different selection methods

or the role of individual differences in performance. We consider some HRM-specific topics, such as strategic resourcing and a consideration of the cost-effectiveness of different recruitment channels, as well as the influence of wider OB issues such as global labour mobility and stereotype threats. This chapter can be seen as setting the stage for the employment relationship, providing a bridge between the foundational aspects we have considered in Chapters 1 and 2 and the elements of the employment relationship that we turn to in more detail in Part 2.

*Getty Images/sturti*

---

## LEARNING FEATURES

Applications: PEST analysis for workforce planning

Applications: Writing a competency-based job description

Applications: Personality at work

Weighing the Evidence: Racial and sex differences in intellectual ability

Web Explorer: Migrant or expat?

In the News: Ageist selection?

Transferrable Skills: Interview skills

Practice Insights: Kirsten Henderson

---

 Video overview

Julian Perkins

Go online to www.macmillanihe.com/sutton-people to access a video of Anna Sutton introducing the chapter's main themes.

# RESOURCING STRATEGY AND PLANNING

We can see how HR concerns are integrated with wider organizational issues in selection and recruitment when we consider the strategic approach to resourcing. Strategic resourcing involves analysing the organizational strategy for its implications for the human resource requirements and consists of four key phases: planning, attracting potential applicants, selecting the best applicants, and then retaining high-quality employees. We focus here on the first three stages and consider the elements that contribute to the final stage in detail in Part 2 where we discuss the employment relationship.

In the planning stage we need to take account of the macro-level issues of workforce planning as well as the micro-level issues of *job analysis*.

## Macro level: workforce planning

Strategic workforce planning clarifies how the business strategy will be operationalized through the human resources of the organization (DeFazio, 2014). It can be defined as 'a process to ensure the right number of people with the right skills are employed in the right place at the right time to deliver an organisation's short- and long-term objectives' (CIPD, 2011a). As the key to supporting sustainable, competitive performance by matching the future needs of the organization to its human resources, workforce planning involves the integration of several different HR activities, such as succession planning, flexible working arrangements, supply and demand forecasting, skills audit and gap analysis, and *talent management*.

To be effective, workforce planning must be agile, responding to short- and long-term issues. For example, if the organization has a short-term objective to reduce the time customers have to wait to speak to an adviser in a call centre, they also need to consider how the recruitment and training of new staff might impact on the long-term goal of reducing staff costs. It is the HR professional's role to raise awareness of potential conflicts like this and find solutions that will allow the organization to prioritize and reach its goals.

Another important outcome of effective workforce planning is that it can help the organization avoid a cycle of downsizing by reducing the number of employees followed by skills shortages and a resultant need for recruitment (Mayo, 2015). A short-term focus on downsizing can cost the organization significantly in redundancy payouts and, if not managed well, can quite often result in the more experienced staff members leaving. This then leaves the organization in the difficult position of having a shortage of key skills, meaning it will need to recruit again. But good planning is not an easy task and faces some significant challenges.

PHOTODISC

*A short-term focus on downsizing may cost the organization significantly in the longer term.*

## Planning challenges

The main challenge in workforce planning is predicting the future. The further we try to see into the future requirements of the organization or the supply of appropriate employees, the more uncertain it becomes. Cappelli (2009) has suggested that supply chain management models and techniques can be used in workforce planning because they face similar tasks: how to ensure a match between supply and demand in an environment of uncertainty. We can overcome some of this uncertainty by:

- Developing a more accurate assessment of supply, particularly the skills of individual employees.

- Creating better simulations of demand based on the business plan.

- Understanding the impact of assumptions in our demand simulations, and how changes in these assumptions will influence the models.

- Being aware of the costs involved in a mismatch of supply and demand and adjusting the forecast to the risks of uncertainty.

Because uncertainty plays such a large role in how successful a forecast is, Cappelli (2009) suggests that we adopt a simple approach to planning which can be adapted with unforeseen changes. He also notes that it is surprisingly easy to improve workforce planning, simply because most organizations do very little. This means that any efforts we make to develop a plan will help the organization to be proactive rather than expensively reactive.

## Workforce planning flowchart

Figure 3.1 is a basic model for workforce planning, which starts with the organizational strategy, collects and analyses relevant data to develop a forecast and then constructs an action plan to operationalize it.

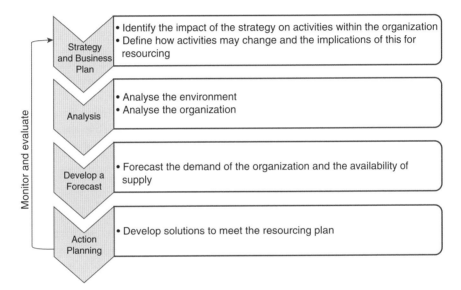

*Figure 3.1 Workforce planning flowchart*

In the first stage, the organization's strategy and business plan need to be understood in terms of their implications for the activities the organization carries out. Here, the HR function needs to determine whether the changes that are planned can be met with the organization's current human resources. It may be the case that existing personnel can be developed to take on new roles, or there may be the need to recruit further staff. Another possibility is that the organization actually needs to downsize or restructure in order to meet its goals, in which case HR needs to identify which **knowledge, skills and abilities (KSAs)** will need to be retained, where they are best deployed and which roles are to be made redundant.

The second stage is a detailed analysis of the organization and its environment. This is the basis for the forecast that will be developed in stage three. Essentially, it is about gathering and understanding information that will help to make an informed decision about future developments. We need to know the current features of the organization's workforce that will have an influence on its future capabilities and the demand for employees. This includes current staffing and performance levels, absence rates, turnover and demographics such as the age of the workforce or key staff members. If, for example, we currently have a good supply of key machine operatives, but the majority of them are approaching retirement age, we need to include this in a plan for recruitment.

In terms of environmental analysis, we need to identify the external drivers that might impact on the workforce plan and the potential supply of employees with the needed KSAs and competencies. A good framework for conducting an environmental analysis is PEST, explored in detail for workforce planning in the Applications box. Originally developed as a framework for analysing markets, it is now used in a variety of settings as a succinct framework for identifying and analysing issues in an organization's environment that are likely to have an impact on its success. PEST analysis can be helpful for HR functions to consider the organization's environment in terms of a labour market and analyse the main issues that can impact on their ability to recruit and retain the staff they need. The four PEST letters stand for:

- **Political:** governmental policies and change, pressure or lobbying groups, legislation (home and international), regulations

- **Economic:** home and international economic trends, taxation, seasonal changes and market cycles, exchange rates

- **Social:** consumer attitudes, demographics (of the potential workforce or consumers), ethnic or religious factors, brand and company image, media

- **Technological:** maturity of technology, new or emergent technologies, competing and replacement technologies, innovation, intellectual property.

There are several other headings suggested for inclusion in a PEST analysis, which means you might see extra letters added to the acronym, for example L (legal or legislative), another E (environmental or ecological), D (demographics), I (industry analysis) and a different E (ethical). If you find it helpful, or one of these extra areas is of particular concern to you, you can always include it as an extra heading in your analysis. However, for most analyses, the effects of these areas will be considered as part of the basic PEST model. For example, ethical considerations are relevant for each of the four basic areas and legal is often subsumed under the political heading. It is also worth noting that particular issues may sometimes overlap into two or more categories. The PEST framework is not definitive and its headings are not mutually exclusive, but it gives us a good basis for a thorough analysis.

 Applications: **PEST analysis for workforce planning**

In order to conduct the PEST analysis, you first need to clearly specify *why* you are doing it. If we take the example of using PEST to support workforce planning, we will be focusing on all the factors to do with the current and future potential workforce. So, under each of the headings, you will gather information on the potential drivers. For example, if our organization is heavily reliant on recent business studies graduates, some of the things we would need to consider are:

- **Political:** Is the government planning to change funding for business degrees? Are new routes into university being developed? What regulations are there to ensure degree equivalence from different universities and even countries?

- **Economic:** Are graduates paying off student loans? How will this affect their salary expectations? If ours is a multinational company, is it worth considering economic strength and taxation levels in determining where to recruit?

- **Social:** How is our organization perceived by potential applicants? What is its image like and how attractive is it? What is the demographic of our potential workforce?

- **Technological:** How will developments in technology influence the kind or number of employees we will need? What technologies are available to assist with recruitment and selection? How familiar will graduates be with these?

Now imagine you work in the HR department of a fast-food restaurant chain. You have been told that the company is considering expanding to a new country: Singapore. The company has been successfully expanding within Western and Eastern Europe over the past decade or so, but this will be the first attempt to enter the market outside Europe. Conduct a PEST analysis to identify the issues that the HR department will need to consider when putting together a workforce plan.

It is this second level of analysis that is key to creating a proactive workforce plan. Using data to inform decisions rather than relying on 'gut feeling' ensures that the plan is fact based and results in better decisions (DeFazio, 2014).

The third stage is to develop a forecast of supply and demand: an understanding of the available human resources within and outside the organization allied with a clear outline of what roles and KSAs the organization needs in order to meet its goal. We should note here that any forecast is tentative. The best forecasts are based on thorough research and analysis, drawing well-evidenced conclusions as to the implications for the organization. However, even the best forecast can change when new information comes to light and, of course, no prediction of the future can be entirely accurate. This is an area where HR has the opportunity to demonstrate its value to the rest of the organization by providing the leadership and support needed to adapt to changing circumstances.

Finally, the fourth stage is to turn the strategy, analysis and forecasting into a concrete plan of action. This is likely to involve efforts towards retaining important existing staff, recruiting new staff, developing succession plans, drawing up *learning* and development activities and possibly also dealing with downsizing issues.

It is important to note that this is not simply a linear process: there must be constant monitoring and evaluation of the process as it continues to ensure that the current activities are still meeting the strategic requirements. It is entirely possible (and indeed, with longer term plans, probable) that the strategy and the balance of supply and demand will change over the course of the plan.

## Micro level: job analysis

Once the higher level planning has been done, the more detailed job-level work needs to be carried out. This means developing a clear outline of what a job will entail, by conducting job analyses. A thorough job analysis identifies the knowledge, skills and behaviours that contribute to good job performance for a specific role. The analysis is then developed into a role profile or job description, and includes the activities that the job holder will carry out, and how the job fits into the organizational structure, for example who the post reports to. It should include the hours of work, terms and conditions of employment and any specific requirements such as mobility. It can also include any planned development activities or career opportunities.

The job description is used as a basis for the person specification. The activities and requirements of the job are 'translated' into an outline of the skills and competencies that an ideal job candidate would have. It is important to remember here that the person specification should only include those aspects that are relevant and important to being able to carry out the tasks effectively. Defining the behavioural and psychological contributors to high job performance is a complex task, but one effective and popular way of doing so is to use a competency-based approach.

## Competencies

**Competencies** can be thought of as sets of behaviours that are key to good job performance (Bartram et al., 2002). Sometimes, competency descriptions in person specifications may include individual characteristics that are thought to contribute to job performance, such as personality traits or years of experience (Boyatzis, 1982); but if we want to use competencies as a basis for accurate selection or assessment of performance, it is better to ensure that we focus on specific behaviours rather than more subjective ideas about the personal approach to a task. The use of competencies is widespread in HR practice and literature because of this focus on performance. Competencies capture not only what a potential job holder can do, but also what they want to do (Ryan et al., 2009). In fact, the use of competencies is seen by many HR researchers as lying 'at the heart of HRM' because it is the basis for the horizontal and vertical integration of HR activities (Soderquist et al., 2010, p. 326). Matching employee competencies and job requirements is claimed to improve employee and organizational performance, as well as lead to increased satisfaction (Spencer et al., 1992).

Competencies need to be written in such a way that they capture observable behaviours associated with different levels of performance. Although we often focus on the use of competencies in identifying good or high-level performance in order to assist selection or promotion decisions, it can be equally useful to have indicators of bad performance, which can be used to underpin later development plans or even dismissal from the organization.

It is worth taking a moment to consider the practicalities of developing a competency-based job description for every role in an organization. Done properly, this is a time-consuming task. And some researchers have suggested that, instead of starting from scratch with each role, we could adapt a general **competency framework** to the specific requirements of individual jobs or organizations. According to this approach, a manager in a research and development department in a pharmaceutical company is likely to need many of the same competencies as a production manager in a manufacturing company, for example good communication skills, effective administration and skills in developing others. Coming from this point of view, Tett et al. (2000) grouped 53 different managerial competencies into nine higher level groups. For example, the 'traditional functions'

group contained competencies such as decision-making and strategic planning, while the 'developing self and others' group contained performance assessment and **job enrichment**. Tett et al. suggest that this comprehensive taxonomy or framework can provide the basis for managerial job analysis.

If a general competency model is chosen, it is still important that the relevance of each of the components is assessed for the job under scrutiny. Competencies only work as a basis for selection procedures if they are clearly relevant to the post. Many job descriptions now include organization-level competencies, which are considered important for everyone in the organization to demonstrate, and job-level competencies, which are specific to the role. The Applications box guides you through developing a competency-based job description.

---

 Applications: **Writing a competency-based job description**

Although competencies are often summarized in terms of abstract titles such as 'planning and organizing', we have seen that, to be effective, they must be described in terms of observable behaviours. With a partner, look through the following list of competencies and develop some clear explanations of what they mean:

- planning and organizing

- delivering excellent customer service

- demonstrating initiative.

Remember that competencies should also be contextualized: that is, clearly described in terms

of the specific job they are for. For example, the 'planning and organizing' competency would look very different for a facilities team leader than it would for a CEO. It would also look different if the job holder was expected to plan and organize only their own work or that of a whole team. So, start by choosing a particular job, then construct a description for each competency, including examples of behaviours that illustrate high and low performance. The more precise these definitions and behavioural indicators, the more useful they will be for selection activities.

---

# ATTRACTING CANDIDATES

We saw that a key element in a strategic approach to resourcing in the organization is to attract high-quality candidates. The aim of the recruitment process is to develop a pool of candidates from which the best can be selected. All the HR processes that follow on from this stage, such as selection and development, rely on the recruitment stage in order to be effective (Orlitzky, 2007). In a review of studies on recruitment and organizational effectiveness, Orlitzky found that there was evidence that good recruitment could improve productivity and financial outcomes.

# Recruitment strategy

There are different recruitment strategies available to organizations to deal with the basic questions of recruitment (Orlitzky, 2007). Who should be recruited? Where and when should they be recruited? And what message should the organization communicate? Windolf (1986) developed a typology that can be used to describe types of recruitment strategies based on an organization's **labour market power** and *internal resources*. Organizations with high labour market power have greater choice over the recruitment strategy they will adopt. Often, these organizations are the ones offering the best remuneration packages – salary, benefits, working conditions and so on. Sometimes, however, the market leader in a particular labour market can offer low wages because there are few viable employment alternatives. Windolf noted that the most relevant internal resource is organizational intelligence, that is, the extent to which the organization can collect and process information, use its knowledge and develop complex strategy. Combining these two variables gives an outline of five basic strategies that organizations tend to adopt to a greater or lesser extent, as shown in Figure 3.2.

| | Low organizational intelligence | High organizational intelligence |
|---|---|---|
| **High labour market power** | **Status quo**<br>Organizations using this strategy have high labour market power and so have little difficulty attracting applicants. They tend to simply recruit applicants with similar backgrounds, skills and experience to current employees. With low organizational intelligence, they use restricted recruitment channels such as friends and family referral and the local community. Because these recruitment channels are so restrictive, there tend to be fewer selection procedures in place. | With high labour market power, these organizations are attractive to applicants and make good use of organizational knowledge to develop the applicant pool.<br><br>**Autonomous**<br>Use very precisely defined job descriptions and expectations: the organization's position as a labour market leader allows it to maintain these strict requirements even in difficult times. Strategy is implemented through specific recruitment channels, e.g. professional publications for specific professions.<br><br>**Innovative**<br>Does not precisely define the type of person they are looking for. These organizations tend to use the full range of recruitment channels and attract a diverse group of applicants, which is then filtered down using sophisticated selection procedures. |
| **Low labour market power** | **Muddling through**<br>If an organization has low labour market power and is not able to make good use of its professional knowledge (i.e. has low organizational intelligence), it can best be described as 'muddling through' recruitment. This type is not really a 'strategy' as such because it does not involve planning or strategic thinking. | **Flexible**<br>If an organization has low labour market power, perhaps because of its small size or remote location, it will find it difficult to attract high-quality candidates. Instead of trying to find an ideal candidate, it is more likely to adapt its own internal structure to take advantage of what is available in the labour market. It may also seek ways of educating or training applicants in order to help them meet the required standards. |

*Figure 3.2 Types of recruitment strategy*
Source: Based on Windolf, P. (1986) 'Recruitment, selection, and internal labour markets in Britain and Germany', *Organization Studies*, 7(3), pp. 235–54.

There are other ways of envisioning the impact of labour market conditions on the choice of recruitment strategy, but the important thing to bear in mind is that the strategy should adapt to the current conditions and make best use of the organizational expertise and knowledge already available. This is one of the advantages of Windolf's typology: although it is a basic outline, it highlights the critical importance of these two factors. Besides this, there are a couple more important labour market issues that deserve further exploration when we are considering the impact on recruitment: *global labour mobility* and skills shortages.

## Global labour mobility

The International Labour Organization (ILO, 2015) estimates that there are 150 million migrant workers in the world, that is, people who have moved to another country to find work. Nearly 80% of migrant workers are found in high-income countries, a reflection of the fact that this is where the higher paid, better work is found. Migrants in general have higher work participation rates that is, they are more likely to be in paid employment than the population at large (73% compared to 64%) and this difference is primarily because migrant women are more likely to be in employment than non-migrant women.

The topic of migrant workers is often highly politically loaded. Many countries, for example Australia, New Zealand and Canada, have points-based immigration systems, which give extra points to people with specific occupational skills when determining which migrants are more desirable and should be allowed into the country. On the other hand, migrant workers are also often a source of cheap labour and may find themselves being blamed for a country's ills, as happened in some of the campaigning for the UK's referendum on EU membership in 2016. Interestingly, there is often a difference in how these migrant workers are referred to in the academic literature and the popular media. People from developed countries who move for work are often called 'expatriates' (or 'expats'), while those from less developed countries are labelled 'migrants' or 'immigrants' and viewed in a less favourable light (Al Ariss and Crowley Henry, 2013). This false distinction can cover up the fact that people who are willing to move country in order to find work are a valuable source of labour and competitive advantage for organizations (Guo and Al Ariss, 2015). The Web Explorer exercise considers these different approaches in detail.

---

 ## Web Explorer: Migrant or expat?

In this exercise, we will investigate how people who move country for work are described in the popular media. To start, look up and read these articles:

- 'In Hong Kong, just who is an expat, anyway?': http://blogs.wsj.com/expat/2014/12/29/in-hong-kong-just-who-is-an-expat-anyway/

- 'Why are white people expats when the rest of us are immigrants?': www.theguardian.com/global-development-professionals-network/2015/mar/13/white-people-expats-immigrants-migration

- UNESCO's definition of migrants/migration: www.unesco.org/new/en/social-and-human-sciences/themes/international—migration/glossary/migrant/

- ILO's report on migrant workers: www.ilo.org/global/topics/labour-migration/news-statements/WCMS_436140/lang-en/index.htm

You could also read a couple of articles from different newspapers in your country. Note how they use terms to describe workers from other countries, as well as the overall tone of the articles.

Having read these different views, address these questions:

» To what extent are workers from other countries seen as a positive addition to the country's workforce or as a threat to the indigenous population? Why do you think that is?

» Why do you think the terms 'migrant' and 'expat' are used so differently? Do you think there is a difference between what the two words mean?

» With mobility being so much easier than it was even 50 years ago, how much do you think countries should try to restrict migrants' access to work in favour of those who were born in that country?

In recruitment terms, the increasing level of international migration for work means that organizations can draw on a much larger and more diverse pool of candidates. There are, of course, challenges in this, ranging from ensuring that language skills meet a sufficient level required for particular jobs to evaluating the comparability of qualifications, skills and experiences of workers from different countries.

## Skills shortages

In a labour market with near full employment, it can be difficult for organizations to recruit and retain individuals with the skills they need. New Zealand is a good example of a country with fairly low unemployment, 4–7% over the past decade, where organizations can sometimes struggle to recruit and retain skilled workers (IndexMundi, 2015). In a study of call centres in New Zealand, which are renowned for boring and stressful work and traditionally have high staff turnover, Hunt and Rasmussen (2007) noted that this tight labour market had inspired some managers to become creative in their approach to recruitment. For example, they expanded the pool of potential applicants by specifically targeting return-to-work mothers by advertising in crèches and inviting them to open days to see what the work involved. They also offered benefits such as family-friendly working practices, including flexible rosters over the school holidays, or extensive development and training opportunities in an effort to attract motivated and skilled workers. These approaches were so successful that one call centre had no staff turnover in two years.

While increased mobility and skills shortages can present recruitment challenges to organizations, they also present the opportunity to develop creative solutions that can ultimately benefit the organization by attracting a pool of high-quality candidates even in a tight labour market. The video interview in this

*FANCY*

*Companies can expand their recruitment pool by targeting specific groups, such as return-to-work mothers.*

chapter is with an international executive search consultant who conducts international searches for high-level candidates.

## Recruitment channels

There are many different **recruitment channels** (or potential ways to recruit candidates) available and one of the key decisions to be made in any recruitment process is which of these to use. The channel needs to provide access to as many qualified candidates as possible, while providing a cost-effective solution. In a recent CIPD survey (CIPD, 2015), HR respondents were asked which of the following 18 different channels were most effective for recruiting different employee groups:

Search consultants
Recruitment consultants
Own corporate website
Specialist journals/trade press
National and local newspapers
Commercial job boards
Professional referral schemes

Speculative applications/word of
    mouth
Alumni (previous employees)
Secondments
Professional networking sites
    (e.g. LinkedIn)
Social networking sites
    (e.g. Facebook)

Links with local organizations
    making redundancies
Jobcentre Plus
Apprenticeships
Local employment partnership
    (LEP)
Links with schools/colleges/
    universities

The corporate website emerged in the top three most effective methods for all groups, from directors to specialist/professional employees to manual employees. Many of the channels, however, were most effective for specific groups. For example, commercial job boards were particularly useful for specialist professional recruitment and administrative roles, while local newspapers were in the top three for manual/shop-floor employees but less effective for other roles. While recruitment consultants were reported as being useful for all the different employee groups, specialist search consultants were the most useful channel for the highest level jobs. Social media also played a role, with professional networking sites like LinkedIn seen as increasingly effective at higher levels in the organization, but social networking sites (like Facebook) much less so. Finally, structured graduate recruitment programmes remain popular, with 38% of organizations specifically targeting and training university graduates.

The same report (CIPD, 2015) summarized the ways that employers in the UK are attempting to attract candidates and found that over the previous two years, a large majority of organizations (86%) had put effort into improving their employer brand, particularly in terms of emphasizing their organizational values and good working practices. An employer brand is not the same as the brand the organization promotes for products and services, but is instead its image *as an employer*. An effective employer brand captures the unique experience of working for that specific organization and is the basis for employees' expectations (Edwards, 2010). It is therefore important that the brand is an honest portrayal of the employee experience; otherwise it could cause more problems if employees find they are disappointed by the reality of working in that organization.

Given this wide variety of recruitment channels, it is perhaps not surprising that the average cost of recruitment also varies. For managerial-level employees, the cost of recruitment only (before the selection procedure even begins) was around £7,000 per hire and for other employees around £2,000. This figure varies a lot depending on the industry, the size of the organization and so on, but it serves to emphasize how important it is to plan the recruitment process in order to make best use of the organization's resources.

Finally, of course, rather than looking outside the organization, a good source of candidates for a job could well be those who are already employed there.

The organization may already have the people it needs, just in a different position. So, resourcing can also include redeploying high-quality employees within the organization; there may well be no need to go through the expense of advertising and recruiting outside if the talent already exists within the organization.

## SELECTION METHODS

If the attraction of candidates goes well, the next stage is to select the best applicant for the job. There are a wide variety of different selection methods that can be used and the choice of the most appropriate or valid method is essential. The cost of hiring the 'wrong' person can be substantial. Schmidt and Hunter (1998), for example, suggested that using selection methods with higher validity, that is, they predict job performance more accurately, can be worth approximately $18,000 in increased output *per hire per year*. The wider impacts of selection errors include decreased team and organization morale, customer dissatisfaction and increased pressure on line managers to deal with poor performance (Sutherland and Wöcke, 2011). In this section, we review the most popular selection methods and consider their advantages and disadvantages in choosing the right person for the job.

### CVs and application forms

Generally, the first level of selection takes place based on the candidate's curriculum vitae (CV)/résumé or application form. These are used to assess a candidate's experience and qualifications against the advertised person or job specification and act as a first filter to remove applicants from the pool who do not meet basic requirements. However, annual surveys indicate that about a third of applicants will exaggerate their academic qualifications when applying for jobs (Rowley, 2014), which makes the subsequent stages of selection and fact-checking procedures important in finding the appropriate candidates for a post.

### Interviews

Interviews are by far the most popular method used in employee selection (Anderson and Cunningham-Snell, 2000) and are rated positively by job candidates (Anderson, 2003). Interviews are usually done in person, in face-to-face meetings, but they can also be carried out over the phone or online using Skype, Google Hangouts or other programmes. In fact, an increasing number of organizations are using distance interviews (CIPD, 2015). The popularity of interviews is easy to understand: if we want to select people for our organization, it is a basic assumption that we will want to meet them. Interviews also provide one of the few two-way selection methods, allowing the candidate to engage with the organization and determine their own fit as well.

However, we do need to be aware that because they rely on an interviewer's judgement, interviews can have a high potential for **bias** and subjectivity. Reliable selection interviews depend on having well-trained interviewers who can recognize natural human biases and misconceptions, and can take steps to counteract them. The following are common biases that we are subject to in coming to decisions in interviews:

- **Halo/horns:** we use a single piece of information to make an overall judgement about a person. For example, if a person arrives at the interview dressed neatly in business wear, we might make a general judgement of them as being competent and professional.

- **Primacy/recency:** the first or most recent piece of information is easiest for us to remember. For example, it is easiest for us to recall the first and the last person we interviewed in a long day of interviews, while the ones in the middle tend to blur together.

- **Stereotypes:** we automatically notice similarities and tend to categorize people based on their similarity, for example skin colour, accent or nationality. Stereotypes are a problem because we then assume that, based on their membership of this superficial category, all members will share other characteristics too.

- **Attribution bias:** this is when we assume we know the reasons behind someone's behaviour. Often, we attribute people's behaviour to personal characteristics (e.g. he arrived late because he is lazy) rather than external circumstances (e.g. he arrived late because someone drove into his car).

## Overcoming bias

Interviewer training is essential to overcome these biases and should focus on the following three areas:

1. The assessment criteria need to be clear and unambiguous, including only information that is related directly to performance ability.

2. Interviewers should record and justify their decisions, not only to reduce the effect of their own biases but also so that the organization has a written record and evidence of the fairness of the selection process.

3. Creating standardized and structured interviews ensures that interviewees are all asked the same questions and their responses assessed in a fair and consistent manner. An unstructured interview is essentially one without a plan and results in a lack of consistency and more scope for bias in the selection process.

Structured interviews can take two forms: behavioural or situational. A behavioural interview asks candidates to describe a time they have demonstrated a specific behaviour. A situational interview, in contrast, presents candidates with a hypothetical situation and asks them how they would deal with it. There is some evidence that situational interviews may be more valid than behavioural ones (Robertson and Smith, 2001) and they do have the advantage that they uncover potential in applicants who may not have as much work experience. The Transferrable Skills activity guides you through a process of developing your own interview skills.

## Transferrable Skills: Interview skills

In this exercise, you will gain practice in conducting an interview and in being interviewed. Interviewing is a complex skill and a good interviewer is able to deal with many different demands and tasks at once, such as putting the interviewee at ease, asking clear and appropriate questions, drawing out their best responses, being aware of potential biases and working to overcome them, and, of course, making notes or otherwise keeping track of responses so that a justified decision can be made at the end of the interview.

To start, get into a group with two other people and find an advert for a job you are interested in and would be qualified for. If it has a person specification, you can use this as the basis for developing your interview questions. If not, read through the advert carefully and see if you can develop a basic outline of what the organization might be looking for in a candidate.

Next, identify four or five key competencies, skills or attributes you think the potential employer will be looking for in the applicants and develop interview questions that will assess them. Remember, you will need the question to be open-ended so that the candidate can provide a full response. It is also useful if you can develop a couple of 'prompts' that the interviewer could use to explore the issue in more detail.

Look back at the differences between behavioural and situational interviews. See if you can develop both types of questions. To take it a step further, you could also construct rating scales for the interviewee's potential responses.

Now, decide in your group who will take on each of these three roles:

- Interviewer: you will conduct the interview, take notes as you see fit and make a decision at the end as to whether the candidate could be offered the job.

- Interviewee: you will play the part of the candidate applying for this job.

- Observer: your role is to observe the interviewer so that you can give them some feedback to improve the interviewing technique.

When you have role-played the interview, conduct a debrief in the group, covering the following issues:

» What was the experience of the interview like for the interviewer? How well did your questions work? What could you do to improve them?

» What was the experience of the interview like for the interviewee? To what extent were you able to communicate your suitability for the post? How positive would you feel about joining an organization after an interview like this?

» What did the observer notice that you could work on to develop your skills as an interviewer further?

You will probably find it most helpful if you repeat the exercise so that you can take turns in each of the roles: you will learn different things from experiencing each of the roles.

A further angle you could explore (perhaps particularly relevant if you already have a fair amount of experience in interviewing) would be to compare the experience of in-person and online or phone interviews. For this, develop your questions as above, but conduct the interview in a different format to your usual experience. What issues do the different formats raise? How can you develop your interview technique to make best use of each of these formats?

---

**Interview question**: What would you do if a team colleague was not completing tasks and it was negatively impacting on your team's performance?

| Score | Interviewee response |
|-------|----------------------|
| 5 | Discuss directly with the team member to see if there's a problem we can resolve together; for example, find out if the colleague has too much other work on |
| 4 | Raise it with our team leader before it becomes too big a problem |
| 3 | Try to do some of my colleague's work as well as mine |
| 2 | Ignore the problem and just get on with my own work |
| 1 | Reduce the amount of effort I am putting in so that it's fairer |

*Figure 3.3 Example BARS*

Another way to counteract natural biases in interviews is to rate the candidates' responses using **behaviourally anchored rating scales (BARS)**. BARS essentially consist of a scale with descriptions of better or worse responses to questions and the interviewee is scored according to how well they meet the criteria, as illustrated in Figure 3.3. This kind of scale helps to make decision-making more objective and ensure that each interviewee is being rated in a consistent way.

## References

*References* are the second most popular method used in selection, despite having one of the lowest validities (Anderson and Cunningham-Snell, 2000). They tend to fall into two main categories. The first is a factual type of reference, which is used to check an applicant's claims about job tenure, educational attainments and so on. Testimonials, on the other hand, are personal opinions about a potential candidate's suitability and fit for a job. These testimonials are, of course, subject to all the same biases of unstructured interviews and have the added drawback that the testimonial author may not even have a clear understanding of the job that is being applied for.

## Psychometric testing

Psychometric tests are quantifiable, standardized methods used to measure a candidate's ability or personality, which allow comparison across different candidates in a fair and consistent manner (Smith and Smith, 2005). A candidate's scores on a test are usually compared to a 'norm' group of similar people, such as graduates, experienced managers, equivalent professionals, so that an informed decision can be made as to the candidate's abilities and characteristics.

One advantage of psychometric tests is that they are cost-effective for filtering a large pool of candidates. They can also identify hidden potential, for example critical reasoning skills in a candidate who may not have a degree but still has the potential to function at that level. It is perhaps because of these advantages that **psychometrics** are used by up to 40% of organizations in the UK (CIPD, 2011b). There are two types of psychometric tests: ability and personality.

### Ability tests

Ability tests include cognitive tests, such as mathematical ability or verbal problem-solving, and physical/sensory motor tests, such as visual acuity or motor coordination, and the aim here is to determine a person's maximum performance. Abilities can be measured at a broad level, for example general mental ability, or at a more specific level such as dexterity. General intelligence, which is measured as how accurately and quickly we can process complex information, is a good predictor of job performance and training success, particularly for complex jobs (Salgado et al., 2003). Frequently, however, we will want to measure more specific abilities, such as numerical reasoning or manual dexterity. While these types of tests are not necessarily any better at predicting job performance than general intelligence tests, candidates are likely to view them as more relevant (Smither et al., 1993).

### Personality tests

Personality tests assess our typical ways of doing things, but can also include values and interest inventories, which can give a picture of how well a candidate might fit with the organizational culture. This type of test gives a more standardized method for assessing a candidate's personality than assumptions that might be made in an interview setting.

There is some controversy over whether personality is important when it comes to evaluating potential job performance. However, some clear conclusions have emerged from the decades of research in this area, especially when using the **Big Five** model of personality as a framework. The Big Five model is a simple yet reliable way of describing an individual's personality on five broad traits (see the Applications box for further information). The conscientiousness and emotional stability traits are the best predictors of work performance, with higher scores on each associated with better performance across a range of jobs (Barrick et al., 2001). The remaining three traits (extraversion, agreeableness and openness to change) are found to be related to performance when considered for individual jobs, but their effect varies across different jobs. For example, a high score on openness to change, which measures a person's creativity and curiosity might be very beneficial for a graphic designer but less useful for an accountant, who would be expected to follow conventions and rules.

Individual test publishers often develop their own systems for measuring personality and may also measure specific valued traits such as **resilience**. In addition, value inventories can be helpful in

## Applications: **Personality at work**

The Big Five are five broad, universal personality traits, which summarize our general patterns of thinking, feeling and behaving (Barrick and Mount, 1991). For each trait, an individual can score anywhere on the continuum from low to high, as shown in Figure 3.4.

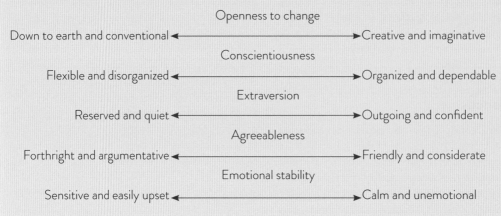

Openness to change

Down to earth and conventional ◄──────────────► Creative and imaginative

Conscientiousness

Flexible and disorganized ◄──────────────► Organized and dependable

Extraversion

Reserved and quiet ◄──────────────► Outgoing and confident

Agreeableness

Forthright and argumentative ◄──────────────► Friendly and considerate

Emotional stability

Sensitive and easily upset ◄──────────────► Calm and unemotional

*Figure 3.4 The Big Five personality traits*

- Put an X on the line where you think you score for each of these traits. For example, if you think you are more down to earth and conventional than creative and imaginative, put an X towards the left hand side of the openness trait. You can then take an online Big Five test here: www.ocf.berkeley.edu/~johnlab/bfi.htm and compare your score from the questionnaire to this quick overview.

- Once you have done this, think about how your scores on these traits might affect your work. Are there particular strengths you have? Is there anything that might cause problems and what could you do about it?

identifying candidates whose values match the organization's and can therefore be expected to have higher levels of commitment (Kristof-Brown et al., 2005). The choice of which tests to use should be based on the specific job competencies and abilities as well as a clear understanding of what needs to be measured.

### Can tests be faked?

There is evidence that about 30–50% of job applicants fake their answers to personality questionnaires, attempting to portray themselves in as positive a light as possible and better suited to the job than they really are (Griffith et al., 2007). It is possible, however, that successful candidates then try to live up to the personality description they believe the job requires. In fact, differences between 'home' and 'work' personalities are recognized in the literature and are not necessarily evidence of faking, but rather of adaptability to different situations.

### Biodata

*Biodata* consists of information about an individual's qualifications, work experience and so on that can be used to predict job performance. Rather than the hypothetical questions common in interviews, biodata extracts a candidate's concrete experiences (Gunter et al., 1993). This data is collated across many different job holders and applicants and, when correctly developed, biodata does a fairly good job of predicting job performance (Anderson and Cunningham-Snell, 2000). It is particularly helpful when sifting through a large number of applicants for jobs requiring certain levels of qualifications or experience.

On the downside, biodata selection is resource intensive to develop and not very popular, particularly among job applicants, as items can seem unconnected with the job (Anderson et al., 2008). It is important when implementing a biodata questionnaire that care is taken to ensure that the items do not inadvertently discriminate against particular groups. For example, if all our current high performers came from a specific university, we need to consider why this is so: is it because that university is very good at developing the skills our organization needs, or could it be that the manager in charge of recruitment up till now was only hiring candidates from their own university?

## Work sample

*Work samples* are excellent selection methods: not only do they predict job performance very well, they are also perceived as good selection methods by the candidates themselves (Anderson and Cunningham-Snell, 2000). These advantages come from the fact that they assess how the candidate actually does the job, rather than looking for indicators that they might perform well. Examples of work sample assessments include:

- **Group exercises:** candidates take part in a group task such as business strategy discussions, budget planning, expansions and so on. Assessors evaluate the individuals using a consistent scoring scheme.

- **In-tray exercises:** the candidate is given a collection of documents, memos and emails to prioritize and develop an action plan for. These samples are particularly useful for managerial or administrative roles.

- **Role-plays:** these may overlap with group exercises, but generally involve scenarios that a candidate would face during the job and the assessor determines how well the candidate prepares for and deals with the situation. Examples could include a medic assessing a 'patient' (played by an actor) to diagnose an illness or a manager conducting a performance review.

- **Presentations:** as a key skill for many jobs, presentations are increasingly common elements of a selection procedure. They give assessors the opportunity to evaluate a candidate's ability to communicate information to appropriate audiences.

*Getty Images/Blend Images/Sam Diephuis*

*Presentation skills are a key requirement in many jobs.*

Although work samples are popular and fairly effective methods for selection, they do have the drawback that it can sometimes be unclear what is being assessed. For example, a role-play may inadvertently assess a candidate's acting skills rather than their real ability to deal with the situation. In addition, work samples can be costly to develop and particularly difficult for more complex jobs.

## Assessment centres

Any or all of the methods outlined above can be combined into an **assessment centre**. Assessment centres use a multi-method approach to evaluating applicants. Based on a list of competencies for the job, a series of measures such as tests, interviews and role-plays may be developed so that the competencies can be assessed more than once. Assessment centre ratings tend to show fairly good association with performance ratings (Hermelin et al., 2012), although it is important that the raters are properly trained (Lievens, 2001). However, caution should be exercised because research has indicated that competency ratings across different exercises were less consistent than within an exercise (Sackett and Dreher, 1982), meaning that different raters

within an exercise might be evaluating a candidate very differently from each other. This issue of fairness and reliability in selection is one that we have encountered several times in this chapter and it deserves detailed consideration so that we can make informed decisions about what methods to choose.

# FAIRNESS IN SELECTION

Given the wide variety of different selection methods, it is important to be aware of the criteria we can use to decide how good each of those methods are and how they should be used to develop a complete picture to inform decisions about employee resourcing. There are three main criteria to bear in mind when judging a selection method: reliability, validity and fairness.

## Reliability

**Reliability** is a way of thinking about the consistency of a measure: a reliable measure will give the same results every time it is used. There are several different kinds of reliability that are relevant to selection processes, shown in Table 3.1.

## Table 3.1 Types of reliability

| Type of reliability | Definition | Example |
|---|---|---|
| **Inter-rater** | The extent to which different raters will give similar scores | A candidate's communication skills in a teamwork role-play at an assessment centre are judged by three different observers who give similar ratings. This means the measure of communication skills can be considered reliable |
| **Test-retest** | How consistent a person's scores are if they complete the measure on a second occasion | A candidate takes a test of verbal reasoning and then completes the same test two months later and receives a similar score. An exception to this might be if the candidate has undertaken specific, tailored training in the interim to improve skills in this area |
| **Internal consistency** | The different parts of a measure give similar results – it is consistent *within* the measure | Someone's personality trait scores are similar when the first half and the second half of the test are compared. There are different ways to check this and it obviously depends on how the test is structured: sometimes odd and even questions are compared instead |
| Parallel forms | Some psychometric tests have more than one version: to be reliable they need to give consistent scores on both versions | A job candidate has completed a mathematical reasoning test as part of the application process for Company A and completes a different version of this test for Company B. The scores on the two tests should be the same if it is reliable |

# Validity

Perhaps even more important than reliability is *validity*. A valid selection method is one that measures what it claims to. For example, if we ask a question about teamworking in an interview, to what extent are we really measuring someone's teamworking ability? As with reliability, there are different forms of validity that we need to consider, outlined in Table 3.2.

## Table 3.2 Types of validity

| Type of validity | Definition | Example |
|---|---|---|
| *Face* | The measure 'looks' like a sensible way of assessing a particular characteristic | A candidate who is told that a role-play will be assessing their teamworking abilities but finds that they are asked to deal with a difficult customer phone call on their own will not feel that the method was really assessing what it claimed to |
| *Content* | The measure is based in contemporary research and theory about what the ability or characteristic consists of | A personality test that is based on expert knowledge of the personality field and rigorous testing with a large sample of people will have greater content validity than one put together by a manager who wants to 'test' how approachable and friendly the candidates are |
| *Criterion* | This is the 'gold standard' to use when judging selection methods. It is how well a method or measure predicts an outcome we want (for example, job performance). It can be concurrent (related to current employee performance) or predictive (related to future employee performance) | An HR manager wants to know which of three selection methods are most closely related to job performance. They ask all members of a team to complete a personality test, an ability test and a structured interview and then compare the scores to performance ratings by their manager. The HR manager finds that, in this case, the interview predicts performance best – it has the highest criterion validity |

By being aware of these different forms of reliability and validity, we can make better decisions about which selection methods to use and how to interpret the results to select the best candidates for jobs. In addition, using valid and reliable methods is a key part of designing a selection procedure that is fair.

# Fairness

*Fairness* is not an easy issue to address in selection because the whole process of hiring revolves around what might be considered an unfair outcome: one person gets the job and another does not. But what we mean by fairness in assessment and selection is that candidates are treated equally and that the decision is made based on fair and balanced procedures. There are three main determinants of how we perceive fairness in selection (Arvey and Renz, 1992):

1. **The elements of the selection procedure:** how objective are they and how consistently are they applied to all the candidates?

2. **The information that is used to make selection decisions:** information that seems relevant to the job, for example based on the job description and person specification, is perceived as fairer than irrelevant information. Organizations also need to avoid collecting information that might be seen as invading a candidate's privacy.

3. **The actual results of the selection procedure:** including, for example, the extent to which minorities are represented in the chosen candidates.

We saw in Chapter 2 that there are several different approaches to trying to improve the diversity in the workforce and counteract problems with discrimination, such as affirmative action and preferential treatment. Alongside these attempts to improve diversity, many countries have equality laws designed to reduce discrimination in the workplace, but unfortunately it still happens. And it is not limited to discrimination against recognized groups such as minority ethnicities, sexuality or gender.

For example, a study showed that people can be discriminated against because they look overweight (Kutcher and Bragger, 2004). But the same study also highlighted the beneficial effects of using better selection methods: the discrimination was most obvious in unstructured interviews, where overweight applicants were rated lower and given lower salary recommendations; using structured interviews reduced this discrimination. The In the News feature illustrates a possible age-based discrimination case.

## In the News: Ageist selection?

Many large organizations actively recruit recent graduates and devote substantial resources to attracting and selecting these young people as they leave university. One of these is PricewaterhouseCoopers (PwC) and a recent law suit brought against the company in the USA alleges that candidates for entry-level positions who are over 40 years old are routinely screened out (Gershman, 2017).

The plaintiffs (two qualified men over 40 who were denied entry-level positions) claim that discriminating against them based on age runs counter to the US law against age discrimination. They point out that PwC actively promotes itself as a 'young' company (the vast majority of its workers were born after 1980) and that by having university campus recruitment drives, PwC is effectively discriminating against people who are not at university. PwC has countered this by claiming

that the age discrimination law only covers people already employed at the organization.

There are many reasons that age discrimination might take place and discrimination may occur for both younger and older job applicants. Older applicants may be assumed to be more experienced, stable and committed to staying with the organization long term. Younger applicants may be seen as more technologically adept, adaptable and having creative ideas. There is also the issue of pay, particularly in economic downturns, when organizations may prefer to hire younger, cheaper labour than older candidates with higher salary expectations.

» Why do so many companies target recent graduates? To what extent do you think this approach is ageist?
» How might age stereotypes impact on fairness in selection and what could be done to minimize their effect?

It can be particularly difficult to stop discrimination in selection procedures, where the methods, by their very design, differentiate between people. In a selection procedure, one person scoring less well on a measure than another is not in itself evidence for it being an unfair measure. Where it becomes unfair, or even discriminatory against particular groups, is if there is **adverse impact**. Adverse impact occurs when two groups score differently on a particular measure and it results in differential hiring rates for the people in each group. For example, one ethnic group may score lower than another on average on a measure, which then leads to less of that first group being hired. Hough et al. (2001) conducted a study of various selection measures in the USA, including

general intelligence, verbal ability, memory, processing speed and personality. They found that there were significant subgroup differences between different ethnic groups, between men and women, and between age groups. In many cases, these differences were such that some groups would have a greater chance of selection if those measures were used in assessments. This is important to recognize because there are many possible reasons why these test score differences exist that mean they do not necessarily reflect differences in ability (Hough et al., 2001):

• **Measurement method:** Some ways of measuring the attributes we are selecting for can increase between-group differences and some methods can reduce it. For example, work samples reduce the differences between white and other ethnicities' scores. As we have already seen, work samples are also some of the most valid selection methods.

- **Test coaching:** There is evidence that test coaching programmes have a small but positive effect on test scores. They help candidates become familiar with the test-taking environment and the style of questions, as well as increase motivation and reduce anxiety. This means that subgroups with a greater familiarity with test-taking are likely to perform better than those unfamiliar with the processes.

- **Applicant perceptions:** People tend to score better in tests when they are convinced of the test's validity and are motivated to do it. This demonstrates how important face validity is when choosing a selection method: the higher the face validity, the more likely applicants will engage with it to the best of their ability.

- **Stereotype perceptions:** An intriguing issue that is especially relevant to selection procedures is the role of stereotype threat, also sometimes called the 'self-fulfilling prophecy'. There is strong

evidence that if we are told that people of our gender/race/ethnicity tend to score worse on a particular test, we do actually score worse on it than if we are not given this information (Steele and Aronson, 1995). If candidates are aware that they are not expected to do well in a particular test, therefore, it can have a negative impact on their performance. See the Weighing the Evidence box for further information on this.

- **Criterion composition:** We saw above how criterion validity was essential in choosing an appropriate selection method. One of the complexities we face in this is that defining the 'criterion' or outcome we want to predict is challenging. While it seems straightforward to say that a selection method needs to predict future job performance, the way that performance is evaluated leaves a lot of room for subjective interpretation. For example, if job performance is restricted to considering performance on individual tasks, minority differences are accentuated. But if job performance is defined as 'contextual', that is, those behaviours that support task performance and build an organization's climate, minority differences are dramatically reduced.

---

 Weighing the Evidence: **Racial and sex differences in intellectual ability**

In the USA, substantial research has been carried out comparing scores of different race groups on standardized ability tests. A consistently emerging result seemed to be that African Americans scored significantly lower on intelligence tests than did white Americans, and Americans of East Asian descent scored higher again (Hough et al., 2001). Similarly, men scored better on measures of mechanical intelligence and women on measures of verbal intelligence. On face value, these kinds of results can be interpreted as providing evidence that people of different racial groups or sexes have different intellectual abilities – not only a controversial finding but potentially very damaging to individuals' self-esteem and educational/career prospects. So is it true?

As we saw above, Hough et al. showed that there were many plausible underlying reasons for this difference that do not mean there is a real difference in ability, but the issue of stereotype threat is particularly important. Stereotype threat

is the term used for a 'social stigma' that people experience where they are aware they are seen as intellectually inferior by their society. This threat then undermines their actual performance. A ground-breaking study demonstrating this was reported in 1995, when African American students scored worse than white students on a test that was presented to them as a measure of their intellectual abilities, but scored equally as well as white students when the test was presented as a problem-solving task (Steele and Aronson, 1995).

Further studies showed that stereotype threat could affect any group when the stereotype was elicited before the test took place; for example, women doing maths (Good et al., 2008), people from lower socioeconomic groups (Croizet and Claire, 1998) and elderly people (Levy, 1996). In fact, stereotype threat can even happen for people who have previously not had any exposure to a negative stereotype. Aronson et al. (1999) selected a group of maths-proficient white males, then told half of them that Asian men tended to do better in this kind of test than white men. The half who had the stereotype induced did worse than those who did not. And the stereotype itself can be induced by something as simple as being asked to indicate race on a test paper.

Given the dramatic effects of stereotype threat, and the ease with which it can be induced, what can we do to try and minimize its impact in selection environments? One of the methods of

reducing stereotype threat is to contextualize the test as non-evaluative, but this will not work in a selection environment where candidates are aware that the purpose of tests is to evaluate their abilities. However, another effective method is simply to tell test-takers that the test is gender and race fair (Quinn and Spencer, 2001), which well-designed and researched tests should be. This seems to remove the anxiety that many people feel because of stereotypes and helps them to perform to the best of their ability.

Given the many possible underlying reasons for subgroup differences in test scores, some might suggest that we should not use them at all because they discriminate unfairly against certain groups. However, we also need to bear in mind that discrimination happens using other selection methods and the advantage of using well-researched psychometric tests is that scores can be compared to relevant norm groups as a way of overcoming these differences. Overcoming discrimination in other methods can be much more difficult and complex. This may be one reason why minority groups often feel that testing is a fairer way of selecting people for jobs (Hough et al., 2001).

But how do we know if a particular selection method is having an adverse impact on a subgroup of applicants? Evaluating adverse impact requires some detailed statistical analysis (for a review of different methods, see the Hough et al. 2001 paper), but there is a simpler rule of thumb that can be used. The so-called '4/5ths rule' states that if the selection rate for one subgroup is less than 4/5ths that of another group, it is an indication that adverse impact might be occurring. That is, if one subgroup tends to be selected 20% less often, it may well be due to inappropriate selection methods and should be investigated further. As we have seen throughout this chapter, the issues of fairness are closely bound up with decisions that HR professionals and others make in choosing selection methods with high reliability and validity.

## SUMMARY

In this chapter, we have looked at some of the key OB and HRM issues that set the stage for the beginning of the employment relationship. We started by noting

### Practice Insights: Kirsten Henderson

Kirsten Henderson is a consultant with Jo Fisher Executive in New Zealand, an international executive search company which specializes in helping clients to find high-calibre candidates for leadership and specialist positions. With her years of experience in international search, Kirsten also has some great insights into the challenges of finding rare skill sets in an international market and the challenges of cross-cultural working.

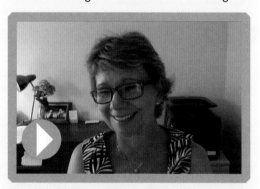

Go online to www.macmillanihe.com/sutton-people to access the interview with Kirsten.

how essential it is that the recruitment strategy is aligned with the organization's overall strategy so that it can support the future development of the organization, and considered job-level and organization-level challenges.

We then gained an overview of the practical methods used by organizations and HR professionals in attracting and recruiting candidates, including how they can deal with issues of global labour mobility and skills shortages. Once candidates have applied for a post, the next major challenge is choosing the right person for the job, and we have looked at the popularity and utility of various methods for selection. Finally, we brought the chapter together by considering fairness in selection, noting how important it is to use reliable and valid selection methods if we are to avoid bias and adverse impact in selection.

## FURTHER READING

- The CIPD's full report on recruitment channels gives a good introduction to the practical aspects of resourcing, see CIPD (2015) *Resourcing and Talent Planning*. Available at: www.cipd.co.uk/hr-resources/survey-reports/resourcing-talent-planning-2015.aspx.

- More details on the reliability and validity of different selection methods can be found in Anderson, N. and Cunningham-Snell, N. (2000) 'Personnel selection', in N. Chmiel (ed.) *Introduction to Work and Organizational Psychology: A European Perspective*. Oxford: Blackwell, pp. 69–99.

## REVIEW QUESTIONS

1. Why is it important to consider both micro- and macro-level issues when determining a resourcing strategy?

2. What impact do skills shortages have on recruitment and selection? Consider the impact on an organization from both a local and an international perspective.

3. How can we ensure selection for job roles is fair? Which methods of selection would you recommend as fairest and why?

## ONLINE RESOURCES

Go online to www.macmillanihe.com/sutton-people to access a MCQ quiz for this chapter and for further resources to support your learning.

## REFERENCES

Anderson, N. (2003) 'Applicant and recruiter reactions to new technology in selection: a critical review and agenda for future research', *International Journal of Selection and Assessment*, 11(2/3), pp. 121–36. doi: 10.1111/1468-2389.00235.

Anderson, N. and Cunningham-Snell, N. (2000) 'Personnel selection', in N. Chmiel (ed.) *Introduction to Work and Organizational Psychology: A European Perspective*. Oxford: Blackwell, pp. 69–99.

Anderson, N., Salgado, J., Schinkel, S. and Cunningham-Snell, N. (2008) 'Staffing the organization: an introduction to personnel selection and assessment', in N. Chmiel (ed.) *An Introduction to Work and Organizational Psychology: A European Perspective*, 2nd edn. Oxford: Blackwell, pp. 257–80.

Al Ariss, A. and Crowley Henry, M. (2013) 'Self-initiated expatriation and migration in the management literature', *Career Development International*, 18(1), pp. 78–96. doi: 10.1108/13620431311305962.

Aronson, J., Lustina, M. J., Good, C. et al. (1999) 'When white men can't do math: necessary and sufficient factors in stereotype threat', *Journal of Experimental Social Psychology*, 35(1), pp. 29–46. doi: 10.1006/jesp.1998.1371.

Arvey, R. and Renz, G. (1992) 'Fairness in the selection of employees', *Journal of Business Ethics*, 11(5/6), pp. 331–40. doi: 10.1007/BF00870545.

Barrick, M. R. and Mount, M. K. (1991) 'The big five personality dimensions and job performance: a meta-analysis', *Personnel Psychology*, 44(1), pp. 1–26.

Barrick, M. R., Mount, M. K. and Judge, T. A. (2001) 'Personality and performance at the beginning of the new millennium: What do we know and where do we go next?', *International Journal of Selection and Assessment*, 9(1/2), pp. 9–30. doi: 10.1111/1468-2389.00160.

Bartram, D., Robertson, I. T. and Callinan, M. (2002) 'Introduction: a framework for examining organizational effectiveness', in *Organizational Effectiveness: The Role of Psychology*. New York: John Wiley & Sons, pp. 1–10.

Boyatzis, R. E. (1982) *The Competent Manager: A Model for Effective Performance*. New York: Wiley.

Cappelli, P. (2009) 'A supply chain approach to workforce planning', *Organizational Dynamics*, 38(1), pp. 8–15. doi: 10.1016/j.orgdyn.2008.10.004.

CIPD (2011a) *Workforce Planning Factsheet*. Available at: www.cipd.co.uk/hr-resources/factsheets/workforce-planning.aspx.

CIPD (2011b) *Resourcing and Talent Planning Annual Survey*. London: CIPD.

CIPD (2015) *Resourcing and Talent Planning*. Available at: www.cipd.co.uk/hr-resources/survey-reports/resourcing-talent-planning-2015.aspx.

Croizet, J.-C. and Claire, T. (1998) 'Extending the concept of stereotype threat to social class: the intellectual underperformance of students from low socioeconomic backgrounds', *Personality and Social Psychology Bulletin*, 24(6), pp. 588–94. doi: 10.1177/0146167298246003.

DeFazio, S. (2014) 'Future-proof your workforce', *Workforce Solutions Review*, March, pp. 40–3.

Edwards, M. R. (2010) 'An integrative review of employer branding and OB theory', *Personnel Review*, 39(1), pp. 5–23.

Gershman, J. (2017) 'Older workers challenge PwC's pursuit of young graduates', *The Australian*, 17 April. Available at: www.theaustralian.com.au/business/older-workers-challenge-pwcs-pursuit-of-young-graduates/news-story/be2550432ec18bfc9b7920d92bd293a8.

Good, C., Aronson, J. and Harder, J. A. (2008) 'Problems in the pipeline: stereotype threat and women's achievement in high-level math courses', *Journal of Applied Developmental Psychology*, 29(1), pp. 17–28. doi: 10.1016/j.appdev.2007.10.004.

Griffith, R. L., Chmielowski, T. and Yoshita, Y. (2007) 'Do applicants fake? An examination of the frequency of applicant faking behavior', *Personnel Review*, 36(3), pp. 341–355. doi: 10.1108/00483480710731310.

Gunter, B., Furnham, A. and Drakely, R. (1993) *Biodata: Biographical Indicators of Business Performance*. London: Routledge.

Guo, C. and Al Ariss, A. (2015) 'Human resource management of international migrants: current theories and future research', *International Journal of Human Resource Management*, 26(10), pp. 1287–97. doi: 10.1080/09585192.2015.1011844.

Hermelin, E., Lievens, F. and Robertson, I. T. (2012) 'The validity of assessment centres for the prediction of supervisory performance ratings: a meta-analysis', *International Journal of Selection and Assessment*, 15(4), pp. 405–11.

Hough, L. M., Oswald, F. L. and Ployhart, R. E. (2001) 'Determinants, detection and amelioration of adverse impact in personnel selection procedures: issues, evidence and lessons learnt', *International Journal of Selection and Assessment*, 9(1/2), pp. 152–94. doi: 10.1111/1468-2389.00171.

Hunt, V. and Rasmussen, E. (2007) 'Turnover and retention in a tight labour market: reflection on New Zealand research', *New Zealand Journal of Employment Relations*, 32(1), pp. 45–58.

IndexMundi (2015) *New Zealand Unemployment Rate*. Available at: www.indexmundi.com/new_zealand/unemployment_rate.html (Accessed 20 September 2016).

ILO (2015) *ILO Global Estimates of Migrant Workers and Migrant Domestic Workers: Results And Methodology*. Geneva. Available at: www.ilo.org/global/topics/labour-migration/publications/WCMS_436343/lang--en/index.htm.

Kristof-Brown, A. L., Zimmerman, R. D. and Johnson, E. C. (2005) 'Consequences of individuals' fit at work: a meta-analysis of person-job, person-organization, person-group, and person-supervisor fit', *Personnel Psychology*, 58(2), pp. 281–342. doi: 10.1111/j.1744-6570.2005.00672.x.

Kutcher, E. J. and Bragger, J. D. (2004) 'Selection interviews of overweight job applicants: Can structure reduce the bias?', *Journal of Applied Social Psychology*, 34(10), pp. 1993–2022. doi: 10.1111/j.1559-1816.2004.tb02688.x.

Levy, B. (1996) 'Improving memory in old age through implicit self-stereotyping', 71(6), pp. 1092–107.

Lievens, F. (2001) 'Assessor training strategies and their effects on accuracy, interrater reliability, and discriminant validity', *Journal of Applied Psychology*, 86(2), pp. 255–64. doi: 10.1037/0021-9010.86.2.255.

Mayo, A. (2015) 'Strategic workforce planning: a vital business activity', *Strategic HR Review*, 14(5), pp. 174–81. doi: 10.1108/SHR-08-2015-0063.

Orlitzky, M. (2007) 'Recruitment strategy', in *The Oxford Handbook of Human Resource Management*. Oxford: Oxford University Press.

Quinn, D. M. and Spencer, S. J. (2001) 'The interference of stereotype threat with women's generation of mathematical problem-solving strategies', *Journal of Social Issues*, 57(1), pp. 55–71. doi: 10.1111/0022-4537.00201.

Robertson, I. T. and Smith, M. (2001) 'Personnel selection', *Journal of Occupational & Organizational Psychology*, 74(4), pp. 441–72.

Rowley, J. (2014) 'Degree deceit: Does it pay to lie on your CV?', *The Guardian*, 18 June. Available at: www.theguardian.com/careers/careers-blog/lie-degree-cv-jobseekers-graduate.

Ryan, G., Emmerling, R. J. and Spencer, L. M. (2009) 'Distinguishing high-performing European executives: the role of emotional, social and cognitive competencies', *Journal of Management Development*, 28(9), pp. 859–75. doi: 10.1108/02621710910987692.

Sackett, P. R. and Dreher, G. F. (1982) 'Constructs and assessment center dimensions: some troubling empirical findings', *Journal of Applied Psychology*, 67(4), pp. 401–10. doi: 10.1037/0021-9010.67.4.401.

Salgado, J. F., Anderson, N., Moscoso, S. et al. (2003) 'International validity generalization of GMA and cognitive abilities: a European Community meta-analysis', *Personnel Psychology*, 56(3), pp. 573–605.

Schmidt, F. L. and Hunter, J. E. (1998) 'The validity and utility of selection methods in personnel psychology: practical and theoretical implications of 85 years of research findings', *Psychological Bulletin*, 124(2), pp. 262–74. doi: 10.1037/0033-2909.124.2.262.

Smith, M. and Smith, P. (2005) *Testing People at Work: Competencies in Psychometric Testing*. Oxford: Blackwell.

Smither, J. W., Reilly, R. R., Millsap, R. E. et al. (1993) 'Applicant reactions to selection procedures', *Personnel Psychology*, 46(1), pp. 49–76. doi: 10.1111/j.1744-6570.1993.tb00867.x.

Soderquist, K. E., Papalexandris, A., Ioannou, G. and Prastacos, G. (2010) 'From task-based to competency-based: a typology and process supporting a critical HRM transition', *Personnel Review*, 39(3), pp. 325–46. doi: 10.1108/00483481011030520.

Spencer, L. M., McClelland, D. C. and Spencer, S. M. (1992) *Competency Assessment Methods: History and State of the Art*. London: Hay/McBer Research Press.

Steele, C. M. and Aronson, J. (1995) 'Stereotype threat and the intellectual test performance of African Americans', *Journal of Personality and Social Psychology*, 69(5), pp. 797–811.

Sutherland, M. and Wöcke, A. (2011) 'The symptoms of and consequences to selection errors in recruitment decisions', *South African Journal of Business*, 42(4), pp. 23–32. Available at: http://reference.sabinet.co.za/sa_epublication_article/busman_v42_n4_a2.

Tett, R. P., Guterman, H. A., Bleier, A. and Murphy, P. J. (2000) 'Development and content validation of a "hyperdimensional" taxonomy of managerial competence', *Human Performance*, 13(3), p. 205.

Windolf, P. (1986) 'Recruitment, selection, and internal labour markets in Britain and Germany', *Organization Studies*, 7(3), pp. 235–54. doi: 10.1177/017084068600700302.

# PART 1 CASE STUDY: CARE WORKERS

Care workers aim to help people who need care and support to live as independently as possible and *domiciliary* care workers provide these services within a client's own home. Care duties range from practical tasks such as making beds and helping with mobility, through more medical tasks like monitoring temperature and ensuring clients have their medications, to more informal aspects such as providing emotional support and engaging activities for their clients (Skills for Care Ltd, 2016). But it is proving increasingly difficult to recruit care workers and the reliance by many firms on informal methods such as word of mouth results in low quantity and quality of applications and ultimately an untrained and low-skilled workforce (Atkinson et al., 2016).

PhotoDisc/Getty Images

Despite doing what many would see as an essential and incredibly important job, care workers in the UK typically experience very poor terms and conditions. They have little job security and are often employed on zero-hour contracts, that is, a contract where the employee is not guaranteed any specific number of hours of work but is essentially employed on an as-and-when-required basis. Until recently, many of them were not even paid the minimum wage (UNISON, 2016), with employers even withholding pay for the time spent travelling between appointments. As one manager put it in a recent report for the Welsh government (Atkinson et al., 2016): 'I think pay is a massive issue ... [care workers] aren't recognised for the work they do – they should be paid a lot more.' Another manager recognized the impact of low pay on the quality of workers they could recruit: 'It's a horrible phrase, but if you pay peanuts you get monkeys. I'm not being disrespectful but to get the real quality of staff we need to pay them more.'

The care workers themselves feel that their contributions are rarely recognized: 'It's one of the hardest jobs I think, caring, and people don't realize it.' They also reflected that working practices were not based on an understanding of the complexity of their tasks:

> We deal with morphine and warfarin and all them sorts of things that you would expect a nurse to deal with. And when you have to do that in a fifteen minute call – like medication is such an important thing and it needs your whole concentration and then you're having

to do meds, food, toileting, in that short amount of time.

If workers have to rush between jobs, they are unable to provide that essential social connection that many of them feel is an important and rewarding part of the job.

Care workers also have to deal with the fact that they have very little status in their job, with some of them saying they have been told their job is 'worthless, you don't even earn anything, you don't earn much money' and 'you're seen as, you're only a carer ... you're more or less the servant'. Male care workers experience further discrimination, as one reported:

> a lot of elderly gentlemen are quite set in their ways shall we say and they think it's a female's job. It is a woman's job, and I don't want a man doing that sort of thing. Is he gay? Is he what? That's what they think. And they don't want you there

There are typically no experience requirements for entry into care work in the UK, yet these workers have responsibility for their clients' health and well-being and may sometimes be the only human contact that a housebound client has all day. While there is a move towards increasing the status and 'professionalization' of care work by introducing registration and mandatory qualifications, there is, as yet, little or no funding to provide this training. One care worker said: 'I was out [in service users' homes] after three hours' training and on my third day I was training someone else. I knew what to do but not why, it was difficult.' Others reported that there were never enough places on essential courses like training them in how to deal with dementia.

So, if the pay, development and status is so poor for this job, why do people still go into it rather than other similarly paid jobs such as retail? Care workers say that the work is rewarding and they can see the positive impact they are having on people's lives. As one carer put it, 'I want to be a carer because I care' and another 'you stay because you love it' despite the poor terms and conditions. However, the sector experiences very high turnover and clearly this internal motivation needs to be supported by appropriate HR structures and practices.

- To what extent do you think employers may take advantage of care workers' motivation to care for other people?

- Why do you think 'caring' professions are generally paid so poorly?

- What kind of recruitment and selection methods would you recommend to care worker employers, bearing in mind their lack of funding? How might you try to convince an employer that a certain level of investment in appropriate selection methods would be worthwhile?

## REFERENCES

Atkinson, C., Crozier, S. and Lewis, L. (2016) *Factors that Affect the Recruitment and Retention of Domiciliary Care Workers and the Extent to which these Factors Impact upon the Quality of Domiciliary*. Cardiff: Welsh Government.

Skills for Care Ltd (2016) Care worker. Available at: www.skillsforcare.org.uk/Care-careers/Think-Care-Careers/Jobs/Care-Worker/Care-worker.aspx.

UNISON (2016) 'Care workers continue to be denied the minimum wage', *UNISON News*.

part
**2**

# THE MANAGEMENT RELATIONSHIP

In Part 1, we laid the foundations for understanding the management relationship, looking at how OB and HRM have developed, evaluating the meaning of work and seeing how the employment relationship is first initiated. Now we turn to look at the management relationship in more detail. In Chapter 4 we start by considering the relationship that individual employees have with their organizations, from how it is formally contracted to how it is informally understood and interpreted. We look at ways managers can influence and change this relationship and particularly the key role of communication in maintaining the relationship. Chapter 5 then considers that essential element of the management relationship, how to encourage and manage performance. Here we take account of the influence of job design and individual

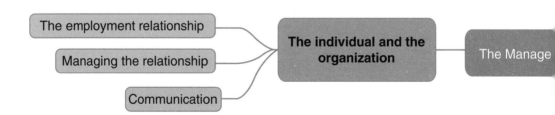

motivation in determining performance as well as the approaches managers take to appraising performance. We also look at the role of benefits and rewards in encouraging performance. In Chapter 6 we move on to look at a specific relationship in organizations, that of leader and follower. We consider the elements that contribute to leader success and evaluate several different models that help us to understand what leadership is all about. Finally, we look at the specific interactions between HRM and leadership in work organizations. The Part 2 case study explores how leaders' use of social media can influence the relationships and trust between employees and their organizations, as well as encourage higher performance.

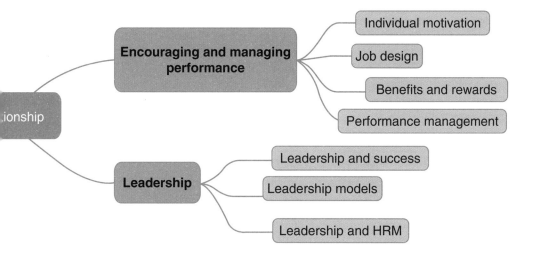

# 4 THE INDIVIDUAL AND THE ORGANIZATION

## INTRODUCTION

In Chapter 3 we considered what happens before an individual joins the organization. In this chapter we look at the developing relationship between the individual and the organization in more detail, drawing on a range of OB and HRM issues. The basis of this relationship could be considered the formal employment contract, where HR plays a key role, but the individual–organization relationship is far more complex than what is captured in a legal contract. So we will also consider the *psychological* contract: the set of unwritten and often unvoiced expectations and obligations that individuals and organizations have of how the employment relationship will work.

We will move on to look at the different ways individuals and organizations try to manage their relationship. We start by considering a key issue in the OB literature: our *frames of reference* or the structures we use to try and make sense of what is happening at work. We then look at how employees can seek collective representation to raise issues with how they are being managed and, finally, we give thorough consideration to the role of trust in the relationship between individuals and organizations.

Building and maintaining good relationships is reliant on good communication, so we close this chapter by looking at how communication can be thought of as an active process with specific goals. We include a discussion of employee voice: the ways that employees can have a say in the running of the organization and how it helps to make communication a two-way process. By integrating the relevant knowledge from the HRM and OB fields, we can develop better ways of understanding the individual–organization relationship.

Getty Images/Blend Images/Erik Isakson

## LEARNING FEATURES

Applications: The psychological contract

Applications: Trust at work

Applications: Communicating difficult messages

Applications: Informal networks and rumour

Weighing the Evidence: High commitment HR practices

Web Explorer: Workers vs management

In the News: Uber and the gig economy

Transferrable Skills: Negotiation

Practice Insights: Mark Harcourt

 Video overview

Julian Perkins

Go online to www.macmillanihe.com/sutton-people to access a video of Anna Sutton introducing the chapter's main themes.

# THE EMPLOYMENT RELATIONSHIP

The relationship between the individual and organization, just like any other relationship, is dynamic and complex. Understanding the employment relationship starts with a recognition that employee and employer needs and expectations are not always the same. In fact, in some cases, they can even be incompatible. Take, for example, an employee who believes that her work is worth higher pay, compared to an employer who wishes to reduce staffing costs as much as possible. The way these conflicting needs are negotiated depends on the past employment relationship and affects the future relationship.

Of course, there are also examples of mutually compatible needs. For example, a teacher may want to help his pupils to learn as much as possible and the employing school may wish to provide a good level of education. Even in this case, however, the relationship between the organization and the individual is key. The organization needs to ensure that any changes it initiates will not adversely impact on these mutual gains or inadvertently restrict the individual's effectiveness.

Because the employment relationship is the basis for determining the rights and obligations of the employer and the employees and has knock-on effects for how workers are treated, it is important that we define what we mean by it and ensure that our definition is not limited to 'traditional' employment relationships where the employee has a clear contract, place of work and is directly remunerated for carrying out the work. Otherwise, workers engaged in a non-traditional or not legally recognized employment relationship may not be entitled to the same rights and protections as other workers. The International Labour Organization (ILO, 2007) identified a range of criteria that could be used to identify employment relationships, the most important being:

- Control: The employer gives instructions on what work should be carried out and exerts control over the process or the result of the work. This was traditionally the main way of determining an employment relationship, but it has become less useful as work has changed. For example, many more people are now able to work from home, so the manager can no longer physically watch what they are doing or regulate how and when the work is done.

- Integration: To address the issue of control, the ILO recognized that newly evolving forms of work often have less control but more integration. That is, workers may have freedom in how they work but their work or products are *integrated into* the organization. For example, someone employed by a cleaning company may spend most of her time working independently on various sites around a city, but might attend regular team meetings or wear a company uniform, and the work that is carried out is considered an integral part of the company's service.

- Dependence: The worker is economically dependent on the employer. This criterion recognizes that an employer may, in fact, exert little control over the work and the employee might not be integrated into the organization, but an employment relationship nevertheless exists because there is an exchange of work for remuneration. An example here might be a subcontractor who works exclusively for one organization and is dependent on it.

- Financial risk: In an employment relationship, the employer's risks (such as reduced profits) are likely to affect employees indirectly but generally they are not exposed to personal financial risks. Instead, it is the employer who assumes the direct financial risk. For example, workers will still be paid weekly or monthly wages even when the employer has lower profits.

In summarizing this lengthy report, the ILO (2016) gives a brief definition of the employment relationship as 'the legal link between employers and employees. It exists when a person performs work or services under certain conditions in return for remuneration.' However, it also recommended that individual nations develop their own definitions to include a range of criteria to capture the variety of employment relationships that exist in their contexts. The In the News box looks at how technological changes are impacting on traditional notions of the employment relationship, using the example of Uber.

Many have argued that the employment relationship is not just the legal contract between workers and employers. Spooner and Haidar (2006) note that the employment relationship does not just affect the work lives of employees, but has wide-ranging impacts on their economic, social and psychological lives, and even affects the lives of those not in an employment relationship. They urge us to recognize that issues of power and control lie at the core of the employment relationship. In fact, we can view the employment relationship as consisting of an economic exchange *and* a power relationship (Dibben et al., 2011), which is why it is important to consider the management and details of that relationship from an HRM and an OB perspective. It is this broader understanding of the employment relationship that we are taking in this chapter.

 In the News: **Uber and the gig economy**

The **'gig economy'** is a phrase used to describe the increasing prevalence of on-demand, short-term work that is replacing traditional secure employment. It is often enabled by technological advances and innovations and a good example is Uber. Initially launched as a 'ride-sharing' app that connected drivers to customers needing lifts, it quickly developed into a multi-million dollar company that is active around the world. Instead of being employed as taxi drivers by Uber, the drivers are effectively self-employed and providing services on demand.

Many people see the gig economy as encouraging innovation and flexibility, with people being able to work whenever they want to and fitting that work around their other commitments. But others have emphasized the downsides: workers with no rights or stability who take on all the risks themselves and a company that makes money no matter what and does not need to provide paid holidays or sick leave. Uber has faced legal challenges in many countries over tax payments and the safety issues involved in having unregistered or unlicensed 'taxi' drivers. In October 2016, Uber drivers in the UK won a tribunal case against Uber: the court upheld their claim that they were workers who were entitled to holiday pay and the minimum wage (O'Connor et al., 2016).

**For discussion**

» What other companies do you know of that use the gig economy model?
» Do you agree that Uber and companies like it should be responsible for ensuring worker rights in the same way as traditional employers? Why or why not?

## Contracting the employment relationship

### Formal contract

The formal contract of employment is often seen as the basis of the employment relationship. It is a way of regulating the relationship between employer and employee, setting out the expectations the organization has of the employee in terms of job scope, working hours and performance, as well as what the employee can expect of the organization in terms of pay and conditions. The contract is itself subject to the legal frameworks of the country in which the employment occurs. But the legal regulations are only one part of the different types of regulation of employment (Dibben et al., 2011):

1. Statutory: This is regulation by law. Laws can be seen as a way of regulating social power (Pound, 1942), that is, protecting those with less power and making efforts to create a fair environment, so they are naturally a key element of regulating employment relations. Legal frameworks provide a certain amount of transparency, equity and security, but can also be excessively rigid or complex.

2. Social: The relationship can also be managed through bargaining between employers and employees. This can be done on an individual level between an employee and manager or at a collective level, for example between management representatives and trade unions. For this to work to the benefit of both sides, there needs to be a fairly even balance of power between the two sides. Social regulation has the advantages of introducing reciprocity into the relationship and maintaining a sustainable balance between the desires of each side. However, it does have disadvantages such as the time-consuming nature of negotiations and the scope for political manoeuvring by both parties.

3. **Market:** There are also market influences, such as supply and demand for skills, on the employment relationship. Legal frameworks in different countries allow these market forces greater or lesser influence. For example, the default position in the USA is 'at-will employment', meaning that employers can dismiss employees whenever they want to and for any reason. This is rare in the rest of the world and in Europe employers must demonstrate that they have just cause for dismissal. Regulation of the relationship through market forces allows for greater flexibility in employment and does not require any expensive administration, but also has several disadvantages. These include a focus on short-termism, decreasing the obligations of employers to their employees and increasing social inequalities.

Getty Images/Blend Images/Jose Luis Pelaez Inc.

*Formal employment contracts form the basis of the employment relationship.*

While an employment contract, as a formal representation of the work for remuneration exchange, may seem simple on the surface, it is a rare job for which a contract can specify exactly all the details of the work that should be carried out. Instead, contracts tend to state that the employer has a general right to direct the employee's work and the employee has the obligation to follow these instructions, which raises the issue of the psychological elements of the relationship between the employer and employee. This psychological contract may be more important in converting employees' potential labour into actual labour.

## Psychological contract

The **psychological contract** is defined by Guest and Conway (2002, p. 22) as the perceptions the individual and the organization have of the 'reciprocal promises and obligations' implied in the employment relationship. The psychological contract is useful as a framework for understanding and managing the employment relationship, and there is evidence that where communication is more effective in organizations, the psychological contract is clearer and there is a perception that exchange is fairer (Guest and Conway, 2002). In addition, because the main focus of the psychological contract is the perceived 'fairness' of the employment relationship, it involves trust. For example, the employee might trust that the employer will not suddenly change the conditions of the work without consultation. The employer, on the other hand, might need to trust that the employee will work to an acceptable level even without constant monitoring. If the psychological contract is violated, this trust breaks down. Interestingly, if the psychological contract is breached within the first year of employment, there are indications that employees actually adjust their expectations of their employer rather than seeing it as a sign of injustice (Payne et al., 2015). We return to the issues of trust and communication later in this chapter.

It is important to remember that the psychological contract is all about perceptions of the 'bargain' we make with our employer and how fair we think it is. Work through the Applications activity to see a simple example of how these expectations form.

## Applications: **The psychological contract**

Here is an extract from an example contract:

> Your base will be at Company HQ in Thistown; however, the Company reserves the right, with appropriate consultation with you, to change your base should the needs of the Company require this. Your working hours will be 37.5 per week. The Company may require you to vary the pattern of your working hours if required on a temporary or permanent basis should the needs of the post require this.

Take a moment to think through the expectations that you would have if you started work for this company. Consider the following questions:

- What would be your expectations of normal working hours for this job?

- Do you expect to be paid for break times?

- What changes to your working hours would you consider reasonable and when would it get to the point you would start to think it was unreasonable?

Imagine you have now been in this job for three months. You generally enjoy your work but have found that most people tend to do about 40 hours' work a week and there is a definite unspoken expectation that you will too. Discuss with your colleagues: Would you personally increase your working hours to match this expectation? Why or why not?

Six months into your job, you are told that the company is considering moving your whole department to a new site because it will cut logistical and facilities costs in the long term. For some people in the department, this will reduce their commuting time, but it will add an extra half an hour on to your commute. How would you respond to this?

If you were the line manager of this department and were faced with managing this move, how would you approach it? Assume that your team is currently performing very well and you want to keep them if at all possible.

There is good evidence that the psychological contract has a larger influence on employees' attitudes and behaviour than the formal work contract (Guest, 2004a). A positive psychological contract, where there is good trust and perceived fairness, is associated with greater commitment to the organization and satisfaction in work. Dabos and Rousseau (2004) found that shared beliefs about the terms of the exchange and reciprocity in commitment between the employee and employer had a positive influence on performance and career development, indicating that positive psychological contracts are beneficial for the organization and the individual. Latorre et al. (2016) confirmed this finding in a study that showed that high commitment HR practices – that is, HR practices that are designed to increase employees' commitment to the organization, for example providing training and development and equitable pay – had a positive impact on the psychological contract, which in turn increased job satisfaction and performance.

We can distinguish between transactional and relational psychological contracts (Rousseau, 2000):

- Transactional psychological contracts tend to be short term and easy to exit, with a focus on narrow and well-defined performance criteria. **Organizational commitment** is low, and turnover or rotation in jobs can be high. An example might be a student who has a summer job in a warehouse and is uninterested in a long-term career with the employer: the focus from employee and employer is simply on making sure that he picks and packs the required number of items and receives wages promptly.

- Relational psychological contracts are more open-ended and have loose performance criteria. Commitment tends to be high and there is long-term security and loyalty. For example, a marketing manager who envisions a long career with the company may be given a high level of flexibility and control over choosing her own projects.

These two types of psychological contract can, of course, be blended to produce balanced or hybrid contracts, which maintain a long-term focus but also allow for flexibility.

You may be wondering what effect the terms of the employment contract might have on individual psychological contracts. An interesting study in Portugal looked at the relationship of temporary agency workers with their temping agency and the client organization where they worked (Giunchi et al., 2015). It found that the type of contract agency workers were on affected their perceptions of organizational support and commitment to the agency, although not with the client organization. In a review of the evidence, Guest (2004b) found that employees on flexible employment contracts had positive psychological contracts, sometimes even more positive than those on permanent contracts. He suggested that this might be because people on flexible contracts had a 'narrower' psychological contract, that is, they had a more limited set of expectations that were more easily fulfilled.

Given the importance of the psychological contract as a collection of expectations and obligations that affect the employment relationship,

we now turn to consider how to manage that relationship in detail.

# MANAGING THE RELATIONSHIP BETWEEN INDIVIDUALS AND ORGANIZATIONS

Now that we have established the role of the formal and psychological contracts, we will move on to discuss the ways this working relationship may be actively managed. It is worth noting here that the vast majority of research in this area is based on the assumption that we want to improve this relationship and that a better relationship and understanding between the individual and the employer will result in benefits to both. We begin by considering some of these underlying assumptions in more detail by discussing our frames of reference, before moving on to discuss two approaches to collective representation and finally, the role of trust.

## Frames of reference

The employment relationship occurs within a context and that context exerts a significant effect on how the actions and communications of each side are interpreted. Alan Fox (1974), an industrial sociologist, introduced the idea of three different 'frames of reference' we use when we are trying to make sense of our experiences at work: the unitarist, **pluralist** or **radical** frames.

The unitarist approach sees managers as the legitimate (and only) source of power in the organization. Employees are assumed to share the same goals as the organization as a whole and any conflict is seen as a threat to the organization and a sign of something going wrong. After all, if everyone shares the same goals, there should be nothing to fight about. HRM often assumes this unitarist approach and aims to create a workplace where everyone is working harmoniously towards the goals of the organization.

In contrast to this, a pluralist view recognizes that there are a range of sources of power in an organization and they are not limited to those with formal authority. For example, if someone depends on you completing your job before they can do theirs, you have a certain degree of power over them. In addition, different groups of employees will have different interests and will actively pursue them. In this view, intra-organizational politics is not only unavoidable, but an important part of the organization's functioning because it is the way these different groups work towards their aims. The employment relationship in this view is a dynamic process that can be continually renegotiated.

Finally, a radical view holds that management and workers will always be in conflict because there is an elite group that maintains control of everything, including socialization processes and political agendas. This group engages in manipulation and suppression of the interests of conflicting groups. Understanding the employment relationship in this frame of reference involves trying to identify

attempts at covert influence and, particularly, identifying what knowledge it is important to have. Those who lose out in the employment relationship are usually lacking in knowledge, or the knowledge they have discourages resistance. For example, if the rules around promotion are hidden, people may be discouraged from applying because they are worried they will fail, or if they do fail, will not know why. Promotion can therefore be retained for people the elite group wish to advance.

Understanding the frame of reference of your manager or your subordinates can help you to understand how your communication will be received and interpreted. It is also an essential element of good negotiation, as we see in the Transferrable Skills exercise.

## Transferrable Skills: Negotiation

Negotiation is a process of trying to create an agreement between two or more people or parties who hold differing views. It is particularly relevant to our consideration of the individual–organization relationship because your negotiation skills may be called on in a variety of ways: you might want to negotiate your salary, you may take part in negotiations between trade unions and management, or you may need to negotiate changes with a team you are responsible for. Whatever the situation, effective negotiation skills can really benefit you and the organization you work for.

Negotiation can either result in a win-win or a win-lose situation. Or even, if it goes really badly, a lose-lose situation. Here, we focus on developing skills for a win-win result because it integrates well with the topics of trust, relationship-building and fairness that we consider in this chapter. We will use the example of a salary negotiation with three roles: a job applicant, a line manager and an HR officer. Get into a group with two other people and have a go at the role-play.

Part of good negotiation is preparation. Before you enter a negotiation, take some time to work out two important things. First, identify your target or ideal outcome as well as the minimum you would accept. Second, work out what power you have in this negotiation. This will help to build your confidence in responding to the other people's offers.

Once you have decided who will play which part, read through the relevant outline below. (Try not to read the other people's roles.) Then carry out the role-play: the job applicant is about to be offered the job and the three of you will be involved in negotiating an appropriate salary.

### Job applicant
You are currently working as an office temp and earn £14,000 a year. You're searching for your first full-time permanent job after graduating and have been looking for about four months now. A friend told you that a position has opened up in exactly the field you want, at a company you have heard good things about. You applied and have just had your interview, which you think went well.

You have in mind a salary that you want (as no salary was stated in the job description), based on your research of what similar positions pay: £20,000. You are really keen to get this job because it is in the field you are passionate about and you think the company will be good at helping you to develop your career.

### Line manager
You are really impressed with this candidate. They have all the skills and qualifications you are looking for and also seem to be really enthusiastic and passionate about the job. You think they will be a great addition to the team and want to do what you can to get them on board. You have a maximum budget of £18,000 for the salary and some

flexibility to offer extra holidays and benefits, such as free training programmes, healthcare and so on, if needed.

**HR officer**

You can tell that the line manager really wants this candidate, and you are satisfied that they are the best of the applicants. You know that the salary on offer is below market rate and that the line manager will want to promise lots of things to try and get the candidate to agree. However, you are also aware that budgets for staff are tight and it is likely that the flexibility that managers currently

have to offer extra holidays and benefits is going to be reduced in future. You also know that it is a tough job market and although this candidate is good, they are not the only one who could do the job.

When you have finished the negotiation, have a debrief with each other. Find out what things your colleagues would have been prepared to negotiate on that you might not have realized. What kind of tactics seemed to work well for you? What things could you improve on next time? Ask your colleagues to make suggestions too.

## Collective representation

### Trade unions

One of the ways employees can negotiate the terms of the employment relationship is by forming groups and having **collective representation**. Trade unions are probably the most prominent or best known of these kinds of collective approaches. They are membership-based organizations that usually exist independently of the employer and represent the views and interests of their members as well as providing some protection to them when needed. Unions can have general membership or be based around a particular industry or profession.

Noon et al. (2013) outline three main reasons that employees may join trade unions or otherwise seek collective representation. The first is that employees recognize that their own and the employer's interests may differ and therefore want to make sure that their own interests are taken into account. While some interests are usually shared, such as continuing survival of the organization, others may be different or even contradictory. For example, it may be in the employer's interest that tasks are standardized and divided up to maximize efficiency but employees may find this approach results in tedious and monotonous work.

A second reason is that employees wish to redress the power imbalance in the employment relationship. If the power in the relationship were equally balanced, there would be no need for employees to seek collective representation: if there was a problem with underpayment, for example, an employee would simply be able to rectify it. But if there is a power imbalance in favour of the employer, an individual employee would not be able to do anything about it. Finally, employees may recognize

that they share some interests with other employees and that joining together will enable them to pursue those interests.

Unions often take different approaches in their negotiations and interactions with employers. Hyman and Gumbrell-McCormick (2013) outline three basic ways of viewing what trade unions are for. These are:

- **Business unionism:** sees unions as organizations representing the interests of a specific group of occupationally allied members. This type of union seeks to promote the interests of its members through collective bargaining, for example in increasing wages.

- **Unions as social movements:** they are part of and sometimes leading the class struggle for equality. They see inequality at work as rooted in wider social inequity and take a radical stance, often becoming closely allied with political parties.

- **Integratist:** they are partners in socioeconomic development or in the success of the organization. While these types of unions can be influential in working with the government or organizational leaders, they also face the challenge of knowing when cooperation becomes too great a compromise for their members.

The Web Explorer activity considers the idea of trade unions for professional managers and illustrates some of the tensions that managers may face in their dual roles as employer-representative and employee.

Much has been written about the declining membership of trade unions in industrialized countries. It is certainly true that trade union membership in the UK, for example, peaked in 1979, with a membership of 13 million (Department for Business Innovation and Skills, 2015) and there was a decline from 32%

## Web Explorer: Workers vs management

It is common for workplace disputes to be couched in terms of workers versus management and for trade unions to be thought of as fighting *for* workers *against* management. But what of the actual managers? They are employees of the organization just as much as non-managerial workers and they too may find that their interests do not coincide perfectly with those of the organization. Are they able to join a union to have collective representation? In fact, several unions do include managers in their membership alongside other professionals, and unions themselves need people with managerial skills in order to organize and use their resources effectively, so the traditional 'worker/management' divide is not that straightforward.

Use a web search to find a trade union in your country that includes managers in the membership. Examples in the UK include:

• FDA, for senior public sector managers and professionals: www.fda.org.uk

• Prospect, for scientists, engineers, managers and specialists: www.prospect.org.uk

Read through the websites to find the answers to these questions:

» What are the aims of the union and how does it go about achieving them?

» How big is the union? Does it give any details on membership composition?

» What are the main issues the union is currently campaigning on?

Imagine that you are a middle manager in a medium-sized organization and you are also a member of a union. To what extent do you think you may experience conflict between the two roles? Would there be specific situations where the conflict might be greater? What advantages do you think you might experience as a member of a union?

of employees being trade union members in 1995 to 25% in 2014. This decline is mirrored in many other countries too, but for historical reasons there is also a dramatic difference in membership between different countries, as illustrated in Figure 4.1, which

means that we need to be careful about making sweeping statements. Scandinavian countries, such as Iceland, Finland, Sweden and Denmark, have very high membership (70–90%), while the USA, Korea and France have the lowest membership at around

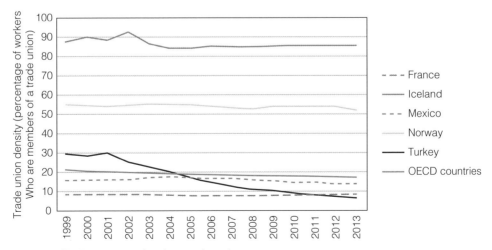

*Figure 4.1 Trade union membership in selected countries*

Source: Compiled using data from Organisation for Economic Co-operation and Development and Visser, J. (2016) *Trade Union Density, ICTWSS database (Institutional Characteristics of Trade Unions, Wage Setting, State Intervention and Social Pacts, 1960-2010).* Available at: https://stats.oecd.org/Index.aspx?DataSetCode=UN_DEN (Accessed 23 August 2016).

7–12%. The average for the 28 OECD (Organisation for Economic Co-operation and Development) countries is around 20% and it shows only a small decline over the past 15 years.

What has led to this general decline in membership? Several suggestions have been put forward, including management dealing more directly with employees rather than through unions, society perhaps becoming more individualistic so that people are less inclined to try to join collective groups, or changes in the workforce composition. As we will see in the section on Employee voice, there are many different ways that management can engage with employees and it may be that these alternatives are proving more useful than trade unions. Some have even suggested that the increased use of HR practices has caused a decline in union membership because they act as a kind of 'substitute', allowing employees to voice their concerns or pursue their interests in cooperation with management rather than via a union. However, research on British workplaces contradicts this suggestion, finding that union membership did not decline faster in organizations with HRM practices (Machin and Wood, 2005). Instead, there seems to be a complementarity between HRM practices and union membership.

Visser (2006) argues that trends for increased global competition, privatization of governmental employment and increased flexible contracts, among other things, may have reduced the power of unions and membership levels. But, in contrast, where there are direct incentives or benefits for membership, such as nationwide bargaining or union-administered unemployment funds, there is a higher rate of membership. The factors underpinning union membership, therefore, need to be understood in the national and local context rather than simply looking at broad international trends.

## Work councils

While trade unions may be the most well-known form of collective arrangement for promoting workers' interests, there are other arrangements too. **Work councils** consist of employees specifically elected to that role by the workforce and are formal, independent representations of workers' interests within the organization. They are based on the idea that work organizations should be accountable to their employees as well as to external stakeholders, an idea we return to in Chapter 12. Work councils are particularly strong in Germany where there is a legal

requirement to have them, and in organizations with over 2,000 employees, the work council must also be represented on the supervisory board. However, in Germany, the employer is under no obligation to form a council, instead the initiative must come from the employees. In Belgium and France, in contrast, the employer is required to take steps to establish the council (Hyman and Gumbrell-McCormick, 2013) and also takes on the role of chair of the council.

These work councils have a say in a wide range of organizational issues including pay, hiring and firing, and working time. Their effectiveness, however, relies on the extent to which the employer cooperates (Hyman and Gumbrell-McCormick, 2013). An employer may be slow in providing the information the council needs or may simply go through the motions of consultation without actually taking account of the representatives' input. Just as with other forms of representation or employee voice, their effectiveness depends on genuine trust and engagement from both sides. Given this, we now move on to discussing the role of trust in the relationship.

## Building trust

So far, in considering the relationship between the individual and the organization, we have looked at the contractual elements (formal and psychological) and the role of frames of reference and collective representation in managing the relationship. We now turn to consider the role of trust in building and maintaining relationships at work.

### What is trust?

Trust is essential to human relations, just as much at work as it is in the rest of life (Argyle, 1972). Yet trust also involves risk: to trust someone means that you will risk being vulnerable to them and you do this because you have a positive expectation that they will not let you down. The Great Place to Work Institute is active in over 40 countries measuring the best places to work and includes measures of trust in its surveys because it believes that trust is a key driver of **engagement** and successful workplace cultures (Great Place to Work Institute, 2016).

Trust is often conceptualized in terms of its causes or benefits and many studies of trust tend to try and determine how much trust there is, its longevity and strength, rather than exploring in detail what people actually mean when they say they trust someone (Young and Daniel, 2003). A conceptual paper by Davis et al. (1995) distinguished trust from related concepts like cooperation, confidence and predictability and positioned it as a primary determinant of risk-taking behaviour in a relationship. Davis et al. noted the importance of the trustor's *propensity to trust* and the other party's *perceived trustworthiness* in determining levels of trust. Factors the authors suggested would increase someone's trustworthiness were their ability in a relevant domain as well as their benevolence and integrity.

Studies on the nature of trust often focus on it as either calculative/rational or as emotional. The first view of trust defines it as a calculated decision to cooperate based on a rational weighing up of the costs and benefits. This has been criticized, and for good reason, as it ignores the emotional element to trust, which is much deeper and longer lasting than a dry cost–benefit analysis could produce. Disappointingly, this rational view of trust still maintains some traction in the OB literature because of the continuing prejudice against emotions in the business world as 'impulsive' or leading to poorer decision-making. Young and Daniel (2003) present a much more complex and integrative model of trust in the workplace as consisting of several different factors and contextual elements, adding a whole range of emotional components to the calculative element:

- Cognitions and calculations around cost–benefit, value and risk: this is a rational weighing up of the potential consequences of trusting a person or an organization. Will the risk of trusting them be worth the outcome?

- Context: including the relationship dynamics, history and relative levels of power. If the context is of a company with high levels of participation and empowerment, trust will be more likely. But if the organization has a history of exploiting workers, trust is far less likely to develop.

- External factors: such as culture, uncertainty and social structures.

- Internal factors: such as individual personality: some people are naturally inclined to trust more than others are.

- Perceptions of others' motivations and competence: to what extent do we think the other will be competent to deliver on promises or actually motivated to do so?

- Emotions: the extent to which we experience relationship-building (interest, admiration, liking, respect), relationship-sustaining (affection, gratitude, security, confidence and acceptance) and relationship-enjoying emotions (appreciation, contentment, satisfaction).

The Applications box (overleaf) explores how this model can be applied to your own experience.

Young and Daniel (2003) note that building trust, especially where there has been a previous breakdown in trust, requires significant effort and should focus on two main issues: communication and personalized relationship-building. Clear and honest communication from management helps to create transparency and reduce the perceived risk in trusting management. When we recognize that trust is inherently an emotional concept that develops between individual people we can see how important that personalized relationship with a manager or supervisor is.

## How trust can be created or destroyed

Employees' trust in their work organizations and management has dropped over the past couple of decades (Kochan, 2007). Kochan suggests that the pressure to work longer hours only to be rewarded with job insecurity has created a sceptical workforce but that the HR profession can assist in rebuilding trust by helping to create transparent and open organizations. Building high trust relationships provides organizations with a source of competitive advantage and can be done by developing 'mutuality' in the employment relationship, that is, the extent to which the capabilities, commitment and contribution of the individual and organization are aligned. If the relationship is one-sided, for example the individual is highly committed to the organization but the organization is not committed to the employee, there is no mutuality and the trust is reduced.

Trust is positively associated with information transparency and justice (Kernan and Hanges, 2002). Even when people are going through a downsizing process, they are more trusting of management when they experience clear and transparent communication and believe that they

## Applications: **Trust at work**

*Getty Images/Caiaimage/Sam Edwards*

Think of someone you trust (if possible, within a work context). Take some time to think about what it means to you to be able to trust them. Using Young and Daniel's framework, see whether you can think of examples from your own experience with, or feelings about, this person that correspond to each of their elements.

Now think of someone you mistrust. Again, using the framework, can you identify the key things that have contributed to this mistrust?

Do you think there are any elements of trust that are missing from this model?

are being dealt with fairly. This tells us that negative events do not necessarily destroy trust, but it is the way these events are handled that is the deciding factor.

At the beginning of this chapter we considered the role of formal contracts as the basis for the relationship between the individual and the organization. So how does trust relate to formal contracts? We could argue that where there is a formal contract, such as in an employment relationship, trust is not important. In fact, the management literature has long argued that control and trust are in opposition: the more management

wishes to control, the less they trust and vice versa (Knights et al., 2001). Woolthuis et al. (2005) explored this issue of trust and control by looking at inter-organizational contracts and came to some fascinating conclusions. They found that trust and contracts were *not*, in fact, in opposition but were often used in a complementary manner to develop working relationships. Woolthuis et al. (2005, p. 835) suggested that contracts should be placed in a social context, with particular emphasis on relationship development: contracts and trust can both be seen as 'the basis and the outcome of cooperation'.

## Outcomes of trust

Fox (1974) suggested that organizations can develop a positive psychological contract and employment relationship by developing a high trust workplace. Trust can be seen as the outcome of the organization's delivery on the psychological contract and its perceived fairness and is critical to determining organizational commitment, motivation, attendance and job performance (Guest, 2004a). Deci et al. (1989) found that managers who supported their workers' autonomy by such things as acknowledging their perspectives and offering choice rather than behaving in a controlling manner increased their subordinates' trust in the organization as well as their job satisfaction.

There is also a link between trust and organizational performance. If employees trust that they will be treated fairly and honestly, they may work harder and thereby improve organizational performance. This suggestion was tested using data from 17,000 workers in the 2004 and 2011 Workplace Employment Relations Surveys in the UK (Brown et al., 2014). Employees were asked questions about how much they trusted management, including whether management could be relied on to keep promises, dealt with employees fairly and honestly, and were sincere in their efforts to understand the employees. Brown et al. (2014) found clear support for a positive link between the average level of employee trust and organizational performance. They also found that individual workers' levels of trust were affected by the types of measures that employers used to deal with the recession: reducing paid overtime or access to training and initiating job or organization restructuring reduced employee trust.

Brown et al.'s study illustrates how changes to the psychological contract can impact on trust and subsequently negatively affect the organization's performance. For example, an employee who has come to expect a certain number of hours of paid overtime will feel that the removal of this is a violation of the unwritten (psychological) contract and will be less inclined to trust the organization. Or someone who has been expecting a new training or development programme may feel betrayed if that training is taken away. When the psychological contract is breached, trust suffers (Zhao et al., 2007). High commitment HR practices are key to developing a long-term and high trust employment relationship. By demonstrating its commitment to the employees, an organization provides the basis for a trusting relationship. In fact, trust has been found to be a moderator of the positive relationship between high commitment HRM practices and employee commitment (Farndale et al., 2010). We explore these high commitment HRM practices in more detail in the Weighing the Evidence activity.

 Weighing the Evidence: **High commitment HR practices**

High commitment HRM refers to a bundle of HR practices that are hypothesized to increase employee commitment and thereby organizational performance. (We will return to the concept of HR bundles when we discuss strategic HRM in Chapter 8.) There is some debate over precisely which practices should be included in a high commitment bundle, but a useful list is provided by Marchington and Wilkinson (2005):

- Employment security and the use of internal labour markets, such as promotion or redeployment within the organization

- Sophisticated selection procedures

- Extensive training and development opportunities

- Employee involvement and voice, information-sharing

- Teamworking, especially self-managed teams

- High performance-related compensation

- Reduction of status differentials in the organization and harmonizing differences, such as harmonizing holiday allowances across all staff.

There is certainly evidence that many of these practices coexist and so could be referred to as a 'bundle'. Having a bundle of practices that complement one another and provide synergy, it is argued, demonstrates that the high commitment approach is deeply embedded in the organization and is more likely to lead to success. While there is some variation in which practices are used, Benson and Lawler (2003) note that this general approach *does* outperform the more traditional controlling type of work systems.

Yet, despite the promising findings that high commitment practices have a positive impact on performance, there are still criticisms. Most of these centre around research methodology issues that then call into question some of the conclusions. For example, there are questions about the direction of causality: does high commitment HRM lead to increased performance or does increased performance 'fund' high commitment HRM? Second, the variability in the practices included in the bundle is also a cause for concern as it makes clear comparisons between organizations more difficult and does not help us to identify precisely which practices actually contribute to performance. Finally, there is the recurrent issue of how cross-culturally applicable these practices are. High commitment HRM was originally developed in the USA and although research has been conducted in several other countries, the different cultures may make some of these practices inappropriate. For example, clear differences in status are more important in China and many Arab countries than the USA and trying to equalize employee benefits may be unsuitable.

So, the jury is still out on this one. In fact, it may make more sense to consider each individual HRM practice in terms of its impact on commitment and performance rather than try to compare bundles of varying composition.

We should note, however, that trust is not the only way to create organizational success. García-Castro et al. (2008) differentiated between two types of employment relationship systems, which were largely formed by the cultural and national context of the organization: market type and internal. A market type has high performance-based incentives, low job security and hires mainly from outside the organization. In contrast, an internal type has few performance-based incentives, high job security and promotes and develops within the organization. This latter type is argued to create success by developing close-knit relationships and high levels of trust, which lead to cooperative action. The market type apparently does not need such high levels of trust because it rewards individual-level efforts and can buy in the skills it needs, although we should bear in mind that at least some trust is necessary for individual employees to believe their efforts will be rewarded.

Having discussed the various aspects of managing the employment relationship and building trust, we now turn to the integral element of communication at work.

# COMMUNICATION

We have seen the importance of good communication emphasized through this chapter: it is essential to a positive psychological contract, to effective negotiation and in building trust. Communication is a central component of any relationship, and within the employment relationship, it is important to understand how and why organizations and employees communicate. Both parties in the employment relationship will try to find ways of communicating their expectations and in this section we will consider both sides: how the organization communicates with employees and how employees communicate with the organization.

We do need to bear in mind that when we talk about the 'organization' communicating, it will be individuals within the organization who make the decisions about how and what to communicate. So, when we refer to the 'organization' throughout this section, remember that it is still communication between people, but some of those people represent the organization as a whole.

## The communication process

We often think of communication in terms of the message content only but it can be helpful to think of it as a simple three-stage process, as shown in Figure 4.2. This will help us to see where and how communication can go wrong and what can be done to improve it.

*Figure 4.2 Communication as a three-stage process*

The first thing to note with this model is that it represents an *active* process: communication is not simply the passive transmission of a message. First, the sender has to find a way to represent the message they wish to communicate. For example, if a supervisor feels that their team is not performing as well as they could, they need to decide how they are going to try and tell them, that is, how they will encode the message. Will the supervisor write it down or speak to the team? Will the message include emotional content, such as disappointment with the current work or perhaps optimism about future performance?

The second part of the communication process is how the message is transmitted. A message about poor performance could be transmitted informally, in a short chat with an individual, or formally in a written warning. The choice of channel through which to communicate can change how a message might be understood. Consider the example of our supervisor deciding they will just have an informal chat with some of the team about the performance concerns. It is quite possible that the team member will think this is not a serious issue. On the other hand, transmitting the message through a formal written warning sends a strong message that it is serious and needs to be addressed as a matter of priority.

This leads us into the final stage of the process: how the receiver decodes the message. Just as there are individual differences in how we choose to encode and transmit a message, there are individual differences in how we decode a message. This can range from our personal relationship with the person communicating with us to the context of the organization we work in. For example, do we like the supervisor and interpret the messages in a positive manner, or do we not get on and believe that they are always trying to find fault with us? Are conversations about performance a normal part of the way things are done at this organization, or are they so unusual that it causes concern among the team?

Besides communication being an active process, it is also a symbolic one. We use words, expressions, tone of voice, pictures and so on as a way of symbolizing something we want to transmit to someone else. It is easy to see that even in a simple model of communication such as this, there is plenty of potential for the message that the sender believes is being transmitted to be changed by the way the receiver decodes it. And, of course, communication is usually a two-way process, with the receiver then becoming the sender for a response to the message, adding further layers of complexity. Work through the Applications exercise to see the whole process in action.

 Applications: **Communicating difficult messages**

Imagine that you are the team leader for a small team of five sales representatives. Your team generally gets on well with each other: they all have a competitive streak but also enjoy working together to boost the sales of the whole team. They work hard and are recognized as good salespeople by the rest of the company: you are proud of them.

Your direct supervisor has just told you that sales need to be increased by 10% over the next six months. This represents a challenging target and you have some doubts as to whether the team will manage. If the team does not meet this new target, your supervisor has said there is a strong possibility that at least one person could be made redundant. You now need to tell your team. Using the model of communication above, take some time to analyse a few different approaches to doing this, with a particular focus on the possible ways that the message you want to transmit could be misinterpreted or result in unexpected or unwanted consequences. What do you think is the best way to communicate this message?

## Goals of communication

Communication at work aims to achieve four broad goals, each of which is important to developing and maintaining the employment relationship: control, motivation, emotional expression and provision of information (Scott and Mitchell, 1976). These functions can often overlap but are useful in gaining an overview of the main reasons we communicate at work:

1. Communication for control can be formal and informal. For example, formal control can be communicated by your boss outlining what your tasks are for the day, while informal control can be exerted by a senior colleague making suggestions about the best ways to approach those tasks.

2. Communication that aims to improve motivation tends to focus on clarifying goals for employees

and providing them with feedback, which helps them to judge how well they are meeting those goals.

3. Emotional expression, such as sharing enthusiasm about a project or having a moan about a boss, is a way of creating and maintaining the social bonds that help groups to function effectively.

4. Informational communication can include a wide range of different types of information, from a monthly newsletter telling employees how the company is doing or the new direction it is moving in, to colleagues keeping each other informed of their progress on a team task.

An alternative conceptualization of organizational communication looks at the types of networks that exist and identifies how they contribute to different organizational goals. In this approach, four main organizational goals are identified (Greenbaum, 1974):

1. Institutionalization: This is about communicating the organization's norms, **values** and so on to all employees in such a way that they will begin to share these. It is based on an informative-instructive communication network, which uses in-house publications and training to get the message across to employees about what is important in this organization. This informative-instructive type of network is all about getting and giving information and contributes to all the following goals as well as institutionalization.

2. Conformity: The extent to which employees behave in the same way and have a consistency of approach to their work. This is particularly important in organizations that value a certain quality and consistency in their products or services. This is achieved using a regulative communication network, with clear policies and procedures that serve to control and direct employees' efforts.

3. Adaptiveness: All organizations need to adapt to their environment if they are to continue to survive and succeed, although the degree to which they do so varies. An innovative communication network can include elements such as suggestion systems or participative problem-solving meetings; the aim being to develop new strategy, implement ideas and solve problems.

4. Morale: An important element of communication is its ability to enhance employees' positive feelings about themselves and their colleagues as well as the organization as a whole. An integrative or maintenance communication network can help to achieve this by providing praise and rewards, promotions and even status symbols to employees.

Besides the formal communication networks in organizations, there are informal groups and networks too, which can sometimes be even more important than the formal ones in terms of contributing to organizational effectiveness and impacting on the employment relationship. Informal networks emerge spontaneously and tend to be a lot more fluid than formal networks, with membership changing frequently and with shorter communication 'chains' (Langan-Fox, 2002). They also often exist outside the organizational hierarchy, with the status of members being less important than in formal networks. Examples of informal networks might be a group of employees who all started on the same day or employees who play sport together outside work.

Although it is difficult to control the communication in these informal networks, it remains important for organizations to be aware of them because they are often a source of innovations and rumours. Organizations will want to try and capture the innovative ideas, while exerting some control over the rumours. Rumours can be seen as an attempt to make sense of some ambiguity at work (DiFonzo, 2010): if the organization's formal communication is not clear, employees will try to make sense of a situation among themselves. Rumour is a type of 'group problem-solving' in response to uncertainty and can be driven by three motivations: fact-finding (using rumours to find out as much as possible about the uncertain situation), relationship-building (using a rumour to try to build positive relationships with each other) and self-enhancement (using rumours to make us feel better about ourselves) (DiFonzo and Bordia, 2007). Seeing the motivations for rumours illustrates the kinds of things that organizations can address when dealing with an ambiguous and possibly threatening situation. We explore this further on the next page.

## Organizational structure

Studies on communication in small groups give us some useful insights into how structure can impact

## Applications: **Informal networks and rumour**

You are the communications officer for a large national organization and have been tasked with preparing an internal communication explaining a proposed organizational restructure. No job losses or salary cuts are envisaged, although the restructure is likely to involve some changes to individual job roles. You are aware that this restructure has the potential to cause anxiety for a lot of the staff and part of your role will be to try and keep this anxiety to a minimum. Drawing on the explanation of the three motivations for rumours by DiFonzo

and Bordia (2007) outlined above, what elements will you want to try and ensure you include in your communication? How would you choose to do this communication?

If you are in a group with colleagues, you could take this activity further by preparing a company-wide communication about this restructure. Remember that you will want to try and maintain motivation and loyalty, while minimizing any negative consequences or anxieties.

on communication in organizations. Bavelas's (1950) study, for example, found that centralized networks, where communication and decision-making had to go through a single person, were faster at completing tasks but had higher error rates and lower member satisfaction. On the other hand, networks that had free communication between all members were slower but provided better results for innovative thinking tasks. As we saw earlier, informal networks are particularly useful for developing innovation and this work indicates that it may well be because these informal networks have much freer communication than formal networks tend to. We will discuss organizational structure in more detail in Chapter 9, so here we focus on the interaction between structure and communication.

© Royalty-Free/Corbis

*Medical specialists need to communicate well in order to provide good patient care.*

Jensen (2003) notes four structural dimensions that influence communication in organizations. The first is the configuration or shape of the organization, including size, hierarchical levels and number of subordinates a supervisor is responsible for. With smaller supervisory teams, there is greater potential for communication but a larger number of levels in the hierarchy tends to reduce the quality of the communication with subordinates.

The second structural dimension is the complexity of the organization. As the number of departments increases, frequency of communication between them tends to decrease. But an opposite pattern is noticed when the number of occupational specialities increases. This may be because specialists need to communicate frequently with each other in order to complete an overall task. For example, a medical team will consist of several specialists who need to integrate their efforts in order to help individual patients, whereas departments are often organized around functional areas and individuals may have very little need to communicate with other departments in order to carry out their day-to-day tasks.

The third dimension is the degree of *formalization*. Where there is greater formalization, for example clear policies covering most of the job behaviours, there is little need for widespread or frequent communication and it can become difficult to communicate outside the formal channels.

The final dimension is *centralization*, or the extent to which decision-making and power are concentrated in senior management or dispersed through the organization. Greater *decentralization* allows for and encourages better communication – in terms of frequency and flow – because more employees are involved in making decisions.

This involvement of employees in decision-making leads us into a discussion of employee voice.

## Employee voice

Discussions of effective communication at work often focus on how management can express itself clearly to employees. But we also need to consider how employees can make themselves heard in the organization at large. 'Employee voice' is the term used for this contribution or the 'say' that employees have in the organization. It is a broad term and in their review of the concept, Wilkinson et al. (2014) recognize that it is understood in slightly different ways by practitioners and academics from different backgrounds. For example, OB approaches tend to focus on voice as an individual's 'verbal communication that is constructive to management' (p. 4) while HRM approaches may define voice as employee involvement or grievance procedures.

Voice mechanisms can include anything from suggestion systems to decentralized decision-making and empowerment, and even the grievance system that allows employees to lodge official complaints, which then require action from higher management. In fact, Benson (2000) notes 18 different employee voice mechanisms in his study of Australian workplaces, including collective organizations (e.g. unions), consultation mechanisms (e.g. suggestion schemes, quality circles, employee surveys), appraisals, grievance and equality procedures, joint committees and elected representatives. And although trade union membership has been declining in Australia for the past couple of decades, 15 of these 18 different mechanisms were more likely to exist in unionized workplaces than non-unionized, indicating that collective representation may encourage the use of other voice mechanisms.

Some authors suggest that absence or sabotage can also be considered forms of voice because they are ways of employees attempting to send a message to the organization (Benson, 2000). In fact, Hirschmann (1970), one of the first proponents of the idea of employee voice, contrasted *voice* with *exit*: he said that if employees felt loyal to the organization, they would attempt to change the issue that was causing them a problem. But if they did not feel loyal, or found they could not effect change, they would leave. Interestingly, however, more recent research indicates that more loyal employees might be less likely to voice their concerns, effectively 'suffering in silence', while those who are less loyal are more likely to complain (Boroff and Lewin, 1997). How, then, can organizations ensure that their efforts to encourage employee voice are effective?

## Effectiveness of voice

It is in the area of employee voice that the tensions between organizational and individual goals, which we discussed at the beginning of this chapter and which are so central to the individual–organization relationship, become most apparent. 'Indirect voice' is the term for contact between managers and employees that goes via an intermediary, such as a trade union representative. Direct voice is where the employee and manager can discuss and communicate directly. We can distinguish between three types of direct voice and see how each of them can be used to address sometimes conflicting worker and managerial goals (Marchington, 2007). These are:

1. Task-based participation: for example, high-performance work systems or self-managed teams give workers more interesting work as well as greater control over their work. At the same time, they help to fulfil managerial goals such as improvements in quality or customer service and in worker commitment and satisfaction.

2. Upward problem-solving: this allows workers to make suggestions to improve the work while providing recognition of their skills. For example, a quality circle is a group of employees who do similar work in the organization and meet regularly to discuss ways to solve problems and improve quality. This quality improvement is beneficial to the organization, as is the way this type of system makes better use of employee skills.

3. Complaints systems: these allow employees to express their dissatisfaction and attempt to rectify problems. Examples here include grievance procedures, for example to raise concerns over bullying in the workplace, and direct complaints to supervisors. These types of systems are important in allowing workers to voice concerns rather than ignoring them.

The effectiveness of these voice mechanisms depends on how they are perceived by workers and management, which, in turn, is based on how well embedded they are in the organization (Marchington, 2007). The *breadth* of voice refers to the number of different voice mechanisms an organization has: the greater the range of mechanisms, the more effective they will be. If there is just a single voice mechanism, for example, workers are unlikely to believe that it is taken seriously by management, perhaps viewing it as merely a token gesture with no commitment behind it. Having a range of different mechanisms, on the other hand, sends a message that the organization respects and wants employee input. The *depth* of voice embeddedness includes the extent to which voice mechanisms are valued in the organization and the frequency with which voice takes place or the speed of response. For example, taking action on a suggestion to improve the workflow in a department within a week will send a clear message to the workers

that their suggestions are valued and important. On the other hand, if workers make suggestions that are routinely ignored, they will soon realize that the voice mechanisms are simply for show.

Evidence that employee voice can have a positive impact on the employee experience can be found in studies using large workplace datasets, which show that consultative management is associated with improved employee well-being (Wood, 2008). The research regarding the impact of employee voice on performance, however, is mixed, perhaps because of the range of other factors that can influence performance but also because there is some debate over the direction of the relationship. Does increased voice lead to higher performance, or is it the case that better performing organizations are able to devote more time and attention to establishing effective voice mechanisms (Marchington, 2007)? Despite these questions, on balance, the research seems to indicate a positive role for voice in organizational performance (Harley, 2014), and reinforces the importance of providing avenues for employees to have a say in the running of the organization.

 ## Practice Insights: Mark Harcourt

Mark Harcourt is Professor of Strategy and Human Resource Management at the University of Waikato, Hamilton, New Zealand. He conducts research into the employment relationship, justice and health and safety at work, and lectures in HRM and strategy. In the video, Mark talks about the changing nature of the employment relationship and the impact of our default ways of thinking on what we accept as 'normal' in that relationship.

Go online to www.macmillanihe.com/sutton-people to access the interview with Mark.

## SUMMARY

In this chapter we have looked at the essential elements of the individual–organization relationship. We started by considering the role of the formal employment contract and the range of expectations and obligations that form the psychological contract. We then looked at the different ways the employment relationship is managed, starting by noting the importance of recognizing the frames of reference we have when we approach this topic: unitarist, pluralist and radical. This led into an overview of the role of trade unions and work councils in representing employee interests and then the important role of trust in the individual–organization relationship, considering how it may be broken down as well as how it can be built up.

We then moved on to discuss communication in organizations and how it contributes to the ongoing dynamic nature of individual–organization interactions. Here, we considered the process and goals of communication as well as how organizational structure can constrain or encourage communication. We also discussed the role of employee voice, or how employees can have their say in the organization and its decisions, continually negotiating the dynamically evolving relationship between individuals and their organizations.

## FURTHER READING

- The psychological contract is a rich area of research and this paper provides a good basis for understanding its basic tenets; Rousseau, D. M. (2001) 'Schema, promise and mutuality: the building blocks of the psychological contract', *Journal of Occupational and Organizational Psychology*, 74(4), pp. 511–41.

- To find out more about the relationship between trust and performance, see Brown, S. Gray, D., McHardy, J. and Taylor, K. (2014) 'Employee trust and workplace performance', *Journal of Economic Behavior and Organization*, 116(8284), pp. 361–78.

- This website provides lots of data on trade union membership that you can use to find out about different countries. It allows you to construct your own graphs: https://stats.oecd.org/Index. aspx?DataSetCode=UN_DEN.

## REVIEW QUESTIONS

1. What is the psychological contract and why is it an important element in understanding the employment relationship?

2. Why might an organization wish to increase employee feedback and how could it go about doing this?

3. Evaluate the role of collective representation in the modern workplace: to what extent does HRM promote an individually based rather than collective employment relationship?

## ONLINE RESOURCES

Go online to www.macmillanihe.com/sutton-people to access a MCQ quiz for this chapter and for further resources to support your learning.

## REFERENCES

Argyle, M. (1972) *The Social Psychology of Work*. Harmondsworth: Penguin.

Bavelas, A. (1950) 'Communication patterns in task-oriented groups', *Journal of the Acoustical Society of America*, 22(6), pp. 725–30.

Benson, J. (2000) 'Employee voice in union and non-union Australian workplaces', *British Journal of Industrial Relations*, 38(3), pp. 453–9. doi: 10.1111/1467-8543.00173.

Benson, G. and Lawler, E. (2003) 'Employee involvement: utilization, impacts, and future prospects', in D. Holman, T. D. Wall, C. W. Clegg et al. (eds) *The New Workplace: A Guide to the Human Impact of Modern Working Practices*. Chichester: John Wiley & Sons.

Boroff, K. E. and Lewin, D. (1997) 'Loyalty, voice, and intent to exit a union firm: a conceptual and empirical analysis', *Industrial and Labor Relations Review*, 51(1), pp. 50–63.

Boxall, P. (2013) 'Mutuality in the management of human resources: assessing the quality of alignment in employment relationships', *Human Resource Management Journal*, 23(1), pp. 3–17. doi: 10.1111/1748-8583.12015.

Brown, S., Gray, D., McHardy, J. and Taylor, K. (2014) 'Employee trust and workplace performance', *Journal of Economic Behavior and Organization*, 116(8284), pp. 361–78. doi: 10.1016/j.jebo.2015.05.001.

Dabos, G. E. and Rousseau, D. M. (2004) 'Mutuality and reciprocity in the psychological contracts of employees and employers', *Journal of Applied Psychology*, 89(1), pp. 52–72. doi: 10.1037/0021-9010.89.1.52.

Davis, J. H., Mayer, R. C. and Schoorman, F. D. (1995) 'An integrative model of organizational trust', *Academy of Management Review*, 20(3), pp. 709–34. doi: 10.2307/258792.

Deci, E. L., Connell, J. P. E. and Ryan, R. M. (1989) 'Self-determination in a work organization', *Journal of Applied Psychology*, 74(4), pp. 580–90. doi: 10.1037/0021-9010.74.4.580.

Department for Business Innovation and Skills (2015) 'Trade Union Membership 2014: Statistical Bulletin', pp. 1–56. Available at: www.gov.uk/government/uploads/system/uploads/attachment_data/file/431564/Trade_Union_Membership_Statistics_2014.pdf.

Dibben, P., Klerck, G. and Wood, G. (2011) 'Introduction', in *Employment Relations: A Critical and International Approach*. London: CIPD, pp. 1–25.

DiFonzo, N. (2010) 'Ferreting facts or fashioning fallacies? Factors in rumor accuracy', *Social and Personality Psychology Compass*, 4(11), pp. 1124–37.

DiFonzo, N. and Bordia, P. (2007) *Rumor Psychology: Social and Organizational Approaches*. Washington DC: American Psychological Association.

Farndale, E., Hope-Hailey, V. and Kelliher, C. (2010) 'High commitment performance management: the roles of justice and trust', *Personnel Review*, 40(1), pp. 5–23.

Fox, A. (1974) *Beyond Contract: Work, Power and Trust Relations*. London: Faber and Faber.

García-Castro, R., Ariño, M. A., Rodriguez, M. A. and Ayuso, S. (2008) 'A cross-national study of corporate governance and employment contracts', *Business Ethics: A European Review*, 17(3), pp. 259–84. doi: 10.1111/j.1467-8608.2008.00535.x.

Giunchi, M., Chambel, M. J. and Ghislieri, C. (2015) 'Contract moderation effects on temporary agency workers' affective organizational commitment and perceptions of support', *Personnel Review*, 44(1), pp. 22–38. doi: http://dx.doi.org/10.1108/PR-03-2014-0061.

Great Place to Work Institute (2016) *Measuring Trust in your Organization*. Available at: www.greatplacetowork.co.uk/our-services/assess-your-organisation/trust-index-assessment (Accessed 24 August 2016).

Greenbaum, H. H. (1974) 'The audit of organizational communication', *Academy of Management Journal*, 17(4), pp. 739–54. doi: 10.2307/255650.

Guest, D. E. (2004a) 'The psychology of the employment relationship: an analysis based on the psychological contract', *Applied Psychology: An International Review*, 53(4), pp. 541–55. doi: 10.1111/j.1464-0597.2004.00187.x.

Guest, D. E. (2004b) 'Flexible employment contracts, the psychological contract and employee outcomes: an analysis and review of the evidence', *International Journal of Management Reviews*, 5/6(1), pp. 1–19. doi: 10.1111/j.1460-8545.2004.00094.x.

Guest, D. E. and Conway, N. (2002) 'Communicating the psychological contract: an employer perspective', *Human Resource Management Journal*, 12(2), pp. 22–38. doi: 10.1111/j.1748-8583.2002.tb00062.x.

Harley, B. (2014) 'High performance work systems and employee voice', in A. Wilkinson, J. Donaghey, T. Dundon and R. Freeman (eds) *Handbook of Research on Employee Voice*. Cheltenham: Edward Elgar, pp. 82–96.

Hirschmann, A. (1970) *Exit, Voice, and Loyalty: Responses to Decline in Firms, Organizations, and States*. Cambridge, MA: Harvard University Press.

Hyman, R. and Gumbrell-McCormick, R. (2013) 'Collective representation at work: institutions and dynamics', in C. Frege and J. Kelly (eds) *Comparative Employment Relations in the Global Economy*. London: Routledge, pp. 49–70.

ILO (2007) *The Employment Relationship: An Annotated Guide to ILO Recommendation No. 198*. Available at: www.ilo.org/ifpdial/areas-of-work/labour-law/WCMS_172417/lang--en/index.htm.

ILO (2016) *Employment Relationship*. Available at: www.ilo.org/ifpdial/areas-of-work/labour-law/WCMS_CON_TXT_IFPDIAL_EMPREL_EN/lang--en/index.htm (Accessed 9 August 2016).

Jensen, M. T. (2003) *Organizational Communication: A Review*. Kristiansand, Norway: Agderforskning Serviceboks.

Kernan, M. C. and Hanges, P. J. (2002) 'Survivor reactions to reorganization: antecedents and consequences of procedural, interpersonal, and informational justice', *Journal of Applied Psychology*, 87(5), pp. 916–28. doi: 10.1037//0021-9010.87.5.916.

Knights, D., Noble, F., Vurdubakis, T. and Willmott, H. (2001) 'Chasing shadows: control, virtuality and the production of trust', *Organization Studies*, 22(2), pp. 311–36. doi: 10.1177/0170840601222006.

Kochan, T. A. (2007) 'Social legitimacy of the HRM profession: a US perspective', in P. Boxall, J. Purcell, and P. M. Wright (eds) *The Oxford Handbook of Human Resource Management*. Oxford: Oxford University Press, pp. 599–620.

Langan-Fox, J. (2002) 'Communication in organizations: speed, diversity, networks, and influence on organizational effectiveness, human health, and relationships', in *Handbook of Industrial, Work And Organizational Psychology*, vol. 2: *Organizational Psychology*. Thousand Oaks, CA: Sage, pp. 188–205.

Latorre, F., Guest, D., Ramos, J. and Gracia, F. J. (2016) 'High commitment HR practices, the employment relationship and job performance: a test of a mediation model', *European Management Journal*, 34, pp. 328–37. doi: 10.1016/j.emj.2016.05.005.

Machin, S. and Wood, S. (2005) 'Human resource management as a substitute for trade unions in British Workplaces', *Industrial and Labor Relations Review*, 58(2), pp. 201–18.

Marchington, M. (2007) 'Employee voice systems', in *The Oxford Handbook of Human Resource Management*. Oxford: Oxford University Press, pp. 231–72.

Marchington, M. and Wilkinson, A. (2005) *Human Resource Management at Work: People Management and Development*. London: CIPD.

Noon, M., Blyton, P. and Morrell, K. (2013) *The Realities of Work*, 4th edn. Basingstoke: Palgrave Macmillan.

O'Connor, S., Croft, J. and Murgia, M. (2016) 'Uber drivers win UK legal battle for workers' rights', *Financial Times*, 28 October.

Organisation for Economic Co-operation and Development and Visser, J. (2016) *Trade Union Density, ICTWSS Database (Institutional Characteristics of Trade Unions, Wage Setting, State Intervention and Social Pacts, 1960-2010)*. Available at: https://stats.oecd.org/Index.aspx?DataSetCode=UN_DEN (Accessed 23 August 2016).

Payne, S. C., Culbertson, S. S., Lopez, Y. P. et al. (2015) 'Contract breach as a trigger for adjustment to the psychological contract during the first year of employment', *Journal of Occupational and Organizational Psychology*, 88(1), pp. 41–60. doi: 10.1111/joop.12077.

Pound, R. (1942) *Social Control Through Law*. London: Transaction.

Rousseau, D. M. (2000) *Psychological Contract Inventory Technical Report*. Pittsburgh, PA: Carnegie Mellon University.

Scott, W. G. and Mitchell, T. R. (1976) *Organization Theory: A Structural and Behavioral Analysis*. Homewood, IL: Irwin.

Spooner, K. and Haidar, A. (2006) 'Defining the employment relationship', *International Journal of Employment Studies*, 14(2), pp. 63–82. Available at: http://iera.net.au/International-Journal-of-Employment-Studies.php.

Visser, J. (2006) 'Union membership statistics in 24 countries', *Monthly Labor Review*, 129(1), pp. 38–49.

Wilkinson, A., Donaghey, J., Dundon, T. and Freeman, R. (eds) (2014) *Handbook of Research on Employee Voice*. Cheltenham: Edward Elgar.

Wood, S. (2008) 'Job characteristics, employee voice and well-being in Britain', *Industrial Relations Journal*, 39(2), pp. 153–68. doi: 10.1111/j.1468-2338.2007.00482.x.

Woolthuis, R. K., Hillebrand, B. and Nooteboom, B. (2005) 'Trust, contract and relationship development', *Organization Studies*, 26(6), pp. 813–40. doi: 10.1177/0170840605054594.

Young, L. and Daniel, K. (2003) 'Affectual trust in the workplace', *International Journal of Human Resource Management*, 14(1), pp. 139–55. doi: 10.1080/09585190210158565.

Zhao, H., Wayne, S. J., Glibkowski, B. C. and Bravo, J. (2007) 'The impact of psychological contract breach on work-related outcomes: a meta-analysis', *Personnel Psychology*, 60(3), pp. 647–80. doi: 10.1111/j.1744-6570.2007.00087.x.

# 5 ENCOURAGING AND MANAGING PERFORMANCE

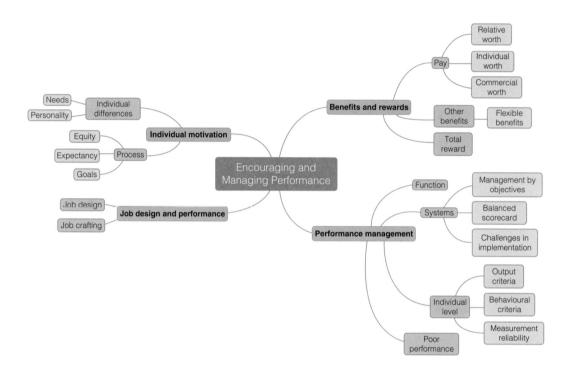

## INTRODUCTION

In this chapter we will be looking at performance, arguably the most important issue that individual managers and organizations deal with. To manage performance effectively, we need to start by finding out what motivates people to do a good job. The OB and HRM literature has a wide range of approaches to trying to understand motivation at work, which tend to fall into three broad areas. First, there are theories that focus on individual differences and personality, looking for internal explanations for people's motivation. Second, there is the role of the job itself in motivating people and, third, there is the role of rewards in helping or hindering motivation. In advising on the provision of rewards and designing of jobs, HR can have a large influence on employee performance. Essentially, we are aiming to find out what contributes to good performance at work and

what managers and HR practitioners can do to enhance it.

The models we consider in these first three sections will then lead us into a discussion of the practicalities of performance management. Here, we will gain an insight into why organizations attempt to manage performance and the different approaches they can use to do so, including looking at the challenges around measuring performance at the individual and organizational level. We will also evaluate the formal performance appraisal and address the issues that managers face in trying to deal with poor performance. In much of the literature on performance management, there is a recognition that people will perform better when they are well motivated, so we start our discussion with an overview of the work *motivation theory*.

*Getty Images/Yuri Arcurs*

---

**LEARNING FEATURES**

Applications: Hiring motivated people

Applications: Job crafting

Applications: Flexible and voluntary benefits

Weighing the Evidence: Does performance management deliver?

Web Explorer: Total rewards

In the News: Instant performance feedback

Transferrable Skills: Holding a performance conversation

Practice Insights: Roger Longden

---

 **Video overview**

Julian Perkins

**Go online to** www.macmillanihe.com/sutton-people to access a video of Anna Sutton introducing the chapter's main themes.

# INDIVIDUAL MOTIVATION

What do we mean when we talk about motivation? It is generally understood to consist of three elements determining the effort we put into our work: direction, intensity and persistence. Direction is our end goal, or what we channel our efforts towards; intensity is the level of effort we put into that particular task or attempt to achieve a goal; and persistence is how long we continue these efforts in the face of difficulties. For an individual's efforts to benefit the organization as a whole, they need to be channelled in the right direction, be at an appropriate level of intensity and be supported through whatever challenges they might face.

## Individual differences

As soon as we start thinking about motivation, it is fairly obvious that there are individual differences in people's levels of motivation and what they are motivated to do. In attempting to explain why this is so, we will consider two broad approaches: needs based and personality based. The first suggests that we are motivated to do things in order to meet our needs and that those needs are different for each of us. The second suggests that levels of motivation are part of our personality: some people seem inherently 'more motivated' than others.

### Needs

Universal needs theories suggest that all of us have a limited set of 'needs' that motivate us. Individual differences come into play because we vary in terms of which of those needs is currently most salient or active in the moment. Several different theories attempt to delineate exactly what those needs are but there is relatively little evidence to support them. So, while we will briefly outline them here, we will not go into them in detail.

Maslow's (1954) hierarchy of needs is probably one of the most well-known models. It claims that each of us has a hierarchy of five basic needs: physiological, safety, social, self-esteem and self-actualization. As we fulfil each need in the hierarchy, the next need becomes activated. However, research evidence indicates that we can be motivated by more than one need at a time and do not progress neatly up a hierarchy (Wahba and Bridwell, 1976). Although Maslow's theory is still prominent in many OB textbooks as an important element in the history

of motivation studies, the consensus among OB experts is that the scientific evidence to support the theory is poor (Miner, 2003).

Alderfer (1969) developed and adapted Maslow's theory specifically for the workplace, reducing the hierarchy to three basic needs, known as **'ERG theory'**, each of which could be active at the same time:

1. Existence: need for survival and physical well-being
2. Relatedness: need for interpersonal relationships, status and recognition
3. Growth: desire for personal development and self-fulfilment.

While there is some evidence that needs may affect performance (e.g. Arnolds and Boshoff, 2002), overall, the evidence is inconsistent (Miner, 2003) and perhaps the best contribution of both of these needs theories was in recognizing that different people may be motivated to meet different needs at any one time.

McClelland's (1987) theory of motivation also centres on needs, but instead of suggesting that there are 'universal' needs that are more or less active, it views needs as **implicit** and therefore more similar to personality traits. Each of us has a different level or strength of three main needs:

1. Achievement (nAch): The need for achievement is a drive to do well, to succeed and to do things better. People with a high nAch will want to succeed for their own personal satisfaction rather than for the external rewards.
2. Affiliation (nAff): The need for affiliation is the desire to build friendly, cooperative relationships and people with a strong nAff will be motivated to do teamwork, where they can work in an interdependent way with others.
3. Power (nPow): People with a high need for power want to have influence over others and will be motivated by the opportunity to gain prestige and control at work.

Unlike the previous two approaches, there is some good evidence that the strengths of these needs are directly related to work performance. For example, a longitudinal study of managers found that those with a moderate to high nPow and low nAff were more successful at gaining promotion 8 and 16 years later (McClelland and Boyatzis, 1982).

## Personality

McClelland's needs theory starts to edge into the field of personality traits and addresses the question of whether some of us are inherently more motivated than others. There have been many studies conducted on personality and motivation and a review of past studies by Judge and Ilies (2002) using the Big Five model of personality (discussed in Chapter 3) found that personality traits had a substantial impact on people's level of performance motivation. Two traits in particular were important: emotional stability and conscientiousness. If part of motivation is down to our personality, it suggests that an organization could conceivably recruit people who will naturally be more motivated, for example by using appropriate psychometric tests (see Chapter 3). We explore the practical implications of this in the Applications activity.

### Applications: Hiring motivated people

Your manager has just read an article entitled 'Scientists prove motivation is genetic'. It claimed that, because there is evidence of a heritable component in personality and certain personality traits are related to motivation levels, some people are naturally more motivated than others. For businesses to succeed, the article suggests, they should hire only these people. Your manager is excited by the idea that motivation can be tested using personality tests and wants to get the whole team to do a Big Five questionnaire and then select members for a new, high-profile project based on their trait scores. He asks you to organize this. What will you do?

## Process

Process theories of motivation focus on explaining *how* we are motivated to perform, taking account of the way we think about work and particularly the outcomes of our efforts: whether they are equitable, whether we believe our efforts will result in a desired goal, and how we work towards our goals.

## Equity

There is good evidence that judgements about fairness or equity are an essential part of what motivates our performance. The **equity theory** of motivation holds that we engage in social comparisons (Carrell and Dittrich, 1978): we compare the effort we put into our work with the effort other people seem to, and expect to be rewarded fairly in comparison to them. We effectively try to achieve a balance between our own and others' input/outcome ratio at work. A perceived inequity can arise in several ways. For example, we may feel we are putting more effort into our work than a colleague, but we both gain the same reward, or perhaps a colleague is paid more for doing the same job. If we recognize an inequity, we will do our best to rectify it by, for example, increasing or decreasing our own performance.

However, there are some important caveats to this that the research has identified. First, although inequity does motivate us to redress the balance, there is evidence that we are less motivated to correct an inequity if we are benefitting from it. Second, the motivational effects of inequity on performance tend to be fairly short term as we adapt our expectations to the current situation. So, for example, if we got a raise, we would initially work harder in an attempt to 'earn' it but would fairly soon start to believe that this was a normal and fair reward for our work and performance levels would reduce again.

## Expectancy

Closely related to the perception of equity is the role of our *expectations* in motivation. Vroom (1964) suggested that we are more motivated when we expect that our effort will result in a desired outcome. The **expectancy theory** of motivation holds that by understanding three key perceptions that individuals have about the outcomes, we can predict the amount of effort they will put into their work:

1. Valence: how desirable the end result or outcome is for the individual.

2. Instrumentality: how likely the individual believes it is that a certain level of performance will actually result in the desired outcome.

3. Expectancy: how much an individual expects that their efforts will manage to achieve the level of performance needed for the outcome.

The model provides a concise summary of how motivated someone will be for any task as well as helping to explain some of the differences between people. Different people will value outcomes to different degrees and have differing beliefs about their own instrumentality or expectations of achievement.

Although this model is intuitively satisfying, the research support is somewhat mixed. The three elements of valence, instrumentality and expectancy are related to attitudes such as turnover intention, that is, whether a person intends to leave the organization, or intended effort, but less clearly related to actual behavioural outcomes (van Eerde and Thierry, 1996). As with many motivational theories, it remains difficult to make the link from our internal processes to workplace performance.

## Goals

Although we have considered the environmental and individual aspects of motivation separately, they do, of course, interact in our daily work lives. Perhaps one of the best ways of understanding how these interactions occur is to consider the role of our personal goals in motivating us to work. **Goal-setting theory** was first proposed in the 1960s and since then has been refined, tested and developed to become not only well supported by research evidence but also one of the most popular models of motivation in active use in workplaces today to enhance employee motivation and performance. The high performance cycle (Locke and Latham, 2002) is a model that combines key elements of several decades of research to show how goals are related to performance, as illustrated in Figure 5.1.

Two core findings form the basis of goal-setting theory (Locke and Latham, 1990). The first is

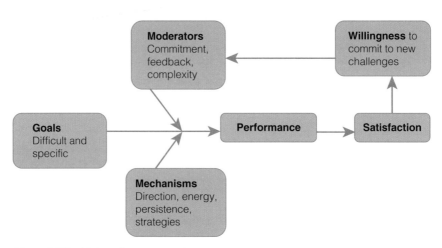

*Figure 5.1 The high performance cycle*

Source: Adapted with permission from Locke, E. A. and Latham, G. P. (2002) 'Building a practically useful theory of goal setting and task motivation', *American Psychologist*, 57(9), 705–17. Copyright © 2002 American Psychological Association.

that people put in more effort and have higher performance when they have more difficult (but achievable) goals. And second is that people perform better when they have specific and challenging goals than when they are simply told to do their best. So, having goals clearly affects our level of performance. But how does this happen? There are four mechanisms (Locke and Latham, 2002):

1. Goals give direction: they ensure that we focus on the right tasks, those things that are related to the end result we want.

2. Goals are energizing: more difficult goals energize us more than easier goals.

3. Goals improve persistence: having a goal encourages us to 'stick with' a task rather than abandon it.

4. Goals activate our knowledge and skills: for tasks where we lack the skills, having a goal can also encourage us to develop the necessary skills. It should be noted here, however, that if a goal is too difficult or complex, anxiety can cause us to perform worse than if we do not have a specific goal. So, with very challenging tasks, it is best to provide specific and structured support to enable people to learn the necessary skills.

BRAND X

*Having a goal to aim for improves persistence.*

The high-performance cycle also demonstrates the impact of some important moderators on the goals–performance relationship. The first is commitment: the more committed people are to a goal, the more effort they will put into achieving that goal. The second is feedback: we need good feedback so that we know how we are progressing towards the goal and what we need to do to adjust our efforts. Third, complexity can also affect the strength of the relationship between goals and performance, as goal-setting has less effect on performance as the task becomes more complex. In more complex goals, the effect of variables such as knowledge, ability or skill levels have more of an impact on performance than the goal-setting itself.

Finally, goal-setting theory also points out how important satisfaction is to performance. Achieving our goals gives us a sense of satisfaction, which then makes us more willing to commit to further challenges. This provides an important counterpoint to the core finding that difficult goals increase performance: if the goals are too difficult and we fail to meet them, we will become discouraged and be less willing to commit to future goals. In managing performance, then, we need to build people's confidence by ensuring that the goals are attainable.

## JOB DESIGN AND PERFORMANCE

If we approach work motivation from an external viewpoint, we will want to know what kinds of things in the job or the work environment itself might motivate people more. From an organizational perspective, being able to design work in a way that encourages people to work more efficiently and effectively has a long history. The early efforts aimed at efficiency and used division of labour and simplification of individual jobs but ran into the problem of worker dissatisfaction and turnover. So, the idea of trying to make the job itself more motivating was developed.

# Job design

Hackman and Oldham's (1975) **model of job characteristics** remains one of the best known ways of conceptualizing the impact of different job dimensions on motivation. They suggested that *enriched* jobs would be more motivating. That is, specific elements of a job, which they called 'core job dimensions', can be improved in order to influence our psychological states and this, in turn, would determine outcomes such as motivation, work quality, satisfaction with work and ultimately absenteeism and turnover. This general model of work design, illustrated in Figure 5.2, has been supported in recent meta-analyses (Humphrey et al., 2007).

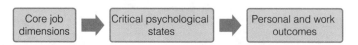

*Figure 5.2 Hackman and Oldman's job characteristics model*

Source: Adapted with permission from Hackman, J. R. and Oldham, G. R. (1975) 'Development of the job diagnostic survey', *Journal of Applied Psychology*, 60(2), 159–70. Copyright © 1975 by the American Psychological Association.

Hackman and Oldham (1976) suggested there were five core job dimensions (numbers 1–5 in the list below) but the number of dimensions has been expanded since then and a distinction drawn between 'job-related' and 'social' dimensions (Humphrey et al., 2007). These social dimensions are still characteristics of the job, but relate to our interactions with other people in our work. An *enriched* job is one that has more of each of these elements in it:

The job-related dimensions are:

1. Skill variety: How many different skills do I use in order to complete my job?

2. Task identity: To what extent do I complete a 'whole' piece of work?

3. Task significance: How much impact does my work have on other people?

4. Autonomy: How much freedom and discretion do I have to decide how and when I will do my work?

5. Feedback: To what extent do I receive clear and direct information on my effectiveness?

6. Task variety: How many different tasks do I complete in my work?

The social dimensions are:

1. Interdependence: How much is my job dependent on others and theirs on mine?

2. Feedback from others: How much feedback do I get on my performance from other people?

3. Social support: To what extent can I get advice and assistance from colleagues or supervisors?

The relationship of these job-related and social dimensions to work outcomes is complex but there is good evidence that both are important in explaining performance, organizational commitment and stress. In addition, there are differences between them, with social dimensions being related to turnover intentions and job-related dimensions related to job involvement and internal work motivation (Humphrey et al., 2007). Humphrey et al. also discovered that the social characteristics have become increasingly important over the years, perhaps because of the increase in the use of teamwork, an important reminder that motivational theories need to be constantly updated to reflect the realities of current working practices.

The extent to which these job dimensions are present in our work determines some of the psychological states that are critical to work outcomes. Hackman and Oldham (1976) suggested that three main states are important:

1. Experienced meaningfulness of the work: Do I think my work is genuinely meaningful, valuable and worthwhile?

2. Experienced responsibility for the outcomes: Do I think I am personally responsible and accountable for the results of my work?

3. Knowledge of the actual results of the work: Do I know how well I am performing my job?

These psychological states are then hypothesized to influence a variety of different behavioural and attitudinal work outcomes. Behavioural outcomes include absenteeism, performance and turnover, while attitudinal outcomes include job satisfaction, internal work motivation and organizational commitment. However, the research (Humphrey et al., 2007) seems to indicate that meaningfulness is the most critical link between the job dimensions and outcomes, and Barrick et al. (2013) have suggested that experienced meaningfulness is the essential interface between our personality traits and job characteristics that triggers motivation.

This framework provides HR professionals and managers with clear guidelines for designing individual jobs to be more motivating. But **job design** is important for more than motivation. In a recent review, Parker (2014) highlighted how the design of work can improve learning and development and is key to enhancing employees' mental and physical health, as well as an important consideration in achieving control and flexibility within the organization.

## Job crafting

Job design focuses on how the organization can redesign work in order to try and motivate employees or reap other positive outcomes of enriched jobs. Wrzesniewski and Dutton (2001) suggested that there was a different way to look at the process of job redesign, and that was to focus on how employees themselves can 'craft' their jobs to better suit them. Employees can do this by changing the task or relational boundaries of their work. Changing *task* boundaries can be done cognitively (by adjusting how we see the work, which elements we focus on or how we see it all interacting) or physically (by changing how we do the work or even what activities we do). We can change the *relational* boundaries of the job by choosing who we interact with. When we do this, it impacts on the meaning of the work and our identity in the job. Wrzesniewski and Dutton give several examples of how people have done this, including how nurses had recrafted their jobs by engaging with patients' families and passing on seemingly unimportant information to colleagues that ultimately resulted in better care for patients. This meant that the meaning of their work included patient advocacy rather than just high-quality technical care. In the Application activity, we explore how someone could actively engage with their job in order to recraft it to suit them better.

## Applications: **Job crafting**

Daniel has recently been promoted to manager of his team of IT support officers. After six months on the job he is starting to regret his move. When he took the job, he was hoping to be able to make things better for his team by addressing some of their concerns, but is worried that he might be losing touch with the details of what is important to them. He no longer has much to do with the day-to-day IT support: he used to really enjoy talking to people and helping them solve their IT problems. He knows he is good at the technical and the social side of IT support but feels like he is now missing out on both as his time is spent checking targets and drawing up action plans. He was also moved out of the open-plan office to an office on his own when he was promoted and he finds it too quiet.

He is feeling rather isolated and prefers having the buzz of other people around him at work.

» What could Daniel do to craft his job? Start by thinking about what *meaning* Daniel seems to want in his work. Then consider how he could change cognitive or physical task boundaries as well as relational boundaries to craft his job to better suit his skills and values and provide this meaning.

» Do you think there is opportunity for **job crafting** in every job? What might be some of the limitations to this kind of approach to adapting our jobs to suit us? From an organizational point of view, should job crafting be encouraged or discouraged?

## BENEFITS AND REWARDS

Probably the most obvious approach to trying to motivate employees and manage their performance is to provide them with material rewards. Piece-rate or commission-based pay is based on this idea: employees are paid per item they produce or amount they sell rather than a flat rate, with the idea that they will be motivated to work harder and be more productive in order to earn more money. We considered the role of pay at work in Chapter 2, when we were thinking about the meaning of work and discussed the research showing that people's primary reason for working was for financial reward, although the financial reward for work can have different meanings to different people. We also saw that people have different approaches to money. For some, more is not always better and they would be happy to earn a certain amount and then stop putting any further effort into their work. So, when we are considering the role of reward in motivation, it is worth going further and taking into account the different types of rewards people want.

## Pay

Our take-home pay is probably the most important element of the whole benefits and rewards package and it is certainly the element that organizations spend the most money on. While pay is often considered as a key element of performance management and motivation of current employees, it is worth remembering that it has wider effects on the organization as well. The organization's approach to pay and reward influence the attraction and retention of employees, thereby having an impact on the talent mix in the organization (Guthrie, 2007). Financial incentives serve more than one purpose: pay is not simply an exchange for the work an employee does, but is also a symbolic exchange, representing status and recognition (Jenkins et al., 1998).

Here, we will consider three different strategies that can be taken to determine pay, which can be differentiated in terms of how they assign 'worth' to a particular role or person (Pilbeam, 2009):

1. Pay based on the relative worth of the job to the organization gives greater pay to jobs that are valued more highly within the organization. Also known as job-based or graded pay, a common example is how pay tends to increase as one progresses up through the hierarchy of the organization, so an HR director is paid more than an HR assistant. The assumption is that the jobs at the top of the organization are worth more (or contribute more) to the organization than those at the bottom.

2. Performance-related pay reflects the individual worth of employees in terms of an assessment of their performance. Those who perform at

a higher level will be rewarded with higher pay. An example of this is when sales reps are given performance bonuses for achieving certain sales targets.

3. Pay is based on the commercial worth of the employee, that is, a labour-market approach, which is centred on the levels of supply and demand: employees with skills that are in short supply will be paid more. A good example of this is how doctors in community practices tend to be paid more than the managers of those practices.

We will consider each of these approaches in more detail now and as we discuss them it will become obvious that the majority of jobs have a mixture of two or even three of these elements.

## Relative worth: graded pay

'Relative worth' to the organization can be determined in two different ways. The traditional way is to grade the job itself, while a more flexible approach grades the value of specific skills. The distinctions between the two are illustrated in Table 5.1.

Some organizations aim for an egalitarian pay structure, based on the belief that fairness in pay is an important element of motivation for their employees (we saw how important equity is to motivation earlier in this chapter). Others use a much more hierarchical approach, with a steep increase in pay as employees progress 'up' the organization. The benefit of this approach is expected to be that employees are attracted to the high salaries and will work hard to compete for them, thus improving organizational performance. The evidence on which approach is more effective is mixed, partly because few organizations adopt an extreme form of either of these approaches. In some cases, pay dispersion has a positive effect on performance; in others it has been shown to have a negative effect on cooperation and commitment, and hence organizational performance (Guthrie, 2007). An interesting and increasingly important debate on the fairness of pay based on relative worth is that around CEO pay, which we consider in detail in Chapter 6.

## Individual worth: performance-based pay

Pay that is linked to performance has clear and established effects on increasing work performance,

Table 5.1 **Graded pay**

| Job-based pay | Person-based pay |
|---|---|
| Traditional approach, attaches a certain level of pay to particular jobs | Pay is associated with specific skills, competencies and knowledge |
| Jobs are evaluated internally and a 'value' attached to them according to their skills, responsibility, working conditions and so on | Skills and competencies needed for particular roles are evaluated and assessed in terms of the value they add |
| Higher value jobs are paid at a higher level | People who demonstrate or achieve greater levels of specified skills or knowledge are paid more |
| Pay levels are often determined by reference to competitors or market analysis | Market data is used to try and evaluate pay levels with competitors, but can be complicated when there are no direct equivalents |
| Reinforces hierarchy, associated with command and control style of management | Thought to promote a flexible and multiskilled workforce |

both for individuals and groups (Guthrie, 2007). Although, as we will explore further in our discussion of intrinsic and extrinsic rewards later in this chapter, this effect seems to be limited to performance quantity rather than quality (Jenkins et al., 1998). The positive effect of *performance-based pay* is partly down to direct incentive effects (higher performance leads to greater pay) and partly down to sorting effects: particular approaches to pay will attract and retain particular employees, specifically those who will respond well to the approach and perform at a higher level.

An important consideration in performance-related pay is that it is subject to 'endowment' bias: the tendency we have to overestimate our own contributions and skills. We are predisposed to feel that we perhaps perform better than our colleagues and that any performance-related pay we gain is not quite as good as we deserve. Lupton et al. (2015) suggest that the best way of combatting this bias is to make the reward system transparent and equitable, so that employees can see how and why different levels of performance are rewarded.

One of the challenges with performance-based pay is how performance can be effectively evaluated and monitored. Some jobs have quantifiable outcomes that can be easily measured, but even with these jobs the quality of the work is often important too, and judging quality can be difficult. Unless the performance criteria are well constructed, other essential components of the job can be ignored. In fact, attempts to introduce inappropriate measures of

performance are notorious for their often unwanted consequences. For example, teachers in Atlanta, USA were convicted of inflating their students' scores by giving them answers to standardized tests or changing answers after submission, in an effort to receive bonuses, increase school funding or even to try and keep their jobs (Brumback, 2015). There is certainly evidence that the design of performance-based pay for professionals needs to take account of the values and overall goals of the organization and the individuals working in it if it is going to promote higher performance (Young et al., 2012) and not conflict with ethical values.

## Commercial worth: market-based pay

There is clear evidence that organizations paying above-market wages are more attractive to potential candidates and current employees, but the evidence regarding the impact of this on organizational competitiveness is not as clear (Guthrie, 2007). Problems may arise with identifying the point at which the above-market rates become too high and developing effective selection procedures if the organization is attractive to many potential candidates.

In addition to considering the market levels of pay, we also need to be aware of the individual's subjective evaluation of the pay and their own worth, which varies over time depending on external and internal factors (Lupton et al., 2015). For example, during a recession, an employee may simply be relieved to have continued employment and satisfied with a level of pay that, during a time of increased labour demand, might seem unsatisfactory. One thing that is important in determining pay is to consider carefully the perceptions of fairness that employees will have. We have seen how essential equity is to motivation and need to bear in mind that these perceptions of equity can change over time, so pay levels may need to be constantly monitored and adjusted.

## Other benefits

### Flexible benefits

One approach to reward at work that recognizes individual differences is to use flexible benefit frameworks or salary sacrifice schemes. Salary sacrifice schemes involve employees deciding to 'sacrifice' some salary in exchange for particular benefits such as extra holidays. In flexible benefit frameworks, the organization offers employees a range of different benefits of varying value and each employee can choose the ones they prefer, adjusting the salary up or down as appropriate. For example, some organizations allow their employees to 'trade-in' holidays. In these schemes, employees who want more time off can 'buy' extra holiday and those who find they just do not want or need as many days off can exchange them for extra pay. A range of other benefits can be offered too. In the Applications activity, we look at how these benefits could be used to motivate and reward different employees.

However, there is a note of caution to sound in considering these **flexible benefits** and that is that *too much choice* can actually have a negative impact

 Applications: **Flexible and voluntary benefits**

*Image Source/Bjarte Rettedal*

Your organization is replacing its current 'one-size-fits-all' benefits with a new flexible benefits programme, in which each employee may choose from a list of discretionary benefits up to a maximum of 15% of their current salary. The benefits will be provided in addition to the normal salary and any unused entitlement may be paid to the employee as a bonus at the end of the year (subject to tax).

- Private healthcare:
  - Plan A (£50 excess and pays 90% of health costs) = £2,000
  - To include dependants, add £1,300
  - Plan B (£500 excess and pays 70% of health costs) = £300
  - To include dependants add £300
- Life insurance
  - Plan A (£25,000 coverage) = £300
  - Plan B (£200,000 coverage) = £2,000
- Extra annual leave: 2% of annual pay for each week, up to 4 weeks a year (in addition to statutory holidays)

- Four-day week during the three summer months (available only to full-time employees) = 4% of annual pay
- Childcare vouchers: £50 per month can be exchanged for £100 of vouchers paid directly to the approved childminder or nursery
- Language class reimbursement = £350

» Imagine that you are earning £20,000, so you have up to £2,500 to spend on these extra benefits. What would you choose to do? Would you find this kind of scheme motivating? Why or why not?

» Find out how your answer compares to your colleagues and discuss the kinds of things that affect your choices.

on employees (Lupton et al., 2015). If faced with an overly complicated or extensive list of possible benefits, it can be difficult for many people to decide which is 'best' and make them worry they may lose out. This can mean that the benefits become more of a cost to the employee than a reward, making them feel they have not gained the best benefit from the package. In addition, the subjective value of these benefits can reduce over time, so that after a while the employee no longer sees them as a valued reward. There are also potential costs to the employer that need to be considered when constructing the benefits. For example, the organization may need to ensure that employees who buy extra leave are still able to keep up with the workload or that those who sell leave are not overworking and risking burnout.

In summary, it is important to take account of the behavioural and subjective aspects of reward (Lupton et al., 2015). Our responses to reward are dynamic, that is, they change over time. So, for example, a single graduate first starting a new job may initially value benefits such as free gym membership or subsidized meals in a work canteen. But later in life, issues such as childcare or life insurance may become more important and benefits that can help with these will be of greater value to the individual. We also continually make comparisons with others and judge whether we believe we are being treated fairly. For these reasons, it is in the organization's interests to help employees to recognize the real value of the various benefits and rewards they receive. This may be done using a **total reward** approach.

## Total reward

As we have seen, one of the challenges that organizations face in implementing their reward systems or reaping the benefits of providing rewards to employees is that employees may often be unaware of the true value of those rewards. Many organizations invest a considerable amount of money into the various rewards for employees, yet the majority of employees often do not think beyond their take-home pay when considering what they gain from an employer. In addition, employees tend to underestimate the value of deferred rewards, that is, incentives they will benefit from at some future point, for example shares and pensions. So, organizations need to continually communicate their value to employees if they hope to use these kinds of benefits to encourage performance (Lupton et al., 2015). This has led to the development of the 'total reward concept', which is an attempt to provide employees with a clearer understanding of the value of their total reward package.

The total reward package may also include learning and development opportunities and perhaps even more intangible elements of the working environment that improve employees' working life, such as a positive climate or involvement in decision-making. Raising employees' awareness of these more intangible rewards is complex, but one approach that many organizations are adopting in dealing with the tangible rewards is to provide employees with a Total Rewards Statement (TRS). A TRS attempts to demonstrate the cash value of all the benefits and rewards of working at a particular organization in a way employees will understand. It typically shows not only employees' pay, but also the employer contribution

to pension, the cash value of paid-for benefits and the value of any tax gains through salary sacrifice or charity donations. Below is a simplified example.

---

### Example Total Rewards Statement: ABC Ltd

This statement shows you your annual rewards as an employee of ABC Ltd. As you will see, the benefits of being an employee here go far beyond your salary.

First, a summary of the value of your salary, pension and other benefits:

| | | |
|---|---|---|
| Financial | Basic salary | £20,000 |
| | Overtime | £1,500 |
| | Employer pension contributions | £2,000 |
| | Share scheme | £100 |
| Value of benefits you have chosen | Gym membership | £360 |
| | Subsidized lunch | £250 |
| Value of pre-tax benefits you have chosen | Childcare vouchers | £500 |
| | Give as you earn charity donations | £100 |
| TOTAL | | £24,810 |

In addition, as a valued employee of ABC Ltd, you have access to the Employee Assistance Programme, which provides free legal help and counselling services, which could be worth in excess of £300 as well as providing peace of mind and assistance with your well-being.

We also have a range of discounts negotiated with local and national organizations, from 10% off at restaurants to discounts on holidays and home insurance. Last year, one of our colleagues, Joe Bloggs, saved a total of £225 using all these different discounts. Let us know if you can do better.

And there is a range of further training opportunities that you as an employee of ABC Ltd can access, which can help you develop your career or simply learn a new skill. We provide free management and leadership training as well as computer software and foreign languages courses. These courses can be worth up to £1,000. Why not try one?

---

Giancola (2006) recommends using advertising principles in order to effectively market the TRS to employees. One of the key issues here is clarity on the value of the various elements. Organizations need to be careful they are not 'overpromising' or claiming greater value for elements than they are

really worth. For some elements, this value will be difficult to express. For example, an EAP can cost the organization only £10 per employee, yet the benefit an individual gains from it could range from zero to several hundred pounds. The Web Explorer activity explores how a TRS can be developed.

---

 ### Web Explorer: Total rewards

If you are currently in employment, design a Total Rewards Statement for your current job. If you are not in employment, base the TRS on a friend or family member's job. Here are two websites with

some examples of total reward packages, so you can see the kinds of things that could be included:

- John Lewis: www.johnlewispartnership.co.uk/work/pay-and-benefits.html

- Siemens USA: www.benefitsquickstart.com/siemens/index.html

Read Robert Crawford's article on ways to create a TRS: www.employeebenefits.co.uk/issues/may-2015/top-five-ways-to-create-an-engaging-total-reward-statement. He suggests five things are important in creating a TRS:

1. **An engaging design:** it should be attractive, using illustrations where possible instead of dense financial information

2. **Easy accessibility:** it could be designed to be accessed online and perhaps linked to an online benefits hub

3. **Captivating content:** it should be creative and include all the different benefits that employees can access

4. **Timing the delivery:** it is common for a TRS to be annual, but technology now permits a much more frequent update

5. **Communication:** let employees know about the TRS, including line managers, in the roll-out.

» To what extent do you think that seeing a full statement of rewards and benefits can help organizations and individuals?

» If organizations want to introduce a TRS, is there anything they should be wary of?

# PERFORMANCE MANAGEMENT

We have looked at how motivation theories can help us understand the effort that people put into their work and how their motivation and performance may be enhanced and supported. But *performance management (PM)* goes beyond simply encouraging motivation. It is about ensuring that the individual's performance contributes effectively to the overall organizational performance and includes a consideration of the most effective or efficient ways of doing this.

At one level, PM could be thought of as the basic role of any kind of management at work. And indeed, this is what many definitions emphasize. Armstrong and Baron (2005) note that one of the key elements of effective performance management is creating a shared understanding between individuals and the organization about what should be achieved, and managing people in a way that leads to higher organizational performance. Good performance management will integrate the individual's efforts with organizational goals and manage individuals and teams in order to achieve higher levels of performance.

In much of the HR literature, there is an assumption that PM will have a positive impact on the individual, to the extent that it is sometimes even defined as supporting and developing underperformers rather than removing them from post (e.g. Armstrong and Baron, 2005, p. 2). However, this positive approach does not always reflect the reality of what happens in organizations. While it is true that in some organizations there certainly is an emphasis on developing and supporting employees in order to improve performance, there are also plenty of other organizations that take a more hardline approach of hiring and firing based on current performance. In looking at PM here, we will take a balanced view, considering different approaches to improving and managing performance in the organization but not assuming that all these approaches will be of benefit to all employees. We start by considering the different types of systems that may be used, before moving on to look at the detail of how PM is often conducted at the individual level.

## Function of performance management

From the organization's point of view, performance management is seen as a means of improving performance by:

- Providing feedback on good and bad performance: motivating good performance through praise and recognition and providing clarity on poor performance

- Differentiating between employees so that performance-related rewards can be distributed

- Identifying areas for development and training.

In the Weighing the Evidence activity, we have a closer look at whether PM delivers on these aims.

Weighing the Evidence: **Does performance management deliver?**

Great claims are made for performance management; that it can improve profitability and increase employee engagement. Certainly, these are the aims when new PM systems are implemented. But do they actually deliver? At a CIPD conference on PM, Keith Grint is reported to have said: 'rarely in the history of management can a system have promised so much and delivered so little' (cited in Brown, 2010, p. 1) and the majority of organizations report being dissatisfied with their PM systems despite continuous efforts to improve them (Brown, 2010). In a survey of 200 companies, 60% of senior managers did not believe that their PM approach was helping to improve their business (Longden, 2016).

Combs et al. (2006) showed that high-performance work practices have a significant correlation with organizational performance, but that performance appraisals alone seem to have very limited, if any, effect. The authors note that this may be due to appraisals having too many different aims: they can be developmental, control-oriented, or results-oriented.

An essential element of any PM system is the measurement of performance. There are many reports of PM systems that fail, and van Camp and Braet (2016) focus on the role of measurements in failure. They suggested that these failures in performance measurement can be classified into three different levels, as shown in Table 5.2.

**Table 5.2 Failures due to performance measurement**

| Level | Failure due to problems with | Example |
|---|---|---|
| Metrics | Measurements of performance, parameters, key performance indicators | Using 'off the shelf' metrics without adapting them appropriately to the specific organization means that the measures are inappropriate or the wording is simply not understood |
| Framework | Development of the performance model, how the measures are processed | Misuse or misunderstanding of the statistics associated with different performance measures |
| Management | Implementation or operation of the performance measurement model, support given by management, decision-making | Performance measures are misaligned with the organizational strategy or managers lack the necessary skills to implement the system appropriately |

Source: Based on van Camp, J. and Braet, J. (2016) 'Taxonomizing performance measurement systems' failures', *International Journal of Productivity and Performance Management*, 65(5), pp. 672–93.

This research reinforces how important it is to implement a performance management system in which the aims, processes and measures are clearly defined and integrated. A PM system without these aspects will not be able to deliver on its promises.

To assume that everyone involved in the PM process is aiming for the same thing would be simplistic. In fact, PM systems and processes can be used for a variety of ends by different organizational actors, and their 'unofficial' functions can be just as substantial as or even more so than their official functions. For example, the person conducting the performance management (usually the direct supervisor) may give performance ratings based on political factors in order to achieve their own aims rather than the official aim of the PM (Fletcher, 2008). Sims et al. (1987) found that many executives actively manipulated performance appraisals in order to do precisely this. These managers were fully aware of the potential longer term outcomes of performance ratings and were focused on these rather than the accurate rating of an employee's current performance. They might inflate a performance rating in order to avoid demotivating staff or avoid an uncomfortable discussion around negative feedback. Some even admitted to inflating the performance ratings to try and promote a difficult employee out of the department.

It is worth noting that the stated organizational aims for PM may also be incompatible with each other because of how the employees respond to the system. For example, if employees view the performance management process as a means of gaining rewards or avoiding negative outcomes, they are likely to try and improve the supervisor's opinion of their performance. If, however, employees see the performance management as primarily supportive and development-based, they will be more likely to be honest about shortcomings and seek help to improve performance.

## Performance management systems

The aim of PM systems is to support individual employees in contributing to the overall performance of the organization. They can consist of policies and practices that help to align employee goals with organizational goals and enable and motivate employee or team performance. There may be many and varied approaches to doing this within a single organization, so an effective PM system will need to integrate these different elements in order to provide strategic management of performance.

According to a survey by the CIPD (Armstrong and Baron, 2009), the key elements of an effective PM system include:

- **Alignment of objectives:** by providing greater clarity on roles and objectives, PM not only makes it clear to individuals what their specific goals are, but also how and why they contribute to the organization's success

- **Building engagement:** good PM encourages better relationships between employees and their managers and builds commitment

- **Central role of line managers:** respondents in the survey noted that good managers will be good at performance management 'whatever the process' but that a good system can support and enable this process

- **Evaluation:** it is important to have ongoing evaluation of the PM system to ensure it is delivering on its objectives

- **Impact on other organizational processes:** PM is seen as a vehicle for identifying potential, can be linked to learning and development activities and is often used as a method for providing performance-related pay.

However, survey respondents also noted that a PM system may often not have a direct impact on the organization's bottom line and again emphasized the role of line managers rather than a specific type of PM system in managing the day-to-day performance of employees. The take-away from this and similar research in the area is that 'performance management' is essentially the key role of managers and that any PM system should support and enable this if it is to have any impact on individual and organizational performance. This is perhaps worth remembering when we consider the different systems that are used.

In line with this view of PM as equating to management, Armstrong and Taylor (2014) suggest that the PM cycle can be modelled using a simple management cycle of 'plan–act–monitor–review'. The planning phase involves setting and agreeing performance objectives and the measures that will be used to check performance, as well as identifying any personal development needs in order to meet those objectives. The act phase involves individuals carrying out their roles and attempting to meet the objectives and engaging with necessary development. Armstrong and Taylor emphasize that monitoring should be carried out continuously, reflecting the findings in the research above that PM should be a continuous process carried out by line managers. In this way, employees receive feedback and are able to adjust their performance throughout the year and managers can deal with underperformance before it results in critical issues. Finally, the review stage could include a formal performance appraisal: it provides a focal point for the manager and employee to reflect on past progress and development and the basis for planning the next cycle.

Other approaches to PM focus on how the performance goals can be set or measured and we consider these next.

## Management by objectives

The concept of **managing by objectives (MBO)** was introduced by Peter Drucker in his book *The Practice of Management* (1955). He suggested that management, although a crucial part of business, was poorly understood and that a key element of good management was to control and alter the environment by 'direct, conscious action' (p. 11). This could only be done by having clear objectives and working towards them. Management by objectives, therefore, became a systematic approach based on cascading the organizational objectives down to individuals in order to align everyone's efforts at all levels of the company.

MBO shows great similarity with Locke and Latham's goal-setting theory. In MBO programmes, there is a set of company-wide, high-level goals that is then cascaded down to individual employees to try and encourage them to work towards the same goals. There are four key elements to MBO that can be drawn out of goal-setting theory:

1. **Goals have to be specific:** Managers cannot simply tell employees to 'work hard', but have to be specific about what work they should do and how they will know they are achieving their goals.

2. **Commitment:** To ensure that people are committed to the goals, participative decision-making is key. That means managers should avoid imposing goals on employees, but encourage them to be involved in the choice of the goals.

3. **Time-specific:** Goals need to have time limits in order for performance assessment to function.

4. **Feedback:** Continual feedback is best, so that employees can adjust and improve their performance as they go along.

Cascading organizational objectives to individual goals is not, of course, a straightforward task and it is here again that the skills and abilities of line managers come into their own. But when done effectively, this kind of PM system, which directs individual efforts through goal-setting to the wider organizational objectives, can reap the benefits of individual motivation and integrated organizational performance.

## The balanced scorecard

The **balanced scorecard** was originally introduced by Kaplan and Norton (1993) as a way of linking non-financial measurements to an organization's strategy in order to give a balanced view of the organization's performance. An organization's success is not judged simply in terms of profits (or 'value for money' in the

non-profit sector). Instead, it includes a consideration of the customer's perspective, the internal business processes and organizational learning and growth. We consider these wider perspectives on organizational success in Chapter 12. Essentially, it is similar to the MBO approach in that it identifies goals at the highest level of the organization and then cascades these goals down to individuals, thereby integrating and encouraging efforts in the required directions, but has the added benefit of ensuring that there is a balanced set of goals.

When used for performance management, goals for each of these four broad areas are set and specific measurements developed that will enable progress towards those goals to be evaluated. The balanced scorecard approach does not assume that every employee will contribute to every goal of the organization, that is, that all the organization's goals are equally relevant to each person. Instead, the goals should be assigned to the relevant teams or departments and cascaded down. Just as with MBO, the individual performance appraisal provides the opportunity to review progress against these goals.

## Challenges in implementing PM systems

The criticisms of these PM systems are fairly similar, and they revolve around the challenges of implementation. As we have seen, PM is reliant on the skills and abilities of line managers: they need to be able to translate higher level organizational goals into specific objectives for their team. They need to understand their staff, be able to motivate them appropriately and provide good feedback. The In the News feature illustrates how technology is impacting on traditional PM systems.

The role of HR, rather than being one of carrying out performance appraisals, is primarily in developing the system and ensuring that managers are empowered and trained to carry it out effectively. No matter how good the system, it relies on the individual manager–employee relationship, so we turn now to consider that individual level.

## PM at the individual level: the appraisal

There are three significant challenges that any PM system will face when it comes down to the individual employee. First, there is the issue of politics and power. The potential rewards, and even sanctions,

## In the News: **Instant performance feedback**

In 2015, General Electric decided to stop its annual performance reviews, joining many other big names like Microsoft and Adobe. Prior to this it had been a vocal promoter of the 'rank and yank' system of appraisal, where employees had their performances ranked against each other and the lowest performers were removed from the organization. The ranking process was dropped a decade ago and more recently, the organization introduced an app that allows employees to give and get instant feedback on how they are doing (Nisen, 2015). Managers keep in regular contact with their team and discuss their progress towards the priorities or goals that are stored on the app. The app also records summaries or notes related to each goal, which can be accessed and checked at any time.

There is no grading of employees against each other: instead, the focus is on supporting **coaching** conversations between managers and individual employees, that is, a collaborative approach to performance improvements based on insights from everyone they work with. While more frequent feedback is certainly essential for improving performance, this new approach does mean that staff are having to learn a new way of distributing performance-based pay. Some critics have suggested that removing the formal performance appraisal has simply pushed the pay decisions behind closed doors and that unfair discrimination may well be the result.

### For discussion

» Should pay increases be based on performance?
» If so, how should performance be judged and who should make the judgements?
» If not, what do you think pay should be based on?

---

associated with performance appraisals can be substantial and the individuals involved may well be aiming for different outcomes from each other and the organization at large. For example, an employee may view the performance management system as an opportunity to gain higher wages by convincing the manager that he is performing at a high level. On the other hand, the manager may well believe that this individual employee is having a negative impact on the overall team but not feel confident enough to address the issue. The organization itself may be facing difficult economic challenges and be attempting to reduce the spend on staffing costs and therefore limiting the budget available for performance-related bonuses. All these different elements will combine to potentially shift the focus of any performance-related discussions away from actual performance.

Second, there is the issue of how the information gathered in performance appraisals is used. We saw earlier that PM systems often aim to achieve a range of outcomes, but that these aims are sometimes incompatible. Research consistently demonstrates this, with the information from performance appraisals being used for salary decisions, feedback on performance to employees and identification of strengths and weaknesses (Cleveland et al., 1989). PM systems face the challenge that they are often

used for two competing outcomes: identifying development needs and providing performance-related pay. The difficulty here lies in how honestly and fairly the process is conducted. Individuals who know that their pay or promotion prospects depend on their appraisal will respond differently from those who see it as a development opportunity. HR professionals and line managers need to be clear about what the PM system is aiming to do and not try to achieve both these ends with a single process.

Related to both these challenges is the third issue of how performance can accurately be measured. We considered this briefly above in our discussion of performance-related pay, but here we will review the practical measures that can be used in assessing performance.

### Output criteria

The most straightforward criterion for performance measurements could be considered the output criterion, especially where they are clearly linked to organizational goals. Output criteria focus on the end results of an employee's efforts and can be based on quantity, for example sales volume, or quality, for example number of errors made. Sometimes, these judgements will be objective but often, and especially for more complex jobs, outputs can be ambiguous

*Getty Images/laflor*

*Managers can find it difficult to address poor performance.*

and measurements very subjective. In addition, they do not take account of situational effects and may often be based on judgements about a person's qualities rather than performance, which are difficult to measure on a scale.

## Behavioural criteria

Specific behavioural criteria can be more useful than outputs if employees' actions can be directly observed and rated in terms of their effectiveness or desirability to the organization. Whatever it is that we choose to evaluate in a performance measurement, it is important that the element is clearly defined and an appropriate method is chosen to assess it. Measures can be standardized across many employees or be individual to each employee.

While we need to have some kind of standardization if we are comparing performance ratings across employees, there is also a place for more individualized measures. These are useful when it is difficult to define clear outcome measures across different jobs or where there may be different, equally effective, behaviours associated with high performance. MBO is a good example of how this

can be done, with individual goals agreed between the manager and the employee.

## Performance measurement reliability

In all kinds of performance measurements, managers need to be aware of the issue of how reliable the ratings are. Performance appraisals are subject to the same kinds of biases we discussed in the section on interviews, for example halo or recency effects (in Chapter 3). Research indicates that while each rater tends to be fairly consistent in how they judge performance, the difference *between* raters can be quite substantial (Viswesvaran et al., 1996). Direct supervisors tend to give more reliable ratings than peers, possibly because they are less subject to the halo bias than peers (Viswesvaran et al., 2005).

A lack of agreement between raters could be a problem if performance-related rewards are involved because it introduces some ambiguity into how those rewards can be fairly distributed. However, in other respects, having more than one rater for an employee's performance could be beneficial; **360-degree appraisal**, where an employee's performance is rated by supervisors, peers and subordinates (and sometimes even external clients or customers), is increasingly popular because it provides a more rounded picture of an individual's performance. Each rater will have a different experience of the individual's performance and, while their ratings may not agree completely, they will be valid (Bozeman, 1997) and can be particularly useful in identifying areas for development (DeNisi and Kluger, 2000).

Interestingly, there does appear to be a common factor that underlies good performance ratings, regardless of who is doing the rating. Viswesvaran et al. (2005) suggest that employees who engage in more organizational citizenship behaviours, that is, make contributions to the organization that go beyond the formal job role, and appear more intelligent and conscientious, will have higher performance ratings than those who are simply good at specific aspects of their jobs.

## Dealing with poor performance

Although one of the primary reasons for having performance management is to deal with poor performance, many managers find this very difficult. Goodhew et al. (2008) note that frontline managers are often reluctant to address the issue with poor performers and tend to be inconsistent when they do, although there is evidence that those managers with greater experience tend to be more consistent. At the extreme, managing poor performance can result in dismissal of the employee. Yet, in their survey of 13,000 managers, Axelrod et al. (2002) found that only 19% believed that their organization removed low performers effectively, while 96% of them wished that it happened more quickly. Axelrod et al. identified three main reasons that managers avoid removing poor performers. First is an emotional attachment to the person and not wishing to harm them. Second is a belief that poor performers can be developed and that this investment will result in improved performance. Finally, there are practical barriers: a fear of litigation or concern that dismissal will result in widespread resentment.

There is no doubt that dealing with poor performance is difficult because it essentially involves giving someone negative feedback, and we explore this in the Transferrable Skills activity. However, it is an important part of performance management and there are some things that managers can do to make the process consistent and fair. First, the organization needs to have a clear policy and process in place for how poor performance will be dealt with. In this way, there is clarity for the manager and the employee on what steps will be taken, as well as what the employee can do to resolve the issue. Second, managers should ensure they use an 'evidence-based' approach, in order to demonstrate to the employee how and where the performance is not up to standard. This is, of course, dependent on having a good performance management system and measurements.

## Transferrable Skills: Holding a performance conversation

As we've seen, conversations about performance at work are among the most important tasks a manager can have, yet are also often avoided. In this activity, you will practise your skills at doing this. It is inspired by advice given by ACAS (the Advisory, Conciliation and Arbitration Service), an organization focused on improving workplace relations and with many years' experience in dealing with difficult conversations. More details can be found at www.acas.org.uk/index.aspx?articleid=3799.

There are three practical steps you can take to make difficult conversations a little easier:

1. **Face the problem:** Although it can be tempting to avoid the issue, putting off the conversation can escalate the problem. For example, not addressing poor performance can have a negative impact on the organization's effectiveness and lower the morale of other workers.

2. **Prepare:** This involves gathering the information you need and planning how you will approach the problem. Start by establishing the facts. What evidence is there of the poor performance? What were the employee's targets and were they made aware of them? Also, reflect on what you know about the employee. Are there extenuating factors? Is this a recurrent problem? Finally, check your organization's policies so that you are confident in what your next steps will be.

3. **Remember your skills:** Skills in dealing with difficult conversations are built by practice, but

you may be surprised at how many of them you already have experience of. For example, active listening skills can be developed in any conversation. You can also draw on your skills of self-control: often being able to control your own reactions to an emotional event is key to a good resolution.

Finally, you can also use a simple framework to help guide the conversation, making sure that you check the other person's understanding at each stage:

- **Introduction:** Set the right tone, explain the purpose of the meeting and adopt a calm and professional manner

- **Explain the problem:** Be specific and explain the wider impact of the problem if necessary (e.g. how it is affecting the team)

- **Ask for explanation:** Give the other person the opportunity to explain why this has happened. Explore the issues together.

- **Agree a way forward:** If possible, do this jointly, basing it on the other person's proposals. But

remember that you will need to make a decision and make it clear what will happen next.

You can practise this with a friend using the role-play below.

**Employee**
You have regular biweekly meetings with your manager and usually they are fine. But today you're not in the best frame of mind because you and your partner recently broke up. You're upset and feeling on edge and know that your work has suffered a bit. But you have worked well at this company for three years so you're hoping they will cut you some slack.

**Manager**
Your employee is usually a very good worker but over the last couple of weeks there have been some fairly serious problems. They have missed a couple of deadlines with reports for your own superiors and been short-tempered with other members of your team. You want to address this problem before it gets worse but are quite nervous about it because they can be a bit intimidating.

## Practice Insights: Roger Longden

Roger Longden is Managing Director of There Be Giants, a management consultancy based in Manchester, UK, specializing in helping organizations to develop systems and cultures to support high performance. In the video he talks about why performance management is so important, as well as challenges and new approaches to managing performance that take advantage of recent technological developments.

Go online to www.macmillanihe.com/sutton-people to access the interview with Roger.

## SUMMARY

There are, of course, many influences on an individual employee's day-to-day performance and in this chapter we have outlined some of the larger issues. We started by considering the role of individual motivation: how people differ in what motivates them as well as how motivation can be turned into performance. We then looked at elements of the job role itself in influencing motivation and performance, focusing on how these could be changed by management as well as how employees themselves craft their jobs once they are in post. Finally we considered the role of benefits and rewards in encouraging high levels of performance.

In the final section of this chapter, we looked at the practicalities of performance management. We saw that the success or otherwise of a PM system relies on careful choice of performance measures and clear integration of individual and organizational goals. Throughout this chapter we have also been reminded of how important the line manager's role is in PM: to such an extent that some people have even suggested that the management of performance is the manager's main role.

# FURTHER READING

- For an in-depth review of the current state of research on work design, see Parker, S. K. (2014) 'Beyond motivation: job and work design for development, health, ambidexterity, and more', *Annual Review of Psychology*, 65(1), pp. 661–91.

- For a concise and practically focused review of reward and benefit at work, see Lupton, B., Rowe, A. and Whittle, R. (2015) *Show Me the Money! The Behavioural Science of Reward.* CIPD Research Report. Available at www.cipd.co.uk/binaries/show-me-the-money_2015-behavioural-science-of-reward.pdf.

# REVIEW QUESTIONS

1. To what extent can theories of individual motivation help managers to encourage their staff to higher performance?

2. Is there such a thing as an inherently motivating job?

3. How effective is the annual performance appraisal in managing performance?

# ONLINE RESOURCES

Go online to www.macmillanihe.com/sutton-people to access a MCQ quiz for this chapter and for further resources to support your learning.

# REFERENCES

Alderfer, C. P. (1969) 'An empirical test of a new theory of human needs', *Organizational Behavior and Human Performance*, 4(2), pp. 142–75.

Armstrong, M. and Baron, A. (2005) *Managing Performance: Performance Management in Action.* London: CIPD.

Armstrong, M. and Baron, A. (2009) *Performance Management in Action: Current Trends and Practice.* London: CIPD.

Armstrong, M. and Taylor, S. (2014) *Handbook of Human Resource Management*, 13th edn. London: Kogan Page.

Arnolds, C. A. and Boshoff, C. (2002) 'Compensation, esteem valence and job performance: an empirical assessment of Alderfer's ERG theory', *International Journal of Human Resource Management*, 13(4), pp. 697–719. doi: 10.1080/09585190210125868.

Axelrod, B., Handfield-Jones, H. and Michaels, E. (2002) 'A new game plan for C players', *Harvard Business Review*, 80(1), pp. 80–8.

Barrick, M. R., Mount, M. K. and Li, N. (2013) 'The theory of purposeful work behavior: the role of personality, higher-order goals, and job characteristics', *Academy of Management Review*, 38(1), pp. 132–53. doi: 10.5465/amr.2010.0479.

Bozeman, D. P. (1997) 'Interrater agreement in multi-source performance appraisal: a commentary', *Journal of Organizational Behavior*, 18(4), pp. 313–16.

Brown, D. (2010) *Performance Management: Can the Practice ever Deliver the Policy?* IES Opinion Paper 23. Available at: www.employment-studies.co.uk/system/files/resources/files/op23.pdf.

Brumback, K. (2015) '11 educators convicted in Atlanta test cheating conspiracy', *Huffington Post*, 1 April. Available at: www.huffingtonpost.com/2015/04/01/educators-convicted-atlan_n_6987044.html.

Carrell, M. and Dittrich, J. (1978) 'Equity theory: the recent literature, methodological considerations, and new directions', *Academy of Management Review*, 3(2), pp. 202–10. doi: citeulike-article-id:7426698.

Cleveland, J. N., Murphy, K. R. and Williams, R. E. (1989) 'Multiple uses of performance appraisal: Prevalence and correlates', *Journal of Applied Psychology*, 74(1), pp. 130–5. doi: 10.1037/0021-9010.74.1.130.

Combs, J. G., Liu, Y. Y., Hall, A. and Ketchen, D. (2006) 'How much do high-performance work practices matter? A meta-analysis of their effects on organizational performance', *Personnel Psychology*, 59, pp. 501–28. doi: 10.1111/j.1744-6570.2006.00045.x.

DeNisi, A. S. and Kluger, A. N. (2000) 'Feedback effectiveness: Can 360-degree appraisals be improved?', *The Academy of Management Executive*, 14(1), pp.129–39. doi:10.5465/AME.2000.2909845.

Drucker, P. F. (1955) *The Practice of Management*. Oxford: Elsevier.

Fletcher, C. (2008) 'Performance appraisal', in N. Chmiel (ed.) *An Introduction to Work and Organizational Psychology: A European Perspective*, 2nd edn. Oxford: Blackwell, pp. 76–96.

Giancola, F. L. (2006) 'Using advertising principles to sell total rewards', *Compensation & Benefits Review*, 38(5), pp. 35–9. doi: 10.1177/0886368706289998.

Goodhew, G. W., Cammock, P. A. and Hamilton, R. T. (2008) 'The management of poor performance by front-line managers', *Journal of Management Development*, 27(9), pp. 951–62. doi: 10.1108/02621710810901291.

Guthrie, J. (2007) 'Remuneration: pay effects at work', in P. Boxall, J. Purcell and P. Wright (eds) *The Oxford Handbook of Human Resource Management*. Oxford: Oxford University Press, pp. 344–63.

Hackman, J. R. and Oldham, G. R. (1975) 'Development of the job diagnostic survey', *Journal of Applied Psychology*, 60(2), pp. 159–70. doi: 10.1037/h0076546.

Hackman, J. and Oldham, G. R. (1976) 'Motivation through the design of work: test of a theory', *Organizational Behavior & Human Performance*, 16(2), pp. 250–79.

Humphrey, S. E., Nahrgang, J. D. and Morgeson, F. P. (2007) 'Integrating motivational, social, and contextual work design features: a meta-analytic summary and theoretical extension of the work design literature', *Journal of Applied Psychology*, 92(5), pp. 1332–56. doi: 10.1037/0021-9010.92.5.1332.

Jenkins, G., Douglas, J., Mitra, A., Gupta, N. and Shaw, J. D. (1998) 'Are financial incentives related to performance? A meta-analytic review of empirical research', *Journal of Applied Psychology*, 83(5), pp. 777–87. doi: 10.1037/0021-9010.83.5.777.

Judge, T. A. and Ilies, R. (2002) 'Relationship of personality to performance motivation: a meta-analytic review', *Journal of Applied Psychology*, 87(4), pp. 797–807.

Kaplan, R. S. and Norton, D. P. (1993) 'Putting the balanced scorecard to work', *Harvard Business Review*, 71(5), pp. 134–47.

Locke, E. A. and Latham, G. P. (1990) *A Theory of Goal Setting and Task Performance*. Englewood Cliffs, NJ: Prentice-Hall.

Locke, E. A. and Latham, G. P. (2002) 'Building a practically useful theory of goal setting and task motivation', *American Psychologist*, 57(9), pp. 705–17.

Longden, R. (2016) *Priming for Performance*. There Be Giants.

Lupton, B., Rowe, A. and Whittle, R. (2015) *Show Me the Money! The Behavioural Science of Reward*, CIPD Research Report, March, pp. 1–49.

McClelland, D. (1987) *Human Motivation*. Cambridge: Cambridge University Press.

McClelland, D. C. and Boyatzis, R. E. (1982) 'Leadership motive pattern and long-term success in management', *Journal of Applied Psychology*, 67(6), pp. 737–43.

Maslow, A. H. (1954) *Motivation and Personality*. New York: Harper & Row.

Miner, J. B. (2003) 'The rated importance, scientific validity, and practical usefulness of organizational behavior theories: a quantitative review', *Academy of Management Learning & Education*, 2(3), pp. 250–68. doi: 10.5465/AMLE.2003.10932132.

Nisen, M. (2015) *General Electric is ending annual performance reviews*, Quartz. Available at: http://qz.com/428813/ge-performance-review-strategy-shift/ (Accessed 23 December 2016).

Parker, S. K. (2014) 'Beyond motivation: job and work design for development, health, ambidexterity, and more', *Annual Review of Psychology*, 65, pp. 661–91. doi: 10.1146/annurev-psych-010213-115208.

Pilbeam, S. (2009) 'Rewarding people at work', in S. Gilmore and S. Williams (eds) *Human Resource Management*. Oxford: Oxford University Press, pp. 168–92.

Sims, J. H. P., Gioia, D. A. and Longenecker, C. O. (1987) 'Behind the mask: the politics of employee appraisal', *Academy of Management Executive*, 1(3), pp. 183–93. doi: 10.5465/AME.1987.4275731.

Van Camp, J. and Braet, J. (2016) 'Taxonomizing performance measurement systems' failures', *International Journal of Productivity and Performance Management*, 65(5), pp. 672–93. doi: 10.1108/IJPPM-03-2015-0054.

Van Eerde, W. and Thierry, H. (1996) 'Vroom's expectancy models and work-related criteria: a meta-analysis', *Journal of Applied Psychology*, 81(5), pp. 575–86. doi: 10.1037//0021-9010.81.5.575.

Viswesvaran, C., Ones, D. S. and Schmidt, F. L. (1996) 'Comparative analysis of the reliability of job performance ratings', *Journal of Applied Psychology*, 81(5), pp. 557–74.

Viswesvaran, C., Schmidt, F. L. and Ones, D. S. (2005) 'Is there a general factor in ratings of job performance? A meta-analytic framework for disentangling substantive and error influences', *Journal of Applied Psychology*, 90(1), pp. 108–31. doi: 10.1037/0021-9010.90.1.108.

Vroom, V. (1964) *Work and Motivation*. New York: John Wiley and Sons.

Wahba, M. A. and Bridwell, L. G. (1976) 'Maslow reconsidered: a review of research on the need hierarchy theory', *Organizational Behavior & Human Performance*, 15(2), pp. 212–40.

Wrzesniewski, A. and Dutton, J. E. (2001) 'Crafting a job: revisioning employees as active crafters of their work', *Academy of Management Review*, 26(2), pp. 179–201. doi: 10.5465/AMR.2001.4378011.

Young, G. J., Beckman, H. and Baker, E. (2012) 'Financial incentives, professional values and performance: a study of pay-for-performance in a professional organization', *Journal of Organizational Behavior*, 33(7), pp. 964–83. doi: 10.1002/job.1770.

# 6 LEADERSHIP: MANAGING LEADERS AND LEADING MANAGEMENT

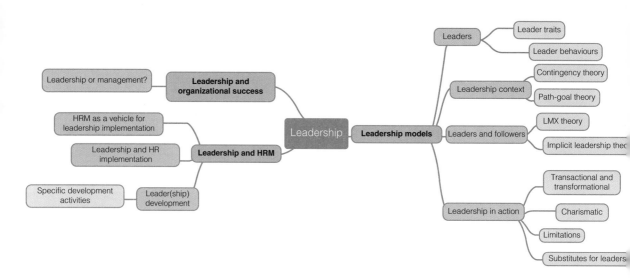

## INTRODUCTION

In this chapter we will consider current leadership models and debates as a foundation for exploring how HR practitioners can develop their own leadership capabilities, as well as how they can support the development of leaders within their organizations.

We start with an evaluation of the role of leadership in organizational success and of the ways to identify effective leaders. This leads us into a detailed discussion of different leadership theories and models, looking at the kinds of people who are most likely to emerge as leaders and the types of leadership behaviours that are most effective. Of course, the context the leader is in can have a significant impact on whether they are successful, so we also draw on theories that evaluate the interaction between a leader's style and the situation.

One element of leadership that is often overlooked is the role of the followers, so we will also consider how leaders and followers build relationships with each other and the impact that followers' perceptions can have on a leader's success. We draw our consideration of leadership theories to a conclusion by discussing newer leadership theories, including transformational and charismatic leadership, and the suggestion that the role of leaders can sometimes be replaced by specific structures.

Finally, we move our discussion from the general to the specific: How does leadership interact with HR practice? Here, we look at how HR practices can help to implement a leader's vision and how individual leaders' styles may impact on how HR practices are implemented across the organization. We draw the chapter to a close with a discussion of leadership development activities and how we can help employees to develop their leadership skills.

Getty Images/Hero Images

## LEARNING FEATURES

Applications: Should all managers be leaders?

Applications: Leading in a new context

Applications: Managing leaders

Weighing the Evidence: Leadership is inherently moral

Web Explorer: How to be a good leader

In the News: Volkswagen cheats emissions tests

Transferrable Skills: Leading a group

Practice Insights: Claudia Nario

 Video overview

Julian Perkins

Go online to www.macmillanihe.com/sutton-people to access a video of Anna Sutton introducing the chapter's main themes.

# LEADERSHIP AND ORGANIZATIONAL SUCCESS

How important is a good leader to an organization's success? If we look solely at the amount of money organizations invest in their top leaders, the answer seems very clear. The FTSE 100 companies paid their CEOs an average of £5.5 million in 2015, which was 147 times the average wage of their other employees (High Pay Centre, 2016). While many different factors affect CEO pay, we can conclude from this that the biggest companies believe that their leaders make a substantial contribution to the organization's success and it is worthwhile to pay them large salaries. The In the News activity illustrates how CEO leadership style is associated with high-profile organizational successes and failures.

 ## In the News: Volkswagen cheats emissions tests

Volkswagen hit the news in 2015 when it emerged that the company had programmed its diesel engines to meet emissions output limits during testing but not in normal driving. The reason for this discrepancy was that reducing emissions in these engines also caused reduced fuel efficiency, which would have discouraged potential purchasers from buying the vehicles.

CEO Martin Winterkorn claimed not to have known about the emissions cheating and in a video apology called it a 'terrible mistake by a few people' that should not detract from the hard work of the thousands of other employees at VW. However, some commentators have blamed his style of leadership as contributing to the scandal. He is reported to have been a perfectionist who would publicly criticize employees who did not meet his standards, leading to the suggestion that employees could have been motivated to hide things from him or even to believe it was acceptable to cheat as long as they met the overall goal (Dishman, 2015). VW stock dropped by a third and Winterkorn resigned a few days after the news broke. It has since emerged that many managers were complicit in the cheating (Hawranek, 2015) and the ongoing costs to VW are in the billions of dollars as it struggles to redress the problems and resolve claims from regulators in the USA, the EU and worldwide (*The Guardian*, 2016).

### For discussion

» To what extent do you think the cheating at VW could be blamed on Martin Winterkorn?
» It is fairly common for CEOs and other leaders to resign when a scandal of this proportion hits the headlines. Why do you think this is so?

When it comes to measuring leadership success, however, we need to look beyond how much the top leaders are paid. Three main elements emerge from the leadership literature as important in defining leadership success (Brodbeck, 2008):

1. The leader can influence others. This can be at the individual level by influencing people's behaviour, values and attitudes or at the group level by influencing group climate or norms.

2. The extent to which a leader affects aspects of individual and organizational performance. This could include employee job satisfaction, organizational turnover, quality and, ultimately, work and organizational performance.

3. How well recognized that leader is. This recognition comes from a leader's position in the organizational hierarchy as well as symbols of status such as a high income.

We should note, however, that these signs of a 'successful leader' are not all synonymous with an 'effective leader'. For example, people can acquire status symbols or be promoted up the organizational hierarchy by political influence rather than by demonstrating effective leadership of a department, just as an effective leader may be overlooked for promotion due to discrimination. Consideration also needs to be given to the timescale on which we measure these elements. For example, increasing organizational performance in the short term can be done at the expense of long-term *sustainability*.

In short, an effective leader is one who can influence other people towards the achievement of a goal (Robbins and Judge, 2007). That influence can come from many different sources and be enacted in different ways, as we will see in the rest of this chapter.

## Leadership or management?

The organizational behaviour literature helps us to differentiate between leadership and management.

Kotter (2001) summed up the distinction by suggesting that good leadership helps the organization cope with change and good management helps the organization cope with complexity. Both are important to organizational effectiveness and have similar tasks, but they achieve these tasks in different ways. Table 6.1 illustrates this distinction and the Applications activity explores the issue further.

Table 6.1 **The tasks of management and leadership**

| Task | Management: dealing with complexity | Leadership: dealing with change |
|---|---|---|
| Decide what needs to be done | Planning and budgeting | Setting a direction i.e. vision and strategy |
| Create networks to achieve these aims | Organizing and staffing | Aligning people with the vision |
| Ensure people do the job | Controlling and problem-solving | Motivating and inspiring people |

## Applications: Should all managers be leaders?

Leadership is such a popular and all-consuming topic in business studies that is easy to be convinced by the rhetoric that everyone should be a good leader. There are, of course, problems with this idea, not least of which is that if we are all leaders, there is no one to be a follower. If we consider the distinction between management and leadership outlined by Kotter, we can see that a successful organization needs both sets of skills.

» Think of a manager you have worked for. Using Table 6.1 to structure your analysis, to what extent do you think that person demonstrated leadership and/or management skills? Was this manager better at one set of skills than another? What kind of impact did that have on you and the rest of the work group?

» Do you think all managers should have leadership skills? Why or why not?

In this chapter we are focusing specifically on the leadership role and we turn now to look at models of leadership in detail.

## LEADERSHIP MODELS

There are many different ways of conceptualizing leadership and attempting to understand what makes leaders effective. We will start by considering what it is about individual leaders that makes them more or less likely to emerge as leaders and how personality and leadership style may influence effectiveness.

## Leader traits and behaviours

### Leadership traits

When we first think about leadership and what makes a good leader, we tend to focus on particular characteristics or personality traits they might have. Many of the early leadership studies tried to uncover precisely which qualities differentiated leaders from non-leaders. Unfortunately, this approach led to the identification of a wide range of variables, the majority of which differed from study to study (Geier, 1967). Order was brought to this confusion with the emergence of the Big

Five personality trait model (see Chapters 3 and 5 for further details of this model), which could be used as a framework for integrating all the different findings.

Reviews using the Big Five model have identified clear links between certain personality traits and leader emergence and effectiveness (Judge et al., 2002). These findings are summarized in Table 6.2.

Table 6.2 **Leadership traits**

| Big Five trait | Relationship to leadership |
| --- | --- |
| Extraversion | Leaders are likely to be confident, outgoing and assertive |
| Conscientiousness | Leaders are self-disciplined and reliable |
| Openness to experience | Leaders tend to be flexible and open to new solutions to problems |
| Emotional stability | Leaders are usually calm and do not get emotionally reactive |
| Agreeableness | While those who are more agreeable tend to go along with others in the group and thus are less likely to emerge as a leader, when in a leadership position, a more agreeable person is likely to be more effective |

The relationship of some of these traits with leadership shows variation across different situations. For example, agreeableness is more strongly related to leadership in student groups than organizational settings. This could be because student groups tend to be non-hierarchical and it is therefore more important for the leader of the group to rely on agreeableness to encourage other group members to follow their lead, whereas in work organizations, the leader is more likely to have some formal authority.

We saw in Chapter 5 that one of the ways to understand what motivates people is to consider the internal needs they are trying to fulfil. Taking on leadership roles is one way that people can meet some of these needs or motives. McClelland and Boyatzis (1982), for example, identified a pattern of motives that was associated with long-term (16-year) managerial success. This pattern included a low need for affiliation and, at lower levels of management, a high need for achievement. In addition, a high need for power, particularly in terms of wanting to enable followers' development, was important. So, it seems that people who are motivated to achieve goals and recognition and to exercise some control over others, but are not as concerned with building rewarding relationships, are more likely to seek out leadership roles.

While the **personality approach to leadership** can help us to identify what kinds of people may take on leadership roles and even give us some insight into their effectiveness, it tells us little about how those leaders behave. For that, we need to turn to behavioural theories.

## Leader behaviours

The **leader behaviour approach** was an attempt to identify the behaviours associated with leader success. Rather than viewing leadership ability as an inborn quality, it sought to describe the behaviours that leaders demonstrated, often with the hope that these behaviours could then be taught in leader development initiatives. The consensus from several different studies and a recent **meta-analysis** (Judge et al., 2004) is that there are two broad dimensions on which leader behaviours differ: the extent to which the leader is considerate of the people, or the extent to which the leader is focused on the task. Research groups at different institutions gave these dimensions different names but they share similar characteristics, as shown in Table 6.3.

The two dimensions are positively related to important organizational outcomes, such as job satisfaction, motivation, group-organization performance, with most of the relationships generally stronger for the consideration dimension. There is also some evidence that while employees are more *satisfied* with a considerate leader, they will *perform* better for a leader who is more focused on initiating structure (Judge et al., 2004).

One of the main criticisms of the trait and the behaviour approach was that they ignored the role of

Table 6.3 **Leadership behaviours**

| Naming conventions | Ohio State University | Consideration | Initiating structure |
|---|---|---|---|
| | University of Michigan | Employee-centred | Production-centred |
| | Harvard University | Person-oriented | Task-oriented |
| Example behaviours | | Supporting employees, listening to them, helping them solve problems, being friendly | Setting targets and monitoring performance, ensuring resources are available, planning |

context or situational factors in influencing a leader's effectiveness. So the next section moves on to the role of context.

## Leadership context

### Contingency theory

In the late 1960s, Fred Fiedler developed a model of leadership effectiveness based on a simple premise: that leaders would be more effective when their style matched the requirements of the situation. Because effectiveness is 'contingent' on the situation, rather than being inherent in a particular person or style, this approach is called *'contingency theory'*. Fiedler (1967) suggests that our leadership style is fairly fixed and stable and is oriented towards either task or relationship, similar to the behavioural approaches we looked at above.

One of the controversial elements of this theory is how leadership style is measured (Schneider, 1985). Fiedler used a questionnaire called the 'least preferred co-worker' (LPC) scale. The LPC asks respondents to rate the person they *work least well with* on 16 pairs of adjectives, such as efficient–inefficient, hostile–supportive, friendly–unfriendly. The theory holds that if you describe this least preferred co-worker in relatively positive terms even though you may not work well together, you have a relationship orientation. On the other hand, if you describe them in relatively negative terms, you are more focused on the task and productivity rather than positive relationships. Some authors have suggested that the scale does not measure task or relationship orientation at all, but instead *cognitive complexity* (Vecchio, 1979). They argue that a person who can recognize positive and negative points about a colleague is more cognitively complex than someone who rates the colleague solely in negative terms. There is also evidence that the LPC score can

change over time, which runs contrary to Fiedler's claim that leader style is fixed (Schriesheim et al., 1979).

However leader style is measured, the next element of the contingency theory of leadership is to identify the key variables in the situation that will influence how effective that style is. While measuring elements of the situation is difficult, Fiedler's theory focuses on three variables:

1. Leader–member relations: How confident followers are in their leader, how much they trust and respect their leader.

2. Task structure: How procedural or structured the task is.

3. Position power: How much influence a leader has over rewards and punishments, such as hiring, firing, salary and disciplinary measures such as formal warnings.

Contexts can be summarized as favourable (good leader–member relations, high task structure and strong position power) or unfavourable (low on all three variables).

Bringing leader style and situation favourability together, we see that effective leaders are those whose style matches the situation. Task-oriented leaders are more effective at the extremes of very favourable or very unfavourable situations, whereas relationship-oriented leaders are more effective in intermediate situations. There is good evidence to support the model (Strube and Garcia, 1981), despite the criticisms outlined above, and contingency theory is a welcome reminder to us to take account of the situation when evaluating leader effectiveness.

### Path–goal theory

An alternative approach to integrating the leader behaviour dimensions with situational complexity is

**path–goal theory** (House, 1996). This theory views leadership as essentially motivational, and effective leaders as those who clarify the path or route an employee needs to take in order to achieve goals, adapting their styles to complement the situation and the employee characteristics.

Getty Images/iStockphoto/pawel_p

*Are leaders like sat navs for their employees?*

It is a fairly complex theory in that it delineates four types of leader behaviours – directive, supportive, participative and achievement-oriented – with three environmental variables – task structure, formal authority and work group autonomy – and three personal factors specific to each follower – experience, ability and locus of control, that is, the extent to which followers believe they are in control of their own lives – that will influence how effective the leader is. Table 6.4 gives examples to illustrate some of these interactions.

Subsequent developments of the theory have defined these leader behaviours differently. For example, directive behaviours were broken into path-goal clarifying (clarifying goals and the means of achieving them) and work facilitation (planning, scheduling, organizing) behaviours, while participative

behaviours included facilitating interaction and using group-oriented decision processes (House, 1996). The complexity of the theory is the main barrier to its widespread use, although it is possible to use it as a framework for improving your own practice, as shown in the Applications activity. While there is good evidence for some of the propositions, research is a long way from supporting all of it (Schriesheim and Neider, 1996).

## Leaders and followers

Path-goal and contingency theory both recognize the importance of the followers in a leader's effectiveness, but they tend to view followers as elements of the situation. The 'effective' leader is one who will adapt their style to suit these situational

Table 6.4 **Examples of path–goal theory**

| Leader style | Aim | Specific leader behaviours | Best suited to |
|---|---|---|---|
| Directive | Reduce role ambiguity, clarify perceptions of how effort will result in performance and how performance is linked to rewards | Scheduling work, giving specific guidance, clarifying policies | Situations where task roles are ambiguous or employees highly experienced/capable |
| Supportive | Satisfy followers' needs and preferences, decrease stress | Displaying concern for welfare, creating supportive work environment, being friendly | Situations with structured tasks, especially where tasks are emotionally or physically distressing |
| Participative | Encourage followers to contribute to decision-making, facilitate communication | Consulting with subordinates, involving them in setting goals | Employees with an internal locus of control undertaking tasks with a high level of interdependence |
| Achievement-oriented | Encourage excellent performance and individual pride in work | Setting challenging goals, showing confidence in followers' ability, seeking improvement | Employees who have high achievement motivation in tasks requiring personal competence |

## Applications: **Leading in a new context**

Mohammed was a successful sales manager in a catering company for five years, leading his team of 8 sales reps to increased performance every year and greatly expanding his organization's share of the local catering market. However, as his company was fairly small and there was no further opportunity for career development there, he has recently moved to a new post at an IT company. Here, he is leading a team of 20 sales reps and faces competition at the national rather than just the local level. The sales reps in this team are used to having a substantial amount of autonomy in how they conduct their work and from his first few days in the job, Mohammed has realized that many of them are also quite competitive with each other. However, he is already wondering if the team could perform better if they cooperated more rather than being so individualistic.

» To what extent will Mohammed's previous experience as a sales manager be of use in this new industry and new team?

» What challenges do you think Mohammed will face in his first few months in the new job? Using insights from contingency theory and path-goal theory, what would you recommend he focuses on first?

elements, whether that be the followers' experience or their trust and confidence in the leader. However, followers have a more active role to play in leader effectiveness, as the two theories we consider in this section will show. Followers and leaders build up complex and dynamic relationships.

## Leader–member exchange theory

The **leader–member exchange (LMX)** theory of leadership suggests that we can understand more about the dynamics of these leader–follower relationships by viewing followers in terms of a leader's *ingroup* and *outgroup* (Dansereau et al., 1975). LMX focuses on the quality of exchange that followers have with their leaders:

- **High LMX:** a high quality of leader–member exchange is characteristic of those followers in the ingroup. The leader trusts these members more, spends more time with them and gives them special privileges or extra support. Members in this group have greater loyalty to the leader and put in more effort to their work.

- **Low LMX:** a low quality of exchange between the leader and members is characteristic of followers in the outgroup. The relationship between leader and members here is much more formal. Followers in this group are given less attention and fewer rewards and rarely go beyond the formal work expectations.

A meta-analysis of LMX research found that good quality of exchange with the leader (high LMX) is associated with increased performance and satisfaction with the job as well as increased commitment and lower turnover intentions (Gerstner and Day, 1997). In addition, followers with high LMX feel empowered and the relationship with the leader is more two-way, with followers able to influence the leader as well (Schriesheim et al., 2001).

It is perhaps no surprise that a better quality of relationship with the leader should have such positive outcomes, but this leads us to consider how those relationships develop. Initially, it was thought that personality similarity was an important factor in determining whether a follower was in a leader's ingroup or outgroup (Gerstner and Day, 1997), because the leader would be attracted to people more like themselves. But there is growing evidence that some dissimilarity in personality may be more important (Oren et al., 2012), which is perhaps a good sign for the development of diversity in groups.

The importance of LMX has been found to vary, depending on the national culture of the followers. In a review of over 250 studies across 23 countries, Rockstuhl et al. (2012) compared LMX outcomes for two broad culture types: those that are individualistic and have a low power distance, where people see themselves as independent and of equal status to others, such as Australia, the USA and the UK; and those that are collectivist and have a high power distance, where people see themselves as interdependent and respect authority, such as China, India and Portugal. Although LMX was positively associated with outcomes such as job satisfaction and leader trust in both cultures, the relationships were weaker in the latter countries. This implies that although building good leader–member relationships is important in both types of culture, leaders in more collectivist/high power distance cultures can also draw on their role-based authority and their followers' loyalty and deference in achieving positive organizational outcomes.

Because it is a dynamic relationship, LMX quality develops over time. When the leader–follower relationship first starts, the relationship is based on formal contractual arrangements and immediate reciprocity. As it develops, there is increased social exchange and sharing of information and resources until the relationship can reach a mature stage where there is trust and respect as well as longer term exchange (Graen and Uhl-Bien, 1995). This relationship is the responsibility of the leader and the follower to develop, which highlights one of the important contributions of LMX theory: that leadership is based on a mutual relationship between leaders and followers rather than being something inherent in the leader.

## Implicit leadership theory

This role of the followers in co-determining a leader's effectiveness is highlighted further in **implicit leadership theory**. Developed by Lord and Maher (1991), this approach notes that our perceptions are often influenced by preconceived notions and stereotypes and so our judgements about a leader's effectiveness will be too. A 'schema' is an unconscious (or *implicit*) representation of what a leader should be like: the more closely a leader matches this implicit picture, the more effective we will perceive them to be. This theory helps to explain not only why some leaders can be seen as less effective than others even when they may objectively have achieved very similar outcomes, but also some of the ways discrimination may occur in promotion to leadership positions in organizations.

We can see this in action by looking at the prejudice against women in leadership that has been and still is a widespread problem worldwide. One of the issues that women face in leadership is that they are caught between two stereotypes. First, one of the basic elements of many people's leadership schemas is that leadership is inherently a masculine attribute and, second, many of the behaviours associated with leadership, such as being assertive and confident, are viewed as more appropriate for men than women (Eagly and Karau, 2002). This means that a woman's leadership potential is not only less likely to be recognized in the first place, but many of the behaviours she would have to demonstrate for effective leadership would be viewed less favourably in her than they would in a man. There is evidence that these views are slowly changing (Newport, 2011) and also mounting evidence of the effectiveness of female leaders (Eagly et al., 2003), but there is still a way to go before many people's judgements of a leader's effectiveness are unaffected by whether the leader is male or female.

*Getty Images/Hero Images*

*Prejudice against women in leadership positions is still a widespread problem.*

The implicit leadership model is also useful for understanding cultural differences in leader effectiveness. The GLOBE (Global Leadership and Organizational Behavior Effectiveness) project surveyed 17,300 middle managers in 951 organizations around the world, assessing how their cultural values impacted on their views of leadership (House et al., 2004). Managers rated leadership attributes in terms of how much they *contribute to* or *inhibit* outstanding leadership. The results showed that many attributes were universally recognized as positive, such as dynamic, encouraging, dependable, and a few were universally considered to be negative, such as irritable, dictatorial, asocial. But the majority of the attributes were culturally contingent, that is, they were seen as positive in some cultures and negative in others: sensitive, cunning, class-conscious and sincere. For example, being cunning was viewed positively in Columbia but negatively in Switzerland.

All these attributes were combined into six broad dimensions describing leadership around the world:

1. Charismatic/value-based leadership: the ability to inspire, motivate and expect high performance from others, based on firmly held values

2. Team-oriented leadership: effective team-building and developing a common purpose among team members

3. Participative leadership: degree to which the leader involves others in decision-making

4. Humane-oriented leadership: supportive, considerate and compassionate leadership

5. **Self-protective leadership:** ensuring the safety and status of the individual or group member; includes such attributes as face saving, status conscious and conflict inducer

6. **Autonomous leadership:** individualistic and independent leadership.

The charismatic dimension was seen as contributing to effective leadership across all cultures, and team-oriented and participative leadership were viewed positively by most cultures. In contrast, the self-protective and autonomous dimensions were seen as negative in some cultures but neutral in others. Countries with similar cultural values had similar leadership concepts, for example Germanic countries like Austria and Germany saw autonomous leaders as more effective than Latin European countries like Portugal and Italy (Brodbeck et al., 2000). This finding sounds a word of caution for us. Most of the leadership theories and research reviewed in this chapter have emerged from the USA and may therefore reflect the unique values of American leadership: while perhaps being applicable to similar cultures, these theories may well become less and less applicable to cultures with very different values.

Implicit leadership theory shows us that a mismatch between a leader's behaviours and the followers' expectations is likely to result in performance losses or misunderstandings (House et al., 2004). Organizations and individuals need to develop cultural flexibility if they are going to have effective international leadership, identifying and developing the leader behaviours that are universally perceived as contributing to effectiveness (like the charismatic dimension) as well as those attributes specific to different countries in question. It is clear that the implicit schemas we have about leaders can influence not only how we view individuals but also the kind of advice we might give on 'good leadership' to others. The Web Explorer activity explores this issue in more detail.

 **Web Explorer: How to be a good leader**

Do an internet search for 'How to be a good leader' and identify five results you would like to explore in more detail. Here are some suggested sites:

- www.notredameonline.com/resources/leadership-and-management/what-makes-an-effective-leader

- www.forbes.com/sites/tanyaprive/2012/12/19/top-10-qualities-that-make-a-great-leader

- www.ted.com/talks/roselinde_torres_what_it_takes_to_be_a_great_leader

» Taking each of them in turn, analyse the suggestions that are made and see if you can identify what kind of underlying leadership model(s) the author is drawing on.

» Do any of the articles or videos provide evidence or support for their suggestions? If not, where do you think the author is getting the ideas? What does this tell us about their implicit leader schema?

When you have finished this chapter, you could write your own blog post or make a vlog with the title 'How to be a good leader'. See if you can provide a simple, practical guide that still has good evidence to support your recommendations.

## Leadership in action

Because leadership is such an important issue for organizations, a wealth of theories and models have been developed to help us try to understand the key elements of effective leadership. We have seen how we can use some of these theories to identify effective leader traits and behaviours, how the leader needs to adapt to the situation, and the pivotal role of followers. But in terms of practical applicability, there are a couple of more recent developments that can help managers and HR practitioners to gain an understanding of leadership in action in organizations. One of these is the distinction between **transformational** and **transactional leadership** (Bass, 1985).

## Transactional and transformational leadership

Leadership that is based on a transaction between the leader and followers is fairly widespread and could be seen as the most basic type of leadership in organizations. Transactional leaders reward their followers' good performance and punish their poor performance. In contrast to this focus on task and behavioural exchange, transformational leadership engages the emotions of followers. Table 6.5 illustrates the differences between the three forms of transactional leadership and transformational leadership.

Table 6.5 **Transactional and transformational leadership compared**

| Form of leadership | Definition | Organizational outcomes |
|---|---|---|
| Transactional: contingent reward | Leader clarifies expectations and recognizes followers' achievements. A constructive approach where the leader creates exchanges (or transactions) that encourage followers to reach high levels of performance | Positive impact on subordinates' commitment, satisfaction and performance |
| Transactional: active management by exception | Leader closely monitors followers' performance and only intervenes when followers do not reach the required performance levels. At this point, the leader will take corrective action in an attempt to improve performance again | Less effective than the contingent reward approach |
| Transactional: passive management by exception | Leaders do not provide clarity on what is expected of their followers but wait for problems to arise before taking action. At the extreme (called 'laissez-faire'), leaders may not even take action when there *are* problems | Least effective of all the approaches. Laissez-faire approach even has negative impact on organizational outcomes |
| Transformational | 1. Idealized influence: Leaders appear to put followers' needs first, take a share in the risks and demonstrate consistency between conduct and principles. Followers admire, trust, respect and identify with their leader 2. Inspirational motivation: Leaders give their followers a vision, providing a meaning to their work and a challenge to work towards. They also demonstrate enthusiasm and optimism, convincing their followers that the vision is attainable 3. Intellectual stimulation: Leaders actively solicit new and creative ideas from their followers, questioning assumptions and reframing problems to encourage innovation. They do not engage in public criticism of followers' mistakes 4. Individualized consideration: Leaders act as coaches or mentors, paying attention to their followers' individual needs and helping them to reach their potential. They encourage personal development and create a supportive climate | Largest effects on organizational outcomes such as performance and satisfaction. In addition, it is seen to be particularly well suited to the constantly changing modern workplace, as it helps followers to engage with and make sense of the changes |

Source: Based on Bass, B. M. (1999) 'Two decades of research and development in transformational leadership', *European Journal of Work and Organizational Psychology*, 8(1), pp. 9–32; Judge, T. A. and Piccolo, R. F. (2004) 'Transformational and transactional leadership: a meta-analytic test of their relative validity', *Journal of Applied Psychology*, 89(5), pp. 755–68; Avolio, B. J., Bass, B. M. and Jung, D. I. (1999) 'Re-examining the components of transformational and transactional leadership using the Multifactor Leadership Questionnaire', *Journal of Occupational and Organizational Psychology*, 72(4), pp. 441–62.

Meta-analysis has shown that transformational leadership is the most effective type of leadership, but also that it is closely related to contingent reward transactional leadership (Judge and Piccolo, 2004). Research certainly demonstrates a positive, cross-cultural impact of transformational leadership on organizational outcomes. Wang et al. (2011) showed that transformational leadership is associated with higher individual, team and organizational performance. It is particularly effective in increasing extra voluntary effort, although, interestingly, contingent reward seems more effective at increasing specific, task-based performance. Bass (1999) has suggested that contingent reward can provide the basis for the development of a more transformational style: providing clarity and rewards helps to build the trust that is necessary for transformational leadership.

## Charismatic leadership

'Charisma' is defined by the *Oxford English Dictionary* as 'compelling attractiveness or charm that can inspire devotion in others'. It has been the subject of research and theory in leadership because charismatic leaders are so successful at influencing their followers. Charismatic leadership is highly valued by organizations: CEOs demonstrating charismatic traits are more likely to be appointed and receive higher compensation packages. However, the evidence to support this value is not so clear. While charismatic CEOs seem to enhance stock prices in uncertain markets, their firms did not perform any better than those headed by less charismatic CEOs (Tosi et al., 2004).

For many researchers, charismatic is simply another word for transformational leadership but some (e.g. Judge et al., 2006) have pointed out that charisma is a personal quality, which is displayed in an expressive communication style. Certainly, some of the elements of a charismatic leadership style show similarities with the definition of transformational, such as a personal identification with leaders and their mission. But perhaps the difference lies in how charismatic leaders are viewed by others, in that they are seen as exceptionally gifted (Trice and Beyer, 1986). This highlights the role of **attributions** that implicit leadership theory raised our awareness of: charisma is at least partially an attribution that followers make.

In fact, Brodbeck (2008) has suggested that the transformational/charismatic leadership concept provides a useful model for integrating the trait, behavioural, context and attributional approaches to

leadership we have looked at in this chapter. It shows us that leadership is a process that is partly determined by the leader's traits and partly by behaviours and skills that can be developed. In addition, the model takes account of context by identifying situations where transformational leadership is more or less effective. The transactional/transformational distinction also integrates the ideas of LMX theory: a leader–member relationship that begins with the transactional type of social exchange can develop into the more effective, high LMX relationship that characterizes transformational leadership (Graen and Uhl-Bien, 1995). Finally, the transformational approach gives a central place to the role of followers' emotional responses. In this model, effective leaders encourage and motivate staff, tapping into their emotional energy to influence them rather than using transactional rewards and punishments.

## Limitations

These leadership theories, which distinguish transactional, transformational and charismatic leadership, all recognize the importance of employees' extra discretionary effort. They go beyond the 'management' of employees to reach acceptable performance levels to focus on how workers may be inspired and led to greater heights: whether that is higher performance levels, prosocial behaviour at work, creative contributions or better well-being (Hannah et al., 2014).

Hannah et al. go on to note that these theories have a few common limitations, but also that we can take some straightforward steps to reduce the impact of these limitations. First, these newer theories of leadership seem to have moved from describing types of *leadership* to types of *leaders*. They often envision a 'super leader' who is detached from normal everyday demands. Although they started as behavioural theories, describing how frequently leaders displayed certain behaviours, they are too often used to describe a type of person. This person is expected to be transformational or charismatic all the time. We can overcome this problem by using the leader behaviour descriptions in a more nuanced way. For example, instead of claiming that we need 'transformational leaders', we should say that organizations can benefit from more transformational leadership *behaviours*. This is a small adjustment but it helps to emphasize that organizations can develop these behaviours in many people, rather than expecting them to be displayed by a single 'super leader'.

The second limitation of these theories is that they often ignore the more functional demands of leadership, that is, they imply that 'leaders' never do any 'management' and that the leader's role is purely ideological. At the beginning of this chapter, we considered the difference between leadership and management and that it is rare to have one without the other; we can reduce this limitation by recognizing that leadership occurs within the context of management roles or functions, and keep working on finding the synergies between leadership and management rather than attempting to separate them out.

A third criticism of these theories concerns the extent to which they often seem to focus on describing how much followers 'like' their leader. While these theories all recognize that our emotional response to leaders is certainly an important element of leadership, we need to remain aware that they also do much more: 'liking' does not explain the whole range of organizational outcomes associated with these kinds of leadership. There are many positive outcomes, such as increased task performance and discretionary effort, which cannot be explained away just by how much followers like their leader.

Finally, there is the issue of how charismatic or transformational leadership theories often have an assumption that the leader is inherently moral. We explore this further in the Weighing the Evidence box.

---

 Weighing the Evidence: **Leadership is inherently moral**

In their critique of leadership theories, Hannah et al. (2014, p. 604) suggested that 'morality is an inherent component of leadership'. They argue that while leadership involves influence, 'leadership' is the term we should use for influence over other people that is *positive and socially acceptable*. Any other influence, especially where it involves manipulation, coercion or other negative behaviours, should not be referred to as leadership and has no place in the study of leadership. This may seem an unusual statement to make, for we can all think of examples of leaders of countries and organizations who definitely do not behave in an ethical way. Yet it is a common and underlying assumption in a lot of the leadership literature, that effective leaders are necessarily ethically 'good' as well. In addition, the newer leadership theories are all overwhelmingly positive: transformational, charismatic and **authentic leadership**, for example, all emphasize a caring and considerate approach to employees and tend to assume that the leader is acting from an ethically positive framework. Indeed, the concept of authentic leadership explicitly includes ethics in its definition: authentic leaders have a high level of self-awareness and act in line with their values (Walumbwa et al., 2008), which are assumed to be ethically sound. There is certainly good evidence that ethical leadership is associated with positive organizational outcomes, such as job satisfaction and extra effort (Brown and Mitchell, 2010).

In fact, this assumption that leadership is inherently ethical is so well rooted that negative behaviours are often not labelled *leader* behaviours at all, but *supervisory* behaviours, as if there is a clear distinction in the concepts. For example, Tepper (2007) reviews hostile behaviours that managers use against their direct reports and suggests that this literature complements the research on leadership behaviours that promote positive outcomes, rather than being part of the same leadership concept.

Why is this, when we have evidence every week in the news that there are very successful business leaders who are behaving in ways that most people would consider ethically suspect at the very least? Part of the answer comes from the approach that many leadership researchers take, which is attempting to describe not just how leadership *is done* in organizations but also what leadership *should* be like. By promoting a view of leadership as inherently ethical, we might hope to encourage future leaders to strive to be more ethical in their dealings with employees and their decision-making. Leaders do not just make ethical decisions about their own work, but have a role in promoting ethical or unethical behaviour in their organizations: what they value and reward becomes what the employees will strive towards (Brown and Mitchell, 2010).

The evidence certainly demonstrates a positive effect of ethical leadership behaviour, but it also demonstrates that many people in leadership positions behave unethically. And this cannot simply be dismissed as 'non-leadership' behaviour. A balanced understanding of leadership, as it is enacted in the workplace, requires us to address ethical and unethical behaviours.

## Substitutes for leadership

All the leadership theories we have reviewed here share a basic assumption. While they may disagree on the best leadership style or the type of person who makes an effective leader, they all assume that some kind of leadership is always needed. A very different approach was put forward by Kerr and Jermier (1978), who suggested that certain task, individual or organizational variables could 'substitute' for leadership. They described a range of these variables in terms of whether they would enhance, neutralize or substitute for relationship- or task-oriented leader behaviours. For example, where a task is unambiguous or routine, there is no need for a leader to provide task structure, while a need for independence on the part of the subordinate will tend to negate any efforts of the leader to provide support or facilitate interaction. Cohesive work groups can substitute for task- and relationship-oriented leadership.

Kerr and Jermier suggest that effective leadership is about providing the guidance or support to employees that they do not receive from other organizational structures. This was tested in a longitudinal study by Keller (2006) in R&D departments, which compared leadership substitutes to transformational leadership and an initiating structure leadership style. Keller found that the substitutes of *subordinates' ability* and an *intrinsically satisfying task* predicted technical quality and profitability, while *ability* also predicted speed to market. He did note, however, that the 'substitutes' acted more like additives to rather than replacements for the other leadership attributes.

Howell et al. (1990) suggest that leadership substitutes can be used to solve organizational problems, distinguishing between actions that serve to enhance or neutralize a leader's influence and those which can substitute for a leader. For example, if a competent leader is being resisted, either actively or passively, the organization can enhance the leader's influence by giving the leader greater control of rewards or substitute for the leader by developing collegiate decision-making systems.

## LEADERSHIP AND HRM

In this section we move on from our discussion of leadership theories to consider some of the ways that leadership in the organization interacts with the HR function and roles. We start by discussing alternate ways to view the relationship between leadership and HRM, before moving on to the complexities of how line manager leadership style may influence the implementation of HR practices. Finally, we examine issues around leadership development, a function that HR is often closely involved in. As we go through this section, take some time to consider how the assumptions people have about what leadership *is* influence how they view the interaction between HRM and leadership. For example, are leadership development programmes aimed at developing leader behaviours in any employee or are they based on an assumption that only certain people are suited to leadership?

## HRM as a vehicle for leadership implementation

There are two different ways of viewing the relationship between organizational leadership and HRM, which depend on how we view each of the concepts (Zhu et al., 2005). If we view HRM narrowly as the organizational administrative system, we might expect that the forms of leadership which engage followers' emotions and inspire them with a vision would have their effects outside this HRM system. However, as we have seen throughout this book, the understanding of HRM we are proposing here is much broader than simply the administration of personnel-related matters. HRM at its best makes a strategic contribution to the organization and aims to develop an engaged and motivated workforce. In this case, we would expect that HRM will have a close relationship with leadership style in affecting organizational outcomes such as performance or absenteeism.

In fact, research on 170 companies in Singapore, which included a substantial number of companies from the USA and Western Europe, has demonstrated that HRM practices mediate the positive effect of transformational leadership on organizational outcomes (Zhu et al., 2005). That is, transformational leadership can have greater positive effects where HRM practices are supportive and effective, but its impact is lessened when HRM processes are inferior. Zhu et al. suggest that this occurs because:

- HR processes help to communicate the leader's vision to employees.

- HRM practitioners can develop effective structuring of the organization and individual jobs in order to empower employees to achieve the leader's vision.

- Transformational leaders could be expected to encourage HRM practices that motivate their followers and provide resources for their development.

Support for this latter proposition may be found in a national survey of Dutch public sector employees, which demonstrated that the transformational leadership style was associated with better developed HRM in the organization (Vermeeren et al., 2014). In this study, the increased use of HR practices also improved employees' job satisfaction and, ultimately, the organization's performance.

As organizations change and increasingly recognize the need for sustainability, the approach to leadership may well need to change too. Waite (2013) notes the difference between leading for innovation and leading for sustainability (we consider sustainability in more detail in Chapter 12). While the former is traditionally focused on delivering new products and services for short-term profit, the latter has broad, long-term aims in the socioeconomic

and environmental arenas. A sustainable approach necessitates nurturing leadership at all levels of the organization so that it can drive innovation and creativity in the longer term. Waite suggests that this can be best achieved by balancing high-performance practices with a concern for employees, their families and communities, something that an organization's HR function can certainly contribute to.

## Leadership and HR implementation

A second issue to consider in this discussion is how the leadership style of different managers might impact on the implementation of organizational-level HRM policies and practices. It would be easy to assume that once the HR function has developed a particular policy, it is then implemented consistently throughout the organization. Indeed, when evaluating the effectiveness of a practice or policy, this assumption is often made. However, because many HR practices are devolved or delegated to line managers, differences in implementation are very likely to arise. The Applications activity explores this problem.

## Applications: **Managing leaders**

Amina is the HR manager of a company that has recently reorganized its performance appraisal process. The previous process was conducted annually, with the appraiser and appraisee together completing the form, which identified good practice and areas for development from the past year and set goals for the following year. But this process was followed rather haphazardly in the company and Amina strongly believes that more frequent feedback is far more helpful to staff members than an annual review. She knows from her studies that effective leaders provide their followers with clear direction and good feedback on their performance, as well as encouraging them to develop, and thinks that the appraisal system should help to support this. She wants the organization to move towards more regular appraisals, which can provide faster feedback to employees and help to identify training needs in a more timely fashion.

After considering various options, Amina decides to bring in a simple software solution, which will allow appraisers and appraisees to complete a brief form monthly via an online interface. It keeps a record of feedback and goals and will send automatic reminders to managers and their staff when it is time to complete the form. It also links to the organization's training provisions so that appraisees and appraisers can book onto courses directly when they identify a particular need for further training.

» What issues will Amina need to consider in implementing this process?

» Is there likely to be any resistance to this change? How should Amina take the lead in order to ensure success of the project?

Research has shown that line managers' leadership style has a substantial impact on the implementation of HR practices in their own work group. Those

managers with a more transformational style were found to implement more commitment-oriented HR practices, such as providing opportunities for training and development, linking rewards to good performance and allowing autonomy in work (Vermeeren, 2014). As well as this, employees' perceptions of how these HR practices were implemented mediated the effect of those practices on the work group's performance. The wide variation in how organizational HR practices were implemented in these different work groups emphasizes the need for HR practitioners to focus on the consistent implementation of systems rather than simply effective design. This could well be through the development of individual line managers or the modification of systems to suit individual leadership styles.

## Leader(ship) development

Day (2001) distinguishes between 'leader development', that is, development activities focused on an individual's knowledge, skills and abilities for a specific leadership role, and 'leadership development', that is, building interpersonal competence. The first is personal development for the leader, focused on self-awareness, self-regulation and motivation, whereas the second aims to develop a person's interpersonal skills and awareness. However, as we noted above, leadership research has a tendency to try and study leaders and leadership somewhat isolated from their context. Practically speaking, both intra- and interpersonal skills are important for effective leadership, so we will consider both approaches simultaneously. In fact, Day suggests that the best approach is to link leader and leadership development so that an organization develops its human *and* social capital, that is, individual knowledge and skills and the interpersonal connections and trust to make best use of them.

One of the largest implications of our leadership theories is the extent to which we believe that leadership can be developed or whether it is an inborn capacity. A review of leadership interventions, that is, ways in which researchers have attempted to improve or enhance leadership, has shown that they do indeed have a positive impact on outcomes, including organizational performance and behavioural change (Avolio et al., 2009). In addition, well-developed interventions can provide a 200% return on investment. But a word of caution here: less well-designed interventions can result in a loss of investment, particularly at the higher levels of the organization where the costs involved are greater.

Getty Images/Compassionate Eye Foundation/Dan Kenyon

*Coaching or mentoring initiatives can help to build leadership capacity.*

Too often, leadership development programmes attempt to 'teach' leadership by providing theoretical models in a classroom setting (Hannah et al., 2014). But if leadership theories show us anything, it is that leadership is a complex skill set that is enacted in a dynamic environment of interpersonal relationships. This has led leadership researchers (e.g. Day, 2001) to recommend that we adopt a *practice context* approach by integrating leadership development into the everyday context. In this approach, more senior leaders provide mentoring and guidance, as well as support for developing leaders by taking supervisory responsibility for any mistakes learners may make: 'In the practice context, leaders develop in the same way that an aspiring doctor does a surgical residency rotation; both expectations and stakes are high, but mistakes are also expected and learnt from' (Hannah et al., 2014, p. 614).

## Specific development activities

We will consider training and development in more detail in Chapter 10, so here we provide just a brief discussion of the different development initiatives and activities used specifically to help organizations develop leadership capacity. These include:

- **360-degree feedback:** employee receives feedback from subordinates, superiors, peers and sometimes clients. Provides a basis for behavioural change through improved self-knowledge.

- **Coaching:** one-to-one learning that is goal-focused and practical. This can help with behavioural change and career development.

- **Mentoring:** a developmental relationship with a more senior manager. Provides guidance on learning from mistakes (or avoiding them) as well as opportunities for career advancement.

- **Networks:** building relationships with peers in other functions or organizations. Can provide insights into alternative ways to solve problems.

- **Job assignments:** assignments in different roles or functions. Provide a broader understanding of the business and the development of individual skills.

- **Action learning:** learning on specific projects. Encourages teamwork skills and develops the ability to implement strategy.

The Transferrable Skills activity guides you through a process of developing your own leadership skills using some of these approaches.

---

 ## Transferrable Skills: **Leading a group**

This chapter shows us that leadership is a complex skill set, which involves managing relationships and influencing people to work together towards a goal. In this activity, we focus on two key areas, clarifying goals and engaging your followers, and look at how you can make use of continuous reflective practice, mentoring and feedback in order to develop your skills.

To carry out this activity, you need to identify a specific project that you can take the lead on. This could be a group project in your university work, a work assignment, organizing an event or taking the lead in a team sport. Whatever you choose, try to identify a specific, time-limited event or project that will have clear performance criteria so that you will be able to benchmark your progress. The two main skills to focus on are:

**Skill 1: Articulate the goal.** Leadership is all about influencing people to work together towards a goal. So, the first step in developing your leadership skills is being able to clearly articulate what that

goal is. You will need to express this goal in a way that makes sense to your followers, shows them how it will benefit them and what their potential contribution could be.

**Skill 2: Engage your followers.** Having a clear goal is not enough on its own. You also need to be able to encourage your followers to work towards it. Working in student or peer groups is a great opportunity to practise this as you do not have any formal authority to fall back on: you have to rely solely on your powers of persuasion and ability to get people on board with your vision. Participative leadership is an ideal way to do this. It involves getting your followers involved with decision-making and encouraging them to take part in crafting the strategy and milestones that will help to measure the progress.

**Mentoring**

As we have seen, one of the best ways to learn leadership is to have a mentor who can provide you with one-to-one support and feedback. To that end, take some time to identify someone in your network whose leadership ability you respect and would like to learn from. It could be a family member, a manager or even a peer who has more leadership experience than you. Ask them if they would be willing to spend some time with you to discuss how you can approach this leadership activity and to provide some structured support as you progress through it.

## Continuous reflective practice

At the beginning of the project, take some time to consider the two main skills and how you will try to practise them in this leadership opportunity. Discuss your plans with your mentor. Depending on how long the project continues, you may also find it helpful to review your progress and development in these two areas at regular intervals. Keeping a log of your reflections is a useful way to keep track of your development and to specify goals for the next team or individual meeting.

## Using feedback

When the project has reached an end, it is time to reflect on what you have learnt as well as your strengths and weaknesses in leading a group. To make the most of this opportunity, you will also need to be open to constructive feedback. The more active a role you take in gathering and using feedback, the faster you will learn and the more quickly you will develop your skills. To help you with this, here are some questions you could ask, which are organized around the two main skills

we are focusing on. Hess (2007) recommended using questions like these as a basis for enhancing leadership development. You can use the questions to guide your own reflections on your performance, your discussions with your mentor and as a basis for gathering feedback from your followers.

### Skill 1: Articulate the goal

To what extent did I provide a clear overview of the project's goals and how did I develop that into specific objectives?

Did I demonstrate an appropriate level of decisiveness and delegate tasks effectively?

How did I ensure completion of a quality project by the deadline?

### Skill 2: Engage your followers

Did I manage to create an environment in which team members felt able to communicate openly and listen properly to each other?

Did I involve everyone and provide plenty of encouragement?

Was I open to other people's ideas?

How did I manage conflict in the team?

At the end of the activity, develop a simple summary of what you have learnt. Identify three things you did well through the course of the leadership task as well as three things that did not go as well. Put together a brief development plan that will enable you to use your strengths even further, as well as develop the areas of weakness. And remember, leadership is like other skills: the more you practise, the better you'll become.

---

Unfortunately, although they are widespread, there is little evidence of the comparative effectiveness of these activities. It seems likely that the precise method adopted is perhaps less important than consistent implementation (Day, 2001) and that they will be most effective when implemented throughout the organization rather than focused at the top levels. HRM has a role here in ensuring that there is commitment and resource available to support the chosen programmes. Insofar as leadership is built on the organization's social capital – trust and positive interpersonal relationships – development of this capital at all levels will promote more effective leadership.

There is, however, another angle to leadership development activities beyond the development of specific skills or competencies. Khoreva (2016) suggests that employees may see these activities

as signs that the organization is investing in them, is committed to them and is providing future opportunities. Employees will feel a need to reciprocate on this investment: a kind of social exchange that results in employees feeling more committed to the organization. In her study, Khoreva found that high-potential employees who engaged in leadership development programmes were not only more committed, but were more likely to accept increased performance demands and build their competencies. In addition, participation in these programmes leads to increased engagement with the organization (Khoreva and van Zalk, 2016). In evaluating leadership development activities, therefore, HR professionals need to keep an eye on these less obvious effects as well as the specific leadership competencies.

## Practice Insights: Claudia Nario

Claudia Nario is a consultant who works with the Center for Creative Leadership, Brussels. Originally from Chile, where she worked as an independent consultant and an HR executive in a large airline, Claudia is now based in Barcelona and travels around Europe conducting leadership development programmes. In the video she talks about what makes a good leader and her essential ingredients for developing leaders.

Go online to www.macmillanihe.com/sutton-people to access the interview with Claudia.

## SUMMARY

We started this chapter by evaluating the role of leadership in organizational success, looking at what makes a leader 'effective'. By reviewing the different models of leadership, we drew out the contributions of leader traits and behaviours as well as the role of the situation in determining how effective a leader is. We have seen that leaders exercise their influence through their relationships with their followers, and cross-cultural work on leadership has highlighted the influence that followers' perceptions can have on this relationship.

While the newer theories of leadership identify the attributes of transformational and charismatic leaders and have demonstrated their link with follower and organizational performance, we have seen that they are not without their criticisms either and that some authors have suggested we can effectively 'substitute' for leadership by developing specific organizational structures. We rounded off the chapter by considering the relationship of HRM with organizational leadership and how leaders can be developed.

## FURTHER READING

• For a detailed review of the strengths and weaknesses of different leadership development programmes, see Day, D. V. (2001) 'Leadership development: a review in context', *Leadership Quarterly*, 11(4), pp. 581–613.

• For more information on how to maximize learning from student leadership development activities, see Hess, P. W. (2007) 'Enhancing leadership skill development by creating practice/feedback opportunities in the classroom', *Journal of Management Education*, 31(2), pp. 195–213.

## REVIEW QUESTIONS

1. What aspects of the leader's situation will influence their effectiveness?

2. Why is transformational leadership considered so effective?

3. Are some people simply better suited to leadership or can anyone be developed into a leadership role?

## ONLINE RESOURCES

Go online to www.macmillanihe.com/sutton-people to access a MCQ quiz for this chapter and for further resources to support your learning.

## REFERENCES

Avolio, B. J., Reichard, R. J., Hannah, S. T. et al. (2009) 'A meta-analytic review of leadership impact research: experimental and quasi-experimental studies', *Leadership Quarterly*, 20(5), pp. 764–84. doi: 10.1016/j.leaqua.2009.06.006.

Bass, B. M. (1985) *Leadership and Performance Beyond Expectations*. New York: Free Press.

Bass, B. M. (1999) 'Two decades of research and development in transformational leadership', *European Journal of Work and Organizational Psychology*, 8(1), pp. 9–32.

Brodbeck, F. (2008) 'Leadership in organizations', in N. Chmiel (ed.) *An Introduction to Work and Organizational Psychology: A European Perspective*, 2nd edn. Malden: Blackwell, pp. 281–304.

Brodbeck, F. C., Frese, M., Akerblom, S. et al. (2000) 'Cultural variation of leadership prototypes across 22 European countries', *Journal of Occupational and Organizational Psychology*, 73(1), pp. 1–29.

Brown, M. E. and Mitchell, M. S. (2010) 'Ethical and unethical leadership: exploring new avenues for future research', *Business Ethics Quarterly*, 20(4), pp. 583–616. doi: 10.1002/pa.363.

Dansereau, F., Graen, G. and Haga, W. J. (1975) 'A vertical dyad linkage approach to leadership within formal organizations: a longitudinal investigation of the role making process', *Organizational Behavior & Human Performance*, 13(1), pp. 46–78.

Day, D. V. (2001) 'Leadership development: a review in context', *Leadership Quarterly*, 11(4), pp. 581–613. doi: 10.1016/S1048-9843(00)00061-8.

Dishman, L. (2015) *The 10 Best and Worst Leaders of 2015*. Available at: www.fastcompany.com/3054777/lessons-learnt/the-10-best-and-worst-leaders-of-2015 (Accessed 23 December 2016).

Eagly, A. H. and Karau, S. J. (2002) 'Role congruity theory of prejudice toward female leaders', *Psychological Review*, 109(3), pp. 573–98.

Eagly, A. H., Johannesen-Schmidt, M. C. and van Engen, M. L. (2003) 'Transformational, transactional, and laissez-faire leadership styles: a meta-analysis comparing women and men', *Psychological Bulletin*, 129(4), pp. 569–91.

Fiedler, F. E. (1967) *A Theory of Leadership Effectiveness*. New York: McGraw-Hill.

Geier, J. G. (1967) 'A trait approach to the study of leadership in small groups', *Journal of Communication*, 17(4), pp. 316–23.

Gerstner, C. R. and Day, D. V (1997) 'Meta-analytic review of leader-member exchange theory: correlates and construct issues', *Journal of Applied Psychology*, 82(6), pp. 827–44.

Graen, G. B. and Uhl-Bien, M. (1995) 'Relationship-based approach to leadership: development of leader-member exchange (LMX) theory of leadership over 25 years: applying a multi-level multi-domain perspective', *Leadership Quarterly*, 6(2), pp. 219–47.

Hannah, S. T., Sumanth, J. J., Lester, P. and Cavarretta, F. (2014) 'Debunking the false dichotomy of leadership idealism and pragmatism: critical evaluation and support of newer genre leadership theories', *Journal of Organizational Behavior*, 35(5), pp. 598–621. doi: 10.1002/job.1931.

Hawranek, D. (2015) 'Dutzende manager in VW-skandal verwickelt', *Der Spiegel*, 14 October.

Hess, P. W. (2007) 'Enhancing leadership skill development by creating practice/feedback opportunities in the classroom', *Journal of Management Education*, 31(2), pp. 195–213. doi: 10.1177/1052562906290933.

High Pay Centre (2016) *The State of Pay: High Pay Centre Briefing on Executive Pay*. Available at: http://highpaycentre.org/files/The_Pay_Today_draft.pdf.

House, R. J. (1996) 'Path-goal theory of leadership: lessons, legacy and a reformulated theory', *Leadership Quarterly*, 7(3), pp. 323–52.

House, R. J., Hanges, P. J., Javidan, M. et al. (2004) *Culture, Leadership, and Organizations*. Thousand Oaks, CA: Sage.

Howell, J. P., Bowen, D. E., Dorfman, P. W. et al. (1990) 'Substitutes for leadership: effective alternatives to ineffective leadership', *Organizational Dynamics*, 19(1), pp. 21–38. doi: 10.1016/0090-2616(90)90046-R.

Judge, T. A. and Piccolo, R. F. (2004) 'Transformational and transactional leadership: a meta-analytic test of their relative validity', *Journal of Applied Psychology*, 89(5), pp. 755–68.

Judge, T. A., Piccolo, R. F. and Ilies, R. (2004) 'The forgotten ones? The validity of consideration and initiating structure in leadership research', *Journal of Applied Psychology*, 89(1), pp. 36–51.

Judge, T. A., Bono, J. E., Ilies, R. and Gerhardt, M. W. (2002) 'Personality and leadership: a qualitative and quantitative review', *Journal of Applied Psychology*, 87(4), pp. 765–80.

Judge, T. A., Woolf, E. F., Hurst, C. and Livingston, B. (2006) 'Charismatic and transformational leadership: a review and an agenda for future research', *Zeitschrift fur Arbeits- und Organisationspsychologie*, 50(4), pp. 203–14.

Keller, R. T. (2006) 'Transformational leadership, initiating structure, and substitutes for leadership: a longitudinal study of research and development project team performance', *Journal of Applied Psychology*, 91(1), pp. 202–10. doi: 10.1037/0021-9010.91.1.202.

Kerr, S. and Jermier, J. M. (1978) 'Substitutes for leadership: their meaning and measurement', *Organizational Behavior and Human Performance*, 22(3), pp. 375–403. doi: 10.1016/0030-5073(78)90023-5.

Khoreva, V. (2016) 'Leadership development practices as drivers of employee attitudes', *Journal of Managerial Psychology*, 31(2), pp. 537–51. doi: 10.1108/JMP-03-2014-0091.

Khoreva, V. and van Zalk, M. (2016) 'Antecedents of work engagement among high potential employees', *Career Development International*, 21(5), pp. 459–76. doi: 10.1108/CDI-10-2015-0131.

Kotter, J. P. (2001) 'What leaders really do', *Harvard Business Review*, 79(11), pp. 85–98.

Lord, R. G. and Maher, K. J. (1991) *Leadership and Information Processing: Linking Perceptions and Performance*. Cambridge, MA: Unwin Hyman.

McClelland, D. C. and Boyatzis, R. E. (1982) 'Leadership motive pattern and long-term success in management', *Journal of Applied Psychology*, 67(6), pp. 737–43.

Newport, F. (2011) 'U.S. still prefers male bosses, but many have no preference'. Available at: www.gallup.com/poll/149360/Americans-Prefer-Male-Bosses-No-Preference.aspx.

Oren, L., Tziner, A., Sharoni, G. et al. (2012) 'Relations between leader-subordinate personality similarity and job attitudes', *Journal of Managerial Psychology*, 27(5), pp. 479–96.

Robbins, S. P. and Judge, T. A. (2007) *Organizational Behavior*, 12th edn. Upper Saddle River, NJ: Pearson/Prentice Hall.

Rockstuhl, T., Dulebohn, J. H., Ang, S. and Shore, L. M. (2012) 'Leader-member exchange (LMX) and culture: a meta-analysis of correlates of LMX across 23 countries', *Journal of Applied Psychology*, 97(6), pp. 1097–130. doi: 10.1037/a0029978.

Schneider, B. (1985) 'Organizational behavior', *Annual Review of Psychology*, 36, pp. 571–611.

Schriesheim, C. A. and Neider, L. L. (1996) 'Path-goal leadership theory: the long and winding road', *Leadership Quarterly*, 7(3), pp. 317–21.

Schriesheim, C. A., Bannister, B. D. and Money, W. H. (1979) 'Psychometric properties of the LPC scale: an extension of rice's review', *Academy of Management Review*, 4(2), pp. 287–90. doi: 10.2307/257783.

Schriesheim, C. A., Castro, S. L., Zhou, X. and Yammarino, F. J. (2001) 'The folly of theorizing "A" but testing "B": a selective level-of-analysis review of the field and a detailed leader-member exchange illustration', *Leadership Quarterly*, 12(4), pp. 515–51.

Strube, M. J. and Garcia, J. E. (1981) 'A meta-analytic investigation of Fiedler's contingency model of leadership effectiveness', *Psychological Bulletin*, 90(2), pp. 307–21.

Tepper, B. J. (2007) 'Abusive supervision in work organizations: review, synthesis, and research agenda', *Journal of Management*, 33(3), pp. 261–89. doi: 10.1177/0149206307300812.

*The Guardian* (2016) 'VW agrees further $1bn settlement deal over emissions scandal', *The Guardian*, 21 December. Available at: www.theguardian.com/business/2016/dec/21/vw-agrees-further-1bn-settlement-deal-regarding-emissions-scandal.

Tosi, H. L., Misangyi, V. F., Fanelli, A. et al. (2004) 'CEO charisma, compensation, and firm performance', *Leadership Quarterly*, 15(3), pp. 405–20.

Trice, H. M. and Beyer, J. M. (1986) 'Charisma and its routinization in two social movement organizations', *Research in Organizational Behavior*, 8, pp. 113–64.

Vecchio, R. P. (1979) 'A test of the cognitive complexity interpretation of the least preferred coworker scale', *Educational and Psychological Measurement*, 39, pp. 523–6.

Vermeeren, B. (2014) 'Variability in HRM implementation among line managers and its effect on performance: a 2-1-2 mediational multilevel approach', *International Journal of Human Resource Management*, 25(22), pp. 3039–59. doi: 10.1080/09585192.2014.934891.

Vermeeren, B., Kuipers, B. and Steijn, B. (2014) 'Does leadership style make a difference? Linking HRM, job satisfaction, and organizational performance', *Review of Public Personnel Administration*, 34(2), pp. 174–95. doi: 10.1177/0734371X13510853.

Waite, M. A. (2013) 'Leadership's influence on innovation and sustainability', *European Journal of Training and Development*, 38(1/2), pp. 15–39. doi: 10.1108/EJTD-09-2013-0094.

Walumbwa, F. O., Avolio, B. J., Gardner, W. L. et al. (2008) 'Authentic leadership: development and validation of a theory-based measure', *Journal of Management*, 34(1), pp. 89–126. doi: 10.1177/0149206307308913.

Wang, G., Oh, I.-S., Courtright, S. H. and Colbert, A. E. (2011) 'Transformational leadership and performance across criteria and levels: a meta-analytic review of 25 years of research', *Group & Organization Management*, 36(2), pp. 223–70. doi: 10.1177/1059601111401017.

Zhu, W., Chew, I. K. H. and Spangler, W. D. (2005) 'CEO transformational leadership and organizational outcomes: the mediating role of human–capital-enhancing human resource management', *Leadership Quarterly*, 16(1), pp. 39–52. doi: 10.1016/j.leaqua.2004.06.001.

# PART 2 CASE STUDY:
## SOCIAL CEOS

*Getty Images/Image Source/heshphoto*

Communication is one of the fundamental elements in building trust and some business leaders have started to recognize how social media can be utilized to communicate and build trust with their employees and their customers. Doing this has a positive effect on organizational outcomes, as was shown in a recent report on the impact of social media by executives. It found that executives in the Australian financial industry who were active on social media had more engaged and higher performing staff (Hootsuite and LinkedIn, 2016). And while the majority (61%) of Fortune 500 CEOs still do not have a social media presence, the number who are engaging with followers on these platforms is slowly increasing (Domo and CEO.com, 2015). These so-called 'social CEOs' can enhance their organization's reputation, attract high-quality candidates and increase sales (Belbey, 2016).

It seems that, on the whole, employees tend to prefer leaders who engage with social media, reporting that they feel proud and inspired by those leaders (Weber Shandwick, 2013). They also see social CEOs as better leaders overall: more open and approachable and better communicators than CEOs who do not engage with social media. Interestingly, social CEOs' posts tend to be seen as aimed more at employees than customers or other stakeholders, which emphasizes the role of these communications in enhancing satisfaction and loyalty in the workforce (Weber Shandwick, 2013).

Richard Branson, who founded the Virgin Group, is one of the most popular business leaders on social media, with over 9 million Twitter followers and an active blog. Virgin was founded in 1970 as a record label and has since grown into a multinational holding company engaged in many different activities. Branson's net worth is now around $5 billion and the Virgin Group had revenues of around $20 billion in 2016. Branson believes that social media is the best way to market a business, because it helps to build networks and communities of like-minded people and present products or information to the right people (Clarkson, 2015). But what makes him so successful at using social media when so many CEOs either do not engage in it or perhaps have their marketing/PR team write their posts for them?

Branson engages directly and personally with his followers. He posts in a way that makes him relatable and human (Belbey, 2016) so that his followers feel a genuine and authentic connection. He posts positively about things he cares about and engages in an interactive relationship with his followers. For example, for his 65th birthday, he asked his followers to suggest 65 challenges for him to complete over the coming year. He picked his favourites and updated everyone as he completed them. All this helps to build interest and trust with employees and customers alike, and make them feel that they are getting to know him as a person rather than just a distant figurehead of the organization.

Despite the positive focus, Branson does not shy away from addressing crises in the company and he does so in a way that addresses customer concerns and shows support for his employees. For example, early in 2016, a passenger on a Virgin Atlantic flight tweeted that they had experienced racial abuse and that the crew had done nothing to stop it. The post went viral and led to online abuse of crew members. Branson quickly posted in English and Mandarin to say the incident was being investigated (Zhang, 2016). He also wrote a full blog post to explain the outcome of the investigation and to encourage people to be patient while all sides of the story were examined (Branson, 2016). He reiterated the company's zero tolerance approach to racism and discrimination and noted his disappointment that people jumping to conclusions based on one side of the story had led to abuse of his crew members who were 'doing their job'.

Finally, Branson uses social media to drive traffic to the company website (Mitchell, 2016), an essential element in building the organization's brand and improving performance. His posts are not just about him as a person, but about him as the founder of Virgin and they help to contribute to the company's brand image. People who follow his social media are aware all the time that he is still engaged with Virgin and his positive actions reflect well on the organization as a whole.

- Why do you think so few leaders engage with social media? To what extent do you think other CEOs and top business leaders should follow Richard Branson's example?

- If your CEO was interested in starting to engage in social media, what advice would you give them?

- How could an organization maintain a unified employer brand while still encouraging individual executives to use social media in a genuine and authentic way?

## REFERENCES

Belbey, J. (2016) 'The social CEO: executives are using social media to transform firms'. Available at: www.forbes.com/sites/joannabelbey/2016/11/30/the-social-ceo-executives-are-using-social-media-to-transform-firms/#3353a4062d80 (Accessed 17 January 2017).

Branson, R. (2016) 'Social media and understanding all sides of the story'. Available at: www.virgin.com/richard-branson/social-media-and-understanding-all-sides-story (Accessed 17 January 2017).

Clarkson, N. (2015) 'Richard Branson: making the most of social media as an entrepreneur'. Available at: www.virgin.com/entrepreneur/richard-branson-making-the-most-of-social-media-as-an-entrepreneur (Accessed 17 January 2017).

Domo and CEO.com (2015) *2015 Social CEO Report.* Available at: www.ceo.com/wp-content/themes/ceov2/assets/CEOcom-Social-CEO-Report-2015.pdf (Accessed 17 January 2017).

Hootsuite and LinkedIn (2016) *How Social Executives are Transforming the Financial Services Industry in Australia.* Available at: https://hootsuite.com/en-gb/resources/transforming-the-financial-services-industry-in-australia (Accessed 17 January 2017).

Mitchell, D. (2016) '4 ways Richard Branson does social media better than you'. Available at: www.entrepreneur.com/article/275472 (Accessed 17 January 2017).

Weber Shandwick (2013) *The Social CEO: Executives Tell All.* Available at: www.webershandwick.com/uploads/news/files/Social-CEO-Study.pdf. (Accessed 17 January 2017).

Zhang, B. (2016) 'Richard Branson warns staff on social media'. Available at: http://uk.businessinsider.com/richard-branson-caution-social-media-virgin-airline-accused-racism-2016-3 (Accessed 17 January 2017).

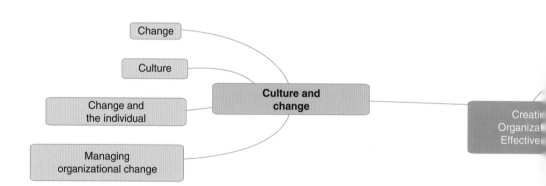

part

# 3

# CREATING ORGANIZATIONAL

# EFFECTIVENESS

In Part 3, we are moving our focus of attention from the management relationship to a discussion of how organizations can build organizational effectiveness. Dealing with change is the focus of Chapter 7 and we consider here the central role of organizational culture in contextualizing change efforts as well as how the individual and organizational elements of change can best be managed. In Chapter 8 we look at how managers create purpose for their organizations by developing strategy. We consider different strategic approaches and their suitability for different organizational aims as well as how strategic HRM can be integrated with, and supports, overall organizational strategy. Finally, in Chapter 9, organizational structure comes under the lens as we explore how it can either support or be a barrier to success. Here we review the basics of how we organize our work as well as the contingencies that influence structural choices. We also look at alternative approaches, including how some organizations are trying out new structures to remove some of the emphasis on hierarchy and control. The Part 3 case study takes a closer look at a recent tech startup and the challenges it faces as it grows and develops.

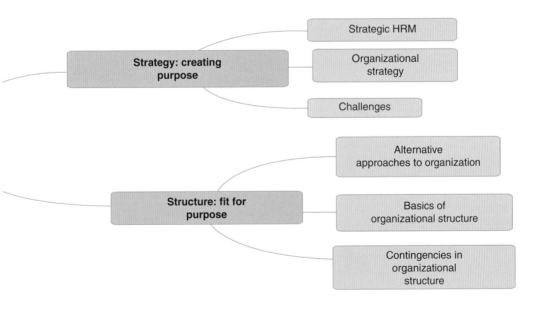

# 7 CULTURE AND CHANGE

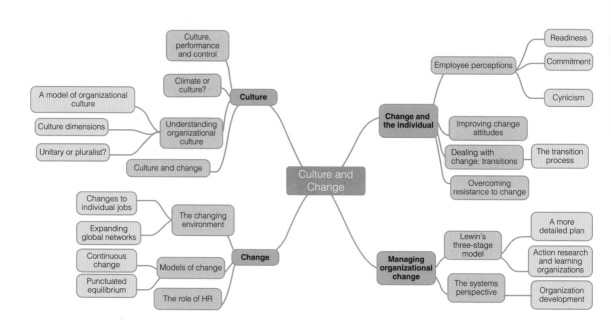

## INTRODUCTION

Culture and change are closely intertwined. Changes to work practices or organizational structure, or myriad other organizational changes, have an impact on the organizational culture and are influenced by it. Failing to take account of culture in a planned change can lead to unexpected results or even complete failure of the change effort (Smith, 2003). In addition, in recent years there has been a move towards culture change itself as a means of maintaining competitive advantage. We start the chapter therefore by discussing the concept of organizational culture before moving on to consider organizational change and its implications.

Change is an increasing fact of organizational life and HR professionals and managers are expected to manage the strategic, organizational aspects of change as well as the implications for individual employees. Kotter (1996) suggests that the rate of change has increased in recent years and it is certainly true that change is a complex topic, with often unforeseen consequences for the organization and its employees. Managing change effectively is essential to organizational success and personal well-being and if it is not managed properly, the HR function can struggle to help the organization to maintain its competitive advantage (Hanson, 2010).

*Image Source/EMMERICHWEBB CM*

## LEARNING FEATURES

Applications: Future changes

Applications: Communicating change

Applications: Action research in action

Weighing the Evidence: Can we plan change?

Web Explorer: Espoused values

In the News: Organizational culture clash

Transferrable Skills: Dealing with change

Practice Insights: Rebecca Lencho

 Video overview

Julian Perkins

Go online to www.macmillanihe.com/sutton-people to access a video of Anna Sutton introducing the chapter's main themes.

# CULTURE

Although there are many different definitions of culture in the OB and HRM literature, they share some common elements. A *culture* is a group's shared understanding of the customary ways of thinking and doing things (their 'norms') and it helps to distinguish one group of people from another. It can be thought of as a set of routines and rules that guide behaviour as well as the dynamic environment that surrounds and gives meaning to the members of a group (Schein, 2004). These elements of culture are neatly summed up in the phrase attributed to Marvin Bower (1966), managing director from 1950 to 1967 of the influential management consultancy firm McKinsey & Co, that culture is 'the way we do things around here'.

## Culture, performance and control

One of the reasons culture is viewed as such an important element of organizational behaviour and HRM practice is its proposed links with performance. Culture links people together so that they are aiming for the same things, behaving in the same way and acting on the same values. So it can seem almost a 'short cut' to getting the organization performing well. The idea is that if an organization has a strong culture binding employees together and guiding their behaviour in the right direction, good performance will flow naturally out of this. Evidence to support this claim is varied: there are some relationships between culture and performance for specific firms, but not a general pattern (Kim Jean Lee and Yu, 2004), which probably reflects the variety that exists in organizational cultures.

Second, culture is often used as a way of controlling employees, even to the level of influencing how they understand and make meaning of their work. Casey (1996) provides an interesting and insightful discussion of the role of corporate culture in organizational change and control. She suggests that the clear division of labour and specialization in the industrial age has given way to more integrated jobs, which have higher skill levels and responsibility but lack the sense of identity that old occupations had. 'Corporate culture', particularly where it is presented as 'family' and 'team', provides workers with this missing sense of identity. This strong culture aims to create *designer employees* who 'believe that their self-development, their source of self-fulfilment and identity are to be found in working for' (p. 320) this organization.

Casey (1999) argues that, while corporate cultures are often couched in terms of employee empowerment and the development of meaningful relationships at work, they are actually another form of management regulation and control of employees. She also noted the impact of culture on employee control. The new culture of team and family was so strong in her field study that employees held strongly to beliefs about the organization 'never letting good workers go' even in the face of clear evidence to the contrary.

## Climate or culture?

The terms 'organizational climate' and 'culture' are often used interchangeably and there is some debate over the extent to which they represent distinct concepts. James et al. (2008) argue that organizational *climate* can be distinguished from culture, with climate being the shared perceptions of individuals in the organization as to how the work environment impacts on their well-being, while culture is the shared system of values and beliefs in an organization. Other authors have suggested the distinction lies in climate being a *description* of the individual's experience rather than an *evaluation* of that experience (Burton et al., 2004), or that climate refers to the current state of affairs while culture represents work behaviours and practices (van den Berg and Wilderom, 2004).

However, Denison (1996) claims that the distinction is largely one of perspective rather than representing differences in the phenomenon itself. Researchers who refer to 'organizational culture' tend to mean the subjective elements of the organizational context, while those who refer to 'climate' prefer objective measurements of the 'dimensions' of this context. But, both climate and culture refer to 'the creation and influence of social contexts in organisations' (p. 646). For the management practitioner, however, a any distinction between climate and culture may be seen as fairly abstract and irrelevant. In discussing the application of these concepts to management in nursing, for example, Sleutel (2000) concludes that in practical terms, culture, climate, context or work environment are all equally valid ways of referring to the social context and practice environment.

# Understanding organizational culture

In trying to understand and describe organizational culture, there are two main approaches we can take. We can either analyse a specific culture in detail, looking at the different levels and symbols of that culture, or we can compare several different cultures using the same basic scales to determine how they differ from one another. We are going to look at each of these approaches in turn in order to evaluate their utility.

## A model of organizational culture

Schein (2004) suggested that we can analyse organizational culture at different levels, from the surface manifestations, to the espoused values and then the underlying basic assumptions. The 'level' is the degree to which that aspect of culture is obvious to the observer, with the deeper levels being the essence of culture, deeply embedded and very often unconscious – so taken for granted that someone who does not conform to them is often dismissed as crazy. For example, in a capitalist environment, it is unimaginable that a company could be designed to operate consistently at a loss. The three levels in Schein's model are:

- **Artefacts:** the physical products or phenomena we encounter in the organization. For example, the language, technology, style of dress or communication, the stories organizational members tell each other, and the organization's ceremonies and rituals.

- **Espoused beliefs or values:** the beliefs that are talked about and expressed in the organization about what is important, the 'right' ways to do things. These espoused beliefs or values may or may not be congruent with the artefacts or underlying assumptions of the organization.

- **Underlying assumptions:** the taken-for-granted beliefs about the way things work. They are so strongly held that it becomes inconceivable that anyone would work in a different way and are extremely difficult to change.

*Getty Images/iStockphoto/mediaphotos*

*How people dress at work can give an insight into the organization's culture.*

Although this model can help us to analyse culture, we do need to be careful how we interpret what we observe. As Schein (2004, p. 26) himself points out, artefacts are 'easy to observe and very difficult to decipher'. For example, if you were to start work at a new company and quickly noticed that everyone dressed in a very formal manner, how would you interpret this? Is it an outward sign that this is an organization that prides itself on its professional approach? Does it mean that you can assume it is an efficient and well-organized company? Or could it mean that it has a strict hierarchy and does not approve of any informality? Is it something that sets this firm apart from its competitors or is this style of dress common to the industry? There are many underlying assumptions that could account for the artefacts we observe, and we look at this further in the Web Explorer exercise.

## Web Explorer: Espoused values

As the notion of organizational culture has gained popularity, management teams around the world have begun to explicitly articulate their organization's values and these are now often displayed prominently on websites and promotional material. But company values are often criticized for being fairly bland or too similar to one another to really give anyone a competitive edge.

» Choose two different organizations within the same industry and explore their websites to find out what they say their values are. How different are these espoused values? For example, you could choose two of the big pharmaceutical companies, Pfizer and Novartis:

- Pfizer's values: Collaboration, Community, Customer Focus, Innovation, Integrity, Leadership, Performance, Respect for People and Quality: http://pfizercareers.com/career-types/mission-purpose-values

- Novartis' values: Innovation, Quality, Collaboration, Performance, Courage, Integrity: www.novartis.co.uk/about-us/who-we-are/our-values

» Do you think it is worthwhile for organizations to develop a specific list of values?

Analysing culture using Schein's model can be a valuable way of identifying a mismatch between the organization's espoused values and its actions or surface manifestations. For example, Nestlé is frequently criticized for its approach to business development and marketing in poorer countries. As the top bottled water company in the world (Nestlé Waters, 2016), it has been criticized for ruining access to clean water in poorer areas (see, for example: http://en.bottledlife.tv/index.html) and for the long-term environmental damage caused by disposable plastic water bottles. Yet Nestlé states on its website that it is dedicated to 'enhancing people's lives' (Nestlé, 2016).

» Search for news articles related to Nestlé and these criticisms, as well as responses from the company itself and its own description of its mission and values. To what extent do you think there is a discrepancy between Nestlé's actions and its espoused values?

## Culture dimensions

Instead of using a model of culture such as Schein's, which allows an individual analysis of an organization, other researchers have been interested in how we might describe the differences between organizational cultures on standardized scales. There have been several proposals for dimensions along which these cultures might differ. For example, the Organizational Culture Profile (OCP) Questionnaire is a popular way of measuring several dimensions to give a detailed description of organizational culture (O'Reilly et al., 1991; Chatman and Jehn, 1994). These dimensions include how employees approach their work, for example their norms around risk-taking and innovation or attention to detail, as well as how competitive or easy-going they are. The OCP also measures the organization's focus on stability or growth, its orientation towards results and towards people, as well as the extent to which teamworking and collaboration are important.

An interesting finding in these studies was that culture varied more across industries than within them, suggesting that organizational culture within an industry is fairly uniform and may not be the source of competitive advantage that it is supposed to be.

## Unitary or pluralist?

One caveat we need to be aware of here is that organizational culture is often discussed as if it is unitary when, in reality, it is likely to be made up of differentiated subgroups or subcultures (Bolon and Bolon, 1994; Li and Jones, 2010). For some authors, a strong, unitary culture is the key to organizational success (see, for example, the very popular book *In Search of Excellence* by Peters and Waterman). However, there is the recurring criticism of unitary approaches that we have seen throughout this book: that they disregard conflict and see dissent as a sign of dysfunction. In fact, too much homogeneity in an organization, including in its culture, can be a disadvantage. For example, homogeneous culture within the research and development function can lead to decreased knowledge creation and productivity (Berliant and Fujita, 2012).

As culture is based on values, there is a common perception that managers can build an 'ethical' culture, which will encourage employees to behave in an ethical manner when carrying out their work. However, this perception is criticized because while strong cultures can encourage commitment to the organization, the homogeneity and lack of dissent means that unethical practices go unchallenged (Sinclair, 1993). Instead, Sinclair suggests that managers who can recognize that there is a plurality of cultures in the organization and work with the variety of subcultures to allow healthy debate on

their conflicting values are more likely to be able to encourage ethical behaviour.

## Culture and change

Culture change is a type of transformational change, that is, change that is multidimensional and aims at large-scale, complex and systematic adjustments. This kind of change is a long-term undertaking: research suggests it can take 2–15 years (Lee et al., 2013). Schein's model helps us to recognize why it is so difficult to change culture, with its basis in unconscious, often unchallengeable, assumptions about how the world operates. And yet, despite a high failure rate and a timescale requiring years for successful implementation, over a quarter of organizational change initiatives are aimed at changing culture (Smith, 2003). Perhaps even more importantly, change of culture was an element in the majority of the change case studies reviewed in Smith's research, which highlights how many organizational changes will, in some way, impact on or be impacted by the culture. An example of the influence of culture on change is given in the In the News box.

It seems that the best way to ensure culture change attempts succeed is to incorporate the change into the strategy and to reward employees for changing: both these approaches emphasize the long-term nature of the change and recognize that for culture to change, employees need to be supported into whole new ways of working. There is also evidence that employees who have more control over their work are more likely to view culture change efforts in a positive light (Gover et al., 2016).

 In the News: **Organizational culture clash**

When companies merge, the clash of organizational cultures can often be a source of their biggest challenges. One example of how this played out in a recent merger was when Molson Coors, a Canadian and US-based brewer, acquired StarBev, a brewer based in the Czech Republic, for €2.65 billion. Added to a language barrier, the values of the two organizations were quite different, which made communication and working together challenging at the beginning.

One of the major differences in how the two companies approached their work was the level of

planning and speed with which they acted. Molson Coors was used to a spontaneous, fast-moving way of working, guided by a confident, entrepreneurial spirit. In contrast, StarBev had a much more ordered and cautious approach, and preferred to work with clear guidelines and timescales in its plans. In addition, Molson Coors takes its social responsibility very seriously and evaluates its impact on the environment and communities using what it calls its 'Beer Print'. Debbie Read, head of corporate social responsibility, notes that having these **CSR** values explicitly stated helps Molson

Coors employees to talk about what is really important to the organization (Kennedy, 2014).

Molson Coors was able to negotiate the cultural differences because it has a history of recognizing and valuing the contribution that people from different backgrounds make (Molson Coors Brewing Company, 2016). In fact, Read says that the acquisition was really a 'two-way learning process', with Molson Coors learning a more structured approach from StarBev, and the Czech company adopting the socially responsible approach that lies at the heart of Molson Coors' approach (Kennedy, 2014).

**For discussion**

» Look up Molson Coors 'Beer Print' and the company values. How do you think that having the Beer Print CSR report helps to reinforce the organization's values? To what extent do you think it helps it to deal effectively with the cultural issues raised by mergers and acquisitions?

# CHANGE

Culture can be thought of as the organizational context within which change takes place. Organizational culture can be both a hindrance and a help when it comes to change efforts. It can provide individual employees with the support they need as they deal with change or can even hamper individual efforts to adapt to new ways of doing things. A culture that encourages innovation and flexibility will obviously be more supportive of change than one that emphasizes stability. We now turn to look at the issues facing change efforts in organizations, starting by considering the drivers for change and then moving on to discuss models of change.

## The changing environment

The changing business environment forces organizations to change in order to survive and sustain their success. Important drivers in the business environment include market conditions, workforce demographics and diversity, technological innovations, focus on customer and quality, shortage of required talent and skills, and larger economic changes (Maheshwari and Vohra, 2015). Frese (2008) conceptualized the future challenges that organizations face in terms of their impact on changes to individual jobs and expanding global networks, and we will look at both of these in detail next. Before we do, take some time to complete the Applications activity to consider your own views of what the future holds.

### Applications: **Future changes**

How do you think the world of work will change over the next five to ten years? Using the following general headings, jot down some notes on what you think will change at work, and why:

- the role of education
- typical working hours and locations
- the role of technology
- diversity at work

» Compare your answers with colleagues to see the range of suggestions. You might like to keep your predictions and look back at them in a few years' time to see how accurate you were.

» Find someone who is nearing retirement from work and ask them about the changes they have experienced using the headings above. Do their answers suggest any new ideas to you or ways you could improve your predictions?

## Changes to individual jobs

The concept of a job for life or a clear career path within one organization has all but disappeared, and employees now are expected to take responsibility for their own career development rather than relying on the organization. There is an increased incidence of temporary contracts and so-called 'precarious work' – that is, jobs which do not provide any security of employment or income – with workers needing to display personal initiative or adaptability in order to succeed in the new workplace. You may wish to look back at Chapter 4 where we reviewed the impact of the 'gig economy' on the individual–organization relationship in order to consider some of the effects of this kind of change.

Alongside this, the complexity of work and the rate of innovation is increasing. Many unskilled jobs are becoming scarcer as technology improves and the jobs that remain make higher intellectual demands on workers. Increased use of teamwork means that social skills and teamwork competencies are becoming as critical to success as technical abilities. Self-managed teams and a reduction in formal supervision result in a delegation of responsibilities, again resulting in more complex jobs. Individuals need to take control of their own training

and organizations need to encourage curiosity and exploration to ensure they stay ahead of the game.

## Expanding global networks

People are now able to communicate with colleagues across the globe using IT solutions and more and more work is being completed outside the physical organization. In this increasingly dispersed working environment, we need new ways of creating and maintaining networks. For example, how can we ensure that a team whose members have never met one another can actually function well as a team?

*Getty Images/Image Source*

*It can be challenging for people who have never met to function well as a team.*

Global competition in a turbulent environment is now the norm for most organizations, giving rise to a need for international cooperation, imagination and employee initiative. This increased global competition is matched by the increasing cultural diversity of the workforce within nations. Workers increasingly have to learn how

to overcome prejudice and bias, as well as dealing with cultural differences and languages. And finally, in this globalized business environment, we need to find ways to pursue organizational justice and fairness.

Clearly, the drivers for change are extensive and unavoidable in the modern business environment, making change an essential for organizational survival. How we approach the change process, however, is based on the understanding we have of how change can be managed.

## Models of change

The way in which we view change determines how (or, indeed, if) we believe it can be managed. In this section, we will review the main approaches to understanding change and their implications for change management. The literature on organizational change often draws on the biological theory of evolution as a metaphor for organizational change: the idea being that change is a gradual incremental process. But this notion was challenged by the idea of punctuated equilibrium, a view of evolution as consisting of sudden large changes interspersed with longer periods of relative stability. Here, we consider each of these models in turn.

### Continuous change

Continuous and rapid change is what underlies some organizations' competitive advantage and Brown and Eisenhardt (1997) suggested that organizations which successfully engage in continuous change typically rely on the following three features:

1. **Semi-structures:** the organization defines and delineates some features of the work, such as responsibilities and project priorities, but leaves other features, such as the design process, flexible. These semi-structures allow organizations to strike a balance between order and chaos, giving freedom for change while still maintaining some control and using order to encourage changes.

2. **Links in time:** successful project managers are able to focus on the current project while having a clear sense of where they are going. These links between current and future projects give the change a direction and help to maintain momentum.

3. **Sequenced steps:** organizations themselves are created through a series of sequenced steps in the implementation of change. Managers gain a detailed understanding of the current situation, determine where they are headed in the future, and then create links between the two. They

ensure that each step is developed and stabilized before moving on to the next.

While some organizations are able to achieve this ideal, continuously adaptive state, most do not. The majority of organizations experience the punctuated equilibrium model that we look at next. They continue as they always have, with perhaps small, incremental changes, until a crisis forces them into dramatic change. The organizations that survive are the ones that can undergo the revolutionary change that is needed.

### Punctuated equilibrium

Gersick (1991) demonstrated how the **punctuated equilibrium model** is useful in the study of organizations. She identified the three main components of this model as: deep structure, equilibrium periods and revolutionary periods. We will look at each of these in detail now, using the example of an organization with which you will be familiar (a university) to illustrate each of the components.

1. **Deep structure** is the durable, underlying foundations of the organization and is very stable. It consists of its culture, strategy, structure, power distribution and control systems (Tushman and Romanelli, 1985). The deep structure is made up of the organization's basic *parts* (how the units of the organization are configured) and basic *activities* (what the organization does to maintain its existence). For example, a university's parts could be the traditional faculties that focus on specific academic areas of study. Its basic activities could be seen as creating and disseminating knowledge.

2. During **equilibrium phases**, this deep structure persists and limits change. For example, if considerable power resided in the heads of the university faculties, the faculty structure would be likely to persist and any change aimed at dissolving those faculties would be severely limited. Equilibrium periods are not 'static', but are periods when the organization carries out its activities and maintains itself in line with its deep structure. There may well be incremental changes during this time that help the organization become better and better at what it does (Tushman and Romanelli, 1985) but, overall, equilibrium is maintained by *organizational inertia*. This inertia is due to three barriers to change:

– *Cognitive barriers* include simply not seeing the problem, as well as the natural human limits on awareness and attention. For example, not seeing any problem with having a faculty structure or not being aware of changes in the research funding environment that might impact on how knowledge should be disseminated.

– *Motivational barriers* include a fear of failure or dislike of uncertainty, as well as an unwillingness to 'lose' all the work that has been done so far. For example, lecturers' unwillingness to have to develop new ways of teaching or an administrative fear that a new system would fail and lead to student complaints.

– *Obligation barriers* build up between people and whole networks to work against change. For example, networks of professional identity, such as chartered engineers or management professionals, are often built up around specific subject areas that would act as a barrier to any attempt to dismantle that group.

3. **Revolutionary periods** occur when the inertial forces are eventually overcome and the whole deep structure is dismantled. The need for revolution can be created either by internal changes that have pulled the basic parts and actions of the organization out of alignment with each other, or by external changes that mean the organization can no longer access the resources it needs. For example, in universities, the basic activity of 'creating knowledge' is increasingly becoming interdisciplinary, which is at odds with a very rigid faculty structure. If the university is unable to find ways of building interdisciplinary networks, it will become increasingly unable to access research funding and ultimately less able to carry out one of its basic activities.

The punctuated equilibrium model of change in organizations has received considerable empirical support (for example, Romanelli et al., 1994). But, of course, a *need* for change does not guarantee change will happen, and some organizations may continue to struggle on as they always have in order to avoid change. But to survive and be successful in the long run, the organization needs to change its deep structure and reassemble itself before embarking on another period of equilibrium. We consider how this might be done when we review detailed models for planning change in the *Managing organizational change* section later in the chapter, but now that we have seen how continuous change can be, the Weighing the Evidence box evaluates the extent to which it is possible to plan for change.

## Weighing the Evidence: **Can we plan change?**

Although we give considerable attention in this chapter to ways of planning for and implementing change, some authors have suggested that change is inherently uncontrollable, unpredictable or chaotic and view the planned approach to change as ineffective and unrealistic. Instead, they see change as 'emergent', meaning that it is made up of ongoing adaptations and alterations which result in fundamental changes that were not planned for or perhaps even expected (Weick, 2000).

Lord et al. (2015), for example, caution against a reliance on linear models of change, which could lead us to view organizational development and evolution as a straightforward, predictable progression. They argue that this perspective on change obscures the complexities and uncertainties of change, particularly the impact of unpredictable events. Instead, they suggest that a more realistic and helpful model of change can be drawn from quantum theory, seeing the future as a 'state of potentiality' that is influenced by many interacting complex systems.

The emergent approach to change emphasizes that change is messy and involves a vast array of different subsystems and contextual factors so that there is no simple linear cause-and-effect model that can effectively capture it. In order to have any hope of influencing the course of the change, managers need to be involved in the continuous process all the time. They need to develop awareness and understanding of the environment. If change is a constant process of mutual interactions between the organization and the environment, the effective management of change is based on the ability to analyse and understand those interactions.

A balanced approach to understanding change recognizes that planned and emergent approaches have their value. Some change in organizations is planned, and there is good evidence that planning well can improve the success of change management. But there is also a lot of **emergent change** and this approach reminds us of the importance of flexibility and continuous adaptation to the environment. Burnes (2004a) notes this in a four-year case study of change at a construction firm, which used an emergent, open-ended approach to changing culture and a planned approach to changing structure. He points out that one of the essential competencies for successful change management is to understand the organizational context. This means that employees within the organization may be better placed to promote change than external 'experts' who come in with a model of planned change. While consultants may be able to help the organization develop a strategy for change or provide models to improve effectiveness, there has to be a heavy reliance on local knowledge and involvement if the change is to succeed.

## The role of HR

Many HR processes and day-to-day activities are aimed towards stability and 'running the system' (Bruns, 2014, p. 27) and so need strategic alignment with the more transformational processes involved in organizational change. Hanson (2010) notes that HR has traditionally been associated with processes for maintaining organizational stability, which can limit its ability to lead change or even function effectively in a changing environment. While the processes for maintaining stability remain essential to the organization's basic functioning, it is increasingly important for HR professionals to lead change effectively. In fact, a strategic approach to implementing new HR practices has been shown to lead to positive and long-term sustained change to organizational culture and day-to-day operations (Molineux, 2013). HR has the potential to enhance the organization's ability to change by implementing practices that shape employee behaviour, increase engagement and build commitment to change (Maheshwari and Vohra, 2015).

HRM can even be seen as one of the core and necessary drivers in organizational change. For example, in the ongoing modernization of the public sector in Germany, which is attempting to improve public service delivery, effective HRM is seen as an essential prerequisite of organizational development and change (Bruns, 2014). However, there is an inherent tension or duality in how HR is involved in change processes: it has a role in leading change and initiating the disruption that this involves and also in ensuring that continuity and stability are maintained in essential areas. Additionally, there is the recurring challenge faced by HR practitioners of balancing individual and organizational needs. We consider both sides of this challenge in the next two sections.

# CHANGE AND THE INDIVIDUAL

## Employee perceptions

Many authors argue that it is the individuals in the organization who can determine the success or failure of change efforts rather than the details of the change effort itself (Shin et al., 2012). It is essential, therefore, to understand employees' attitude towards change in order to provide managers with important information regarding employees' concerns or evaluation of specific changes (Choi, 2011). Attitudes are not fixed but can be changed and are subject to situational effects – thus, they may provide a useful point of leverage for managers wishing to enhance the possibilities of success for change implementation. In a review of the literature, Choi (2011) identified and defined four key attitudes relevant to organizational change: readiness for and openness to change, commitment to change and cynicism about change, which all reflect a person's positive or negative evaluation of a change.

### Readiness for and openness to change

Readiness for change is our belief about how likely the change is to be successful and lead to positive outcomes. It includes an assessment of the extent to which we think our organization is capable of implementing change successfully and the support it is providing. There are several things that influence this evaluative belief, including trust in the leaders and our perceptions of our own competence. Our readiness for change is also influenced by our general openness to change, which is a combination of a willingness to support the change along with generally positive feelings about its consequences.

Although we are considering individual attitudes here, it is worth remembering that readiness for change can be seen at the individual, group and organizational culture level. Individuals are not working in isolation but are part of mutually interacting groups at work and their team's readiness for change will influence their individual attitudes (Vakola, 2013). In addition, organizations may not be ready to change because of fixed organizational structures and processes, so that any readiness to change on the part of individuals or teams might become mired at the organizational level.

## Commitment to change

Commitment to change is our intention to support the change initiative and behave in a way that will promote its success. There are many reasons why employees might be reluctant to commit to change, including a fear it might disrupt their social relationships, increase workload, or drain their emotional resources (Shin et al., 2012).

People with a higher commitment to the change are more likely to comply with organizational directives during the change and go out of their way to ensure the change is implemented as well as possible (Choi, 2011). They are also more likely to express behavioural support for the change and develop creative solutions to issues that emerge as the change progresses (Shin et al., 2012).

HR practices that are likely to have a significant influence on employee behaviour in a change process include (Maheshwari and Vohra, 2015):

- Understanding the current culture and fostering a culture that will support innovation and change, reinforcing desired behaviours and striving to remove unwanted behaviours.

- Providing leadership and motivating leaders in the organization, giving clear vision and goals.

- Increasing cross-functional integration by providing training and measuring and coordinating performance.

- Developing a learning environment and providing continuous training to employees.

- Establishing trust and collaboration through open communication.

- Using technology effectively for administration, to develop connectivity and to increase employee participation.

These practices are expected to improve employee perceptions and thereby their commitment to change. Shin et al. (2012) also identify several factors that can influence the extent to which we are committed to the change, such as how favourable the change is or how turbulent the process is. Commitment to change can be enhanced by the provision of developmental and material rewards by the organization and tends to be higher in employees who are more resilient, as they are more likely to experience positive feelings about the change.

## Cynicism about change

Cynicism about the organization means that an employee views the organization as lacking in integrity and has negative feelings about it. Cynicism about change can be considered a 'subset' of this broader attitude, consisting of pessimism about the change's chances of success and assigning blame for this pessimism to management. It is associated with resistance to change and is heavily influenced by employees' previous experiences of change in that organization, developing as a result of employees' unmet expectations (Barton and Ambrosini, 2012). It is particularly important, therefore, for organizations that have been through unsuccessful changes to expect and be able to deal with cynicism about future changes: cynicism will lead people to be less committed to implementing the change (Barton and Ambrosini, 2012).

## Improving change attitudes

Because these attitudes are situationally variable – that is, they are heavily influenced by an individual's experiences – they can change as those experiences change. That means that managers and HR professionals can have a key influence on these attitudes and make efforts to improve employees' readiness for, commitment to and openness to change as well as reducing their cynicism. Based on the research, Choi (2011) recommends three steps to take in attempting to change attitudes:

- Provide employees with the opportunities to participate in the change process and decision-making

- Provide training to help employees with the change, encouraging them to have confidence in their own abilities

- Develop an open and sharing environment where information about the change is communicated clearly and in a timely fashion. We explore this further in the Applications activity.

The insecurities and uncertainties that are an inherent part of change processes have a large impact on employee attitudes and outcomes. Job insecurity in itself directly reduces commitment but it also has an indirect negative impact on commitment by increasing feelings of unfairness and exhaustion (Schumacher et al., 2016). While it may not be possible to completely remove this insecurity, HR practitioners and managers can reduce its impact by framing change more positively, for example pointing out opportunities for personal development, and providing as much clarity and certainty through the process as is possible.

 Applications: **Communicating change**

On 13 June 2016, Microsoft acquired LinkedIn for $28 billion in one of the top ten biggest tech deals ever (Shen, 2016). The day the acquisition was announced, Jeff Weiner, CEO of LinkedIn, sent an email to his global workforce and published it on his blog. You can read the whole email at www.linkedin.com/pulse/linkedin-microsoft-changing-way-world-works-jeff-weiner but here is an extract:

> No matter what you're feeling now, give yourself some time to process the news. You might feel a sense of excitement, fear, sadness, or some combination of all of those emotions. Every member of the exec team has experienced the same, but we've had months to process. Regardless of the ups and downs, we've come out the other side

> knowing beyond a shadow of a doubt, this is the best thing for our company.

Weiner also emphasizes the congruity of the missions and cultures of the two companies in painting an optimistic picture of the future for LinkedIn employees.

» What do you think of Weiner's approach? What parallels can you see with the strategies for enhancing employees' attitudes towards change outlined above? (Reading the full blog will enable you to see more.)

» Imagine you worked at LinkedIn when this deal was being negotiated and were tasked with coming up with recommendations to make to Jeff Weiner about how to ensure the change went as smoothly as possible. What would you suggest and why?

## Dealing with change: transitions

Whether an individual employee perceives a change in a positive or negative manner can have a large impact on how they respond to that change, and these perceptions may well differ from the organizational view. For example, if the organization is implementing a change to a more flexible workforce by changing contracts, this could be perceived by some employees as an increase in freedom and autonomy and by others as a financial threat or increase in insecurity (Stuart, 1995). Those employees who perceive positive triggers for change

will engage more positively with the process and are likely to resist it less. Those who perceive it negatively and as a threat are more likely to resist the change as well as experience greater stress in dealing with it. Although there is individual variation in the extent to which we enjoy change or find it difficult, change *is* stressful. We turn next to look at the process of dealing with change.

One of the major contributors to our understanding of how change impacts on people at work is William Bridges (2009, p. 3), who said: 'It isn't the changes that do you in, it's the transitions.' He draws a contrast between *change*, which is

*Getty Images*

*Whether we view a change as positive or negative has an impact on how well we transition through it.*

something that happens at a specific place and time (like starting a new job or graduating from university) and *transition*, which is the psychological process of coming to terms with that change.

## The transition process

Transition essentially involves three phases (Bridges, 1980), illustrated in Figure 7.1 and explored further in the Transferrable Skills activity (overleaf).

| Ending | Neutral zone | Beginning |
|---|---|---|
| • Every transition starts with an ending, where we let go of old ways of doing things or an old identity. This is the time where people are dealing with loss | • During this time, the 'old' has gone; for example, we can no longer do things the way we used to or no longer have our old identity, but the 'new' is not yet fully in place. We recognize that we need to change but we are not sure what will happen | • It is only towards the end of the transition process that we truly begin the new way of being. We have a new identity or have discovered the new way of doing things |

*Figure 7.1 The three phases of transition*

## Transferrable Skills: Dealing with change

The ability to deal well with change will be invaluable to you as you progress in your career, as will the skills to help others through the transition process. In this exercise, we will go through some of the management techniques associated with the three stages of Bridges' (2009) model of transition. You can practise these skills on yourself as you go through a change, giving you an insight into how to apply the management techniques to others as well.

First, think about a recent change you experienced. For example, coming to university, starting (or losing) a job, changes in your family circumstances and so on. As you go through each of the stages below, reflect on their application to that transition.

### Stage 1: Ending

At this stage, it is important to accept that you will be experiencing many emotions and may well resist the change. You need to allow yourself time to accept the change – transition is not an instant experience but a process. Specific steps to help in this stage:

- Find someone you can talk to openly about how you are feeling.

- Identify what it is you will have to let go of and acknowledge its importance to you: this is part of respecting the past and the lessons you have learnt.

- Focus on the positives of the change: how you can use or develop new skills. Seek out ways you can gain support or training to help you manage specific aspects of the change.

### Stage 2: Neutral zone

In this stage, we tend to feel quite confused and uncertain, and depending on what the change is, may well be taking on more work as we learn the skills or routines of the new situation. Specific steps to help in this stage:

- Find clarity on the direction in which you are moving, identifying specific goals that will help you deal with the uncertainty.

- Set the bar low and make some of those goals short-term, 'easy wins' that will help you to maintain your motivation through this difficult stage.

- Look for ways to get feedback on how you're doing so that you can adjust course as needed.

- If your workload does become too much, look for ways to manage or prioritize it. Don't be afraid to ask for help.

### Stage 3: Beginning

In the final stage, we are at the point of accepting the change and making it our new norm. We tend to feel excited and committed to the change and are likely to be seeing the benefits of it. Specific steps to help in this stage:

- The aim at this stage is to sustain the change, so keep track of your progress and the goals you've reached already.

- Reward yourself for specific achievements.

- Don't try to rush through to this stage too quickly – be patient.

---

Hayes (2014) has suggested a more detailed transition process, which outlines seven distinct phases:

1. Awareness/shock: at the beginning of a transition, people can be overwhelmed, especially if they had little notice that the change was coming. They feel 'immobilized', unable to take in new information or to plan properly, and the less prepared they were for the change and the more undesirable the change is, the more intense this stage will be. In the case of a gradual dawning of awareness of the change, this stage is associated

with worrying, with people focusing on how they might lose out.

2. Denial: instead of dealing with the change, people tend to deny it for a while. They focus their attention on other things, perhaps convince themselves that the change is not actually going to happen (or has not happened). People are most resistant to change when in this phase and can get angry if forced to face up to it. This stage is important, however, because refusing to accept the change can sometimes give people the time they need to make the **personal transition**,

rehearsing the implications of the change in their minds (Parkes, 1993).

3. Depression: as denial fades, people begin to face reality and recognize that the change is happening. This leads to feelings of helplessness, stress and depression and corresponds with Bridges' neutral zone. It can even happen with changes that were initially perceived as positive, if practical problems surface.

4. Letting go: this is the lowest part of the process in terms of mood. For the transition to continue, the individual needs to let go of the old identity or behaviours and accept the new reality.

5. Testing: now that the new reality has 'arrived', people start to engage more actively with it. They test out new ways of being, using a trial-and-error process to see what works in the 'new world'.

6. Consolidation: the behaviours and patterns that are successful in the testing process now become the new norms.

7. Internalization: the final phase marks the end of the transition. At this point, the new behaviours and norms are fully adopted and the past has been left behind. By reflecting on the process, people can learn from it and use that learning in future changes.

Each of us progresses through these stages at a different speed and sometimes we may not even make it through successfully, but get 'stuck' at a particular stage and be unable to progress. It may make more sense to think of change as a journey through a number of 'fields' or areas of change rather than a set sequence of stages (Stuart, 1995), with each person able to take a different path through these fields in their process of dealing with change. It is helpful to be reminded that people deal with change in different ways and that while transition models are useful in understanding the range of responses we may experience in response to change, they cannot be used in a prescriptive manner that determines how people will react at any one moment.

## Overcoming resistance to change

Given the difficulties and discomfort that employees experience when engaged in the transition process,

it is perhaps not surprising that most organizational changes face resistance from the people involved. There are four main sources of this resistance (Kotter and Schlesinger, 1979):

1. Parochial self-interest: people do not want to lose something of value to them and are focused on their own self-interests. Even if a change is obviously good for the organization or the rest of the team, someone may still resist it if the change is likely to cause extra work or mean a loss of status.

2. Misunderstanding and lack of trust: related to the point above, people may misunderstand the change and believe the costs outweigh the benefits even when this is not the case. This is particularly likely to happen when there is a lack of trust between the change agent and those affected by the change.

3. Different assessments: the change agent may believe that a change will result in many positive effects, such as improved productivity, increased employee motivation and so on. But those affected by the change may see it very differently. This highlights how important it is for change to be transparent so that everyone is aware of all the relevant information.

4. Low tolerance for change: people worry that they may not be able to develop the required new skills and abilities quickly enough or that they simply will not be able to cope with the change. Some people simply find change more difficult than others. People who are more extraverted, agreeable, conscientious and open to experience have more positive attitudes towards organizational change (Vakola et al., 2004).

Understanding individual differences can help managers to identify those people who may need further support or training in dealing with change. In addition, Kotter and Schlesinger (1979) suggested several different strategies that managers can use to reduce resistance and increase the effectiveness of the change, as shown in Table 7.1 (overleaf).

The effects of these management efforts will, of course, be varied, and given the potentially negative consequences of the later strategies, careful thought needs to be given as to when each is appropriate. Through all this, however, it is also

## Table 7.1 **Management strategies**

| | |
|---|---|
| Education and communication | Helps people to understand the reasons for the change. It can also help to build trust as information is shared rather than change being imposed without explanation |
| Participation and involvement | Involve those who are affected by the change in its implementation. This can ensure that potential obstacles are dealt with before they become problems and encourages feedback on the implications of change |
| Facilitation and support | This can be done by providing training in new skills or strategies for dealing with change or simply emotional support for those struggling with the change |
| Negotiation and agreement | Offer incentives to those who are likely to resist the change in order to get them on board |
| Manipulation and cooption | Rather than an open, participative approach like some of the previous strategies, this involves sharing information selectively or consciously structuring events to ensure the change occurs |
| Explicit or implicit coercion | This involves forcing people to change by threatening them. For example, a manager might hint that someone's promotion prospects might be damaged if they resist the change, or even fire them if they do not conform |

Source: Based on Kotter, J. P. and Schlesinger, L. A. (1979) 'Choosing strategies for change', *Harvard Business Review*, 57(2), pp. 106–14.

worth remembering that resistance to change is not in itself a bad thing. It can have positive results, such as slowing the process down so that people have the time they need to adapt, or helping to highlight problems with the change that have not been identified before. For this reason, managing change in a participatory way whenever possible is to be preferred, as it ensures that change managers will have access to as much information as possible in guiding the change and also gives the individuals involved some control over the speed of the change and the ability to manage their own responses.

# MANAGING ORGANIZATIONAL CHANGE

The management of change involves attempting to control the change process and its consequences in order to achieve the desired outcomes. In this section we will look at some basic change models that can help change leaders, whether HR professionals or managers, to consider all the different elements that need to be considered in the change management process.

## Lewin's three-stage model of change

Karl Lewin's approach to understanding change rested on what he called 'force field analysis', which identified the forces for and against change in order to find the best way to introduce and maintain change. He recognized that the current status quo was essentially a 'stable, quasi-stationary equilibrium', in which the driving forces *for* change are balanced by the restraining forces *against* change (Lewin, 1951). Because most people find change uncomfortable, he noted that if we attempt to push change through by focusing on increasing the driving forces, people will become tense and emotional and not engage in constructive behaviours, thereby actually increasing the restraining forces that attempt to keep things as they are and resist the change. Thus, in order to initiate and sustain change, he suggested that the best approach is to reduce the restraining forces. There are three main stages in doing this, depicted in Figure 7.2.

Recent work has confirmed the utility of Lewin's model for implementing organizational change, with change seen to progress through this sequence and more effective changes associated with higher levels of change processes at each stage (Ford and Greer, 2006). We should note, however, that this approach is fairly slow and reliant on group consensus, which

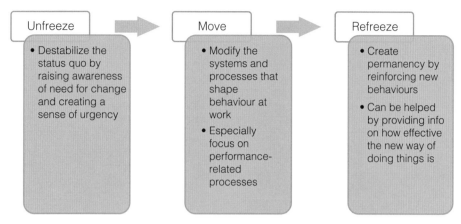

*Figure 7.2 Lewin's three-stage model of change*

Source: Based on Lewin, K. (1997) *Resolving Social Conflicts and Field Theory in Social Science.* © 1997 American Psychological Association.

can seem ineffective or even inappropriate for organizations operating in turbulent, fast-changing environments (Burnes, 2004a). Also, we need to be careful when thinking about what it means to 'refreeze' the organization in the new status quo: to a large extent, organizations might be viewed as fluid, constantly changing entities (Kanter et al., 1992). Lewin's definition of stability as an equilibrium recognizes this and 'refreezing' should perhaps be better thought of as a stage of reinforcing new behaviours in order to reduce regression, rather than a completely stable, new state. Unfortunately, many organizations today forget this final stage and try to introduce one change after another, meaning that they often do not reap the expected benefits of the change because it is not ever properly established. In fact, it may be that introducing popular changes to the organization is more beneficial for the firm's reputation than its actual performance (Staw and Epstein, 2000).

## A more detailed plan

Lewin's simple model is useful in that it shows us the main issues to be aware of in managing change, but more recent developments have suggested more detailed plans. Kotter (1996), for example, reviewed what factors led to change failure and expanded on the *unfreezing* and *moving* parts of Lewin's model to give managers a more detailed guide for avoiding the common pitfalls of change interventions. It also links change back to culture by showing how the change needs to be incorporated into organizational culture in order to stabilize it.

Hayes (2014) takes a slightly different approach in recognizing the different steps in a change process, starting with a recognition of the drivers for change and offering a framework that summarizes many of the other change models that have been proposed and notes the importance of feedback loops throughout the process. Table 7.2 overleaf summarizes each of these approaches and shows how they expand on Lewin's three stages.

## Action research and learning organizations

Lewin's model should be understood as part of his overall model of groups and how they change (Burnes, 2004b). In terms of how change should be implemented, Lewin (1946) recommended an approach called **action research** or 'research that will help the practitioner'. Any actions we take to achieve the change should be based on a thorough analysis and understanding of the situation ('research'), and follow these steps:

* Planning: develop an overall idea of how to reach the objective, which should be based on diagnosis of the problem. Use this to identify possible solutions and choose the preferred option

* Executing: carry out the plan, but maintain an adaptive approach based on constant evaluation

* Evaluation and Fact-finding: evaluate the actions and learn from them by gathering data on impacts

Action research is an iterative process, meaning that change managers need to engage in a constant

Table 7.2 **Expanding the model**

| Lewin | Kotter | Hayes |
|-------|--------|-------|
| | | • Noticing problems or opportunities as a result of external environmental changes |
| • Unfreeze | • Establish a sense of urgency: it is important that everyone realizes that change needs to happen now<br><br>• Create a guiding coalition: gather a group to lead the change who will work well together and have the power to see it through<br><br>• Develop a change vision: create a vision to guide the change and strategies to implement it<br><br>• Communicate the vision for buy-in: get as many people on board as possible | • Recognize the need for change and start the process: this involves recognizing the external pressures or internal circumstances that mean a change is needed and making decisions about who to involve in the change<br><br>• Diagnosis: identifying a future state that the organization wishes to move towards needs to be based on an accurate understanding of the current state: the vision of the desired future needs to be attainable<br><br>• Plan and prepare to change: a thorough change plan will need details of how it is going to be implemented and often this list will be very long. But this stage is also about preparing people for change and dealing with potential political aspects of the change, not just planning the technical changes |
| • Move | • Empower broad-based action: get as many people actively involved in the change as possible by removing barriers to change and encouraging new ideas<br><br>• Generate short-term wins: plan for visible achievements and reward those involved<br><br>• Never let up: consolidate improvements and make continual readjustments to keep change on track | • Implement the change: the plan is put into action. However, this is rarely a straightforward process of just doing what the plan says, it will need to be adapted and refined as the change progresses. Importantly, the implementation needs to be monitored and feedback becomes essential. With change that is more broadly defined and may not have a specific end point, the implementation stage may be more a series of small, incremental steps that are constantly evaluated |
| • Refreeze | • Incorporate change into the culture: make it clear how the changes have increased organizational success | • Sustain the change: this can be done by ensuring that reward systems reinforce the new behaviours and by building on the feedback mechanisms to continue to monitor the change |

cycle of planning, executing and evaluation, adapting the change process to the specific situation incorporating any new or unexpected results of the change. The Applications activity demonstrates how to apply this process to a challenge at work. Hayes (2010), in his integration of various change models, notes the importance of this ongoing review and adaptation of the process, particularly in terms of the impact on people and the implications for their management. Any change at work, no matter how much it seems solely technical, will have an impact on the people who work there, and change agents need to consider issues of motivation, politics, power and so on. We will return

## Applications: **Action research in action**

Miguel is the HR manager in a medium-sized game development company, which primarily employs young computer programmers and animators. The organization is looking for ways to enhance its flexibility and one proposal has been to move to a more flexible working pattern. A survey of current employees has revealed that a popular option is to try a four-day working week. Miguel has decided to use action research to implement and evaluate this change, the aim being to make a final decision on the working pattern in six months' time.

» What steps should Miguel take to ensure that he can make the best decision on the final working pattern? (Use the action research model in Figure 7.3 as a guide.) Think about what level of detail the plan should contain, the kind of data he needs to gather and how he can maintain an adaptive approach.

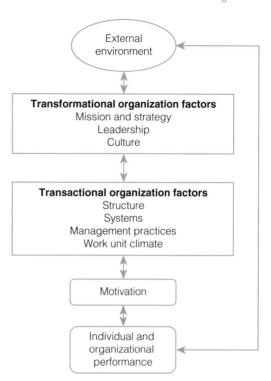

Figure 7.3 A systems model of change

Source: Adapted with permission from Burke, W. and Litwin, G. H. (1992) 'A causal model of organizational performance and change', *Journal of Management*, 18(3), pp. 523–45. Permission conveyed through Copyright Clearance Center, Inc.

to this continual cycle of evaluation in discussions in Chapter 10 about learning organizations, which are defined by their engagement in this cycle of continual transformation and development.

## The systems perspective

Organizational change is a complex process but unfortunately the 'step' models we have considered so far may tempt some people into thinking it can be managed in a fairly simplistic way. A systems perspective can be a good antidote to this, by helping to remind us that any work organization is a system of interrelated and mutually dependent parts. A simplified version of one of these systems models of change is shown in Figure 7.3 (Burke and Litwin, 1992).

This model reminds us that the organization is open to its environment and affected by it, as well as distinguishing between two types of change:

1. Transformational change: in response to the environment and requiring whole new sets of behaviours

2. Transactional change: brought about by short-term reciprocity between organizational members.

Although more complex than the stepped models of change, it helps to highlight how many different factors we need to consider in the management of change. It is not enough simply to develop a good organizational mission and strategy and hope that this will be enough to carry the change through. The impacts of change in any one of these factors will be felt throughout the system and change in one will lead to change in another, sometimes in unexpected ways. A particularly important point of this model is the way it highlights *how* change impacts on organizational performance: it is not a direct effect, but occurs through the changes in employees, and gives particular precedence to the impact on employee motivation.

## *Organization development*

This emphasis on the 'human' side of organizational change is at the root of **organization development (OD)** approaches to change. OD is closely allied with HRM and a subject of study in its own right, but is essentially concerned with organization-wide interventions to ensure continual organizational survival. Organizational effectiveness is measured not only in terms of production and efficiency but also in terms of the quality of working life and employee well-being. The values underlying this approach are collaborative and democratic, treating people as human beings with needs, rather than just as a 'resource' for the organization to use. The OD approach originally sought to develop work so that people had the chance to develop their full potential and the organization could achieve all its goals (Margulies and Raia, 1972).

However, later developments in the field seem to have moved away from the focus on individual learning and involvement to emphasize the role of senior managers in decisions about change and to exclude employees who do not fit with the new culture. For example, an OD approach to culture change (Cummings and Huse, 1989) recommends five steps, of which three involve top management (in creating vision, being committed to the change and providing leadership) and one involves modifying structures and systems. The only step to mention other employees recommends selecting those who fit with the new culture and removing those who do not – a far cry from the collaborative approach that OD was based on.

The OD field seems to have undergone a process of renewal in the past years (Burnes and Cooke, 2012). Recent business scandals have emphasized the importance of ethics and values in organizations, which fits in well with the original basis of OD, and there is an increased rigour and relevance to OD models. Finally, OD is absorbing theories of emergent change and complexity, which were previously seen as challenging the whole approach.

## SUMMARY

We started this chapter by looking at organizational culture as the context in which change happens

 **Practice Insights: Rebecca Lencho**

Rebecca Lencho is a Human Resources Manager at Rockline Industries, an American manufacturing company with five sites in the USA as well as locations in the UK and China. She is based at the Springdale, Arkansas site. In the video she talks about the range of tasks she undertakes as a general HR manager as well as sharing insights into managing culture and change within her organization.

Go online to www.macmillanihe.com/sutton-people to access the interview with Rebecca.

and a subject of change management itself. We then moved on to consider the current trends that organizations and individuals are facing and how they can best be addressed. Dealing with change effectively is an essential skill for today's managers and HR professionals, and we looked at the individual and organizational issues that need to be addressed in change management. These models can help us to understand the basic stages that people go through and that managers can use to plan organizational change. But it is also useful to view change as a continuously evolving process in which we can take an active, experimental role: a process that treats the organization and culture as an integrated whole.

## FURTHER READING

- For an interesting and detailed illustration of culture as a mechanism for control, see Casey, C. (1999) '"Come, join our family": discipline and integration in corporate organizational culture', *Human Relations*, 52(2), pp. 155–78.

- For a discussion of how to enhance success in changing culture, read Smith, M. E. (2003) 'Changing an organisation's culture: correlates of success and failure', *Leadership & Organization Development Journal*, 24(5), pp. 249–61.

• For a more detailed introduction to the psychological process of dealing with change, try Parkes, C. (1971) 'Psycho-social transitions: a field for study', *Social Science & Medicine*, 5(2), pp. 101–115.

## REVIEW QUESTIONS

1. How does organizational culture impact on performance?

2. Why is culture an important element to consider in change management?

3. What can managers do to support their staff through a change process?

## ONLINE RESOURCES

Go online to www.macmillanihe.com/sutton-people to access a MCQ quiz for this chapter and for further resources to support your learning.

## REFERENCES

Barton, L. C. and Ambrosini, V. (2012) 'The moderating effect of organizational change cynicism on middle manager strategy commitment', *International Journal of Human Resource Management*, 24(4), pp. 1–26. doi: 10.1080/09585192.2012.697481.

Berliant, M. and Fujita, M. (2012) 'Culture and diversity in knowledge creation', *Regional Science and Urban Economics*, 42(4), pp. 648–62. doi: 10.1016/j.regsciurbeco.2012.02.008.

Bolon, D. S. and Bolon, D. S. (1994) 'A reconceptualization and analysis of organizational culture', *Journal of Managerial Psychology*, 9(5), pp. 22–7. doi: 10.1108/02683949410066336.

Bower, M. (1966) *The Will to Manage: Corporate Success Through Programmed Management*. New York: McGraw-Hill.

Bridges, W. (1980) *Transitions: Making Sense of Life's Changes*. Cambridge, MA: Addison-Wesley.

Bridges, W. (2009) *Managing Transitions: Making the Most of Change*, 3rd edn. Philadelphia: Da Capo Press.

Brown, S. L. and Eisenhardt, K. M. (1997) 'The art of continuous change: linking complexity theory and time-paced evolution in relentlessly shifting organizations', *Administrative Science Quarterly*, 42(1), pp. 1–34. doi: 10.2307/2393807.

Bruns, H.-J. (2014) 'HR development in local government: how and why does HR strategy matter in organizational change and development?', *Business Research*, 7(1), pp. 1–49. doi: 10.1007/s40685-014-0002-z.

Burke, W. and Litwin, G. H. (1992) 'A causal model of organizational performance and change', *Journal of Management*, 18(3), pp. 523–45.

Burnes, B. (2004a) 'Emergent change and planned change – competitors or allies?: The case of XYZ construction', *International Journal of Operations & Production Management*, 24(9), pp. 886–902. doi: 10.1108/01443570410552108.

Burnes, B. (2004b) 'Kurt Lewin and the planned approach to change: a re-appraisal', *Journal of Management Studies*, 41(6), pp. 977–1002.

Burnes, B. and Cooke, B. (2012) 'The past, present and future of organization development: taking the long view', *Human Relations*, 65(11), pp. 1395–429. doi: 10.1177/0018726712450058.

Burton, R. M., Lauridsen, J. and Obel, B. (2004) 'The impact of organizational climate and strategic fit on firm performance', *Human Resource Management*, 43(1), pp. 67–82. doi: 10.1002/hrm.20003.

Casey, C. (1996) 'Corporate transformations: designer culture, designer employees and "post-occupational" solidarity', *Organization*, 3(3), pp. 317–39.

Casey, C. (1999) '"Come, join our family": discipline and integration in corporate organizational culture', *Human Relations*, 52(2), pp. 155–78.

Chatman, J. A. and Jehn, K. A. (1994) 'Assessing the relationship between industry characteristics and organizational culture: How different can you be?', *Academy of Management Journal*, 37(3), pp. 522–53. doi: 10.2307/256699.

Choi, M. (2011) 'Employees' attitudes toward organizational change: a literature review', *Human Resource Management*, 50(4), pp. 479–500. doi: 10.1002/hrm.20434.

Cummings, T. G. and Huse, E. F. (1989) *Organization Development and Change*. St Paul, MN: West Publishing.

Denison, D. R. (1996) 'What is the difference between organizational culture and organizational climate? A native's point of view on a decade of paradigm wars', *Academy of Management Review*, 21(3), pp. 619–54. Available at: www.jstor.org/stable/258997.

Ford, M. W. and Greer, B. M. (2006) 'Profiling change: an empirical study of change process patterns', *Journal of Applied Behavioral Science*, 42(4), pp. 420–46.

Frese, M. (2008) 'The changing nature of work', in N. Chmiel (ed.) *Introduction to Work and Organizational Psychology: A European Perspective*. Oxford: Blackwell, pp. 397–413.

Gersick, C. J. (1991) 'Revolutionary change theories: a multilevel exploration of the punctuated equilibrium paradigm', *Academy of Management Review*, 16(1), pp. 10–36. doi: 10.5465/AMR.1991.4278988.

Gover, L., Halinski, M. and Duxbury, L. (2016) 'Is it just me? Exploring perceptions of organizational culture change', *British Journal of Management*, 27(3), pp. 567–82. doi: 10.1111/1467-8551.12117.

Hanson, S. (2010) 'Change management and organizational effectiveness for the HR professional', *Cornell HR Review*, pp. 1–7.

Hayes, J. (2010) *The Theory and Practice of Change Management*, 3rd edn. Basingstoke: Palgrave Macmillan.

Hayes, J. (2014) *The Theory and Practice of Change Management*, 4th edn. Basingstoke: Palgrave Macmillan.

James, L. R., Choi, C. C., Ko, C. H. E. et al. (2008) 'Organizational and psychological climate: a review of theory and research', *European Journal of Work and Organizational Psychology*, 17(1), pp. 5–32. doi: Doi 10.1080/13594320701662550.

Kanter, R. M., Stein, B. and Jick, T. (1992) *The Challenge of Organizational Change: How Companies Experience it and Leaders Guide it*. New York: Free Press.

Kennedy, B. (2014) 'When corporate cultures clash: defining company values across borders', *The Guardian*, 29 September. Available at: www.theguardian.com/sustainable-business/2014/sep/29/corporate-social-responsibility-coors-molson-nike-coke.

Kim Jean Lee, S. and Yu, K. (2004) 'Corporate culture and organizational performance', *Journal of Managerial Psychology*, 19(4), pp. 340–59. doi: 10.1108/02683940410537927.

Kotter, J. P. (1996) *Leading Change*. Boston: Harvard Business School Press.

Kotter, J. P. and Schlesinger, L. A. (1979) 'Choosing strategies for change', *Harvard Business Review*, 57(2), pp. 106–14.

Lee, S.-Y. D., Weiner, B. J., Harrison, M. I. and Belden, C. M. (2013) 'Organizational transformation: a systematic review of empirical research in health care and other industries', *Medical Care Research and Review*, 70(2), pp. 115–42. doi: 10.1177/1077558712458539.

Lewin, K. (1946) 'Action research and minority problems', *Journal of Social Issues*, 2(4), pp. 34–46.

Lewin, K. (1951) *Field Theory in Social Science: Selected Theoretical Papers*. New York: Harper & Row.

Lewin, K. (1997) *Resolving Social Conflicts and Field Theory in Social Science*. Washington DC: American Psychological Association.

Li, S. K. and Jones, G. (2010) 'A study of the effect of functional subcultures on the performance of Hong Kong construction companies', *Systemic Practice and Action Research*, 23(6), pp. 509–28. doi: 10.1007/s11213-010-9170-8.

Lord, R. G., Dinh, J. E. and Hoffman, E. L. (2015) 'A quantum approach to time and organizational change', *Academy of Management Review*, 40(2), pp. 263–90. doi: 10.5465/amr.2013.0273.

Maheshwari, S. and Vohra, V. (2015) 'Identifying critical HR practices impacting employee perception and commitment during organizational change', *Journal of Organizational Change Management*, 28(5), pp. 872–94. doi: 10.1108/JOCM-03-2014-0066.

Margulies, N. and Raia, A. P. (1972) *Organizational Development: Values, Processes, and Technology*. New York: McGraw-Hill.

Molineux, J. (2013) 'Enabling organizational cultural change using systemic strategic human resource management: a longitudinal case study', *International Journal of Human Resource Management*, 24(8), pp. 1588–612. doi: 10.1080/09585192.2012.723022.

Molson Coors Brewing Company (2016) *How We Work*. Available at: www.molsoncoors.com/en/responsibility/how we work (Accessed 23 December 2016).

Nestlé (2016) *Nestlé Global: Our Vision*. Available at: www.nestle.com/randd/ourvision (Accessed 20 December 2016).

Nestlé Waters (2016) *Inside Nestlé Waters: Key Figures*. Available at: www.nestle-waters.com/aboutus/key-figures (Accessed 20 December 2016).

O'Reilly, C. A., Chatman, J. and Caldwell, D. F. (1991) 'People and organizational culture: a profile comparison approach to assessing person-organization fit', *Academy of Management Journal*, 34(3), pp. 487–516.

Parkes, C. M. (1993) 'Bereavement as a psychosocial transition: processes of adaptation to change', in *Handbook of Bereavement: Theory, Research, and Intervention*. New York: Cambridge University Press, pp. 91–101.

Romanelli, E., Tushman, M. L. and Michael, L. (1994) 'Organizational transformation as punctuated equilibrium: an empirical test', *Academy of Management Journal*, 37(5), pp. 1141–66. doi: 10.2307/256669.

Schein, E. H. (2004) *Organizational Culture and Leadership*, 3rd edn. San Francisco, CA: Jossey-Bass.

Schumacher, D., Schreurs, B., Van Emmerik, H. and De Witte, H. (2016) 'Explaining the relation between job insecurity and employee outcomes during organizational change: a multiple group comparison', *Human Resource Management*, 55(5), pp. 809–27. doi: 10.1002/hrm.21687.

Shen, L. (2016) *These are the 12 Biggest Mergers and Acquisitions of 2016*. Available at: http://fortune.com/2016/06/13/12-biggest-mergers-and-acquisitions-of-2016/ (Accessed 20 December 2016).

Shin, J., Taylor, M. S. and Seo, M. G. (2012) 'Resources for change: the relationships of organizational inducements and psychological resilience to employees' attitudes and behaviors toward organizational change', *Academy of Management Journal*, 55(3), pp. 727–48. doi: 10.5465/amj.2010.0325.

Sinclair, A. (1993) 'Approaches to organisational culture and ethics approaches to organisational culture and ethics', *Journal of Business Ethics*, 12(1), pp. 63–73.

Sleutel, M. R. (2000) 'Climate, culture, context, or work environment? Organizational factors that influence nursing practice', *Journal of Nursing Administration*, 30(2), pp. 53–8. doi: 10.1097/00005110-200002000-00002.

Smith, M. E. (2003) 'Changing an organisation's culture: correlates of success and failure', *Leadership & Organization Development Journal*, 24(5), pp. 249–61. doi: 10.1108/01437730310485752.

Staw, B. M. and Epstein, L. D. (2000) 'What bandwagons bring: effects of popular management techniques on corporate performance, reputation, and CEO pay', *Administrative Science Quarterly*, 45(3), pp. 523–56.

Stuart, R. (1995) 'Experiencing organizational change: triggers, processes and outcomes of change journeys', *Personnel Review*, 24(2), pp. 3–88. doi: 10.1108/00483489510085726.

Tushman, M. L. and Romanelli, E. (1985) 'Organizational evolution: a metamorphosis model of convergence and reorientation', *Research in Organizational Behavior*, 7, pp. 171–222.

Vakola, M. (2013) 'Multilevel readiness to organizational change: a conceptual approach', *Journal of Change Management*, 13(1), pp. 96–109. doi: 10.1080/14697017.2013.768436.

Vakola, M., Tsaousis, I. and Nikolaou, I. (2004) 'The role of emotional intelligence and personality variables on attitudes toward organisational change', *Journal of Managerial Psychology*, 19(2), pp. 88–110. doi: 10.1108/02683940410526082.

Van den Berg, P. T. and Wilderom, C. P. M. (2004) 'Defining, measuring, and comparing organisational cultures', *Applied Psychology*, 53(4), pp. 570–82. doi: 10.1111/j.1464-0597.2004.00189.x.

Weick, K. E. (2000) 'Emergent change as a universal in organizations', in M. Beer and N. Nohria (eds) *Breaking the Code of Change*. Boston, MA: Harvard Business School Press, pp. 223–41.

# 8 STRATEGY: CREATING PURPOSE

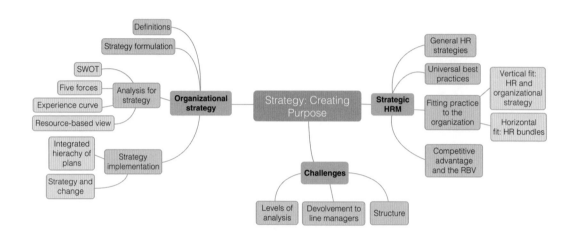

## INTRODUCTION

So far in our discussion of how to create organizational effectiveness we have considered the role of culture and change in creating competitive advantage. In this chapter we are developing this further by considering the integrative and guiding role of organizational strategy. Drawing on the OB and management literature, we start by evaluating what we mean by strategy and how it consists of two main interrelated elements: formulation and implementation. There are several models available to aid us in analysing the organization and its environment as a basis for the formulation of effective strategy, and we will consider the kinds of strategies that can be formulated in response to the different factors picked up by these analyses. A well-formulated strategy is only half the issue though, as

we also need to consider how that strategy can be implemented throughout the organization and how the resultant changes are managed.

With this foundation in strategic management, we then turn to discuss a specific application, that of strategic HRM. There are two important elements here: how HRM can contribute effectively to formulating organizational strategy and HR's key role in implementing strategy. We will look into the debate over whether SHRM should focus on specific practices or try to develop a best fit approach before seeing how a resource-based view of the organization can help to elucidate the contribution of SHRM to organizational performance. We end with a consideration of three main challenges facing SHRM.

*Getty Images*

## LEARNING FEATURES

Applications: Thinking differently

Applications: SWOT analysis

Applications: Developing HR strategy

Weighing the Evidence: Strategy as practice

Web Explorer: How unique are HR strategies?

In the News: SHRM failure?

Transferrable Skills: Scenario planning

Practice Insights: Kris DeLano

 Video overview

Julian Perkins

Go online to www.macmillanihe.com/sutton-people to access a video of Anna Sutton introducing the chapter's main themes.

# ORGANIZATIONAL STRATEGY

## Definitions

An organization's strategy is its understanding of the business it is in (or should be in) and its plan for future success. The Greek and Latin roots of our word 'strategy' include the concept of 'the art of leading an army' as well as the ideas of a 'pathway' or 'coverage/spread' (Linstead et al., 2009, p. 711). Linstead et al. highlight some important considerations for our discussions of organizational strategy from this analysis of strategy's roots. First, strategy is associated with the legitimization of hierarchy: it is seen as something that 'top management' does, separating them from the rest of the workforce. Second, strategy is an art as well as a science, a process that includes data-gathering, decision-making and the ability to engage in nuanced thinking. (We explore this further in the Applications activity.) And, third, strategy contains an element of competition and aims at defeating an opponent. This is reflected in the writing about strategic management, which views it as the source of competitive advantage.

---

## Applications: **Thinking differently**

We often think of business degrees and MBAs as prerequisites for people in top management, but they are not the only ways to success in business. In fact, two of the most important elements of business success in the tech revolution are creativity and the ability to think critically, both of which are developed in arts and humanities degrees. An example of this different approach is found in Slack Technologies.

Slack Technologies, creators of a team messaging app, was the Forbes' top ranked cloud computing company in 2016 (Forbes, 2016) and achieved a valuation of $1 billion in just 15 months – the fastest ever (Kim, 2015). Anna Pickard, editorial director of Slack Technologies, studied theatre. She describes her job as providing users with 'extra bits of surprise and delight' (Anders, 2015). And Stewart Butterfield, the CEO, whose stake in the company is worth an estimated $300 million, studied philosophy and the history of science at university. Butterfield believes his studies taught him three essential things for his role as CEO: clarity of expression, the ability to follow an argument to its underlying assumptions, and an understanding of how and why we believe things to be true. That ability to think differently and to value the role of creativity and social skills even in tech companies is increasingly essential to success.

» Do a quick survey of your fellow students and find out what they have studied in the past. If these people were all part of your team at work, how could you make best use of their different approaches in developing and implementing a strategy?

» What practical steps can a manager take to ensure that they value and utilize the contributions that employees with different backgrounds can make?

---

Because strategy is such a wide-ranging field, Henry Mintzberg (1987a) suggested that it cannot be defined as a single concept. Instead, 'strategy' consists of five interrelated concepts, known as Mintzberg's '5Ps of strategy':

1. **Plan:** a strategy is an intended course of action that can be general or specific. This could be developed, for example, by brainstorming or conducting a PEST or **SWOT analysis** (see Chapter 3 for how to do a PEST analysis and the later section in this chapter for a SWOT analysis).

2. **Ploy:** a more specific strategy that is undertaken to outwit or beat a competitor, for example,

a car dealer could reduce the price of its cars in the same week that a competitor launches a new model. This definition emphasizes the competitive nature of inter-organizational strategies.

3. **Pattern:** consistency in behaviour (whether or not the actions were intended) is also referred to as strategy. Sometimes, this strategy may be inferred after the fact as a way of making sense of the organization's or management's actions. An example might be a researcher in a pharmaceutical company that is known for its innovations finding new ways to improve the

products. The researcher simply acts in line with the company's normal approach to doing business.

4. **Position:** strategy refers to the match or fit between the organization and its environment. As an example, a watchmaker might position itself as a luxury manufacturer and its products and prices would match this place in the market.

5. **Perspective:** strategy can also be seen as a worldview, a shared perspective managers in an organization take when deciding how to act. For example, an innovative company is likely to have a more risk-taking perspective than one which relies on consistency of quality. This is similar to the concept of culture, which we looked at in Chapter 7.

Many of the most popular texts on strategy are essentially Western – and predominantly American – but there are alternative approaches to strategy that it is worth being aware of. For example, a very different point of view is described by Rosalie Tung (1994) in her article summarizing the East Asian approach to business strategy. She identifies 12 themes that guide the East Asian approach to business, drawn from four classical texts including Sun Tzu's *The Art of War*. The first of these themes recognizes the importance of strategies. While a strategy providing a swift victory over an opponent is the most preferred option, the East Asian approach would then prefer diplomacy to a more protracted confrontation, even if it results in victory. There is also a much longer term view in the East Asian approach, with patience recognized as one of the central elements in success. Being aware of these different approaches and our own cultural bias in developing strategies will improve our ability to construct effective, international strategies.

Having a clear strategy is often considered an essential for any organization, and the advantages seem self-evident. For example, strategy helps set direction, focus effort and provide consistency for the organization. But each of those advantages comes with disadvantages too (Mintzberg et al., 1998). In setting direction, an organization may be blind to potential dangers or fail to respond appropriately to changes. Or, in coordinating efforts, it may encourage **groupthink**, that is, when a group of people want coherence and conformity so much that they fail to recognize different ways of doing things and their decision-making is

impaired. This highlights the distinction between the two elements of strategy: formulation and implementation. Even the most carefully and brilliantly formulated strategy can fail if it is not implemented well, or it is formulated so rigidly that implementation cannot be adapted to a changing internal or external environment. In the next sections we will consider the various approaches to developing strategy before moving on to discuss how strategy is implemented.

## Strategy formulation

Approaches to strategic management have developed over the past few decades from a rigid, prescriptive approach that assumed a stable and 'knowable' environment, in which plans could be made and implemented fairly easily, to more contingent, emergent approaches, which recognize instability and ambiguity as essential elements of the business and its environment. Mintzberg and colleagues described ten different schools of thought that have developed in the study of strategy formation (Mintzberg et al., 1998; Mintzberg and Lampel, 1999). Table 8.1 summarizes these schools and the three general categories they are grouped into.

We will not review each of these approaches in detail here (the Further Reading section includes recommendations if you would like to read more about them); instead, the following sections will highlight some of the important strategic *elements* that can be drawn from these approaches. These elements are essentially different ways of analysing important aspects of the organization and its environment in order to formulate effective strategy.

## Analysis for strategy formulation

### SWOT analysis

For many strategy authors, the fit between the organization and its environment is an essential component of a good strategy. This fit is dependent on having a fair idea of the organization's current strengths and weaknesses as well as an understanding of the environmental opportunities and challenges, and a SWOT (strengths, weaknesses, opportunities and threats) analysis is a popular way of analysing and conceptualizing these components. The Applications activity guides you through this analysis and some

Table 8.1 **Schools and categories of strategy formulation**

| Category | Concerned with | School of thought | Strategy formation |
|---|---|---|---|
| Prescriptive or normative | How strategy *should* be devised | Design | Should be a process of conception and informal design. It looks to create a fit between internal strengths and weaknesses and external opportunities and threats. The SWOT model developed in this approach |
| | | Planning | Should be a detached and systematic process of formal planning. The plans are drawn up in a series of clear steps and supported by objectives, budgets and so on |
| | | Positioning | Should be an analytical process to select appropriate position in the market. This approach suggests there are a limited range of specific market positions and accurate analysis is needed to ensure the organization chooses the right one |
| Descriptive | How strategy actually gets made | Entrepreneurial | Develops from the vision of an innovative leader. Often focused on startups but also includes leaders responsible for revitalizing a business. Formulation and implementation tend not to be as distinct in this approach |
| | | Cognitive | Develops through the mental processes in the manager's mind. In this approach, we need to be aware of the **cognitive biases** and distortions that affect the process as well as how we use strategy to interpret reality |
| | | Learning | Is an emergent process as the organization learns and adapts to its environment. Strategy here is no longer the province only of top management but is shared by people throughout the organization, and formulation and implementation are closely interwoven |
| | | Power | Develops through a process of negotiation between the organization and the environment (e.g. using power over partners to negotiate collective strategy in its favour) and between different groups in the organization (e.g. political manoeuvring and bargaining) |
| | | Cultural | Is a collective and social process. Culture can act to restrict strategic change or encourage it, as well as determining the direction of effort |
| | | Environmental | Develops as the organization reacts to its environment. Different elements of the environment will require different strategies and the environment exerts limits on the range of choices available to organizations |
| Transformative | Integrating elements from the other schools in order to transform the organization | Configuration | Changes as the organization develops through different stages or cycles. This approach integrates the other schools by identifying them with different types of organization and environment |

important questions about the process. SWOT analyses are often seen as objective, rational techniques for gathering data, which can be used as a basis for decision-making and strategic development. However, as you engage in the activity you will see that the process of conducting the analysis involves many subjective decisions and evaluations. In fact, a SWOT analysis might be best thought of as a summary of managers' perceptions rather than an objective reflection of the organization and its environment.

 Applications: **SWOT analysis**

This activity works best if you can carry it out in a group. Choose an organization you all know fairly well, for example Amazon or Microsoft. Construct a grid as below and discuss what aspects you would assign to each of the boxes. Strengths and weaknesses refer to elements within the organization, while opportunities and threats are outside the organization, for example competitors or legal challenges.

| Strengths | Weaknesses |
|---|---|
| Opportunities | Threats |

» Based on this analysis, develop a simple strategy for the organization by outlining what it should aim to do over the next five years.

» Once you have completed this, reflect on the process of carrying out a SWOT analysis. How 'objective' do you think your analysis was? How might your analysis change if you had access to further data, such as numbers and abilities of employees, knowledge of competitors and so on? Were there any elements that could be assigned to more than one box in the matrix? For example, having a highly paid workforce could be a strength (low turnover), a weakness (are employees loyal only because of the money?) or a threat (competitors have lower staff costs).

In the SWOT analysis, strengths and weaknesses are seen as fixed entities, as is the environment itself. This lack of dynamism is one of the frequent criticisms of a planned approach to strategizing. But the East Asian approach to strategizing that Tung (1994) describes has a focus on *transforming an adversary's strength into weakness*. It emphasizes instead a flexible approach to strategy, including understanding the interrelationship of situations, finding compromises and acting to take advantage of a competitor's misfortune. So, in using the SWOT analysis, it can be helpful to consider how a strategy might be able to transform a strength or weaknesses rather than simply use it as it is.

### The five forces model and resultant strategies

Fitting the organization to the environment requires an understanding of how forces in the environment impact on the organization's positioning. For Porter (1979, p. 137), coping with these competitive forces was, in fact, the 'essence of strategy formulation' and he identified five basic forces, known as Porter's *'five forces model'*:

1. **Threat of new entrants to the industry:** this is reduced if barriers to entry are high. Barriers include capital requirements, knowledge and experience, and access to distribution channels, among others. An example here is the threat to national postal services brought about by independent delivery companies, particularly with the increase in internet shopping.

2. **Threat of substitutes:** this is the extent to which the product or service is unique or might be replaced by alternatives. For example, mobile phones act as a substitute to watches as a product for telling the time.

3. **Power of suppliers:** powerful suppliers can threaten the profitability and success of an

organization by, for example, increasing the costs of raw materials or reducing their quality.

4. **Power of customers:** customers can have a large impact on an organization. The greater their choice of competitors or alternatives, the larger that impact will be. Consumer groups, for example, may bring together many hundreds or thousands of customers to address an issue of concern with the supplying organization.

5. **Competitive rivalry:** this is with other organizations already operating in the industry. Among other things, competition is more intense where the service or product on offer, for example table salt, is less differentiated or industry growth is slow.

Porter (1980) suggests that, based on the analysis of forces for a particular organization, an appropriate strategy should be chosen to defend against potential threats and to take advantage of changes – and even to create those changes in the industry that would help the organization to greater profitability. Porter suggested three basic competitive strategies:

1. **Cost leadership:** the organization delivers products or services at a lower price than competitors

2. **Differentiation:** the organization delivers products or services that are differentiated from their competitors' offerings on dimensions other than price, for example, higher quality

3. **Focus:** the organization focuses on a narrow segment of the market and aims to meet the needs of those customers specifically, for example by producing a unique product or service.

Porter's recognition that the organization can adopt a strategy to *change* its environment as well as being affected by the environment is an important reminder that organizations are active agents rather than simply responding passively to the forces around them.

## *The experience curve and growth share strategies*

Similar to Porter's suggestion that strategy should be based on analysis of the organization and its environment, and that similar strategies will be appropriate for organizations in similar situations, is the Boston Consulting Group (BCG) approach. BCG based its strategy recommendations on research into the effect of the organization's production experience (as measured by the number of units sold) on the costs of producing those units. BCG found that costs reduced by 20–30% every time experience (the cumulative number of units produced) doubled, as shown in Figure 8.1.

*Creatas*

*National postal services are increasingly threatened by independent delivery companies.*

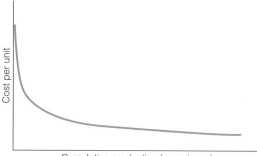

Cumulative production (experience)

*Figure 8.1 The experience curve*

Bruce Henderson (1968), the founder of BCG, did not claim that this reduction in costs was automatic, but that it was the result of managers making a strategic choice to reduce costs in order to remain profitable. These costs are not simply the costs of production, but the R&D, marketing, sales and everything else associated with delivering the product to the end user. The implication is that an organization with a dominant market share will be able to accumulate experience more rapidly than its competitors and therefore maintain a self-perpetuating advantage. Based on this curve, BCG developed a 'growth share matrix', which recommended different strategies for products dependent on their market share and the level of growth in the market: investing in those that had potential and withdrawing those products that had reached the end of their life-cycle.

The experience curve and its associated strategies are particularly relevant for organizations that operate by *fulfilling* demand but not so helpful for those that succeed by *shaping* demand – which BCG argues is essential for the majority of organizations today (Reeves et al., 2013). Instead, these organizations need to operate in a cycle of shaping and fulfilling demand, and each of these processes will require different strategies. For example, one of the key issues for an organization to address here is to 'unlink' the management of existing products from the development of new ones. While the former requires a cost-cutting approach, the latter requires risk-taking and experimentation. An organization that can effectively engage in both strategies simultaneously is referred to as 'ambidextrous'.

## Resource-based view

An alternative to the product- and market-focused strategies of Porter and BCG was suggested by Wernerfelt in the early 1980s. He recommended that strategists should analyse their organizations using a **'resource-based view'** (Wernerfelt, 1984). He saw resources and products as two sides of the same coin. We can either analyse the organization's current product markets and from this develop strategy to ensure the necessary resources are in place for optimum performance, or we can analyse the organization's current resource profile and develop strategy for its optimal activities. Resources can be tangible, such as machinery or capital, or

intangible, such as networks and contacts, skilled employees or technological expertise. Strategies should be developed that balance the exploitation of existing resources with the development of new resources. Resources can be analysed using the VRIO framework (Barney, 1991, 1995):

- Valuable: Does the resource add value by allowing the organization to exploit opportunities or neutralize threats? For example, an organization might have a well-funded and agile R&D team who are at the forefront of developments in their field and able to turn new ideas into practical innovations quickly.

- Rare: How unique is the resource? If many of the competitors have the same resources, the organization is not going to be able to gain advantage from it. For example, all the competitors may have technological expertise in developing computer software, but if only one organization has a well-developed customer service system with socially skilled employees, it will gain an advantage.

- Inimitable: How easily can the resource be copied or substituted? For example, new drugs are protected by patent for 20 years but after that time it is fairly easy for copycat drugs to be made and sold by other companies.

- Organized: Is the firm organized to exploit the resources effectively? For example, an organization that wants to remain at the forefront of its field needs to provide incentives for innovations and the organizational support for risk-taking.

It is only when a resource meets all these criteria that it can be a source of sustained competitive advantage (Barney, 1991). The resource-based view can provide a basis for strategizing that is particularly suitable for turbulent environments, and although most of the research around it has been conducted in private organizations, it seems equally applicable to public organizations looking to improve their flexibility (Szymaniec-Mlicka, 2014).

However, the resource-based view has been criticized for being overly inclusive in its definition of resources and for not clarifying how resources contribute to competitive advantage or how their value can be ascertained (Priem and Butler, 2001). It has also been criticized as 'paradoxical': for example, the resource-based view claims that a resource which is less observable will be harder for competitors to copy and therefore contribute more to competitive advantage. However, if it is unobservable, how can we be sure of its value? Lado et al. (2006) suggest, in contrast, that far from being a problem, recognizing this very paradoxical nature can help us to understand the complexities of strategic management in the real world.

Maintaining awareness of complexity is one of the areas where the East Asian approach to strategy differs from the Western approach. While both approaches emphasize the importance of gathering information and using it to develop understanding, the Western style of analysing and planning tends to try to 'cut through' complexities to find the simplest solution, while the East Asian style is more open to complexities and aims to understand and use contradictions (Tung, 1994). This challenge of dealing with complexity is also central to any attempts to analyse and plan strategy, and is further highlighted in the Transferrable Skills activity, which looks at how we can plan for the future.

## Transferrable Skills: Scenario planning

One of the biggest challenges that managers face when attempting to formulate strategies is the difficulty of predicting the future with any kind of accuracy, especially because we are all subject to biases and errors in decision-making. Schoemaker (1995, p. 25) suggested that managers who can 'expand their imaginations to see a wider range of possible futures' will be better able to take advantage of opportunities. *Scenario planning* allows managers to consider the joint impact of many variables and uncertainties simultaneously and to include objective analysis and subjective interpretation. Scenarios are developed in a way that allows managers to consider the impact of various changes in a somewhat simplified manner. For example, instead of considering hundreds of interest rate changes, it could be simplified to low, medium and high. In this way, the range of possibilities are covered in broad terms.

Scenario development should be a team effort, including line managers and strategists within the organization as well as external people such as regulators, customers or academics. The wider the range of people involved in the development of scenarios, the greater the diversity and the more accurate the perceptions of the future are likely to be.

Scenario planning can be used for any exploration of the future. In this exercise, we will look at how you can use it to explore your future career using a simplified version of the ten stages Schoemaker (1995) describes.

1. **Define the scope:** What timeframe will you limit the scenarios to? Will you consider the possibility of a change in career or focus solely on one predefined career route? What are your geographic limits?

2. **Identify the major stakeholders:** Who has an interest in your career progress or will be affected by it? Here you might consider family responsibilities as well as your current or future employer. Schoemaker suggests involving stakeholders as much as possible in the scenario development.

3. **Identify basic trends and key uncertainties:** You can use a PEST analysis (see Chapter 3) to identify environmental trends that may impact on your career. It is useful to briefly outline what the trends are and how you think they may affect you. For events with uncertain outcomes, consider a limited range of options, that is, not just a single outcome, but also don't get bogged down in trying to think of every single possible result. As you develop the scenarios, you may well find that you need to gather more information. For example, if you are working towards professional accreditation, are there any upcoming changes in how practice and education will be accredited?

4. **Construct scenario themes:** A basic approach here is to combine all the negatives into one 'world' and all the positives into another. This would give you a way of exploring a strategy in an optimistic future as well as having a strategy for dealing with disaster. Another useful approach is to identify the two uncertainties you think are most important and create a grid out of them, as shown in the example above. You then develop scenarios within each of these grid spaces.

|  | Low unemployment | High unemployment |
|---|---|---|
| Need to remain in limited geographic area |  |  |
| Geographically flexible |  |  |

5. **Check scenarios for internal consistency and plausibility:** This is the stage where you make the 'story' of the scenario feasible. For example, how plausible is it that you will face a scenario where *everything* has changed? What about the key stakeholders: are they likely to want to change anything in the scenario?

6. **Brainstorm implications and actions:** Once you have developed the scenarios, think through the implications of each of them and what actions you could take to maximize your success. Rather than having a single 'strategy' for a successful career, you now have a range of options for dealing with an unpredictable future and will be more able to take advantage of any opportunities that come your way.

## Strategy implementation

Once a strategy has been formulated, it needs to be implemented. There can often be a substantial gap between the strategy as it is intended and the actions that actually result in the organization, so in this section we consider some of the main issues to be aware of in implementation.

### Integrated hierarchy of plans

For a strategy to be effective, there needs to be a clear relationship between the global overall goal and direction and the efforts that each business unit or person is making on a day-to-day basis. Different levels of planning are needed at different levels of the organization as the strategy is cascaded down the hierarchy. These levels answer different questions (Linstead et al., 2009), as explained in Figure 8.2 (overleaf).

There is a danger in viewing strategy implementation at distinct levels, which may lead to the separation of plans at different levels and a reduction in responsiveness to change. Although the plans seem to cascade downwards, strategy at lower levels can influence that at higher levels too. For example, an HR strategy to hire candidates with the desired technical skills for a role as well as a commitment to cross-functional learning and development will probably lead to the development

of new resources and opportunities, perhaps even developing new products or markets.

As the strategy is cascaded down the hierarchy and each level of management is expected to implement it, it will be subject to change. Each manager, for example, may choose to emphasize a particular aspect of it depending on their personal priorities, their view of their professional role or even their ability. In this way, even a carefully developed strategy, which aims to give clear direction to the organization, can end up lacking that unifying purpose. Mintzberg (1987b) suggested that top managers should provide only an 'umbrella' strategy with broad guidelines and leave it to middle managers and frontline workers to craft this by developing specific plans.

### Strategy and change

Many organizational strategies aim to change the organization in some way, which means that they will run into all the same issues with implementation that any other change effort does. We considered change in detail in Chapter 7, so here we will only discuss it briefly as it relates specifically to strategy. Johnson (1992) noted that strategy is often assumed to develop through a process of logical analysis and planning, but that, in reality, the organizational culture works to limit managers' perceptions, plans and responses. When faced with the dynamic and complex task of developing strategy that takes

Enterprise strategy
- What is the role of the organization in society?
- Identifies the aim of the organization, e.g. to provide excellent customer satisfaction, to have a positive impact on the environment, and to provide shareholder value

Corporate strategy
- What kinds of businesses can meet that purpose?
- Identifies the markets, products, technologies that the organization will engage with

Business strategy
- How will we allocate resources to meet customer needs better than our competitors?
- Identifies the organization's distinctive offering and integrates the different business functions, e.g. HR and marketing

Functional strategy
- How will each business function contribute to the strategy?
- Identifies offerings at function level, although this is increasingly merged with the level above as organizations operate more cross-functionally

*Figure 8.2 Strategy hierarchy*

into account the many confusing signals and overwhelming amount of information that could be relevant, managers adopt a paradigm (or mindset) to make sense of it. This paradigm is determined by the culture – their shared set of assumptions and beliefs. Johnson suggests that culture can be helpful if it captures the unique resources of the organization and therefore guides action to achieve competitive advantage, but it can also cause blind spots, fixed ways of thinking and even resistance to change.

Over time, this resistance can cause 'strategic drift', where the organization's strategy drifts out of line with its environment and eventually this drift can only be corrected by radical change (Johnson, 1992). In attempting to analyse the organization

and its environment, we are dealing with complex and dynamic entities. One of the dangers of strategic management approaches is that they may encourage managers to feel that simple techniques such as a SWOT analysis are effective ways to understand what is essentially an ever-changing and complex entity. In any large organization, for example, the strength of one department or team may be another's weakness, and the impact of that on the organization as a whole is difficult to judge. The implementation of strategy is where these complexities really take effect. The Weighing the Evidence box looks at an alternative approach to strategy, which starts from a consideration of what practitioners actually do when they are implementing strategy.

 Weighing the Evidence: **Strategy as practice**

There is a different way of looking at strategy, and that is from the perspective of the people doing the strategizing. This is what the 'strategy as practice' (SAP) movement does. It considers strategy as a social practice and, looking at what practitioners do and how they interact, attempts to answer the question: 'What does it take to be an effective strategy practitioner?' (Whittington, 1996, p. 731).

SAP emphasizes the detailed day-to-day practice of getting things done and considers the *inspiration* and the *perspiration* involved in effective strategy: the ideas and opportunity-spotting as well as the routines of budgets, meetings and presentations. Whittington (1996) notes that competence in strategy is highly situational: it relies more on local knowledge and the ability to work with the range of people involved in the strategy's implementation than on textbook knowledge of how strategy 'ought' to be done. This definition is expanded by Jarzabkowski and Spee (2009) to emphasize the SAP focus on the human element of strategy.

Although this approach sounds inherently attractive to managers and practitioners, with its authors emphasizing the 'reality' of how strategy is done, Carter et al. (2008) argue that it does not offer much in the way of new insights and tends to be somewhat oversimplistic and naive. For example, Carter et al. claim that the SAP approach assumes that strategy is the concern only of top management teams rather than taking account of other stakeholders or society at large. This criticism is echoed in a review of the field by some of the supporters of the SAP approach. The review recognizes that although strategy 'practitioners' should include anyone who directly or indirectly influences strategy practice, research thus far has not considered people outside the organization (Jarzabkowski and Spee, 2009). Jarzabkowski and Spee conclude that the SAP approach has potential for substantial contributions to understanding strategy but that research in the field is at an early stage and would benefit from a clearer framework.

## STRATEGIC HRM

The concept of 'strategic HRM' emphasizes a strategic approach to managing human resources within the organization. Ideally, of course, all HRM should be strategic, in the sense of making proactive rather than reactive efforts to align HRM with the overall business goals or, even worse, carrying out HR tasks in a way that is completely unaligned with the business purpose. In fact, as we saw in Chapter 1, for Guest (1987), the integration of HR into strategic management lies at the heart of the distinctiveness of HRM as opposed to earlier personnel management roles and practices. But Boxall and Purcell (2000) advise a more careful approach, distinguishing between a broad and inclusive definition of HRM as everything to do with the management of employment relations and SHRM, which has a targeted focus on how HRM is critical to organizational success. A strategic approach to HRM has, in fact, been shown to be critical to the success of even complex organizational change, such as a major culture change, because it *enables* the change (Molineux, 2013).

In Chapter 1 we introduced the contrast between hard and soft approaches to HRM and this tension is reflected in SHRM too. A 'hard' approach believes 'human' resources should be utilized in the same way as other organizational resources: efficiently. They should be acquired as cheaply as possible, used sparingly, and developed and exploited as fully as possible. In this approach, the organizational strategy is paramount and the HR strategy is entirely dependent on it. In contrast, a 'soft' approach takes account of the relationship between the employer and employee and attempts to integrate the interests of different organizational stakeholders with the overall management objectives. In this approach, there is more of a two-way relationship between HR and organizational strategy, with SHRM contributing to the formulation of the business strategy, not just flowing naturally out of it.

One of the earliest proponents of SHRM defined it simply as 'linking the people with the strategic needs of the business' (Schuler, 1992, p. 18). Schuler went on to note that SHRM has two main tasks: integration and adaptation. These can be seen as corresponding to the formulation and implementation aspects of strategic management that we reviewed earlier in the chapter and is depicted in Figure 8.3.

SHRM has to start with a clear identification of business needs; otherwise HR activities cannot be effectively aligned with them. Once this is done, SHRM is carried out through five main activities (Schuler, 1992), known as the '5-P model of HRM' (not to be confused with Mintzberg's 5Ps of strategy, discussed at the start of this chapter):

1. **The HR philosophy:** how people in the organization are valued and treated, essentially an expression of organizational culture.

2. **HR policies:** provide guidelines for how to act in relation to people matters in the organization.

3. **HR programmes:** coordinate the efforts to introduce and manage change.

4. **HR practices:** ensure that employees are motivated to engage in the needed behaviours

that will contribute to the business objectives. Examples of these practices include performance appraisal, training and development, and reward.

5. **HR processes:** deal with how the other activities are formulated and carried out, for example in terms of the level of involvement of employees.

**Formulation (integration)**

- HRM functions (e.g. recruitment, development, retention, reward) should be formulated in line with the overall business strategy and integrated with each other
- The aim is to ensure that the organization has the human resources in place when needed and that HR systems support high performance

**Implementation (adaptation)**

- HR contributes in communicating strategy throughout the organization
- HR also has a role in ensuring compliance and contribution towards strategy by managing performance
- The aim is to ensure that 'HR practices are adjusted, accepted and used' (Schuler, 1992, p. 18) by all employees

*Figure 8.3 The link between SHRM and strategic management tasks*

## General HR strategies

The SHRM literature underscores the importance of a longer term view of functions such as resourcing, reward and performance, integrating them with the overall business strategy (CIPD, 2016). Although all HR strategies will be slightly different, Armstrong and Taylor (2014) suggest that three general approaches can be taken:

1. **High performance strategy:** aims to improve performance – productivity, quality, profits and so on – using HR practices such as extensive training and development, incentive pay systems and rigorous selection procedures.

2. **High commitment strategy:** aims to enhance employee commitment to the organization using HR practices that promote trust and encourage self-regulation rather than close monitoring of performance, for example developing self-managing teams.

3. **High involvement strategy:** aims to offer employees the opportunity to contribute to the organization by enhancing their involvement in decision-making, devolving power and increasing access to information.

Despite their different names, these three strategies all aim to support and direct employee behaviour in line with organizational objectives. High commitment and high involvement are used as a way to encourage specific employee and organizational performance.

In deciding on the best HRM strategy to adopt, a basic choice managers are faced with is between the choice of specific practices or the development of good fit. The best practice approach argues that there is one best way to manage people that will work regardless of the context. The best fit approach argues that HR strategy is most effective when it is well integrated with the organizational and environmental context. Good fit or integration between HRM and the organizational strategy ensures that people are managed effectively and perform at higher levels.

A different approach is to conceptualize SHRM in terms of its impact on the organization's competitive advantage. Creating unique HRM systems or approaches can contribute to competitive advantage: essentially, the HR management in an organization can become one of its key resources, adding value, being rare and difficult to imitate, and providing the organization needed to allow the firm to effectively utilize its human resources. Whether SHRM has yet fulfilled its promise is still subject to debate, as the In the News feature illustrates.

## Universal best practices

One view on SHRM is to suggest that organizations should adopt a set of best practices, and that these

In the News: **SHRM failure?**

The rise in so-called 'precarious work' – jobs with no security and variable hours – is based on the perceived needs of employers for a flexible workforce and reduced staffing costs. It is a growing issue around the world, including Canada, where Wayne Lewchuck, an economics professor at McMaster University, found that nearly half of the people in the Toronto and Hamilton area were working in insecure jobs (Grant, 2014). The news article highlighted the substantial impact of precarious work on the workers themselves: there is no consistency in working hours so no way of planning the rest of their life and responsibilities, for example childcare or education, no security of income and people often have to work at more than one job.

*Getty Images/iStockphoto/Thinkstock Images*

Fiona McQuarrie (2014), writing in a blog about work and organizations, blames this rise in precarious work on a failure of the HR profession. She notes that while many HR professionals themselves object to precarious work because they can see the long-term consequences on the organization and the wider economy, HRM as a function has failed to become influential in organizations. Instead of having a voice and making a strategic contribution to organizational decisions, HRM is still often only fulfilling an administrative role. This failure of HR to take part in strategy means that employee issues are not taken seriously at higher levels of the organization.

**For discussion**

» How do you think the HR profession can promote itself as capable of making a strong strategic contribution?

» Why do you think so many organizations pay lip service to the idea of their people being their most important asset yet use employment practices that seem to treat people as disposable? Do you see a role for HR in changing this?

practices are best, regardless of the individual organization's context. This is also known as a 'universalist' approach, as it assumes that there is one best way to manage HR. Unfortunately, there is little agreement as to what these best practices are, and while they include some obvious micro-level candidates, like the use of structured rather than unstructured interviews in selection, there is much more ambiguity around issues like employee involvement and voice (Boxall and Purcell, 2000).

There are also the strong influences of culture in determining the impact of specific practices on individual and organizational outcomes. One of the basic differences between cultures is the extent to which they are individualist – people view themselves as independent and value self-reliance – or collectivist – people view themselves as interdependent and expect loyalty to and from the group. While individualistic approaches might be 'best practice' in American organizations, they can be counterproductive in more collectivist cultures. For example, multi-rater feedback on performance is often proposed as a best practice element of performance appraisal, but cross-cultural research has shown that it can actually be detrimental to organizational outcomes in collectivist cultures (Peretz and Fried, 2012). Finally, there is the consideration of who defines 'best practice'. What is best for employees, for example high pay and job security, might not be best for all organizations or industries.

If we cannot base our HRM strategy on a set of universal best practices, how then can we ensure that it is going to support the organization? We move on now to consider the role of strategic fit.

## Fitting practice to the organization

A different, perhaps more sophisticated approach to SHRM is to use a best fit model. HRM strategy that fits or is aligned with the organizational strategy and internal and external context will be more effective than one which is at odds with them. Delery (1998) notes a distinction between vertical and horizontal fit. *Vertical fit* is about aligning HR practices with the organizational context and strategy, while horizontal fit is the integration of different HR practices into a coherent system. We will look at each of these in turn, but bear in mind that good fit requires both vertical and horizontal alignment.

## Vertical fit: HR and organizational strategy

Just as we have seen for strategic management, there is no one HRM strategy that will lead to success in every organization. Instead, success depends on the skills and experience of HR professionals to choose the right course for their unique organization. One of the earliest suggestions for fitting HRM strategy to organizational strategy was a three-part typology of practices that aimed to develop the employee behaviours needed to meet Porter's three competitive strategies (Schuler and Jackson, 1987), explained in Table 8.2. (Note that Schuler and Jackson use slightly different terminology from Porter, calling the differentiation strategy 'quality' and the focus strategy 'innovation'.)

While the various factors that influence HRM strategy formulation are extensive, research from a cross-cultural perspective has developed a framework that we can use to consider and evaluate them (Budhwar and Sparrow, 2002). The framework evaluates factors in three categories: national, contingent and organizational influences:

1. **National factors:** the norms of the national culture, for example the management styles and values, as well as the influence of institutions such as educational systems, governmental bodies and so on. There are also national influences on the specific industrial sector, such as mobility of the labour force, skill requirements and industry-specific regulations, as well as factors in the business environment, such as level of competition and influence of globalization.

2. **Contingent factors:** the age, size and ownership of the organization, as well as stakeholder interests and the product life-cycle stage.

3. **Organizational factors:** the overall strategy, extent of teamwork and how devolved responsibility is within the organization.

Based on an analysis of these elements, Budhwar and Sparrow (2002) suggest four main types of generic HRM strategies that emerge in response to their influence:

1. **Talent acquisition:** aims to attract the best talent from external sources

2. **Effective resource allocation:** aims to make best use of existing human resources

Table 8.2 **Fitting HRM strategy to Porter's competitive strategies**

| Porter's competitive strategies | HRM strategy | Appropriate HRM practices |
| --- | --- | --- |
| **Cost leadership (cost reduction)** | Provide the means for closely monitoring and controlling employee activities in order to maximize efficiency | • Fixed, narrowly defined and explicit job descriptions<br>• Career paths that encourage specialization, expertise and efficiency<br>• Performance assessments that use short-term, result-oriented measures<br>• Compensation based on market levels<br>• Low investment in training and development |
| **Differentiation (quality)** | Develop highly reliable behaviour from employees and encourage them to identify with the goals of the organization<br>Be flexible enough to allow new job assignments and adaptation to technological change | • Fixed and explicit job descriptions<br>• High level of employee participation in job-related decisions<br>• Performance assessment using a mix of individual and group criteria, but still short term and results-oriented<br>• Egalitarian compensation and some degree of job security<br>• Continuous and extensive training and development |
| **Focus (innovation)** | Encourage cooperative, interdependent behaviour with a longer term orientation, as well as fluid exchange of ideas and a relatively high level of risk-taking | • Flexible job design that encourages interaction and coordination<br>• Performance assessment on longer timescales and group achievements<br>• Focus on development activities and broad career paths<br>• Compensation should be internally equitable rather than market based and allow employees to choose reward components |

3. **Talent improvement:** aims to provide continuous training, development and guidance for existing employees in order to maximize their talents and contributions

4. **Cost reduction:** aims to reduce the personnel costs as far as possible.

Despite this range of HRM strategies, Becker and Huselid (2006) make an interesting observation that, although SHRM focuses on how to align HR systems to organizational strategy, most HR professionals still rely solely on cost control practices.

Vertical fit is also concerned with the fit of the organization to its stage of development. So, for example, an innovative startup would be best served by a flexible approach to HRM, while a more formal and differentiated HR system will be better suited to an established firm with a wider range of employees and a more complex range of roles (Boxall and Purcell, 2000).

There are, however, some criticisms of this contingency or fitting approach. It takes a fairly simplistic view of the strategy of the organization, reducing it to a limited number of options, and does not consider how practices or strategies might align with employee interests or wider norms (Boxall and Purcell, 2000). It also gives little consideration to the need for flexibility. HRM can only contribute to the organization's performance to the extent to which it enables the organization to adapt to changing demands (Taylor et al., 1996). The Applications activity explores some of the challenges in fitting HR strategy to organizational strategy.

 Applications: **Developing HR strategy**

Lush Cosmetics Ltd is an international manufacturer and retailer of fresh handmade cosmetics founded in the UK. Launched in 2001, it now has retail outlets in 49 countries and an annual turnover of over £500 million (Lush Cosmetics Ltd, 2015). The company places a high value on ethical and socially responsible activity and gave over £6 million to charity in 2015.

The directors' strategic report outlines four key objectives for the company:

1. Increase the number of shops in prime sites

2. A stretch target of 50% of sales being online

3. 'Launch it right': recognizing that a good launch requires attention to detail and good execution

4. Changing the game: ethically sourced ingredients, working towards a regenerative supply chain that is sustainable for all.

In its annual report, Lush states that it has a policy of communicating openly to employees, providing frequent performance updates, communicating the company values and sharing stories about their buying, innovation and charitable activities. The company places a high value on training and development as well as on employment practices that recognize and value diversity. Internal promotion is encouraged and rewards include little extras like employees being given the day off on their birthdays. The company hopes that these approaches will encourage employees to 'take on more responsibility and progress through the business' (Lush Cosmetics Ltd, 2015, p. 10).

» How would you turn this organizational strategy into an HR strategy? Think about the implications of each of the objectives: how can HR contribute towards their achievement?

» How would you recommend the HR strategy is implemented? Consider here the culture of the company and the kinds of actions that would align with already established norms and values.

## Horizontal fit: HR 'bundles'

In considering **horizontal fit**, or how HR practices fit together to contribute to the organizational strategy, some authors have suggested that it makes sense to consider how they are configured or 'bundled' together in mutually reinforcing sets of practices. While the logic behind creating bundles is clear (it is better to have practices that are synergistic rather than in competition), for a while after they were first proposed, there was little evidence that they were superior to individual HR practices. One of the problems was that the contents of these 'bundles' seemed to vary too much between organizations to provide clear comparisons of their impact on performance (Dyer and Reeves, 1995). In addition,

the effect of individual HR practices on organizational performance could vary significantly: when in a bundle they could act independently or interact with one another in affecting performance (Delery, 1998).

However, a meta-analysis by Subramony (2009) reviewed the findings of 65 studies over a 13-year period and found convincing evidence that bundles of synergistic practices had positive effects on organizational performance and that these effects were greater than for the individual practices. He suggested that **HR bundles** be classified in terms of their overall effect on the key elements of employee empowerment, motivation and skill, which, in turn, are expected to enhance organizational performance. The three bundles are:

*Getty Images/Tetra images RF/Jamie Grill*

*Synergistic HR practices can be bundled together.*

1. **Empowerment-enhancing bundles:** practices such as job enrichment or employee involvement in decision-making, including self-managed teams. Also include systems for employee feedback, such as suggestion schemes or complaint procedures.

2. **Motivation-enhancing bundles:** practices such as performance appraisals and career development, as well as attractive benefit or incentive schemes and performance-linked pay.

3. **Skill-enhancing bundles:** practices focused on identifying and developing employee skills, such as using valid selection methods and job-based training.

Bundles of synergistic practices are expected to have a greater effect on performance because they mutually support and reinforce one another. For example, having a performance appraisal system enables employees to set goals and monitor performance and supporting this with rewards for high performance

increases motivation. Subramony's (2009) meta-analysis found that each of the three bundles had a positive impact on financial, production and overall business performance as well as retention. He also found that using these more compact bundles could lead to a greater increase in performance than a more comprehensive HRM system, which, while it might consist of more practices, could be more costly and contain practices that are not well aligned. This emphasizes again the importance of a strategic, integrated approach to HRM.

We should not, however, fall into the trap of thinking that SHRM is concerned solely with HR practices. In fact, one of the great benefits of SHRM is its reminder that competitive advantage comes from the human resources (the people) that the HR practices contribute towards attracting, managing and retaining (Delery, 1998).

## Competitive advantage and the resource-based view

The resource-based view of the organization can be a useful way to consider SHRM because it proposes that HRM helps the organization to build and utilize its valuable human resources. In exploring this contribution, Huselid et al. (1997) suggest that 'strategic' HRM activities can be distinguished from 'technical' HRM activities. The latter include activities that are well recognized by internal and external stakeholders and often regulated by governments, such as recruitment and selection, performance measurement and compensation. SHRM, in contrast, includes activities such as developing a flexible workforce, talent planning and employee empowerment. Based on their analysis of nearly 300 US firms, Huselid et al. suggested that technical HRM activities, because they are so widespread and institutionalized, cannot provide any source of competitive advantage, whereas SHRM activities can. In addition, they found in their research that SHRM effectiveness was positively related to employee performance and the organization's market value, but there was no relationship between technical HRM and performance. Competence in HRM is highlighted as an important component of multinational firms' competitive advantage in a model of international SHRM too (Taylor et al., 1996), which shows how the firm's unique resources can be mobilized to meet international challenges.

How can an organization protect the competitive advantage it gains from its human capital? There are some distinct barriers to imitation by competitors (Boxall and Purcell, 2000):

- **Timing and learning:** expertise and learning are developed over time and those organizations late to the market will simply not be able to copy that expertise. In fact, acquiring this expertise is often the reason for takeovers and mergers.

- **Social complexity:** many of the organization's advantages will stem from networks and relationships among teams and with external stakeholders. This kind of complexity cannot simply be 'copied' by another organization.

- **Causal ambiguity:** sometimes, competitors will simply be unable to identify which practices contribute to an organization's success.

In contrast to the sometimes prescriptive notions of what SHRM should be about, Colbert (2004) recommends a more emergent and flexible set of principles that could enable the organization to flourish much as a living organism might. He notes that while best practice approaches can help to define specific HR products or practices, as we aim for a coherent approach at higher levels, such as policies and principles, we need a more complex understanding that provides a central place for the unique context. This view of SHRM as a complex and dynamic system emphasizes that, far from being a standard set of practices, SHRM can really provide the organization with unique, inimitable resources. The Web Explorer activity explores this uniqueness in more detail. Developing a sustainable competitive advantage involves a strategic approach to the totality of HR systems rather than reliance on individual HR practices (Molineux, 2013).

## Web Explorer: How unique are HR strategies?

A criticism that could be made of SHRM is that, although the literature recommends that each organization have a uniquely tailored HR strategy, there is little real difference in how these strategies are publicly presented. How likely is it, for example, that an organization will say its HR strategy is to employ people as cheaply as possible, make no investment in their development and not care about their well-being? In this exercise, we will explore two quite different business models and compare their HR strategies.

» The John Lewis Partnership is a UK employee-owned business with annual sales of £11 billion. It is proud to put the 'happiness of Partners at the centre of everything it does' (www.johnlewispartnership.co.uk/about.html). Explore the John Lewis website and look up its strategy (www.johnlewispartnership.co.uk/about/our-strategy.html). To what extent is the HR strategy embedded within the overall organizational strategy? What are its main aims? How does it relate to the models of HR strategy we review in this chapter?

» Goldman Sachs is a global investment banking firm with clients ranging from individuals to corporations and even governments. It sees its people as its greatest asset and has a focus on 'cultivating and sustaining a diverse work environment and workforce' (www.goldmansachs.com/who-we-are/people-and-culture/index.html). At Goldman Sachs, the traditional HR functions are carried out by the Human Capital Management division, which emphasizes a strategic view on the global workforce (www.goldmansachs.com/careers/why-goldman-sachs/our-divisions/human-capital-management). Why do you think it has chosen to use this different title? What impression does it give of the division and the organization? What is the HCM strategy and how is it aiming to achieve it?

» What are the similarities and differences between the approaches of John Lewis and Goldman Sachs to SHRM? To what extent do you think they represent genuinely distinct strategies?

For an in-depth case study of the John Lewis Partnership and the continuing tension with managerial interests, see Cathcart (2014).

# CHALLENGES

During our discussions of organizational and HR strategy, we have explored some of the challenges managers face in formulation and implementation, and we round off this chapter with a brief discussion of some further general challenges that practitioners deal with.

## Levels of analysis

One of the recurring issues in HRM and OB research is the problem of the level at which we conduct our analysis. This is a particular challenge for SHRM because we are proposing that strategic choices at the level of the organization determine the HR practices that affect individual-level behaviour, which is then often measured at the level of organizational performance (Wright and Nishii, 2013). But there are, of course, many different variables that could affect how organizational decisions and practices influence individual performance and then again, how that performance is converted to organizational outcomes. So while we certainly have some support for the relationship between SHRM and performance, there is still more research to be done to determine *how* HR strategy impacts individual and organizational performance.

## Devolvement to line managers

Another challenge in strategic management and SHRM that we consider here is the extent to which strategy is devolved to line managers. Basic models of strategy assume that there is a cascade of strategic intent from top management down through the organization so that everyone works towards the same goals. In fact, this devolution to line managers is a critical element of some definitions of SHRM (Andersen et al., 2007). This devolvement will necessarily entail line managers taking responsibility for delivering HR practices. While this is, to a certain extent, fairly normal in many organizations, for example line managers typically carry out performance appraisals that may be originally developed by HR practitioners, it may not happen with other practices. One of the critical issues here is the extent to which line managers have the skills and training to deliver HR practices effectively.

Andersen et al. (2007) found, in a survey of Australian firms, that even where line managers were involved, they only had moderate levels of training in how to carry out the activities. A study in the USA reinforces these findings: the relationship between HR practices and workplace outcomes was fully mediated by the extent to which line managers implemented the practices that were in place in their organization (Sikora et al., 2015). One of the major factors contributing to implementation was the line managers' HR knowledge, skills and abilities. These findings highlight a significant challenge for HR managers in ensuring that the strategy they so carefully formulate is actually implemented effectively.

## Structuring the HR function

A final challenge is how the organization or HR function should be structured to carry out strategy effectively. Ulrich (1996) distinguished between the transactional and transformational work that the HR department typically carries out. Transactional work, such as payroll administration and absence monitoring, can be standardized and often delivered effectively through technology, while transformational work, such as strategy generation and implementation, requires skills in analysis and insight generation. Based on this distinction, Ulrich suggested that the HR function could be structured so as to provide optimal delivery, with three key elements:

1. Shared services centres are centralized administrative units, which provide all the transactional services, often using technology to do so in a cost-effective and efficient manner.

2. Centres of expertise or excellence consist of small HR teams with specialist knowledge in areas such as learning, reward or engagement that can help the HR function to deliver competitive advantage.

3. Business partners (also known as strategic partners) are HR professionals who work at the top levels of the organization to influence and develop strategy.

While this model helped to emphasize the importance of SHRM as distinct from the administrative work of HR, it also seems to separate HR from the rest of the organization rather than seeing it as an integral function, and was predominantly driven by a desire for standardization and efficiency (CIPD, 2015). Ulrich's more recent developments of the model, suggesting that HR should move to a professional services model similar to accountancy or consulting firms (Ulrich and Grochowski, 2012), can be seen as taking this a step further, although it does

emphasize the importance of ensuring that the HR structure aligns with organizational and HR strategy. We therefore now turn to consider organizational structure in more detail in Chapter 9.

## Practice Insights: Kris DeLano

Kris DeLano is the Corporate HR Director for Rockline Industries, a manufacturing company founded in the USA, which now has sites in Europe and China. With 30 years' experience in HR, Kris has a breadth and depth of understanding of the HR role and the best ways to build personal and professional credibility. In the video she gives her insights into how the HR function contributes to and implements organizational strategy.

Go online to www.macmillanihe.com/sutton-people to access the interview with Kris.

## SUMMARY

In this chapter, we have evaluated the role of strategy in the effective management of organizations and the people who work in them. Strategy formulation involves analysis of the organization and its environment, and this can be carried out in terms of strengths and weaknesses, competitive forces, experience gains or a focus on the unique resources of the organization. Issues to consider in strategy implementation include how the strategy is cascaded through the organization and how change is managed.

Strategic HRM offers a range of perspectives for understanding how HR practitioners are involved in strategy, from formulation to implementation. We have considered best practice, best fit and a resource-based view of the organization here and have seen that there is good evidence for SHRM having a positive impact on organizational performance, although the exact mechanisms of this effect are still being researched. The final section of the chapter drew out some important challenges that managers need to address in formulating and implementing their strategies.

## FURTHER READING

- For more detail on the ten schools of thought in strategy, read Mintzberg, H. and Lampel, J. (1999) 'Reflecting on the strategy process', *Sloan Management Review*, 40(3), 21–30.

- For a review of the East Asian approach to strategic management, see Tung, R. L. (1994) 'Strategic management thought in East Asia', *Organizational Dynamics*, 22(4), 55–65.

## REVIEW QUESTIONS

1. Contrast the resource-based view with a product/market-based view of strategy. What are the implications for HRM?

2. How can SHRM contribute to competitive advantage?

3. What are some of the challenges faced during the implementation of strategy?

## ONLINE RESOURCES

Go online to www.macmillanihe.com/sutton-people to access a MCQ quiz for this chapter and for further resources to support your learning.

## REFERENCES

Anders, G. (2015) 'That "useless" liberal arts degree has become tech's hottest ticket', *Forbes*, July. Available at: http://onforb.es/1OBHNQK.

Andersen, K. K., Cooper, B. K. and Zhu, C. J. (2007) 'The effect of SHRM practices on perceived firm financial performance: some initial evidence from Australia', *Asia Pacific Journal of Human Resources*, 45(2), pp. 168–79. doi: 10.1177/1038411107079111.

Armstrong, M. and Taylor, S. (2014) *Handbook of Human Resource Management*, 13th edn. London: Kogan Page.

Barney, J. (1991) 'Firm resources and sustained competitive advantage', *Journal of Management*, 17(1), pp. 99–120.

Barney, J. B. (1995) 'Looking inside for competitive advantage', *Academy of Management Executive*, 9(4), pp. 49–61.

Becker, B. and Huselid, M. A. (2006) 'Strategic human resources management: Where do we go from here?', *Journal of Management*, 32(6), pp. 898–925. doi: 10.1177/0149206306293668.

Boxall, P. and Purcell, J. (2000) 'Strategic human resource management: Where have we come from and where should we be going?', *International Journal of Management*, 2(2), pp. 183–203. doi: 10.1111/1468-2370.00037.

Budhwar, P. S. and Sparrow, P. R. (2002) 'An integrative framework for understanding cross-national human resource management practices', *Human Resource Management Review*, 12(3), pp. 377–403. doi: 10.1016/S1053-4822(02)00066-9.

Carter, C., Clegg, S. R. and Kornberger, M. (2008) 'Strategy as practice?', *Strategic Organization*, 6(1), pp. 83–99. doi: 10.1177/1476127007087154.

Cathcart, A. (2014) 'Paradoxes of participation: non-union workplace partnership in John Lewis', *International Journal of Human Resource Management*, 25(6), pp. 762–80. doi: 10.1080/09585192.2012.743476.

CIPD (2015) *The Strategic Role of HR: What Does a Strategic HR Function Look Like?*, Changing HR Operating Models. London: CIPD.

CIPD (2016) 'Strategic human resource management factsheet'. Available at: www.cipd.co.uk/knowledge/strategy/hr/strategic-hrm-factsheet.

Colbert, B. A. (2004) 'The complex resource-based view: implications for theory and practice in strategic human resource management', *Academy of Management Review*, 29(3), pp. 341–58. doi: 10.2307/20159047.

Delery, J. E. (1998) 'Issues of fit in strategic human resource management: implications for research', *Human Resource Management Review*, 8(3), pp. 289–309. doi: 10.1016/S1053-4822(98)90006-7.

Dyer, L. and Reeves, T. (1995) 'Human resource strategies and firm performance: What do we know and where do we need to go ?', *International Journal of Human Resource Management*, 6(3), pp. 656–70. doi: 10.1080/09585199500000041.

Forbes (2016) *Cloud 100 2016*. Available at: www.forbes.com/cloud100/#454619076e6e (Accessed 26 December 2016).

Grant, T. (2014) 'The 15-hour workweek: Canada's part-time problem', *The Globe and Mail*, 4 October. Available at: www.theglobeandmail.com/report-on-business/the-15-hour-workweek-canadas-part-time-problem/article20926986/ (Accessed 27 December 2016).

Guest, D. E. (1987) 'Human resource management and industrial relations', *Journal of Management Studies*, 24(5), pp. 503–21. doi: 10.1111/j.1467-6486.1987.tb00460.x.

Henderson, B. (1968) *The Experience Curve*. Available at: www.bcgperspectives.com/content/Classics/strategy_the_experience_curve/ (Accessed 27 December 2016).

Huselid, M. A., Jackson, S. E. and Schuler, R. S. (1997) 'Technical and strategic human resources management effectiveness and determinants of firm performance', *Academy of Management Journal*, 40(1), pp. 171–88. doi: 10.2307/257025.

Jarzabkowski, P. and Spee, A. P. (2009) 'Strategy-as-practice: a review and future directions for the field', *International Journal of Management Reviews*, 11(1), pp. 69–95. doi: 10.1111/j.1468-2370.2008.00250.x.

Johnson, G. (1992) 'Managing strategic change: strategy, culture and action', *Long Range Planning*, 25(1), pp. 28–36. doi: 10.1016/0024-6301(92)90307-N.

Kim, E. (2015) 'The 14 fastest unicorns to reach $1 billion'. Available at: http://uk.businessinsider.com/fastest-startups-to-1-billion-valuation-2015-8 (Accessed 27 December 2016).

Lado, A. A., Boyd, N. G., Wright, P. and Kroll, M. (2006) 'Paradox and theorizing within the resource-based view', *Academy of Management Review*, 31(1), pp. 115–31. doi: 10.5465/amr.2006.19379627.

Linstead, S., Fulop, L. and Lilley, S. (2009) *Management and Organization: A Critical Text*. Basingstoke: Palgrave Macmillan.

Lush Cosmetics Ltd (2015) *Directors' Report and Consolidated Financial Statements*. Cardiff.

McQuarrie, F. (2014) 'Precarious work and the failure of 'human resource management'. Available at: http://allaboutwork.org/2014/10/18/precarious-work-and-the-failure-of-human-resource-management/ (Accessed 30 December 2016).

Mintzberg, H. (1987a) 'The strategy concept I: five Ps for strategy', *California Management Review*, 30(1), pp. 11–24.

Mintzberg, H. (1987b) 'Crafting strategy', *Harvard Business Review*, 65(4), pp. 65–74.

Mintzberg, H. and Lampel, J. (1999) 'Reflecting on the strategy process', *Sloan Management Review*, 40(3), pp. 21–30. doi: 10.1128/JVI.78.19.10303-10309.2004.

Mintzberg, H., Ahlstrand, B. and Lampel, J. (1998) *Strategy Safari: A Guided Tour Through the Wilds of Strategic Management*. New York: Free Press.

Molineux, J. (2013) 'Enabling organizational cultural change using systemic strategic human resource management: a longitudinal case study', *International*

*Journal of Human Resource Management*, 24(8), pp. 1588–612. doi: 10.1080/09585192.2012.723022.

Peretz, H. and Fried, Y. (2012) 'National cultures, performance appraisal practices, and organizational absenteeism and turnover: a study across 21 countries', *Journal of Applied Psychology*, 97(2), pp. 448–59. doi: 10.1037/a0026011.

Porter, M. (1979) 'How competitive forces shape strategy', *Harvard Business Review*, 57(2), pp. 137–45. doi: 10.1097/00006534-199804050-00042.

Porter, M. (1980) *Competitive Strategy*. New York: Free Press.

Priem, R. L. and Butler, J. E. (2001) 'Is the resource-based "view" a useful perspective for strategic management research?', *Academy of Management Review*, 26(1), pp. 22–40. doi: 10.5465/AMR.2001.4011938.

Reeves, M., Stalk, G. and Scognamiglio Pasini, F. (2013) *BCG Classics Revisited: The Experience Curve, The Boston Consulting Group Perspectives*. Available at: www.bcgperspectives.com/content/articles/growth_business_unit_strategy_experience_curve_bcg_classics_revisited/ (Accessed 27 December 2016).

Schoemaker, P. J. H. (1995) 'Scenario planning: a tool for strategic thinking', *Sloan Management Review*, pp. 32–40. doi: 10.1016/0024-6301(95)91604-0.

Schuler, R. S. (1992) 'Strategic human resources management: linking the people with the strategic needs of the business', *Organizational Dynamics*, 21(1), pp. 18–32. doi: 10.1016/0090-2616(92)90083-Y.

Schuler, R. S. and Jackson, S. E. (1987) 'Linking competitive strategies with human resource management practices', *Academy of Management Executive*, 1(3), pp. 207–19. doi: 10.5465/AME.1987.4275740.

Sikora, D. M., Ferris, G. R. and van Iddekinge, C. H. (2015) 'Line manager implementation perceptions as a mediator of relations between high-performance work practices and employee outcomes', *Journal of Applied Psychology*, 100(6), pp. 1908–18. doi: 10.1037/apl0000024.

Subramony, M. (2009) 'A meta-analytic investigation of the relationship between HRM bundles and firm performance', *Human Resource Management*, 48(5), pp. 745–68. doi: 10.1002/hrm.20315.

Szymaniec-Mlicka, K. (2014) 'Resource-based view in strategic management of public organizations: a review of the literature', *Management*, 18(2), pp. 19–30. doi: 10.2478/manment-2014-0039.

Taylor, S., Beechler, S. and Napier, N. (1996) 'Toward an integrative model of strategic international human resource management', *Academy of Management Review*, 21(4), pp. 959–85. doi: 10.5465/AMR.1996.9704071860.

Tung, R. L. (1994) 'Strategic management thought in East Asia', *Organizational Dynamics*, 22(4), pp. 55–65. doi: 10.1016/0090-2616(94)90078-7.

Ulrich, D. (1996) *Human Resource Champions: The Next Agenda for Adding Value and Delivering Results*. Boston, MA: Harvard Business Review Press.

Ulrich, D. and Grochowski, J. (2012) 'From shared services to professional services', *Strategic HR Review*, 11(3), pp. 136–42. doi: 10.1108/14754391211216850.

Wernerfelt, B. (1984) 'A resource based view of the firm', *Strategic Management Journal*, 5(2), pp. 171–80. doi: 10.1002/smj.4250050207.

Whittington, R. (1996) 'Strategy as practice', *Long Range Planning*, 29(5), pp. 731–5.

Wright, P. and Nishii, L. (2013) 'Strategic HRM and organizational behaviour: integrating multiple levels of analysis', in D. E. Guest, J. Paauwe and P. Wright (eds) *HRM and Performance: Achievements and Challenges*. Chichester: John Wiley and Sons, pp. 97–110.

# 9 STRUCTURE: FIT FOR PURPOSE

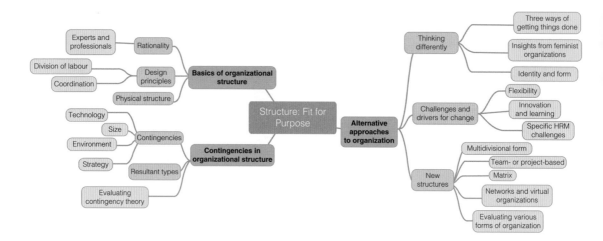

## INTRODUCTION

Having considered the different strategic approaches that organizations can take in order to meet their goals, we now turn to how they structure themselves to support those strategies. For effective performance, the organization's structure needs to be coherent with its task. The theme through this chapter is how organizations can ensure they are 'fit for purpose' and the role that HR plays in facilitating this. How work is organized can be seen as one of the most basic challenges a work institution faces and this chapter will demonstrate how essential it is for an organization to get its structure right if it hopes to direct and integrate workers' efforts to achieve its goals.

We start by discussing the basics of organizational structure, beginning with Max Weber's work, which suggests that there is an ideal way for organizations to structure to enhance effectiveness. We then move on to consider the dimensions that vary between different structures and to see what impact they have on how people work. This approach is the beginning of the contingency approach, which underlies most of modern thought on organizational structure. The contingency approach essentially takes the view that the organizational structure needs to take account of variables in the organization and its environment – *contingencies* – in order to support performance. Different combinations of these contingencies give rise to different types of organization.

Developing the idea of contingencies even further, we consider some of the more critical or theoretical issues in organizational design and look at how modern organizations are developing new structures in order to meet current challenges. Many of these structures are attempts to introduce more flexibility and teamwork into organizations than is possible with the traditional bureaucratic structure.

Getty Images/Caiaimage/Martin Barraud

---

## LEARNING FEATURES

Applications: HR professionals

Applications: Strategic design?

Applications: Developing participation in NGOs

Weighing the Evidence: Bureaucratic or bureaupathic?

Web Explorer: Organizational charts

In the News: Self-managed organizations

Transferrable Skills: Analysing organizational function

Practice Insights: Darren Cook

 Video overview

Julian Perkins

Go online to www.macmillanihe.com/sutton-people to access a video of Anna Sutton introducing the chapter's main themes.

# BASICS OF ORGANIZATIONAL STRUCTURE

In this section we will consider some of the early OB work on organizational structure, which attempted to find the best ways of organizing work. The starting point is bureaucracies, formal and highly structured organizations based on a rational approach to work, and then consider some of the wider organizational structure dimensions and their impact on how work happens.

## Rational organizations

One way to approach organization structure is from a sociological perspective, understanding how people behave in groups and looking at the type of groups that develop around particular leaders. Weber (2015) suggested there are three main ways that leaders can exercise authority and that this determines how the organization forms. Weber called these three types 'ideals', that is, they were rare in these pure forms and most types of organization would be a mixture of two or even three. Weber's three pure leadership types and their associated structures are:

1. **Charismatic:** here, authority comes from the personality and leadership qualities of the individual. Charismatic leaders inspire loyalty and obedience from their followers and tend to be seen as quite revolutionary, challenging preconceived ideas or ways of doing things and inspiring people to change and try to fulfil the leader's vision. (Compare this definition of charismatic leadership with the discussion in Chapter 6 to see how the concept has developed.) The work organization is typified by entrepreneurial firms and tends to be fairly unstable. If the leader leaves, the organization tends to dissolve because no one else is seen as able to take that person's place. And if the organization survives, the charismatic authority will eventually become routinized until it is superseded by a traditional or legal-rational authority.

2. **Traditional (or hereditary):** people obey because that is how things have always been done and the leadership position is a traditional one.

An example of this in work organizations is the family firm where the current leader has inherited the firm from their parents. Quite often, the people in lower levels of authority have family ties with the leader and are appointed because the leader likes them rather than because of any particular skills or qualifications. Authority in this kind of organization is based on an individual's personal relationship with the traditional leader rather than a formal job position.

3. **Legal-rational (or bureaucratic):** leaders gain authority from the position they occupy (the word *bureaucracy* literally means desk-power). This is probably the form of authority at work you are most familiar with, where authority is based on the hierarchical structure and is exercised through rules and regulations: managers are obeyed because they occupy a role within the organization that gives them that legitimate authority. Bureaucratic leadership means that individuals in the business are still free, to a certain extent, to use their judgement but they have to ensure that they are carrying out the wishes of the people higher up in the chain of command.

As we saw in Chapter 1, Weber proposed 'bureaucracies' as the ideal type of organization because they were based on legal-rational authority where work is conducted based on rules and procedures that apply to everyone. People follow those rules and regulations because they are considered rational and conform to legal requirements. The idea here is that a bureaucracy is fair: it applies the same procedures to everyone and does not discriminate. Weber (2015) thought that this type of organization was the way to success, providing greater efficiency, speed and clarity as well as a unity of purpose and reductions in costs.

Modern bureaucracies very rarely conform to Weber's ideal and are often criticized for being inflexible and, unfortunately, given his suggestion that they systematize fairness, inequitable and inhuman because they treat people as numbers. Miner's (1982) critique of the characteristics of modern bureaucracies can be summarized into two broad issues. First is a preoccupation with rules, including regulations, policies and procedures. They have to be based on methods that allow an accurate calculation of outcomes, for example performance

Getty Images/Hero Images

*Bureaucratic leaders gain authority from their position in the organization.*

reviews, using computerized systems for selection and recruitment, or recruiting and promoting people on the bases of merit and qualifications. Rules are established by management and are portrayed as being impartial and equitable, but heavily limit individual employees' freedom of action. In terms of work performance judgements, following the rules is what counts most. For example, correct completion of a quality assurance form becomes more important than any other judgement of the actual quality of the product or service.

The second issue is the importance of hierarchy. Job results are evaluated by superiors and pay levels are based on seniority in the organization. Many decisions and activities are centralized and resources are allocated by management, meaning that senior managers take the risk and the responsibility for failures. The implication of these two preoccupations is that no one is considered irreplaceable. New employees can simply be slotted into the appropriate position and, by following the rules, will be able to function effectively. The Weighing the Evidence activity explores the impact of bureaucracy on work behaviour.

 Weighing the Evidence: **Bureaucratic or bureaupathic?**

One of the positive elements of bureaucratic organization presented by Weber was the potential for this kind of organization to be fair and impartial. The formalized rules and procedures should ensure that everyone is treated equally and that discrimination and bias are reduced or prevented. Unfortunately, research has shown that one of the main disadvantages of a bureaucratic system is the resultant individual employee behaviour, which is often in contrast to the organization's actual goals.

Thompson (1977, p. 23) noted that the 'modern organisation is a prolific generator of anxiety and insecurity' and the way in which employees cope with the anxiety and tension is to ensure that they rigidly follow the rules. This results in them working only to the minimum acceptable level and following rules so rigidly that clients are often treated impersonally and inhumanely. Thompson referred to this as *bureaupathic* behaviour to emphasize the negative, 'illness-like' element. Bureaupathic behaviour essentially involves valuing the rules more highly than the organizational goals.

Bureaucracies are also criticized for the way they formalize power inequalities and are overly rigid, two features seen as unsuitable for a fast-paced, complex environment (Ashcraft, 2001). Further advantages and disadvantages of bureaucracies are summarized in Figure 9.1 (Byrt, 1973).

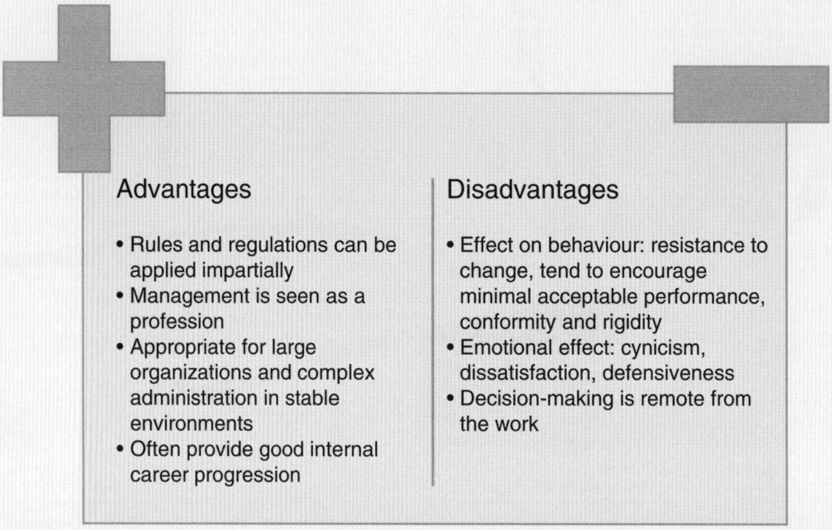

### Advantages

- Rules and regulations can be applied impartially
- Management is seen as a profession
- Appropriate for large organizations and complex administration in stable environments
- Often provide good internal career progression

### Disadvantages

- Effect on behaviour: resistance to change, tend to encourage minimal acceptable performance, conformity and rigidity
- Emotional effect: cynicism, dissatisfaction, defensiveness
- Decision-making is remote from the work

*Figure 9.1 Advantages and disadvantages of bureaucracies*

Because many HR tasks are administrative, often have serious consequences if they are not carried out correctly, and, for large organizations, can be very complex, a bureaucratic structure may be appropriate. For example, in ensuring compliance with legal requirements in selection and recruitment, it is necessary that HR staff closely follow the rules to ensure the organization is not open to charges of discrimination or unfair treatment. The challenge for modern HR professionals is in combining the impartiality, reliability and fairness of the bureaucracy with a more flexible and engaging organizational approach that can treat individual employees as humans rather than numbers.

## Experts and professionals in a bureaucracy

The importance of control in the bureaucracy is clear: the whole structure functions as a way to control and coordinate employees. One of the challenges this kind of structure faces is how to deal with experts and professionals – the people who are not easy to replace. The tension between expert power and control is an ongoing issue for modern organizations: knowledge and expertise are increasingly important for their success and survival, but individuals with that required expertise or who are engaged in tasks that are too complex for their (non-expert) managers to understand have the power to resist organizational control (Reed, 1996). In addition, the training demanded by many professional bodies may emphasize different values or ethical frameworks from those expected by the employing organization, as well as autonomous decision-making and responsibility for actions. May et al. (2002) suggest that expert workers cannot be managed effectively using command-and-control styles but should be given the opportunity to participate in decision-making and co-construct performance evaluations.

If we compare professional systems to bureaucracies, we can see some clear areas where conflict with a bureaucratic structure could occur. Rules are established by the professional group and emphasize the individual professional's judgement and choice of action. Performance is judged and regulated by professional standards. Professionals also have different attitudes towards hierarchy. Hierarchy in a professional occupation is based on qualifications and experience, and only other professionals are deemed competent to judge their results and engage in joint decision-making. The individual professional, rather than a manager, takes on the risk and the responsibility for actions.

Interestingly, the very definition of professional has changed over the years, as Reed (1996) highlighted when he distinguished between three forms of experts in the modern workplace and noted that they were associated with different organizational structures:

- Independent/liberal professionals have a monopoly on specific fields through their expert knowledge and related technical skills. For example, in many countries, doctors have a monopoly on giving medical advice and interventions such as prescribing medication because of their specialist medical knowledge and expertise. They tend to have collegiate structures, where individuals collaborate freely, share knowledge and contribute to each other's work.

- Organizational professionals develop a craft-like understanding of specific situations and, through this, gain educational and organizational credentials. For example, a manager may build up experience-based expertise as well as gain formal qualifications such as an MBA, which can lead to promotion and recognition in the organization. These professionals tend to utilize a centralized and hierarchical bureaucratic structure.

- Entrepreneurial professionals (also known as knowledge workers) use their specialized cognitive and technical skills in complex task domains. For example, business consultants develop analytical and intervention skills in complex areas such as organizational change. They can then gain advantage by marketing these transferable skills to organizations looking for innovation and knowledge creation. Entrepreneurial professionals tend to be structured in networks, which are decentralized and have little hierarchy.

Getty Images/Caiaimage/Paul Bradbury

*Professional practice requires conditions of trust, discretion and competence.*

Julia Evetts (2009), a sociologist who studies professional groups, notes that true professional practice requires conditions of trust, discretion and competence, but that these conditions are constantly being challenged. She suggests that 'professionalism' is increasingly becoming another form of control. Scott (2008), on the other hand, argues that professionals are leading agents in the creation and maintenance of organizational institutions. Scott suggests a different conceptualization of professionals to Reed's, based on their roles in developing, transmitting and utilizing knowledge:

- **creative professionals** develop the knowledge, like researchers

- **carrier professionals** interpret the knowledge for specific fields, like teachers

- **clinical professionals** apply principles to solve specific client problems, like doctors.

All three types of professionals share the role of developing and applying knowledge but with slightly different emphases. We explore the implications of these different definitions of professional in the Applications activity.

## Applications: HR professionals

Write down five occupations you consider to be 'professional'. Using Reed's typology, first classify them as independent, organizational or entrepreneurial. Consider issues such as how someone gains 'entry' into the profession or demonstrates their competence, how it is regulated, and how members of that profession are employed. Second, what role do you think these professionals have in developing/applying knowledge according to Scott's typology of creative, carrier or clinical professionals?

» What kind of professional do you think HR practitioners are? Why? What are the implications of this for the role of HR professionals in organizations?

## Design principles

Henri Fayol (1841–1925) was an engineer who ran a successful mining company at the turn of the 19th century. He believed that management should be guided by principles that determine how work

is structured and organized (Fayol, 1949). Fayol was careful to note that these principles should not be used rigidly; rather, the manager's job is to determine their relevance for each situation and to adapt them as needed. He was a great believer in the importance of education and training for managers and his purpose in developing these principles was to encourage their teaching. He saw management as a skill that was needed at all levels of the organization and the principles should therefore be understood and developed (at an appropriate level) by all workers alongside their technical expertise.

For example, one of the principles was *division of work* into specializations so that employees can develop expertise and improve productivity, while another was *unity of command*, meaning that employees should only have one boss telling them what to do or there will be confusion and productivity will suffer. He also included more abstract concepts such as *esprit de corps*, essentially the promotion of morale among subordinates, and *equity*, or treating employees fairly. These latter elements are often overlooked in organizational design and structure, which tends to focus on the more immediately graspable elements such as chains of command, but they are essential to consider in terms of how the structure influences behaviour and outcomes.

Fayol's principles have evolved into dimensions that we can use to describe and analyse organizational structure. In any organizational structure, there is an inherent tension between the *division of labour* that is necessary for specialized expertise and the *integration or coordination* of individual efforts that is needed in order to achieve the organization's goals.

## Division of labour

Labour can be divided in several ways in an organization: by department or division, by type of role and by job specialization. We will look at each of these in turn.

Departments: Individual jobs can be divided into groups or departments dependent on their function or their market. The functional/process form is widely used and encourages a high level of skill and knowledge development within the particular functions or processes. Examples include marketing, production or HR departments. However, this type of division may lead an organization to be unresponsive to market and customer needs. An alternative is to group jobs around the market they serve. The market could be a product or client group or even a geographical location and these kinds of departments are likely to be more responsive to the market's needs but may find it more difficult to develop the functional expertise.

Divisions: At a higher level, groups of departments are often referred to as 'divisions' and may operate as separate business units with a head office providing overall strategic planning control. Many multinationals or conglomerates operate in this way and there are several advantages, including more finely grained accountability so that each division can be assessed on its own performance. Divisions allow for the development of expertise and can be more closely aligned with their particular markets. But there are also some disadvantages, including the possibility of duplication of resources if each division has its own marketing or HR specialists, competition over corporate resources, or focus on divisional goals at the expense of corporate ones.

Roles: Another aspect of the division of labour is a division between roles that perform the primary work of the business and those that provide support to enable that work to be carried out effectively. This distinction can get quite political: everyone would like to feel that they are essential to the business and add direct value. This is especially fraught if the organization is considering downsizing or outsourcing some functions. But it is perhaps a false distinction: certainly, some roles are more directly involved in providing the service or producing the product and, at an extreme, perhaps almost every role could be outsourced, but this does not make the indirect roles any less essential to the effective, long-term functioning of the organization. As an example, in a hospital, doctors and nurses are directly involved in providing healthcare, but good administration is just as essential in the long run because it ensures adequate staffing levels, organization of patient flow, and prompt and accurate salary payments. In the same way, although IT technicians may not have direct contact with patients, they need to keep the technology running that supports access to patient records. In terms of analysing organizational structure, rather than assigning a relative value to these different roles, we are interested in how the different roles are integrated and coordinated.

Job specialization: The larger an organization gets, the greater the degree of job specialization there will tend to be. Specialization in jobs has the advantage that employees develop expertise in an area, which makes them more effective and efficient.

If the specialization involves very precise definitions of tasks and responsibilities, often through job descriptions, it provides the basis for greater control. Where specialization involves breaking tasks down into simple elements, it means that employees can be trained and replaced more easily too. However, highly skilled specialists become difficult to replace, while simple repetitive work is boring and demotivating. Employees also do not have any sense of the overall product or service, and overspecialization can lead to inflexibility on the part of employees and the organization as a whole.

## Coordination

As jobs become more specialized, there is a greater need for coordination and control of individual employees' efforts by managers. The effectiveness of this coordination depends on several structural factors, including span of control, chain of command and centralization:

Span of control: the number of people whose work the manager is responsible for coordinating. While early writers attempted to identify the ideal number of people in this span, it has been recognized that effective control depends on many different elements, including the subordinates' motivation and skills, the complexity of the tasks involved, and the skill of the supervisor.

Chain of command: the chain of reporting relationships through the organization, and a way of describing the hierarchical structures. Generally, having a clear chain of command with a single reporting relationship (one boss) is associated with better performance and satisfaction. But there is an interesting organizational structure that breaks this 'golden rule': the matrix structure, which we look at later in this chapter.

Centralization: related to chain of command, this is the degree to which authority and decision-making are controlled by the top levels of the organization or delegated down the organization. Both approaches are claimed to result in 'better' decisions, although it depends how those decisions are judged. While centralization provides greater overall control and consistency, decentralization can mean quicker decisions that are made closer to the place they are implemented. And while the delegation and participation involved in decentralization are more motivational for employees, they can result in a lack of integration.

## Physical structure

The physical layout and location of the organization is another important element to consider because it sometimes determines the structure of the organization and also can have a large impact on employee relationships. For example, an HR adviser who works in the same office as the employees she is supporting will have a greater degree of insight into their work demands, have more frequent informal contact with them, and will be experiencing similar working conditions, all of which can strengthen understanding and working relationships. On the other hand, an HR adviser who is located on a different site will have to make much more conscious effort to have contact with other employees, have little first-hand knowledge of the working conditions and will have to rely on other means of gaining insight into their unique challenges and concerns. The Applications activity explores this issue in more detail.

---

 Applications: **Strategic design?**

This case study explores the impact of physical structure on organizational design decisions. A university that was spread out over several different locations was restructuring to centralize onto a single campus. As part of this process, one of the faculties was moving to a brand new building. Previously, the faculty had been organized into six departments but the new building had three floors for staff offices. The top management team decided that the faculty should reorganize into three departments, with the lecturing staff of each department housed on one floor. To do this, pairs of departments (consisting of 20–30 lecturing staff each) were simply merged together and the associated administrators for all departments were moved into a single, large open-plan office. Each new department therefore consisted of 50–60 academic staff members and one head of department with supervisory responsibility.

Within a couple of years, it was realized that this size of department was too unwieldy for a single head of department to act as manager to all staff, so two associate head posts were brought in to each department. A further difficulty was that the departments made by the mergers were too generalized to make best use of the subject expertise of the lecturers. The departments were therefore reorganized again to form several subject groups, each led by a head of group.

» Use the dimensions of structure we have reviewed in this section to analyse the various permutations that the faculty went through. Can they help to explain why subsequent stages of the reorganization happened?

The changes in the faculty are continuing. A recent change in the university's strategic focus has led to an expansion in student numbers, with a resultant need to increase teaching staff numbers. In addition, the faculty is investing in its research efforts, meaning that more research staff are also being recruited. The result is that the faculty's staff can no longer be housed on the original three floors and are spread around the building.

» Matching changing organizational needs to the physical limitations of the building is frequently a challenge for evolving organizations. What suggestions can you make for this case? What kind of challenges might you face in implementing it? For example, staff being reluctant to move offices, overcrowding, issues of privacy for student meetings versus accessibility of staff.

---

# CONTINGENCIES IN ORGANIZATIONAL STRUCTURE

The **contingency approach** to organizational structure looks at how situational factors, known as 'contingencies', influence structure and suggests that the best structure would be one which fits the organization to those situational demands. A well-designed organization with an appropriate management style will meet the needs of employees and the organization. This approach to organizational structure is typified by the 'Aston programme', a series of studies carried out by a research group based at Aston University (was the College of Advanced Technology prior to 1966), Birmingham,

UK in the 1950s–70s. They developed a set of criteria to analyse the structures of a wide variety of organizations in a way that would give them insights into how structure was related to organizational functioning (Pugh and Hickson, 2007). Their five variables indicated how specialized jobs were, how standardized the procedures were, how formalized the documentation was, how the different roles were configured and how centralized authority and decision-making was. They combined these five variables into two basic elements of organization:

1.  Structuring of activities: looks at how structured the various organizational activities and jobs are (first three variables)

2.  Concentration of authority: the extent to which decision-making is concentrated at the top of the organization or spread throughout.

Using these two dimensions, the researchers could distinguish between different types of organizations, from full bureaucracies (high structure and high concentration of authority) to non-bureaucracies, which have little structuring and decentralized authority. They also helped to identify the range of factors that could influence an optimum organizational structure, and it is to a more detailed consideration of these contingencies that we now turn.

## Contingencies

### Technology

Although we probably tend to think of technology these days in terms of IT and computing, the term covers a much wider area than that, and technology is one of the most important contingencies affecting organizational structure. Broadly, technology is how an organization turns inputs into outputs. British academic Joan Woodward studied this in the 1960s and found that there were specific structure–technology patterns that separated successful organizations from unsuccessful ones (Klein, 2006). Essentially, the more routinized the technology was, the more structured the authority relations in the organization needed to be.

### Size

The research on the effect of size can be fairly easily summed up: the larger the organization, the more bureaucratic (structured and centralized) it tends to

be (Pugh and Hickson, 2007). This is simply because having a greater number of employees requires a more standardized approach to coordinating and managing their activities if the organization is to continue to be effective.

### Environment

In the early 1960s, Burns and Stalker (1961) looked at how innovation was managed and in their research noticed a difference between organizations best suited for stable industries and environments and those better suited to unstable and fast-moving environments. The first they called *'mechanistic'* because they were structured and functioned like machines, and the second 'organic' because they grew and adapted like living organisms.

Mechanistic organizations are formal, hierarchical and have extensive job specialization, while organic organizations are much more informal, have flat structures, that is, little hierarchy or levels of authority, and job roles tend to be broad. These structures allow the organizations to be successful in their individual situations and can be seen as extreme forms of the dimensions the Aston Group developed: high structuring and high centralization versus low structuring and decentralization.

### Strategy

In Chapter 8 we looked at organizational strategy in detail and the strategy that an organization adopts will need to have an appropriate structure if it is to succeed. We can use Porter's (1979) three basic strategies to illustrate this. Mechanistic organizations tend to be larger and focused on delivering standardized products or services, often with a cost minimization strategy. **Organic structures** are much better suited to innovation and taking advantage of fast-changing environments. Organizations pursuing an imitation strategy will need a combination of both structures: an organic approach as they move into new areas or products and a mechanistic approach for established activities and products.

## Resultant types of organization: Mintzberg's 'structure in 5s'

Henry Mintzberg (1980) noted that the elements of organizational structure show 'a curious tendency to appear in 5s', from parts based on the division of roles (support staff, operating core, strategic apex, middle line and technostructure) to mechanisms of coordination (including direct supervision and standardization of work processes) to design parameters and contingency factors. Based on this analysis, Mintzberg suggested that there were five basic configurations that organizations could take on in their structure:

1. **Simple structure:** has few layers of management, is highly centralized and is associated with dynamic environments. Young organizations with strong leaders tend to have this structure.

2. **Machine bureaucracy:** has highly formalized and standardized processes with specialized staff and is associated with stable environments. These organizations tend to be older and more established.

3. **Professional bureaucracy:** has standardized skills and relies on highly trained and specialized staff. Associated with stable but complex environments.

4. **Divisionalized form:** decision-making is decentralized to divisions based around particular markets with performance monitored by headquarters. Typical of large, older corporations (often multinational) operating in diversified markets.

5. **Adhocracy:** specialized but informal jobs with collaboration and decentralized decision-making. Associated with complex, dynamic environments.

Mintzberg (1980), in line with contingency theory, claimed that an organization will be more effective where its structure matches the demands of its environment but also noted that conflicting demands may make organizations adopt hybrid structures.

## Evaluating contingency theory

The focus on the variables or contingencies that influence organizational structure can lead us into thinking that organizations simply 'evolve' or are determined by their environment. But it is, of course, managers who make these decisions about what to change and adapt. So, the findings of contingency theory should support managers in making the most effective decisions on how to change organizational structure to match the important demands, rather than encouraging them to think that these changes will happen automatically.

Before we move on to consider alternative approaches to understanding structure, complete the Web Explorer activity to explore the different types of structures that organizations adopt.

# ALTERNATIVE APPROACHES TO ORGANIZATION

In this section, we start by considering some of the theoretical and critical discussions around

---

 ## Web Explorer: Organizational charts

Many organizations produce charts to illustrate or explain their structure on their websites. For example, PricewaterhouseCoopers International Ltd operates as a network of firms providing professional services rather than a multinational corporation because there are legal requirements in some countries that accountancy firms be locally owned. Together, these firms form the PwC network. Read the full description of how the PwC network is organized here:

www.pwc.com/gx/en/about/corporate-governance/network-structure.html.

Compare PwC's organizational structure with that of Macmillan, a charity providing cancer support:

www.macmillan.org.uk/documents/getinvolved/volunteering/onlinecommunity/macmillanorganisational structurechartoctober2011.pdf.

» Which elements of structure do these two very different organizations share? How are they different? Look at elements such as divisionalization, functions, boards and so on. What impression do you get of each organization based on how they are structured?

» Do your own search and see if you can find examples of different types of organizational structure. Do there tend to be similar structures within an industry or sector, or can you see evidence of variety? Why do you think this might be?

organizational structure. These note how widespread the bureaucratic approach is and try to offer alternative ways of thinking that could provide us with new ideas for how to organize work. We then move on to discuss the main challenges facing modern organizations and how they have restructured to meet them, finishing with an overview of several of the new forms that have been adopted to fit an organization's strategy to a dynamic and demanding business environment.

## Thinking differently about organization

Because of the dominance of the bureaucratic model of organization, researchers in OB have long been discussing 'new' forms of organization as alternatives to this model, but there is some confusion over what 'new' actually means (Palmer et al., 2007). Some authors refer to new structures if they are relatively recent, while, for others, a structure is new if it has not been used in a particular industry before.

For a while, it was thought that these 'new' structures would eventually replace the old bureaucratic structure but what is emerging instead is a hybrid of bureaucratic elements of centralization and formalization, with designs that encourage speed, flexibility and innovation (Dunford et al., 2007). Dunford et al. investigated nine of these more recent organizational structure elements, including delayering, short-term staffing, empowerment of employees and flexible work groups, and found that, as expected, they were more likely to be used in more dynamic business environments. Interestingly, however, increased use of these new elements did not

necessitate decentralization and was actually associated with *higher* formalization. This supports the suggestion that modern organizations are using adapted or hybrid bureaucratic forms rather than abandoning the formal, centralized structure completely.

## Three ways of getting things done

We often think of hierarchy as an inescapable and necessary element of work organizations. After all, if no one gave orders, how would workers know what to do? Would they even do anything? Fairtlough (2007) noted that there are actually three ways of 'getting things done' in work organizations, illustrated in Figure 9.2.

Fairtlough (2007) believed that we are 'addicted' to hierarchy in a way that stifles and limits our views of the alternatives, and that major change to blend these three approaches is required to promote effective and responsible action and creativity. The In the News (overleaf) activity illustrates one approach to organization that is attempting to do this.

## Insights from feminist organizations

A feminist critique of management literature has highlighted the role of bureaucracy in maintaining unequal gender power distributions and valuing 'rational professionals' above workers who deal with emotional work (Ashcraft, 2001). These 'rational professionals' are expected to suppress their personal needs and separate their work and home life in order to provide objective-seeming and emotionally neutral work. In contrast to this, organizations designed along more feminist principles reduce hierarchy and

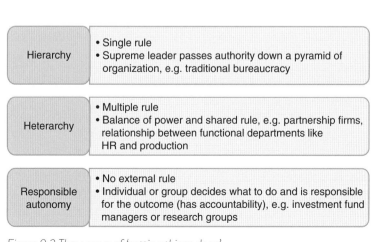

Figure 9.2 Three ways of 'getting things done'

## In the News: Self-managed organizations

HolacracyOne is a company founded in 2007 to promote and train people in a new type of self-managed organization, a form it has named and trademarked as 'holacracy'. (The term 'holacracy' is derived from the term 'holarchy', coined by Arthur Koestler in his 1967 book *The Ghost in the Machine*.) A form of responsible autonomy, this approach replaces traditional hierarchical management with what it calls a 'peer-to-peer operating system' to increase accountability, transparency and flexibility (HolacracyOne, 2017). Instead of a hierarchical structure of management to organize work, which is divided into specific jobs, HolacracyOne combines a transparent set of rules and a specific meeting process to facilitate the self-organization of teams around changing work roles.

One of the most famous companies to use holacracy is Zappos.com, an online shoe retailer led by CEO Tony Hsieh (Zappos Insights, 2016). Although holacracy is often in the news for the assumption that there is no structure, Hsieh says that, in some ways, it is actually more structured than traditional companies (Feloni, 2016). The transparent rules for the organization are captured in a detailed constitution that outlines responsibilities and procedures, and the meeting process is highly structured to ensure that it deals appropriately with all relevant issues (HolacracyOne, 2017). Instead of a hierarchy of managers, there is what Hsieh calls a 'hierarchy of purpose': circles of workers who are dedicated to specific purposes.

There have been criticisms of the holacratic approach and particularly of the claims that it reduces or removes hierarchy. In fact, Denning (2015) called holacracy 'hierarchy on steroids' and noted that even though there are apparently no managers, Tony Hsieh is still the CEO of Zappos. But he also notes that the main critics of the approach are traditional managers who have a vested interest in seeing Zappos, and the idea of self-management, fail. Hsieh recognizes that one of the difficulties with describing how holacracy works is that it is so different to what most people are used to at work that it takes a long time (several months) to learn how to work in this new way (Feloni, 2016). But not only is he convinced that this is the way for the company to continue to innovate and succeed, he also sees it as an important component of his social responsibility to 'deliver happiness' at work.

### For discussion

» Can you see any similarities between this kind of self-managed organization and a traditional bureaucracy?
» How would you feel about having a job with no official job title where you were expected to work with others to organize your work?
» If this kind of organization becomes more popular, what are the implications for traditional managerial and HRM jobs?

have more focus on collective effort (Lemke, 2016). These organizations promote the empowerment of workers and integrate personal and work life so that workers develop a sense of community, which encourages personal emotional expression while still maintaining flexible limits that ensure functional relationships are maintained.

Ashcraft notes that research on organizations constructed along feminist ideals shows they tend to develop into a hybrid form of bureaucracy, merging hierarchical and egalitarian power structures. By comparing the ideal bureaucracy and ideal feminist organization, Ashcraft (2001) develops a description of a *feminist bureaucracy*, characterized as having:

- dual goals of efficiency/productivity and empowerment

- ongoing tension between centralization/decentralization: mixing formal hierarchical structures with egalitarian practices

- formal rules that adapt to individual contexts and needs ('living' rules)

- some formal division of labour alongside flexibility in tasks

- selection and promotion based on a combination of formal qualifications and informal experience, weighing individual advancement against collective good

- a balance between rational and emotional, a view of 'professionalism' as including emotion and personal needs.

A feminist bureaucracy is only one example of many hybrid alternatives, which emphasize empowerment and flexibility while attempting to retain the rationality of bureaucratic structures. Ashcraft (2001) calls these structures 'organised dissonance' form: a strategic blending of forms that many presume are contradictory and mutually exclusive. It recognizes that organizations have to structure in a way that will deal with the tensions we have reviewed above rather than ignoring them, and does not assume that having a single purpose will remove these tensions.

## Identity and form

So far, we have been talking about organizational structure in concrete terms but a different approach is to consider organizational *identity* as a kind of structure. Although the literature on organizational identity is fairly complex, it can be understood at a simple level as 'who the organization is', in much the same way as we think of our own identity. It involves the perceptions and beliefs of organization insiders and external agents. Hsu and Hannan (2005) suggest using organizational identity as a basis for analysing structure and form. Organizational 'forms' in this approach are groups or types of similar organizations and can be described on the following dimensions:

- **Complexity or simplicity of identity**: a simple identity makes it easier for an audience to label and recognize the organization, but complexity will allow the organization to show its relevance to a wide range of activities

- **Generalization or specialization**: similarly, a generalist can tolerate variance in the environment and move into new areas with ease, while a specialist might suffer loss of value if it attempts to enter a new niche

- **Sharpness**: how distinct the organizational form is from others

- **Resonance**: the extent to which the organizational identity embodies taken-for-granted elements of society

- **Authenticity**: how well the forms relate to moral and ethical expectations.

These dimensions help us to see how the identity of an organization can constrain the kinds of strategies it can pursue. For example, a cooperative organization – one that has member participation in decision-making and engagement with the community – is unlikely to succeed if it starts to pursue an aggressively competitive strategy or adopt a hierarchical structure that is at odds with people's perceptions of its values. Instead, by using strategies that emphasize sharing and valuing members' contributions, and having an egalitarian structure, it can capitalize on the authenticity element of its identity.

## Challenges and drivers for changing structure

### Becoming more flexible

One of the primary reasons given for changing organizational structure is 'flexibility' (Dunford et al., 2013). Having a flexible and responsive organization is often seen as essential to survive in a dynamic business environment and to enhance innovation. Recommendations for increasing flexibility include removing barriers such as hierarchy and divisionalization, and encouraging trust-building, sharing and networking.

Holland (2002) recommends adopting a core and periphery structure in order to recruit and retain desirable employees, in this case, highly skilled IT workers, and notes the importance of a challenging work environment as one of the ways to retain these workers. In one organization he studied, the firm itself could not provide suitable career development for their workers within the organization. However, by restructuring to develop a second periphery of employees who were subcontracted to partner organizations, it was able to partner with its network of distributors and customers in order to offer development opportunities externally. This resulted in a turnover of only 5% compared to an industry average of 15%.

But flexibility does come with additional costs. This was demonstrated by Attia et al. (2014) in a study which identified two forms of flexibility that were important in manufacturing companies: working time flexibility and versatility of the operators. They showed that focusing on cost minimization resulted in a reduction in the overall skill range of employees and decreased flexibility, while development of future flexibility required an investment in the organization's human resources.

Getty Images/iStockphoto/Monkey Business Images

*Developing future flexibility requires investment in people.*

## Promoting innovation and learning

Functional divisions within an organization act as barriers to organizational learning because they hamper knowledge-sharing. This problem of 'silo' functioning preventing knowledge workers from carrying out their tasks effectively was highlighted in a South African study of a shared services centre, which combined HR, procurement and finance services but had poor performance because the workers were still facing barriers between the functional groups (Ramsey and Barkhuizen, 2011). A case study of a pharmaceutical company facing a similar challenge demonstrated the importance of aligning HR practices with attempts at restructuring which were aimed at overcoming this problem. The restructure involved the merger of two departments, providing lateral integration to encourage knowledge-sharing. Unfortunately, this change was generally unsuccessful and one of the main problems was that the performance management system was still aligned to the old functional departments and was driven by short-term tasks rather than the new longer term learning objectives (Currie and Kerrin, 2003).

Research and development (R&D) departments are centres of innovation and creativity for many organizations and it is therefore particularly important to design structures to support learning in these departments. Effective management of these departments is dependent on the adoption of innovative HRM practices, specifically support for idea generation and delegation of responsibility. Other HR practices such as job rotation, recruitment policies and network developments are also critical for R&D success. This has led to the suggestion that an organization's general HR practices need to be adapted by R&D managers to their specific challenges. However, research seems to indicate that this adaptation does not take place to the extent that might be expected (Ángel and Sánchez, 2009), perhaps because it creates knock-on problems of perceived injustice. The researchers found that, while there was adaptation for specific work organization, issues such as career management and compensation were determined by HR departments.

The development of internationally focused HR structures, for example by encouraging international networking of HR managers in the organization, is associated with significantly more organizational learning and transfer mechanisms (McDonnell et al., 2010). This is probably because these international HR factors help to develop a supportive learning environment. The adoption of IT systems into HRM, which encourage sharing and dissemination of information, also contributes to higher innovation (Lin, 2011).

## Specific HRM challenges: practice bundles and pay

We looked at the idea of HR bundles in Chapter 8 as a way of aligning HR practice with strategy. Research has investigated the extent to which specific bundles are linked to organizational structure. Verburg et al. (2007) tested four bundles (bureaucratic, professional, market and flexibility), which were hypothesized to align to four of Mintzberg's structure types (machine bureaucracy, professional bureaucracy, simple and **adhocracy**). Each bundle was developed to meet HR goals of ensuring compliance or commitment combined with corporate or individual responsibility for employability. However, the research did not demonstrate any advantage for organizations which adopted an HR bundle that was theorized to be a better fit to its structure. Instead, as with other research on HR bundles, it seemed that internal congruency in the specific practices that were adopted was the key determinant of success.

Bunning (2004) discusses the link between structure and pay, suggesting that the traditional hierarchical structure, which was supported by hierarchical and highly differentiated pay levels, is increasingly disappearing in more organic structures. Flatter organizations have had to adopt fewer pay levels and they deal with the challenges of providing compensation within limited ranges and career paths by providing pay for merit, performance bonuses or tenure increases. Truly organic organizations, however, have fluid structures and therefore no clear foundation for the development of pay systems. Bunning suggests that pay in these kinds of organizations will tend to adopt a 'cafeteria' pay system similar to the flexible benefits packages that already exist. The individual employee will have a core pay that can be increased through knowledge or skill increases, 'gainsharing' – where financial gains from performance improvements are shared among the employees – or performance pay based on peer appraisal.

## New structures

Having considered some of the theoretical critiques of organizational structure and the specific challenges organizations face, we now turn to look at the practical ways organizations structure to meet the demands of today's business world. As we progress through this section, the organizational structures become gradually less formal, although we will see that even in the most informal, there is still a need for unifying concepts and a degree of control.

## Multidivisional form

As organizations have expanded, they have started to operate across many product or service lines, countries and even different industries. The tight and formalized control of a traditional bureaucracy does not allow these multinational corporations to adapt effectively to the different demands of these markets. The need for some control combined with a degree of independence led to the development of the multidivisional or 'M-form' structure. While sometimes suggested as an alternative to bureaucracy, it is more an adaptation of the bureaucratic structure than a replacement. In this structure, there are several autonomous divisions that can be focused on a geographical area, for example a UK division and an Australian division, a product line or even an industry. Each division is its own profit centre: it has to meet performance standards set by the central core company but how it does this is left open, meaning that each division can adapt its practices, structures and policies to its specific needs. While the traditional bureaucracy would keep tight control by having formalized and standardized procedures, the M-form exerts control over outcomes instead.

Large complex multinational organizations face four main challenges (Campbell and Strikwerda, 2013):

1. Attempting to decentralize without allowing one form of division to dominate over others, for example dividing by geography and losing track of products

2. Providing management focus within a certain division without creating silos that restrict sharing of knowledge

3. Enhancing coordination across the organization without losing motivation: greater control means less freedom and initiative

4. Divisional accountability that does not promote destructive inter-division competition.

Campbell and Strikwerda suggest that successful multinational organizations address these challenges with 'power-of-one' solutions, effectively providing the entire organization with one underlying logic, which defines the structures that determine success within that organization, and is built on a unified information system.

## Matrix structure

A matrix structure is often used as a way of integrating people from different functions onto individual projects. A single employee will report to a functional head and a project leader, as Figure 9.3 illustrates.

|  | HR manager | Finance manager | IT manager |
|---|---|---|---|
| Project A leader<br>Developing online access to payslips for employees | HR employee 1 | Finance employee 1 | IT employee 1 |
| Project B leader<br>Improving automatic booking of training events | HR employee 2 | Finance employee 1 | IT employee 1 |

*Figure 9.3 Example matrix structure*

One advantage of a matrix structure is that it encourages cross-functional learning and communication while maintaining specialisms, thus providing a certain degree of flexibility for larger organizations. However, there are disadvantages, including ambiguity over resources and responsibility. And while it can be interesting and developmental for individual employees working on different projects, it can also cause uncertainty over how to deal with conflicting priorities from different bosses.

## Team- or project-based structures

Project-oriented companies, for example construction companies organized around specific sites, conduct their processes through a project structure, which they integrate to create organizational performance. They often have a fairly flat structure and present specific challenges for employees and the HR department, including the dynamic and temporary nature of project teams and goals, as well as issues of multiple role demands and resources (Huemann et al., 2007). There are several outcomes of these challenges that HR practitioners need to deal with. For example, maintaining employee well-being becomes more difficult in a constantly changing internal environment. The basic HR process of recruitment-employment-release also becomes far more complex in an environment where an individual's constant employment is replaced by repeating cycles of *recruitment to a project* followed by *employment on the project* followed by *release from the project*. Huemann et al. (2007) suggest that project-oriented companies can provide advantages such as varied and interesting career paths but HR has a pivotal role by providing systems that ensure fairness and ensuring that this career path actually materializes by having clarity in linking projects together. The role of accountability in project teams is particularly important: where employees on specific projects are only accountable to their original function manager, they will naturally remain focused on them rather than the cross-functional project (Currie and Kerrin, 2003).

Greater use of team-based structures is associated with higher levels of innovation and HRM systems are important moderators of this link (Fay et al., 2015). Higher quality HRM, defined as good practice in key activities such as recruitment and promotion as well as strategic focus, enhances the strength of the relationship between teamwork and innovation. This is because HR has a key role in facilitating or constraining the beneficial effects of teamwork. In project-intensive organizations, HRM faces four key challenges (Söderlund and Bredin, 2006):

1. Competence: HR managers need to consider the required competencies now and in the future, develop ways of tracking competence development and integrating the learning that takes place in project teams at the organizational level.

2. Trust: HR should provide structures that enable trust to develop by building long-term cooperation and coordination. A related issue is how to deal with breaches of trust, and attention needs to be given to mechanisms to reduce the risk of opportunistic behaviours.

3. Change: HR has to address the common challenges of identifying and facilitating change more frequently in this kind of organization than others. Part of addressing this is to ensure that HRM activities are integrated into day-to-day activities.

4. People: Responsibility for career development tends to be on the individual employee but attracting and retaining high-calibre workers necessitates good HR programmes of development and support.

In addition, newer forms of organizational structure, which encourage participation and teamwork, mean that there is a demand for new skills such as problem-solving and communication (Felstead and Ashton, 1997). For HRM, the challenge becomes how to recruit or develop these skills. The Applications activity explores this issue in the non-profit sector.

 Applications: **Developing participation in NGOs**

Concern Worldwide (2016) is an international nongovernmental organization (NGO) that works to reduce hunger and poverty. In the late 1990s, the Mozambique arm of this organization wanted to introduce greater participation by workers in organizational decision-making and management. This approach was seen as fitting very well with the overall ethos of the organization as a vehicle for empowerment and community development, as well as allowing it to respond more quickly and appropriately to local situations (Sheehan, 1998). The change involved three different elements:

1. A move to a flatter organization.

2. Introducing team structures: this included project teams in each of the local areas to design and evaluate work plans and two national teams responsible for formulating and implementing overall strategy.

3. Encouragement of a more open and communicative environment in which learning is supported, for example launching a staff magazine and involving the staff in an evaluation of the organization's strengths and weaknesses.

The result of these changes was an increase in members' levels of participation as well as more effective service delivery. Sheehan (1998) notes the importance of formalizing the *patterns* of participation into *structures*.

» To what extent do you think participatory management is particularly appropriate for charities and NGOs?

» Why do you think it was considered so important to change Concern's structure in order to change behaviour?

» If you were involved in this kind of change, what other recommendations would you make for encouraging greater participation?

## Networks and virtual organizations

Miles and Snow (1986) coined the phrase *dynamic network* for a new form of organizational structure they had noticed emerging in 1980s' America in response to increased complexity and competition. A dynamic network has four main characteristics:

1. Vertical disaggregation: functions that had traditionally all been conducted in-house are undertaken by independent organizations in the network. These functions could include manufacturing, marketing, research, design and so on.

2. **Brokers:** these different functions are integrated and brought together through a broker.

3. **Market mechanisms:** instead of being managed in a traditional way with personal supervision, the functions are held together by contracts and payments for results.

4. **Full disclosure information systems:** trust is a key element in a network, and this is developed quickly through information systems that allow broad access to partners.

Networks allow an entire industry to meet the needs of efficiency and innovation by linking together in a complementary way organizations that specialize in different areas. Miles and Snow claim that networks allow a much more effective use of human resources because people no longer have to be 'maintained' by a single organization.

Lipnack and Stamps (1999) claimed that virtual teams and networks were the latest evolution in organizational structure, although they did note that hierarchies and other bureaucratic elements will not simply disappear. For them, the key advantage of networks and teams was that they could overcome the one-way flow of information that is typical of hierarchies. Virtual teams could take advantage of technology developments such that they could work together without having to be physically in the same place (or even organization). Figure 9.4 illustrates the factors necessary for a successful virtual team (Bergiel et al., 2008).

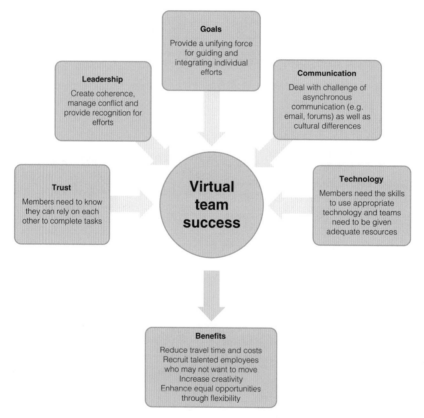

Figure 9.4 Factors contributing to virtual team success

There is a distinct contribution here for HRM in terms of developing the necessary skills and competencies that will ensure virtual team success. A particular area that many employees need support and development in is the effective use of electronic communication, as face-to-face meetings are likely to be minimal. HRM is also critical in contributing to the selection of employees who are able and willing to work effectively in this way.

Many have argued that trust is essential for virtual teams and organizations, but an interesting alternative perspective is suggested by Gallivan (2001) in a study of the open source software (OSS) movement, which he classes as a prototypical virtual organization. The OSS movement supports the voluntary writing of program code to develop software and the use of open-source licensing so that anyone can obtain and modify it. Gallivan argues that the OSS movement demonstrates that trust is not necessary for effective performance; instead, explicit and implicit forms of control can substitute for trust. Explicit forms of control include statements of rules and norms in FAQs, and implicit forms include an emphasis on the individual's reputation. We need to maintain a sense of balance about virtual teams and organizations: trust is important but, as we saw in Chapter 4, it is complemented by formal contracts and controls.

At a simple level, networks are the relationships and connections that employees or whole organizations have with each other. Networks can be described in terms of how closely the members are clustered and the length of the path (or the number of links in the chain) that connects two members. A 'small world network' is one in which there is high clustering and short paths between members (Watts and Strogatz, 1998). This kind of network is very efficient at sharing information and forms naturally. The difficulty for organizations is how to connect these naturally forming networks together because traditional structures actively divide people and departments from each other (Satell, 2015).

Networked organizations tend to function in a 'subcontracting' mode, where a central group sets strategy and maintains the network, bringing in other groups and individuals as needed. A unique element in an industry such as the UK television industry is the intermittent nature of the projects for which networks form (Starkey et al., 2000). That is, the network of actors, directors, producers, camera, sound technicians and so on will be drawn together for a specific project over perhaps a few weeks, and then disband again. Starkey et al. suggest that this challenge is overcome by the formation of 'latent' organizations: networks that only become manifest around certain projects but continue to exist even when not actively engaged. Essentially, the relationships are continuous but the production is episodic. The quality and competitive advantage comes from the unique combination of a specific broker working with specific (talented and trusted) agents. These latent organizations 'make it possible to maintain a constant configuration of the same members that can be used intermittently over time' (p. 300). The Practice Insights video interview in this chapter is with a film director who talks through how these latent organizations rely on personal networks.

It may seem that networked organizations present the opportunity of progression for developing countries by providing strong links for local businesses with international corporations. However, Dhillon et al. (2001) recommend caution if the network is not to become skewed and provide little benefit to the host country. One of the major challenges to balance here is the development of a skilled national workforce that is sought after by foreign companies against the host country becoming competitive in its own right. A mutual flow of knowledge and expertise is needed if the network is to be beneficial to all members.

## Evaluating various forms of organization

Despite the recurring theme in OB and HRM that there is not 'one best way' to manage people and organizations, we still come across writers

---

### Transferrable Skills: Analysing organizational function

An important element of any attempt at restructuring an organization is to understand the functions that are carried out and how they relate to each other. A 'function' is a collection of activities directed towards fulfilling the organization's goals. An effective structure will support and enhance those activities, while ineffective structures can throw up barriers, limit progression or even sabotage people's efforts to achieve them. In this activity, we will go through a simple analysis to enable you to identify key functions and start to think about how to design an appropriate structure.

To start, identify an organization that you know reasonably well. You may find this easier if you use a smaller organization or can talk to some of the people who work there to get their insights. Find the organization's strategy or goals – you will use this as the basis for analysing how different functions contribute to this overall strategy.

» Draw up a list of the different departments or work groups in the organization. This provides you with a basic outline of the functions that are already recognized. For example, it might include an HR department, local store managers and their teams, a marketing department and so on.

» For each group you identify, develop a list of what they do and how that helps the organization to achieve its goals. It can be helpful to divide these functions into those contributing directly to the organization's goals (known as line or business) and those contributing indirectly (support or administrative) functions.

» Identify the critical or 'core' functions from your list, that is, functions that lead to the desired outcomes. You will need to refer to the organizational strategy here: is it aiming for high quality or low cost or good customer satisfaction or some other goal? You may find that these core functions cross over the traditional organizational boundaries. For example, you might decide that a critical function of achieving customer satisfaction in a high-street shop includes a friendly welcome to the shop and good

customer service as well as effective pricing and a reliable and timely logistical chain to ensure that enough stock is available. Give these core functions names and a brief description.

» Now consider how you could use this analysis as the basis for restructuring the organization so that it could pursue its goals more effectively. Can you organize around functions? How will you ensure that different linked elements of a function communicate with each other? Do you want to remove or introduce any extra management or other support?

If your analysis leads you to develop a very different structure to the one that is currently being used, consider how you might have to address some of the people issues involved in radical restructuring. Will there be a need for training or development? Have you created any new positions or removed any old ones and how will you deal with this? It might be worth looking back at Chapter 7 to explore this further.

---

 ### Practice Insights: Darren Cook

Darren Cook is a film director, TV editor and photographer with over 20 years' experience in the film industry. He runs his own company, Scruffy Bear Pictures, and is currently working as Head of Production with Applejack Creative Services. In this video he talks about the way work is organized and structured in this creative industry, where projects are generally short term and rely heavily on personal contacts and networks.

Go online to www.macmillanihe.com/sutton-people to access the interview with Darren.

and policy makers arguing that a particular organizational structure is the most effective. This was demonstrated in an interesting case study of new public management in the Netherlands, which is the attempt to apply market-driven management ideas to the large bureaucracies of public institutions. In their comparison of three different structures (bureaucratic, market and network) for organizations working towards re-employment of those on disability benefits, Svensson et al. (2008, p. 514) concluded that the superiority of one approach is 'wishful thinking'. Hopefully, what you have seen in this chapter is that there are many ways of organizing our work and that what counts is how well the structure supports the aim of the organization: the Transferrable Skills activity works through how we can analyse function in order to do this.

## SUMMARY

We have seen in this chapter that there are many different ways of organizing work and that the structure of the organization should not simply be left to chance. Successful integration and enhancement of individual performance depends on an appropriate structure. Starting with the bureaucratic model as a rational 'ideal' form of organization, we have discussed the different dimensions that organizations can change and the impact this has on work, as well as the importance of considering the organizational contingencies in developing a structure that is 'fit for purpose'.

We have also taken a step back to consider some of the more theoretical critiques, particularly how deeply engrained some of our assumptions are about how organizations 'should' be structured. By evaluating the challenges that organizations face and the drivers advocating a shift from a traditional bureaucratic structure, we have seen there is a demand for increased flexibility and innovation. The chapter concluded with a consideration of some of these more adaptable forms, noting that where innovation and flexibility are needed, a more informal, team-based and organic approach may be most suitable.

## FURTHER READING

* You can read new translations of Max Weber's work in Weber, M. (2015) *Weber's Rationalism and Modern Society: New Translations on Politics, Bureaucracy, and Social Stratification* (eds T. Waters and D. Waters). Basingstoke: Palgrave Macmillan.

* Chapter 1 in Pugh and Hickman's very readable summary of some of the main writers on organizations gives a good introduction to important studies in organizational structure: Pugh, D. and Hickson, D. (2007) *Writers on Organizations*, 6th edn. Thousand Oaks, CA: Sage.

## REVIEW QUESTIONS

1. What are the main design principles of organizational structure? Give examples of how they are implemented in organizations you know.

2. How can contingency theory contribute to the development of effective organizational structures?

3. Why have some organizations started to develop new structures?

## ONLINE RESOURCES

Go online to www.macmillanihe.com/sutton-people to access a MCQ quiz for this chapter and for further resources to support your learning.

## REFERENCES

Ángel, P. O. and Sánchez, L. S. (2009) 'R&D managers' adaptation of firms' HRM practices', *R&D Management*, 39(3), pp. 271–90. doi: 10.1111/j.1467-9310.2009.00552.x.

Ashcraft, K. L. (2001) 'Organized dissonance: feminist bureaucracy as hybrid form', *Academy of Management Journal*, 44(6), pp. 1301–22.

Attia, E.-A., Duquenne, P. and Le-Lann, J.-M. (2014) 'Considering skills evolutions in multi-skilled workforce allocation with flexible working hours', *International Journal of Production Research*, 52(15), pp. 4548–73. doi: 10.1080/00207543.2013.877613.

Bergiel, B. J., Bergiel, E. B. and Balsmeier, P. W. (2008) 'Nature of virtual teams: a summary of their advantages and disadvantages', *Management Research News*, 31(2), pp. 99–110. doi: 10.1108/01409170810846821.

Bunning, R. L. (2004) 'Pay in the organic organisation', *Journal of Management Development*, 23(7), pp. 648–63. doi: 10.1108/02621710410546650.

Burns, T. E. and Stalker, G. M. (1961) *The Management of Innovation*. London: Tavistock.

Byrt, W. J. (1973) *Theories of Organisation*. Sydney: McGraw-Hill.

Campbell, A. and Strikwerda, H. (2013) 'The power of one: towards the new integrated organisation', *Journal of Business Strategy*, 34(2), pp. 4–12. doi: 10.1108/02756661311310404.

Concern Worldwide (2016) 'Our history'. Available at: www.concern.net/en/about/history (Accessed 6 January 2017).

Currie, G. and Kerrin, M. (2003) 'Human resource management and knowledge management: enhancing knowledge sharing in a pharmaceutical company', *International Journal of Human Resource Management*, 14(6), pp. 1027–45. doi: 10.1080/0958519032000124641.

Denning, S. (2015) 'Is holacracy succeeding at Zappos?', *Forbes*, May. Available at: www.forbes.com/sites/stevedenning/2015/05/23/is-holacracy-succeeding-at-zappos/#10998d1540bb (Accessed 6 January 2017).

Dhillon, G., Moores, T. and Hackney, R. (2001) 'The emergence of networked organizations in India: A misalignment of interests?', *Journal of Global Information Management*, 9(1), pp. 25–30.

Dunford, R., Palmer, I., Benveniste, J. and Crawford, J. (2007) 'Coexistence of "old" and "new" organizational practices: Transitory phenomenon or enduring feature?', *Asia Pacific Journal of Human Resources*, 45(1), pp. 24–43. doi: 10.1177/1038411107073597.

Dunford, R., Cuganesan, S., Grant, D. et al. (2013) '"Flexibility" as the rationale for organizational change: a discourse perspective', *Journal of Organizational Change Management*, 26(1), pp. 83–97. doi: 10.1108/09534811311307923.

Evetts, J. (2009) 'The management of professionalism: a contemporary paradox', in S. Gewirtz, P. Mahony, I. Hextall and A. Cribb (eds) Changing Teacher Professionalism: International Trends, *Challenges and Ways Forward*. London: Taylor & Francis, pp. 19–30.

Fairtlough, G. (2007) *The Three Ways of Getting Things Done: Hierarchy, Heterarchy & Responsible Autonomy in Organizations*. Axminster: Triarchy Press.

Fay, D., Shipton, H., West, M. A. and Patterson, M. (2015) 'Teamwork and organizational innovation: the moderating role of the HRM-context', *Teamwork and Organizational Innovation*, 24(2), pp. 17–21.

Fayol, H. (1949) *General and Industrial Management*. London: Pitman.

Feloni, R. (2016) 'Zappos CEO Tony Hsieh reveals what it was like losing 18 % of his employees in a radical management experiment – and why it was worth it', *Business Insider UK*, January. Available at: http://uk.businessinsider.com/tony-hsieh-explains-how-zappos-rebounded-from-employee-exodus-2016-1.

Felstead, A. and Ashton, D. (1997) 'Tracing the link: organisational structures and skill demands', *Human Resource Management Journal*, 10(3), pp. 5–21.

Gallivan, M. J. (2001) 'Striking a balance between trust and control in a virtual organization: a content analysis of open source software case studies', *Information Systems Journal*, 11(4), pp. 277–304. doi: 10.1046/j.1365-2575.2001.00108.x.

HolacracyOne (2017) *How It Works*. Available at: www.holacracy.org/how-it-works/ (Accessed 6 January 2017).

Holland, P. J. (2002) 'Human resource strategies and organisational structures for managing gold-collar workers', *Journal of European Industrial Training*, 26(2), pp. 72–80. doi: 10.1108/03090590210421941.

Hsu, G. and Hannan, M. T. (2005) 'Identity, genres, and organizational forms', *Organization Science*, 16(5), pp. 474–90. doi: 10.1287/orsc.1050.0151.

Huemann, M., Keegan, A. and Turner, J. R. (2007) 'Human resource management in the project-oriented company: a review', *International Journal of Project Management*, 25(3), pp. 315–23. doi: 10.1016/j.ijproman.2006.10.001.

Klein, L. (2006) 'Joan Woodward memorial lecture: applied social science: Is it just common sense?', *Organization Studies*, 59(8), pp. 1155–72. doi: 10.1177/0018726706068804.

Lemke, M. A. (2016) 'Feminist organizations, definition of', in *The Wiley Blackwell Encyclopedia of Gender and Sexuality Studies*. Malden, MA: John Wiley & Sons.

Lin, L.-H. (2011) 'Electronic human resource management and organizational innovation: the roles of information technology and virtual organizational structure', *International Journal of Human Resource Management*, 22(2), pp. 235–57. doi: 10.1080/09585192.2011.540149.

Lipnack, J. and Stamps, J. (1999) 'Virtual teams: the new way to work', *Strategy & Leadership*, 27(1), pp. 14–19. doi: 10.1108/eb054625.

McDonnell, A., Gunnigle, P. and Lavelle, J. (2010) 'Learning transfer in multinational companies: explaining inter-organisation variation', *Human Resource Management Journal*, 20(1), pp. 23–43. doi: 10.1111/j.1748-8583.2009.00104.x.

May, T. Y. M., Korczynski, M. and Frenkel, S. J. (2002) 'Organizational and occupational commitment: knowledge workers in large corporations', *Journal of Management Studies*, 39(6), pp. 775–801. doi: 10.1111/1467-6486.00311.

Miles, R. E. and Snow, C. C. (1986) 'Organizations: new concepts for new forms', *California Management Review*, 28(3), pp. 62–73. doi: 10.2307/41165202.

Miner, J. B. (1982) *Theories of Organizational Structure and Process*. New York: Dryden Press.

Mintzberg, H. (1980) 'Structure in 5's: a synthesis of the research on organization design', *Management Science*, pp. 322–41. doi: 10.1287/mnsc.26.3.322.

Palmer, I., Benveniste, J. and Dunford, R. (2007) 'New organizational forms: towards a generative dialogue', *Organization Studies*, 28(12), pp. 1829–47. doi: 10.1177/0170840607079531.

Porter, M. (1979) 'How competitive forces shape strategy', *Harvard Business Review*, 57(2), pp. 137–45. doi: 10.1097/00006534-199804050-00042.

Pugh, D. and Hickson, D. (2007) *Writers on Organizations*, 6th edn. Thousand Oaks, CA: Sage.

Ramsey, M. and Barkhuizen, N. (2011) 'Organisational design elements and competencies for optimising the expertise of knowledge workers in a shared services centre', *SA Journal of Human Resource Management*, 9(1), pp. 1–15. doi: 10.4102/sajhrm.v9i1.307.

Reed, M. (1996) 'Expert power and control in late modernity: an empirical review and theoretical synthesis', *Organization Studies*, 17(4), pp. 573–97.

Satell, G. (2015) 'What makes an organization "networked"?', *Harvard Business Review*, June, pp. 1–5. Available at: https://hbr.org/2015/06/what-makes-an-organization-networked.

Scott, W. R. (2008) 'Lords of the dance: professionals as institutional agents', *Organization Studies*, 29(2), pp. 219–38. doi: 10.1177/0170840607088151.

Sheehan, J. (1998) 'NGOs and participatory management styles: a case study of Concern Worldwide, Mozambique', *CVO International Working Paper Number 2*. Available at: http://eprints.lse.ac.uk/29090/1/int-work-paper2.pdf.

Söderlund, J. and Bredin, K. (2006) 'HRM in project-intensive firms: changes and challenges', *Human Resource Management*, 45(2), pp. 249–65. doi: 10.1002/hrm.20107.

Starkey, K., Barnatt, C. and Tempest, S. (2000) 'Beyond networks and hierarchies: latent organizations in the U.K. television industry', *Organization Science*, 11(3), pp. 299–305. doi: 10.1287/orsc.11.3.299.12500.

Svensson, J., Trommel, W. and Lantink, T. (2008) 'Reemployment services in the Netherlands: a comparative study of bureaucratic, market, and network forms of organization', *Public Administration Review*, 68(3), pp. 505–15. doi: 10.1111/j.1540-6210.2008.00886.x.

Thompson, V. A. (1977) *Modern Organization*, 2nd edn. Tuscaloosa, AL: University of Alabama Press.

Verburg, R. M., Den Hartog, D. N. and Koopman, P. L. (2007) 'Configurations of human resource management practices: a model and test of internal fit', *International Journal of Human Resource Management*, 18(2), pp. 184–208. doi: 10.1080/09585190601102349.

Watts, D. J. and Strogatz, S. H. (1998) 'Collective dynamics of "small-world" networks', *Nature*, 393(6684), pp. 440–2. doi: 10.1038/30918.

Weber, M. (2015) *Weber's Rationalism and Modern Society: New Translations on Politics, Bureaucracy, and Social Stratification* (eds T. Waters and D. Waters). Basingstoke: Palgrave Macmillan.

Zappos Insights (2016) *Holacracy: Flattening the Organization Structure and Busting Bureaucracy*. Available at: www.zapposinsights.com/about/holacracy (Accessed 6 January 2017).

# PART 3 CASE STUDY: FROM STARTUP TO SCALEUP: TALA

Founded by Shivani Siroya, Tala Mobile is a tech startup that makes microloans to people in developing countries like Kenya and the Philippines. Siroya started the company because there were billions of people in developing markets who, she believed, deserved access to financial services but this could only be achieved if those systems were radically rethought and redesigned around the customer (Siroya, 2016a). She is passionate about providing financial choice and control to everyone.

Getty Images/Blend Images/JGI/Jamie Grill

Before founding Tala (or Inventure as it was originally known), Siroya worked in an investment bank and then with an NGO in India. The NGO was engaged in microfinance, which is a way of offering financial services to people who are otherwise unable to access formal loans and other banking services: the goal being to help people to become self-sufficient. It was during this time that she recognized that one of the biggest challenges facing people in these developing markets was that they could not gain access to the formal credit system (Adams, 2016). A third of the world's population simply do not have access to a credit score and therefore are not 'trusted' by financial systems (Siroya, 2016b). After working on a project for the UN, which involved manually interviewing people to try and build a credit score, Siroya's breakthrough came when she realized that much of this data was on people's phones and could be used to develop a kind of 'financial identity'. This financial identity could be used in the way credit scores are used in formal financial systems to determine what level of risk someone represents.

Siroya then developed her ideas into a business that she launched with her own capital, lending $20,000 to 50 people in countries around the world (Adams, 2016). To start with, she asked questions of potential borrowers using texts and voice messages. The company then developed an app that could extract data from borrowers' phones to verify identity and calculate a credit score. To begin with, they licensed this data to traditional banks and lenders but have since started using their own capital to fund the loans. The app now evaluates 10,000 data points from a borrower's digital identity, including social connectedness and geographic patterns (Tala, 2016). Their data relates how things like the number of people a borrower communicates with daily can increase the likelihood of repaying a loan (Siroya, 2016b). The app now allows borrowers to have a loan in about two minutes and repayment rates are in line with traditional banking.

As a company, Tala is guided by a belief that everyone should have choice and control over their financial lives (Siroya, 2016a). It has a diversity focused culture underpinned by three main values: nimble (efficient and responsive), meritocratic (empowered to work autonomously and recognition for good work) and committed to excellence (in products, customer relationships and employees) (Tala, 2016).

Tala employed around 50 people at the beginning of 2017 according to crunchbase.com, and is currently going through a scaleup process. A scaleup is a high-tech business that is at the development stage and seeking to grow in size, revenue and markets, often by building collaborations with established companies (Onetti, 2014). A lot changes in the move from startup to scaleup, which Glickman (2016), CEO of Ultra Mobile, a company that has gone through this process, summarizes into a few main themes. There is the move from generalist to specialist employees, from a comfort with risk-taking to a focus on consistency in delivery, and a move towards developing processes rather than relying on spontaneous problem-solving. These are all challenges Tala will face and have to overcome if it is going to continue to grow. In addition, Shiroya has identified two unique challenges that the company will have to deal with in the coming years (Bloomberg Philanthropies, 2016). First, there is a lack of awareness on the part of potential investors about the opportunities in Africa and other developing markets. Shiroya says that the company has to somehow undo the perception that African countries are reliant on aid rather than a good business opportunity. Second, Tala is expanding globally and needs to find ways to launch effectively in new countries in Southeast Asia, Latin America and sub-Saharan Africa as well as to expand its product line and offer more financial services to its customers.

Given Tala's history and current challenges, how would you recommend it scales up without losing its unique culture and social mission? Consider the following issues:

- What organizational structure would you recommend Tala develops? What kind of challenges might the company face as it starts to bring in formal processes to a very informal working environment? How could it deal with these challenges effectively?

- How can Tala ensure that it continues to capitalize on the individual and organizational learning that is such a feature of tech startups as it goes through the scaleup process?

- What strategic approach would suit Tala as it moves towards the future? Do you think it will need to change its strategy as it develops?

# REFERENCES

Adams, S. (2016) 'How Tala Mobile is using phone data to revolutionize microfinance'. Available at: www.forbes.com/sites/forbestreptalks/2016/08/29/how-tala-mobile-is-using-phone-data-to-revolutionize-microfinance/#5be2eaa411e2 (Accessed 17 January 2017).

Bloomberg Philanthropies (2016) *Tech Startup Series: Tala*. Available at: https://medium.com/u-s-africa-business-forum-2016/tech-startup-series-tala-f31b9ffb2df6#.ibk6xc53i (Accessed 17 January 2017).

Glickman, D. (2016) 'Don't mistake a scaleup for a startup'. Available at: www.recode.net/2016/6/30/12053144/scaleup-startup-entrepreneur-enterprise-growth-specializing (Accessed 17 January 2017).

Onetti, A. (2014) 'When does a startup turn into a scaleup?' Available at: http://startupeuropepartnership.eu/scaleups-when-does-a-startup-turn-into-a-scaleup/ (Accessed 17 January 2017).

Siroya, S. (2016a) 'Why Tala?' Available at: https://medium.com/tala/why-tala-9726e8112537#.famsy0jah (Accessed 17 January 2017).

Siroya, S. (2016b) 'Shivani Siroya: a smart loan for people with no credit history (yet)'. Available at: www.ted.com/talks/shivani_siroya_a_smart_loan_for_people_with_no_credit_history_yet?utm_source=tedcomshare&utm_medium=referral&utm_campaign=tedspread (Accessed 17 January 2017).

Tala (2016) 'Careers'. Available at: http://tala.co/careers/.

# SUSTAINING ORGANIZATIONAL EFFECTIVENESS

In this final part of the book, we are looking to the future and considering what we can do to build organizations that survive long term. In Chapter 10 we start by finding out how to encourage individual learning and development at work, before considering how this can be captured into organizational learning in order to ensure that the organization is able to be as effective as possible in changing circumstances. In Chapter 11, we look at the different approaches that organizations take to looking after the physical health and safety of their staff, as well the increasing emphasis on developing holistic well-being. This is a key element in building employee engagement at

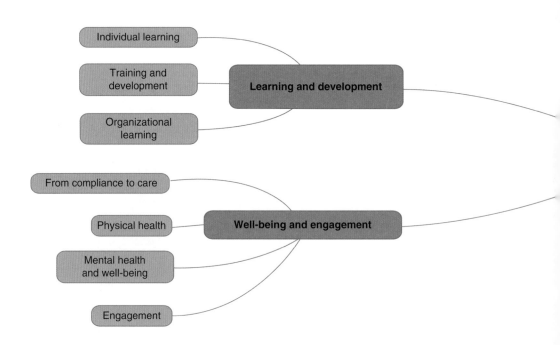

work and we will see how the recent interest in this area is related to organizations attempting to build a high performing and sustainable workforce. Finally, in Chapter 12, we look at how we can 'future-proof' organizations, considering issues around sustainability and its implications for measuring organizational success, as well as how we can evaluate and utilize cutting-edge research in HRM and OB. The Part 4 case study looks at an organization that survived nearly 150 years but finally failed, drawing out our main themes of well-being, organizational learning and sustainability to consider whether anything could have been done to sustain its survival.

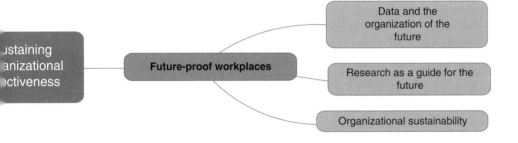

# 10 LEARNING AND DEVELOPMENT

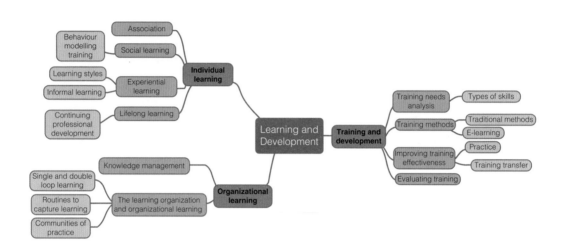

## INTRODUCTION

In this chapter we bring together HR concerns of how to frame and implement learning and training in organizations with OB issues of knowledge management and learning in work organizations. We start by discussing the main ways that people learn, from simple association through to complex learning in a social context. We will also look at the increasing importance of lifelong learning: how people can keep their skills and knowledge up to date in a fast-changing world and the central role of continuing development in maintaining professional credibility.

In keeping with the theme of the final part of the book, namely building organizations that can last, we then move on to the practical side of learning at work, that is, how organizations can provide training to employees that meets the needs of the individual and the future requirements of the organization. Training can be seen as an iterative cycle that starts with good analysis of training needs moves to providing effective learning opportunities, and is evaluated in a balanced way to demonstrate the utility of the training. This leads us into a consideration of learning at the organizational level, including how knowledge can be managed for competitive advantage and the different conceptualizations of organizational learning and learning organizations.

*Stockbyte/Punchstock*

## LEARNING FEATURES

Applications: Using rewards to change behaviour

Applications: Does personality affect how we learn?

Applications: Managing your own CPD

Weighing the Evidence: Are learning organizations real?

Web Explorer: E-learning

In the News: Project ECHO

Transferrable Skills: Designing a training programme

Practice Insights: Paul Walsh

 Video overview

*Julian Perkins*

Go online to www.macmillanihe.com/sutton-people to access a video of Anna Sutton introducing the chapter's main themes.

# INDIVIDUAL LEARNING

Although learning, training and development are interwoven issues in organizations, it is important to distinguish between them so that we can develop effective interventions and ensure that the development activities or training courses the organization provides are meeting their goals. Learning can be thought of as the acquisition of new knowledge, skills and abilities (KSAs), and Sonnentag et al. (2008) distinguish between training and development by considering the timescale over which they operate and their ultimate aims. Training is the process of helping employees to develop the KSAs needed for their current roles or jobs in the near future, whereas development focuses on personal and professional growth relevant to employees' future career. A good understanding of how people learn is an essential foundation for any HR or organizational intervention that attempts to improve learning in the organization or provide training and development opportunities.

## Simple learning: association

Perhaps the most basic element of individual learning is the fact that we learn through association. In early psychological studies this was called 'conditioning'. One of the most famous studies in this area was a set of experiments that Ivan Pavlov conducted on dogs, where they learnt to associate the ringing of a bell with food and started to show the same response to the bell on its own as they did to food. This simple style of learning, called *'classical conditioning'*, is about associating stimulus and response.

A slightly more complex way of learning is called *'operant conditioning'*. This is still an associative form of learning, but in this case it is the association of an action with its consequences or outcomes that influences our actions. If we are rewarded for doing something, we are more likely to do that action again and, if punished, less likely. For example, if a manager praises an employee because he remained calm and polite with a particularly difficult customer, the employee is more likely to behave like that in future. On the other hand, if instead a manager tells off the employee for taking so long to deal with the customer, he will be less likely to take his time with a difficult customer in future. The Applications activity looks at how the schedule of these rewards and punishments, known as 'reinforcers', can influence behaviour modification.

These associative or conditioning theories are good explanations for simple learning and certainly underlie much of our learning. But, these approaches do tend to view the individual as quite passive in the learning process: actions are simply 'determined' by the associations of stimuli and response. They are useful in terms of understanding the basic links that our brains make when we are learning, but less so for understanding more active forms of learning.

---

 Applications: **Using rewards to change behaviour**

One of the important implications of associative learning theories is that rewards and punishments (reinforcers) influence behaviour. We can use these findings to build simple interventions to change behaviour at work by choosing the most appropriate *reinforcement schedule* for the behaviour we want to change, that is, when rewards should be given. There are five types of reinforcement schedules:

1. **Continuous:** reward is given every time the behaviour is shown. Learning of the new behaviour is fast, but people quickly revert to the old behaviour if the reward is stopped.

2. **Fixed interval:** reward is given after a fixed time interval (e.g. at the end of each week). People will show the required behaviour only at average levels and perform it fairly irregularly.

3. **Variable interval:** reward is given at random times. People will do the required behaviour well (high and stable performance) and will continue to do it for a long time after rewards are stopped.

4. **Fixed ratio:** reward is given after a set number of times the behaviour is displayed. People will quickly learn to do the required behaviour and will perform at high levels. But if the rewards are stopped, they will also quickly stop doing the behaviour.

5. **Variable ratio:** reward is given after varying numbers of the desired outputs/behaviours. People will perform at high levels and will continue to do so for a long time after the reward is stopped.

Anastasia is the manager of a team of employees in a customer service call centre. She has noticed that her team often let the phones ring for extended periods before answering and she needs to reduce customer waiting time. She would like to encourage her team to answer phones more quickly using a reward system. She needs the change in behaviour to occur as quickly as possible, but also to continue long term until it becomes the 'new normal' for the team.

» What kinds of rewards could she offer and how should she schedule them? You may decide to combine several schedules.

## Social learning

**Social learning theory** (Bandura, 1977) notes that an important aspect of human learning is that we learn by watching others. The theory also emphasizes our ability to develop hypotheses about what behaviours will be most successful, to gather feedback, and to reflect on that feedback to refine behaviour. As learners, we are not only responding to rewards and punishments, but actively thinking about what we are doing. Learning through trial and error would be extremely laborious in many situations and could sometimes be dangerous. For example, no one would suggest that a new machine operator learns how to operate a million pound machine by trying various things and waiting to see if the efforts are rewarded or punished. Social learning theory shows how we learn complex behaviours by copying other people. It could even be the basis for how we learn the attitudes or elements of professional language or jargon when we start a new job.

In this theory, the people we copy are called 'models' and modelling occurs when that model displays the attitudes or behaviours that we reproduce. This modelling is most obvious when we learn how to do a new task by copying someone who is already able to do it. For example, imagine you have just started work as a receptionist. On your first day, you are shown how to operate the switchboard. Someone demonstrates which buttons to press to answer a call, transfer it to another line, divert to an answering machine and so on. You learn what to do by copying them. But we do not always have to learn by watching a specific person. For example, imagine that it is your first day of work and no one in the building knows how the telephone system works. Instead, you are given an instruction manual. In this case, you could read the instructions and do what the manual said. Instead of imitating a 'real-life' model, you can imitate *verbal modelling*.

## Behaviour modelling training

**Behaviour modelling training (BMT)** is a type of training based on social learning theory. A BMT programme involves five essential 'ingredients':

1. Clearly define the set of behaviours or skills to be learnt and explain them to the trainees.

2. Provide a 'model' of those behaviours. This can be done through a video or demonstrated directly to the trainees. Including 'negative' models (that is, people modelling the undesirable behaviours) seems to enhance the effects of the training on complex job behaviours but reduces the effectiveness of training on attitudes or knowledge (Taylor et al., 2005). This is probably because including negative models helps trainees to transfer their knowledge from the training course to their job, but confuses them when they are trying to learn specific technical skills.

3. Give trainees the opportunity to practise the new skills and behaviours.

4. Provide feedback and reinforcement based on the practice sessions.

5. Maximize the transfer of new skills to the job. This can be done by using practice scenarios generated by the trainees themselves, training managers as well, and introducing rewards for the new behaviours into the trainee's job.

A recent meta-analysis (Taylor et al., 2005) assessed the impact of BMT on several different training outcomes: *procedural knowledge* (this is knowledge of how to do things/skills), *declarative knowledge* (knowledge you can express, for example in a written test), attitudes, job behaviour, work group productivity and work group climate. BMT improved procedural and declarative knowledge substantially, had a modest effect on employee attitudes, showed a small improvement in job behaviour and had very little influence on work group outcomes. The effect of the training on declarative knowledge tended to fade after some time but remained stable and sometimes increased for employees' procedural knowledge, probably because they were practising the skills in their jobs. Overall, then, BMT is an effective way of training employees in a range of outcomes.

## Experiential learning

Perhaps one of the most famous models of learning, particularly when it comes to learning in applied situations, like at work, is Kolb's *experiential learning* theory (ELT), which emphasizes the central role of *experience* in our learning processes (Kolb, 1984). This model suggests that the learner goes through a continuous process from experiencing an event through thinking about it and trying to improve performance next time (Kolb and Kolb, 2005):

1. **Concrete experience:** carrying out an activity, for example conducting a performance conversation with a subordinate.

2. **Reflective observation:** observing and reflecting on the experience, for example drawing out lessons of what went well and what could be improved.

3. **Abstract conceptualization:** developing ideas or theories that would explain the experience. For example, if the conversation became adversarial, was it because the subordinate felt threatened?

4. **Active experimentation:** trying out new ideas to see if the situation can be improved. For example, trying to put the subordinate at ease at the beginning of the conversation by explaining that the aim was to understand their situation.

It is often suggested that people prefer one of these four learning modes, commonly referred to as **'learning styles'** (Kolb and Kolb, 2005). Yet, it is also clear that if learners are to be effective, they need *all four* abilities in the cycle (Kolb, 1984) and the ELT notes that learning is a process of moving through each of the four stages rather than something that happens just at one point. We explore this idea of learning styles in more detail in the next section but for now, it is important to recognize that learning is *the process of creating knowledge 'through the transformation of experience'*

(Kolb, 1984, p. 38). There are some important principles in ELT to bear in mind for understanding learning at work:

- Learning should be viewed as a **continual process**; we should recognize this procedural nature rather than seeing it as the achievement of a specific set of outcomes. This continuous process is grounded in our *experiences*: we constantly test out new knowledge and concepts against our experiences.

- The learning process is **filled with tension and conflict**: as we learn, new concepts come into conflict with our previous knowledge, skills or attitudes and we need to resolve these concepts if we are to learn anything. There is conflict in the learning process itself, between reflection and action, theory and practice.

- Learning is a **holistic process**: that is, it involves all our functioning – thinking, feeling, behaving and perceiving – in a process of adapting to the world. Learning shouldn't be seen as a specialized function but as '*the* major process of human adaptation' (Kolb, 1984, p. 32).

- Learning is an **active process** of transaction between the person and the environment: it is not something that takes place internally within the learner, but is applied in normal life.

It is worth taking a moment to reflect on your learning at university and the extent to which you have experienced these principles during your studies.

## Learning styles

A popular approach to understanding individual learning is to suggest that people have different styles in how they learn and that training should be adapted to the individual's style. There are many suggestions for how these differences might be conceptualized; in fact, a review for the Learning and Skills Research Centre showed there were over 70 different models of learning styles (Coffield et al., 2004). Coffield et al. were able to classify this wide range of models into five broad 'families', which can be arranged on a continuum from 'inborn' or fixed learning styles through to those models that emphasize flexibility and environmental effects, as shown in Figure 10.1. The Applications activity explores one of these, the personality approach to learning styles, in more detail.

| Type of model | View of learning styles |
|---|---|
| Dispositional | People are born with a specific learning style and this does not change over the course of their lives |
| Cognitive | People have generalized patterns or habits of thought and these patterns influence how we learn most effectively |
| Stable personality type | Learning styles are a part of individual personality and remain fairly stable throughout our lives |
| Flexibly stable learning preferences | These models are based on Kolb's four-stage model of learning and suggest that each person has a preference for one stage in the process |
| Learning approaches and strategies | People do not have a fixed style but can adopt different learning strategies to suit different situations |

*Figure 10.1 Categories of learning styles*

Source: Based on Coffield et al.'s (2004) review.

## Applications: Does personality affect how we learn?

Conduct a quick survey of your colleagues on your course, asking two questions:

- Do you prefer to study with background noise/ with a group of people, or on your own and in silence/without distractions?

- Do you consider yourself to be more of an extravert or more of an introvert?

» Do you notice any patterns in your group?

DIGITAL VISION

You will probably find in your survey that people who are more extraverted report that they learn better when there is more activity around them, whereas more introverted people learn better without distractions. Research supporting this difference has been around for decades (e.g. Howarth, 1969; Morgenstern et al., 1974) and a more recent study by Furnham and Allass (1999) found a similar effect on cognitive performance with background music.

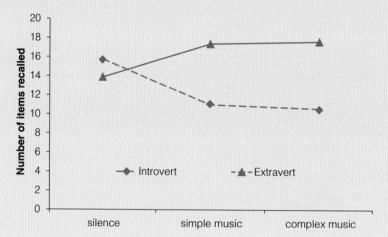

*Figure 10.2 Performance on cognitive tasks (immediate recall) in different background music conditions*

Source: Based on data from Furnham and Allass (1999).

» Why do you think there is this difference in the ideal conditions for learning and cognitive performance for introverts and extraverts?

» What are the implications of this difference for designing learning events?

The learning styles literature can help us to understand some important elements of learning and training. First, it indicates the importance of 'metacognition', that is, how developing an understanding of how we learn can be the basis of our own development. Second, discussion of learning styles can be a 'catalyst for individual, organisational or even systemic change' (Coffield et al., 2004, p. 133). However, these positive elements need to be understood within the generally cautious approach that the reviewers recommend when it comes to specific learning styles theories. They note that there are significant and serious issues with the learning styles literature. These issues include:

- The problem of 'labelling' learners: both trainers and learners may start to use labels as stereotypes. For example, if a learner completes a questionnaire that labels her as an 'activist' learner, she may believe that she can never learn anything from a book.

- There are relatively few models of learning styles that have sufficient and convincing evidence behind them or acceptable psychometric properties for their questionnaires.

- There is very little evidence that adapting the training or teaching style to learners' proposed style makes any difference in the effectiveness of learning.

- Learning styles approaches too often lead to a dismissal of actual 'knowledge'. While different disciplines may require different learning and teaching methods, they all require engagement with existing knowledge.

The criticisms of learning styles were echoed by Pashler et al. (2009) in their discussion of the practical application of learning styles. They concluded that there was no evidence of any interaction between learning style and optimal learning. This means that while we may have preferences for how information is presented to us and differing abilities in how we think, there is no evidence that we learn any better when instruction is tailored to our supposed learning style. Given the popularity of learning styles approaches, these cautions are important to bear in mind. Instead of a blanket acceptance of all learning styles approaches, just as with other models, we need to carefully choose those which are validated before applying them to learning and training at work.

## Informal learning

It is estimated that anywhere from 20–90% of what we learn at work takes place informally (Conlon, 2004), that is, learning that is relevant to job performance but is not organized by the employing organization (Dale and Bell, 1999). Traditionally, an informal approach to learning was the norm, with specific skills being embedded in a more generalized socialization process as people learnt how to do their jobs (Marsick, 2009). *Informal learning* has the benefits of being very flexible and adaptable as it is tailored towards the individual, but has the challenge that it is difficult for organizations to monitor and evaluate it (Dale and Bell, 1999).

There are, however, ways that organizations can incorporate informal learning opportunities into their formal training and development schemes (Cunningham and Hillier, 2013). This can be done, for example, by building learning relationships such as mentoring and peer feedback. There are also opportunities around job enlargement, for example cross training, where an employee is trained on something outside their normal job, and stretch assignments, which involve giving employees assignments that are beyond their current skill set, and job enrichment, for example acting management, discussion forums and temporary assignments. The effectiveness of informal learning can be enhanced by having clear planning processes, encouraging and developing active learning, and having an orientation towards the application of learning to the job. There have been suggestions that, at its best, *e-learning* could be a way of providing this formal and informal learning integration (Svensson et al., 2004) by allowing employees to access the formal learning in whatever order suits them, and at convenient times, in conjunction with their experiential learning. E-learning has the advantage of being more cost-effective to deliver, although the initial development of high-quality materials is a significant factor to consider. We discuss these issues further in the section on training methods later in the chapter.

## Lifelong learning

We have seen how learning in the workplace can best be conceptualized as an ongoing process and this brings us on to a consideration of the increasing importance given to **continuing (or continuous) professional development (CPD)** in many different professional arenas, including HRM. CPD involves the individual engaging in ongoing development of skills and knowledge to ensure that they stay up to date with current practice. A recent report by UNESCO noted the increased global mobility of people and jobs and recognized the importance of lifelong learning and skills development in helping people and countries to prosper in this internationally competitive environment (Keevy and Chakroun, 2015).

## Continuing professional development

Many professional bodies see CPD as an essential part of professional practice. In the UK, for example, the Chartered Institute of Personnel and Development (CIPD, 2016) recommends that members should actively seek to develop their competence in ways that benefit themselves as well as their organizations and clients. The map it provides to guide its members, illustrated in Figure 10.3, is based on the experiential learning theory we discussed above, but with some additions to emphasize the importance of active planning of the learning and how the development is shared with others in order to enhance the community of practice.

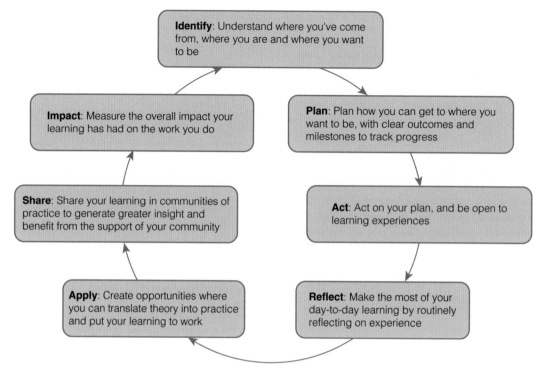

*Figure 10.3 The CIPD's stages of continuing professional development*

Source: CIPD (2016) 'Continuing professional development policy', www.cipd.co.uk/learn/cpd/policy. Adapted with the permission of the publisher, the Chartered Institute of Personnel Development, London (www.cipd.co.uk).

The importance of reflection in and on practice is often highlighted by researchers, but it must be noted that this reflection needs to be critical of any use (Lawless and McQue, 2008). That is, the critically reflective practitioner is able to question underlying assumptions and engage in discussion about taken-for-granted values and practices. Only by engaging in this level of reflection can learning be truly developmental. However, we should also note that critical reflection is not an easy task. First, it is a difficult skill for individuals to develop and, second, even when mastered it can be disruptive. Developing self-awareness has costs and benefits (Sutton, 2016) and critical reflection, by its very nature, increases our awareness of flaws in the systems, or the organizational values within which we work (Rigg and Trehan, 2008), which can be challenging to deal with. You may wish to look at the Transferrable Skills activities in Chapter 1 and 2 for guidance on how to develop your ability to identify assumptions and think critically.

The Applications activity makes recommendations for how you can use a model of continuing professional development to enhance your career.

 Applications: **Managing your own CPD**

It is a common requirement for professional bodies to require their members to engage in CPD and it is a good habit to get into from an early stage in your career. Working through the CIPD model in Figure 10.3 above, draw up a plan for your own development over the next five years, including thinking of ways to meet your overall goals and how to build reflection into your learning at regular intervals. You could, for example keep a portfolio that includes regular reflections on your progress, and ideas for how you can share your learning with others in your professional area, perhaps by participating in professional conferences.

# TRAINING AND DEVELOPMENT

Having considered the ways we learn and the importance of seeing learning as a continuous process, we now move on to discuss some of the practical realities of how learning takes place within organizations. Taking a systematic approach to formal learning and training as an ongoing cycle, we start with an analysis of training needs, then move on to consider the best method for providing training and how we can ensure training is as effective as possible. Finally, bringing us full circle, we look at ways that training can be evaluated to identify further training needs.

## Training needs analysis

If the investment an organization makes in training its staff is to be realized, the training should be based on a thorough needs analysis. It would clearly be a waste of resources to provide training that was not needed by certain individuals or did not contribute to overall organizational aims. So, the analysis should take place at three levels, as shown in Figure 10.4.

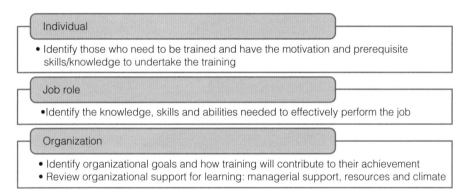

**Individual**
- Identify those who need to be trained and have the motivation and prerequisite skills/knowledge to undertake the training

**Job role**
- Identify the knowledge, skills and abilities needed to effectively perform the job

**Organization**
- Identify organizational goals and how training will contribute to their achievement
- Review organizational support for learning: managerial support, resources and climate

*Figure 10.4 Needs analysis levels*

Training needs analysis has traditionally taken what is called a 'deficit' view of performance. It focuses on the aspects of job performance that an individual cannot yet do or is not very good at, and attempts to improve their performance on these elements. While there is certainly a place for this kind of training, a growing and complementary alternative is strengths-focused development. This approach suggests that deficit-focused development will only ever result in average or mediocre performance, and it is only by using and building on our strengths that we can achieve excellence. For example, a research study found that the best managers are those who can manage the unique talents and abilities of their team (their strengths) rather than those who concentrate on building up their weaker areas and trying to help everyone become 'well-rounded' (Hodges and Clifton, 2004). ***Strengths-based development*** helps employees to identify their strengths and look for ways to use them more in their current or future work, as well as enhancing employee engagement.

## *Types of skills*

In analysing the skills needed for employment around the world, UNESCO (2014) provides a basic taxonomy of types of skills:

- **Foundation skills:** such as literacy and numeracy. These are the outcomes of basic education and allow people to continue their education and training.

- **Transferrable skills:** such as communication or teamworking. These skills are needed in a variety of contexts within and outside employment, and there is a strong expectation that they will be developed in higher education alongside subject-specific knowledge.

- **Technical/vocational skills:** technical abilities and knowledge needed to carry out specific tasks, for example using database software or changing the oil in a car.

*Getty Images/Klaus Vedfelt*

*Transferrable skills such as teamworking can be used in a variety of work situations.*

It is the latter two types of skills that tend to be the cause of skills shortages in employment. In a 2015 report on the skills challenges faced by UK employers, nearly a quarter of all vacancies were defined as 'hard to fill' because of skills shortages (UK Commission for Employment and Skills, 2015) and had led to direct financial impact for two-thirds of employers. The skills that were in short supply were technical (including machine operation and complex analytical skills), personal (such as time management) and people skills (such as customer skills and management). A similar picture is found in many other countries. In Australia, for example, the government conducts research to identify areas of skill shortage and recruitment difficulties, and identified over 40 occupations where there was a lack of suitably qualified and experienced workers, including mechanics, midwives and early childhood teachers (Department of Employment, 2017). The president of Mauritius has stated that the lack of scientific and engineering capability in many African countries is a serious problem for their future growth and prosperity (Harvey, 2016).

Many countries, particularly those with developing economies, face a paradoxical problem of high unemployment alongside severe skills shortages. South Africa, for example, despite being the second largest economy on the continent, has over 200 'high demand' occupations, that is occupations that are experiencing high growth or shortages in the labour market, from managers and teachers to engineers and skilled trade workers (Department of Higher Education and Training, 2016). The government has called on education providers and employers to build responsive training systems to address the issue.

The skills gap goes beyond not being able to find suitable people to fill vacancies. There is also a skills gap for those already employed: about 5% of the currently employed workforce in the UK is considered to be lacking some key skills for their roles (UK Commission for Employment and Skills, 2015). There is clearly a need to develop these missing skills and about two-thirds of employers provide training and development to their staff, averaging about six or seven days per year over the past few years. In total, UK employers spent £45 billion a year on training and development. This represents a huge investment and helps to highlight the importance of using effective training methods to meet organizations' needs.

## Training methods

There are a wide range of different methods available for training and the choice of appropriate methods should be guided by the aims of the programme. Their effectiveness, however, is dependent on a number of contextual factors, such as how well they match the learning outcomes, how skilled the trainer is, and also how engaged trainees are. Table 10.1 summarizes some of the main traditional training methods and techniques for learning. We then consider e-learning in more detail.

Table 10.1 **Traditional training methods**

| Method | Evaluation |
|---|---|
| Demonstration: the trainer explains to trainees how to do something and shows them the process | Trainees can immediately see what needs to be done. Particularly effective for simple tasks but less so for more complex tasks. Only shows trainees one, standardized way of doing things |
| Case study: an outline of a scenario that helps to illustrate the learning topic, it can be hypothetical or a summary of a real situation | Trainees have the time and space to think deeply and analyse a situation in order to develop solutions and learn from it. But may not reflect the reality of situations trainees are faced with, making transfer of learning more difficult |
| Lecture: presents information to trainees, usually in verbal form | Effective way to communicate information to a large number of trainees but little opportunity for interaction. Difficult to tailor to individual levels or needs |
| Simulation: can be equipment simulators or more abstract, for example an in-tray exercise | Excellent way of allowing trainees to practise skills that would normally have high costs associated with failure, for example flight simulators. Can be expensive to set up. Only useful to the extent that they accurately portray real tasks and environment the trainee will be faced with |
| Group discussion: trainees can discuss aspects of the training or specific problems, or share best practice | Helps trainees see other people's points of view, discover new ways of doing things and share and reflect on their own learning. Can be time-consuming. No guarantee it will produce helpful or desirable outcomes |
| Role-play: trainees take on roles and act out how they would handle specific situations | Can give trainees the opportunity to practise skills, especially interpersonal ones, in a non-threatening environment and help them to transfer learning more easily. Usefulness is highly dependent on the type of feedback the trainee receives. Also, many people feel uncomfortable 'acting', especially in front of a group |
| Job rotation/placements: trainees take on temporary assignments within the organization or with clients/competitors | Trainees can become multiskilled and gain a new perspective on their old job or on the organization as a whole. Associated costs can be high, because the employee has to be trained and supported in each new placement/rotation |

## Table 10.1 Traditional training methods (continued)

| Method | Evaluation |
|---|---|
| Coaching and mentoring: based on a one-to-one relationship between the learner and a more experienced or expert person who can give tailored guidance and direction. Mentoring tends to be more informal and intra-organizational, while coaching often uses external professional coaches | Instruction and guidance can be tailored to the individual's current situation and needs. Guidance is usually holistic rather than focusing on an isolated skill. A resource-intensive method, dependent on a good relationship between coach/mentor and protégé |

## E-learning

It is worth considering e-learning in more detail as it is an increasingly important part of training delivery in work organizations and universities. Generally, e-learning refers to a 'learning package' delivered via computer, most commonly through the internet or organizational-specific intranets. The contents of these learning packages can be very varied – from a simple online form with information to be read, through to an integrated package of text, video and activities. This variety presents some problems in examining its effectiveness: just as it would be difficult (and misleading) to evaluate the effectiveness of different kinds of traditional training methods as one entity, grouping all e-learning together fails to distinguish between well and poorly designed packages.

E-learning has two potential benefits over other methods, namely reduced costs and increased flexibility (Macpherson et al., 2004). The reduced costs include a reduced time away from the job as well as the ability to deliver training to large numbers of employees for little extra expense. Flexibility is obvious in how and when the training is delivered, as well as the way employees can engage with it at their own pace. From the learners' point of view, another advantage is that they can take control over their learning (DeRouin et al., 2004).

These advantages come with some disadvantages, however, that need to be addressed if e-learning is going to be implemented effectively. One of the key issues is that e-learning relies on learners taking control of their learning to a much greater extent than face-to-face methods. Learners need to be self-motivated and also able to learn in isolation rather than in a social context. Sorgenfrei and Smolnik (2016) noted how important it was to understand this 'learner control' dimension of e-learning. Their review indicated that providing learners with control over the time and pace of their engagement as well as navigation through and design of the learning materials had a beneficial impact on learning. Control over the content of the learning or task selection, however, should only be given with caution, as these types of control had ambiguous relationships with learning outcomes.

Macpherson et al. (2004) highlight a couple more critical considerations with e-learning. First is the frequent lack of personal support to learners, which detracts from effective learning outcomes. Second, there is the significant problem, inherent in any method attempting to deliver a standardized, generic learning package to a range of employees, of reduced contextualization, making the training less meaningful or relevant to learners. This latter point of the relevance of e-learning to the individual's work was recognized as the central factor in the successful implementation of e-learning programmes (Netteland, 2009).

The research does give organizations some pointers on how to maximize the effectiveness of their e-learning programmes, based on a view of e-learning as essentially a 'socio-technical system', in which the social aspects of employees' skills, relationships with colleagues and authority structures interact with the technical systems of processes, tasks and technology (Upadhyaya and Mallik, 2013). The interaction of these systems was demonstrated in a study by Garavan et al. (2010), which showed that employees' participation in e-learning was influenced by individual factors, such as motivation to learn and social support, as well as design factors, such as the quality of the content and the learning feedback available in the e-learning package. A review of the literature (DeRouin et al., 2004) highlighted guidelines for optimizing e-learning in organizations by focusing on three main areas, summarized in Figure 10.5. The Web Explorer exercise looks at how these guidelines can be used in evaluating e-learning providers.

---

**Preparing trainees for learner-controlled training**

- Make it clear to trainees how much control they have over their learning and give them time to adapt to this new way of learning
- Calibrate their expectations of how challenging the learning will be

**Designing learner-controlled training**

- Allow for individualization to trainees' context, skill level, experience and motivation
- Provide signposting to show trainees how they are progressing
- Give some control over the design, e.g. move windows about on the screen
- Offer help in self-evaluation of learning, e.g. tests or feedback so learners can judge for themselves how much training they need
- Keep each instructional segment self-contained, but provide smooth transitions so that learners can see how they are connected

**Workplace conditions that facilitate learner-controlled training**

- Provide supervisor support and promotion of the learning
- Offer rewards and incentives for participation
- Develop a climate that encourages participation, empowerment and autonomy

*Figure 10.5 Guidelines for e-learning*
Source: Based on DeRouin et al. (2004).

---

 **Web Explorer: E-learning**

For this activity, imagine that you work in a customer service role and your department has recently received some negative feedback on how you are dealing with customers. Your manager has tasked you to find an e-learning solution to help develop the customer service skills of the colleagues in your group. You have been given a budget of £1,000 for training for ten members of staff and told that any money you do not spend on the training can be used on a meal out with the department.

Look online for the range of options available to you:

- You could start with free, instant access options, such as videos on YouTube: www.youtube.com/watch?v=t5KibZuz6Kk

- Or you could investigate companies that require registration and provide free online courses, with payments for certificates when you have completed the course, for example Alison: https://alison.com/company/about/

- Another option is to look into blended learning, which combines a 'live' workshop with an e-learning module, such as that provided by Brilliant Customer Service: www.brilliantcustomerservice.co.uk.

Evaluate the different options using DeRouin et al.'s (2004) guidelines and consider how you might enhance the e-learning's effectiviness on each principle.

We have talked a lot about how effective training may be, so now we turn to considering ways to maximize the effectiveness of whichever methods are chosen.

## Improving training effectiveness

The opportunity to practise the new skills or use new knowledge is one important aspect of how we can improve the effectiveness of training, and another is to consider how we transfer learning from one situation to another.

### Practice

Learning, whether of knowledge or skills, is not a single event but an ongoing process in which practice and review play a key part. How that practice is structured has an effect on how well we learn. Donovan and Radosevich (1999) conducted a review of studies on practice effects and found that *spaced practice*, where learners are given rest periods between the practice sessions, resulted in better learning than *massed practice*, where learners were given continuous practice with no rest periods. For complex learning, longer rest periods were needed and for learning simple tasks, shorter rest periods resulted in better learning.

When designing training, therefore, we need to build in rest or break periods between practice sessions. Unfortunately, the importance of practice is often ignored when training is provided in organizations. For example, a company may introduce a new piece of software to manage staff absences and provide a single 'training' session to show employees how to use it. It would be better to provide several shorter sessions, which allow employees to practise, take a break and then return to practise again.

### Training transfer

**Training transfer** is the extent to which what we learn in one situation is 'transferred' to a new situation. For example, a trainee on an interviewing skills course may perform very well in a role-played interview on the training course but fail to put that learning into action in a real interview.

Many researchers have criticized training and learning studies for failing to show that this training transfer happens, essentially questioning the utility of many training and learning activities. But a review by Barnett and Ceci (2002) suggested that this failure was due to a lack of clarity about the kind of transfer of learning that was being investigated. They noted that

the *content* and the *context* of the learning impacts on how well the training is transferred. Content refers to the type of skill being learnt, for example a specific procedure or a principle to be applied, the kind of performance being changed – is it speed, accuracy or a change in approach? – and the memory demands being made, for example recall or recognize. The simpler the content, the easier it is to transfer the learning.

The context of the learning refers to how similar the learning context and the performance context are. *Near* transfer occurs with more similar contexts and *far* transfer with more different contexts:

- **Knowledge domain:** This is the extent to which a skill learnt in one domain is transferred to another domain. For example, a learner might be expected to transfer logical thinking skills developed in a maths course to problem-solving in a business studies course.

- **Physical context:** Does the learning take place in similar physical surroundings to the performance context?

- **Temporal context:** The time that elapses between learning and performance.

- **Functional context:** How is the skill taught? If it is taught as an academic skill, far transfer would entail transferring that skill to a new functional context such as the workplace, whereas near transfer would simply mean performing the skill within the same academic context.

- **Social context:** The extent to which a skill learnt alone could be applied in a team or vice versa.

- **Modality:** The skill may be learnt in one modality (e.g. auditory) and applied in a different one (e.g. written). An example of this might be learning something in a lecture and then attempting to apply that knowledge or skill in writing an essay.

Essentially, the 'further' the difference between the contexts, the more difficult it is to ensure effective training transfer. Contrary to the pessimism of other researchers about learning transfer, Barnett and Ceci suggest that using this taxonomy helps us to identify that far transfer does indeed occur. A meta-analysis by Blume et al. (2010) identified three main contributors to effective training transfer:

- **Personal characteristics:** Trainees with higher cognitive ability, conscientiousness and self-efficacy demonstrated better learning transfer. In addition, those who were more motivated and took part in the training voluntarily also showed a moderate increase in training transfer effectiveness.

- **Environmental factors:** If the organization has a good transfer climate – availability of equipment and opportunity to practise as well as positive and negative reinforcement – trainees are able to transfer their learning much more effectively. Support from peers and management is also important in encouraging transfer.

- **Learning outcomes of the training:** Where training results in higher self-efficacy and knowledge for the participants, they are more likely to be able to transfer the learning to their job situation.

Understanding the conditions that promote effective training transfer leads us naturally into considerations of how we can evaluate training.

## Evaluating training

One of the challenges that training and development faces in organizations is in terms of demonstrating its impact or value for money. If training is expected to improve organizational performance, we need to be able to demonstrate that improvement, and often this simply does not happen. However, a useful model for training evaluation suggests that it can be carried out at four different levels (Kirkpatrick and Kirkpatrick, 2006):

1. **Reaction:** how the trainees reacted to the training, how they felt about it. This is often assessed by feedback sheets at the end of the training programme asking the participants what they enjoyed or how satisfied they are with the programme.

2. **Learning:** how much the trainees learnt on the programme. This can be assessed using tests or interviews.

3. **Behaviour:** to what extent the trainees change their work behaviour as a result of the training. This is more difficult to assess and can involve further interviews and observations, as well as gathering feedback from the trainees' colleagues or manager.

4. **Results:** this is the extent to which the training impacts on organizational-level outcomes and is the most difficult to assess, primarily because organizational measures have so many contributing factors.

A meta-analysis of studies on the effectiveness of nearly 400 training programmes using Kirkpatrick's model demonstrated that training had demonstrably positive impacts at all four levels of evaluation: trainee reactions, learning, behaviour and organizational results (Arthur et al., 2003). It divided the studies into three groups based on the skills or tasks that were being learnt and identified the most effective training methods for each, as shown in Table 10.2.

## Table 10.2 Training effectiveness for different skills

| Type of skill | Description | Most effective training methods |
|---|---|---|
| Psychomotor | Physical or manual tasks | Equipment simulators, audiovisual and discussion |
| Interpersonal | Skills for interacting with others, such as leadership or communication | Lectures, audiovisual and programmed instruction |
| Cognitive | Understanding, problem-solving and knowledge | Lectures, audiovisual and self-instruction from books or other materials |

Source: Based on Arthur et al. (2003).

In this section, we have considered the key issues to be aware of when designing and delivering training and also seen how continual development and training is an increasingly normal part of every job. In the Transferrable Skills activity, you are guided through an exercise to help develop your own skills in training other people. Our next step in understanding training and learning at work is to move from the individual level up to the organizational level. We will consider how organizations can embed learning throughout their systems and make the most of the knowledge their employees have.

## Transferrable Skills: Designing a training programme

We can use the simple systematic training cycle outlined at the beginning of this section as a basis for developing skills in training design and delivery. We have seen that employers are increasingly looking for transferrable skills such as time management, so, in this activity, you will be guided through how to design a training event to improve people's time management skills: from identifying what the event aims to achieve, through choice of design and delivery and finally how the event could be evaluated.

### 1. Identify the training needs

The first step in designing a training programme or event is to have clarity on what you are aiming to achieve with it. When trainees have completed the programme, what should they be able to do or understand? Although the simple answer might be 'They will be better at time management', we need to have more detail than this if we are to design the training appropriately and be able to evaluate its success at the end. So, start by drawing up a list of specific performance criteria you would use to judge someone's ability to manage their time. What specific things do you think you might be able to do better if you were better at managing your time?

### 2. Design the training event

This step is where most of your planning takes place. Based on the specific criteria you identified in step 1, you will decide on the *content* of the training and the *techniques* you think will be best to help people learn this content and skill. This will lead naturally into decisions about the kinds of facilities or resources you need to do the training properly, how long it will take and who the trainers will be. At this stage, you need

to be aware of the budgetary constraints as well as how much time the participants or trainees will be able to commit to the training. For a skill like time management, this could be particularly tricky as the very people who need the training may not feel they have the time to attend. Think about ways you could address this issue when designing the event.

### 3. Carry out the training

This is where you put the plan into action. It is useful to have backup plans in case you run into problems on the day. For example, if you are planning to use audiovisual equipment and there are technical difficulties, how could you adapt the programme?

### 4. Evaluate the training

In this step, it is best to use a model of evaluation such as the Kirkpatrick four-level model. Remember that effective evaluation above the level of 'reaction' is dependent on accurate and clear identification of performance criteria in step 1 of the training design: you can only evaluate the effectiveness of the learning or its impact on individual behaviour and organizational results if you have been clear about what is expected to improve. If you carried out the training yourself, you can also include self-reflections in this evaluation that could help you to improve your own training skills.

The training cycle is a closed loop: the next cycle starts immediately after the evaluation. In fact, the next iteration of the cycle should use the learning developed through evaluation to improve the next event. Even if the next event aims to develop different skills, the lessons learnt are often transferrable.

# ORGANIZATIONAL LEARNING

Individual learning and development is an essential component of effective performance in the long term, as we have seen. But there is more at stake for the organization than simply having skilled and developed individuals: it needs to make effective use of that individual learning and knowledge at an

organizational level too. In this section we consider how organizations can manage the knowledge they already have as well as consider the concept of a learning organization.

## Knowledge management

Clegg et al. (2015) distinguish between **knowledge** as the resources the organization already has, such as facts, information and skills, and *learning* as the development or acquisition of this knowledge. **Knowledge management**, then, is how the organization manages its knowledge resources to meet its current and future needs.

Discussions of the nature of knowledge can get quite abstract and convoluted, and we will not go into them in detail here, but a useful distinction can be drawn between tacit and explicit knowledge (Polanyi, 1967). *Tacit knowledge* is knowledge we may not be consciously aware of or find difficult to articulate but which we use to do and understand things. For example, you may instinctively 'know' how best to deal with a manager you have worked with for a couple of years, but find it difficult to explain to a new colleague how you do this. On the other hand,

*explicit knowledge* is easier to capture and express to other people. For example, if your new colleague asks you how to submit an expenses claim, you will be able to show her. More recently, these two types of knowledge have been viewed as two ends of a continuum (Nonaka and von Krogh, 2009), which expresses how hidden or readily accessible the knowledge is.

In the late 1980s, tacit knowledge was recognized as one of the sources of an organization's competitive advantage (Winter, 1987). Nonaka (1994) suggested that knowledge is created in organizations through a continuous process of conversion between tacit and explicit knowledge, giving four different modes of knowledge conversion, as shown in Figure 10.6.

| | To | |
|---|---|---|
| | **Tacit** | **Explicit** |
| **From** — **Tacit** | **Socialization**<br>Knowledge is created through shared experience and interactions. For example, a new employee soon learns the new company culture or an apprentice learns through observation and imitation | **Articulation**<br>Knowledge that was previously tacit is made accessible and shared so that it becomes new knowledge for others. For example, a good manager could be asked to describe how she deals with a difficult performance appraisal and this knowledge is developed into a guidance document for other managers |
| **From** — **Explicit** | **Internalization**<br>Knowledge that has been consciously learnt becomes habitual and unconscious. For example, a driver learning how to operate a forklift is eventually able to operate the vehicle without consciously thinking about it | **Combination**<br>Social processes are used to combine explicit knowledge from two different areas. For example, an HR officer and an IT specialist may work together to develop an online platform for employees to register their holiday requests, each of them sharing with the other their explicit knowledge in their area of specialism |

*Figure 10.6 Modes of knowledge conversion*

Source: Adapted with permission from Nonaka, I. (1994) 'A dynamic theory of organization knowledge creation', *Organization Science*, 5(1), pp. 14–37. Copyright (1994) the Institute for Operations Research and the Management Sciences, 5521 Research Park Drive, Catonsville, Maryland 21228. Copyright, INFORMS, www.informs.org.

Understanding this knowledge creation process can help organizations to make the most of their knowledge assets and manage them more effectively. Effective knowledge conversion and creation can help to ensure that tacit knowledge is not lost when

employees leave and that innovation is supported and increased.

The simple tacit/explicit knowledge distinction can be further broken down if we consider the different ways we view knowledge in organizations.

Blackler (1995) identified five different 'images' of knowledge, that is, different ways of viewing knowledge:

1. **Embrained:** conceptual and theoretical knowledge that relies on a person's cognitive abilities, for example the kind of knowledge you might develop on a university course.

2. **Embodied:** action-oriented knowledge that is highly context specific, using physical presence and information from the senses, including conversations with others. An example would be knowing how to deliver some difficult feedback to a specific colleague.

3. **Encultured:** knowledge based on developing shared understandings, for example storytelling that develops a common understanding of how things are done in that organization.

4. **Embedded:** knowledge contained within the organization's routines. For example, a hospital's A&E department has a set of routines for dealing with incoming patients, which represents the 'knowledge' of how to deal with medical emergencies.

5. **Encoded:** knowledge 'encoded' in signs and symbols, including language. An example would be the recipe and manufacturing process for a certain type of shampoo, which is captured in the company's manual.

Blackler (1995) also pointed out that instead of viewing knowledge as a static 'thing' to be created or developed, it would be more helpful to view it in terms of an active process of knowing, which includes the individual, the activity and the community in which the activity takes place. Instead of defining knowledge, then, Blackler suggests that we should consider 'knowing' as a process *mediated* by language, technological, control and collaborative systems, *situated* in a particular context and *pragmatic*, that is, has a purpose. The process of knowing is also constantly developing, meaning that our current state of knowledge is *provisional* and often *contested* as people attempt to use or control it for their own ends. This emphasis on the social nature of organizational knowledge leads us into a deeper consideration of learning within the organization.

## The learning organization and organizational learning

Some authors distinguish between *'organizational learning'* and the *'learning organization'* in order to emphasize different aspects of learning in organizations. Opinion on these two concepts is somewhat divided, with the academic literature focusing on describing and conceptualizing the processes of organizational learning and the practitioner literature seeking to clarify how a learning organization can be created (Easterby-Smith et al., 1998):

- **Organizational learning** is not simply the sum of individual learning in the organization but the integration and embedding of that individual learning into and through the whole organization (Linstead et al., 2009). That is, it takes individual learning a step further to make it useful to the whole organization.

- A **learning organization** has learning as a focus and central tenet; it encourages and facilitates learning by employees in order to continually develop itself. This concept was popularized by Peter Senge (1990), who claimed that the only sustainable competitive advantage was in being able to learn faster than the competition. A learning organization is one that can adapt to its changing environment and survive, much like a biological organism; essentially, it translates new knowledge into new behaviour (Garvin, 1993).

However, it can be argued that this distinction is less than helpful and that 'the task of the learning organization is to integrate individual learning into organisational learning' (Wang and Ahmed, 2003, p. 9). Wang and Ahmed suggest that the organizational learning literature has shifted its focus from knowledge accumulation through incremental changes, systems-based thinking and a competitive focus on continuous improvement to knowledge creation through radical change, creative thinking and a competence-based focus on sustainability. The debate is discussed further in the Weighing the Evidence activity, and in the remainder of this section, we review the main approaches to understanding organizational learning while integrating ideas about how to develop learning organizations.

Weighing the Evidence: **Are learning organizations real?**

The 'learning organization' (LO) is certainly a popular notion in the management and HR literature, but to what extent does it represent a real type of organization? The concept is seen differently by different people. For some, it is pragmatic, representing a set of design criteria that will affect specific organizational outcomes. For others, it is more metaphorical, representing a type of culture that defines some organizations (Garavan, 1997).

Garavan (1997) notes that the idea of a learning organization represented two important shifts in emphasis for how managers viewed their organizations. First, a shift from a focus on lean organizations, which emphasize efficiency, to a focus on organizational development and growth that requires excess capacity. Second, a shift from emphasizing individual learning to collective learning. A learning organization is suggested to have some distinctive characteristics (Garvin, 1993):

- systematic problem-solving

- willingness to experiment with new approaches

- the ability to learn from own experiences and from others'

- efficient transfer of new knowledge throughout the organization.

Despite these characteristics, however, the LO theory does not provide clear or consistent definitions of what a learning organization is, nor is there clarity on how to develop a LO (Santa, 2015). Instead, these general recommendations tend to confine themselves to noting that any best practice approaches will only work within a supportive culture that fosters and supports learning, while removing traditional boundaries between jobs or areas of expertise (Garvin, 1993).

Something that should be clear from this list of characteristics is how disruptive the learning process can be. An organization that truly wishes to prioritize learning will need to be comfortable with constant change and challenges to the status quo, as well as providing the space and support for risk-taking. Not all the experiments will result in better outcomes for the organization and employees need to be supported through the process. One issue that is rarely explored in the LO literature is the role of the individual (Garavan, 1997): what type of person is suited to this kind of organization? Certainly, to meet the requirements of the kind of organization outlined here, they will need to be collaborative, comfortable with ambiguity and mature enough to engage in critical reflection. It could be argued that this kind of employee is fairly rare and that organizations that require all employees to engage in the process will be similarly rare.

A further criticism of the LO concept revolves around its view of leadership. As originally conceptualized by Senge (1990), the LO can be viewed as a form of distributed leadership (Caldwell, 2012), where many different learners participate in shaping the leadership and direction-setting of the organization. However, the issue of power and politics in determining the boundaries of the learning and its implementation are ignored.

The ambiguity over learning organizations has even prompted Tosey (2005) to suggest that the LO is a fantastical creature we are told exists but for which there is no hard evidence. Despite this, he also notes its importance in stimulating experimentation and work in optimizing learning in organizations.

## Single- and double-loop learning

Argyris (1977, p. 116) defines organizational learning as a 'process of detecting and correcting error' and distinguishes between *single-loop* and *double-loop learning*. Single-loop learning is a process that enables the organization to meet its current objectives: it can take in and evaluate information in order to take action within a certain set of parameters. Double-loop learning is the process of questioning and adjusting the underlying objectives or policies, rather than simply trying to meet them. An example will help to illustrate the difference between these two approaches. Imagine an organization that wishes to recruit the highest quality graduates each year to its management training programme. Single-loop learning would be finding the most efficient and valid selection methods to ensure high-quality candidates. Double-loop learning, on the other hand, would involve questioning what the criteria defining 'high quality' actually are and how relevant they are for individual trainee or organizational success. This would enable the organization to continually reassess its definitions of quality candidates and respond quickly to changes in the recruitment market.

Although double-loop learning has many advantages, not least of which is the ability to innovate and adapt more appropriately to the environment, there are also barriers to this kind of learning. Confronting error or raising questions about the organization's routines often goes against cultural norms, so that many people feel pressured to simply carry on and ignore the errors and problems. Argyris (1977) notes that it often takes a crisis, such as a recession or new management, to create the momentum required for double-loop learning. Double-loop learning requires the building of trust and risk-taking, as well as being prepared to be accountable for decisions.

## Routines to capture learning

In contrast to this view of learning as 'error detection' is a definition of learning as the development of routines that guide employee behaviour (Levitt and March, 1988). As the people in the organization experience various events, they develop procedures, policies or beliefs that help the organization to adapt to these events. This means that, even after the original events are no longer remembered (perhaps because all the people who were there at the time have left), the routines guiding current employees' behaviour are still there. Or, as Levitt and March put it (p. 320): 'The experiential lessons of history are captured by routines in a way that makes the lessons, but not the history, accessible to organisations and organisational members who have not themselves experienced the history.' This view of learning sees it as primarily about adaptation to the environment, which is similar to how learning was viewed in the early theories of learning we covered at the beginning of this chapter.

In their review, Levitt and March (1988) outlined the various ways organizations learn, including learning from direct experience, from their interpretation of experience and from the experience of others. The authors also outlined several traps that can prevent organizational learning, including:

- **The competency trap:** the organization accumulates enough experience with an inferior procedure to ensure good performance but does not have enough experience of a better procedure to make it rewarding enough to use.

- **The ambiguity of success:** not only do people change their interpretations of what constitutes 'success', but different groups or individuals within an organization may evaluate an event differently. For some it may be a success and for others a failure, with correspondingly different lessons to be learnt.

March (1991) developed these ideas further when he distinguished between exploitation and exploration of knowledge in organizational learning, using this distinction to draw out the limitations on learning. Exploitation of organizational knowledge includes refining processes, selection between alternatives and issues around implementation. Exploration, on the other hand, involves searching, taking risks, experimenting and discovering. Organizations need to find an appropriate balance between these two approaches because both are costly and can lead to serious problems if pursued exclusively. An organization that focuses too much on exploration will run too many risks without gaining any benefit from established procedures, whereas one that exploits current knowledge but does not explore will be unable to innovate. Exploitation leads to faster and more predictable returns, whereas exploration leads to uncertain and often negative returns, meaning that few organizations adopt this approach and can get trapped in a suboptimal performance.

In an interesting longitudinal study, Coradi et al. (2015) looked at the influence of the physical workspace on knowledge exploitation and exploration in the R&D processes of a pharmaceutical company. They found that for exploitative activities, workspaces should be designed with high proximity to colleagues to allow for faster feedback and gaining first-hand information. Exploration, on the other hand, needs high visibility to encourage cross-functional interactions as well as a certain degree of protection from interruptions. An example of this could be glass-walled offices where people can see each other but also have 'quiet space' when they need to concentrate.

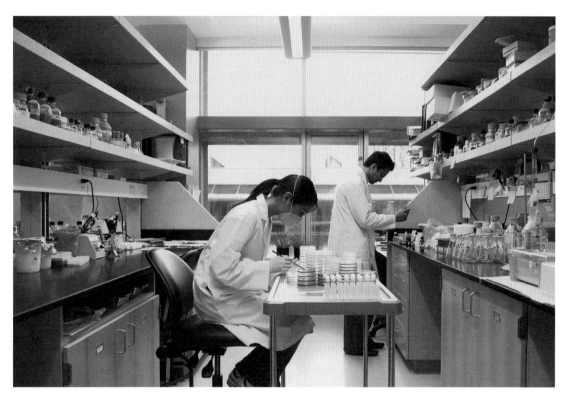

Fancy/Punchstock/Getty Images

*The physical design of a workplace can influence knowledge management.*

## Communities of practice

We saw in our review of learning theories that we learn in a social context and often by mimicking others, for example in social learning theory. Wenger (1998) recognized the importance of social learning and called these groups in which we learn **communities of practice**. He noted that we learn through our participation in communities of people with whom we regularly interact. Communities of practice are not just networks of people in the organization or a specific work unit or department. Instead, Wenger defines them using three criteria as a community of *mutually engaged* members with a *shared repertoire* of routines, vocabulary, styles and so on who are engaged in a *joint enterprise*. The communities of practice that people are engaged with help them to develop the knowledge they need in order to complete their tasks in their teams, departments and so on. The In the News feature explores a community of practice approach in healthcare settings.

 In the News: **Project ECHO**

Project ECHO (Extension for Community Healthcare Outcomes) is a model of education that uses the communities of practice approach to developing and disseminating knowledge (Project ECHO, 2016). It was started in 2003 by the medical doctor Sanjeev Arora, a liver disease specialist who wanted to extend specialist medical care to the many thousands of hepatitis C patients who did not have access to a specialist in their local area. It started fairly simply as a teleconference between Dr Arora and colleagues at the University of New Mexico, USA and various primary care providers across the state. The experts at UNM would provide guidance and specialist knowledge to the providers, who not only learnt from their own cases but from those of the other participants too (Barash, 2016).

Since then, Project ECHO has expanded to include 90 hubs with specialism in over 45 different disease and conditions, providing access to specialist medical knowledge for doctors and their patients worldwide. It is not only used for hepatitis C but also for HIV care in Namibia and India and training in opioid addiction for healthcare teams across the USA. In April 2017, ECHO was launched in New Jersey, USA, to help primary healthcare providers screen for and treat pediatric developmental and behavioural conditions (Robert Wood Johnson Partners, 2017).

### For discussion

This kind of geographically dispersed community of practice with instant communication and feedback would not have been possible without the technological advances that have made teleconferencing so widely available.

» What are the benefits and drawbacks of this kind of 'virtual' community of practice?

» Can you think of any non-medical applications for this approach?

---

Communities of practice do not just develop knowledge but also provide people with a sense of identity. It is worth noting that these communities, while they provide an important means of learning in the organization, tend to be informal and perhaps not well suited to exploitation or control by management. In some cases, they may even propose and support different working practices from those which management might wish to promote. But this social and cultural element of learning systems is an essential component of any understanding of organizational learning and the learning organization.

## SUMMARY

In this chapter we have looked at how learning is of central importance to an organization, not just in terms of developing its own capacity but also for its continued competitive advantage. Starting with a discussion of basic learning theories, we gained an insight into how we learn that can be used to help design training and development and support learning in organizations.

We also discussed in detail the different practical training methods that are available and the impacts they have on organizational outcomes. While detailed evaluation of training remains rare, it is an essential component of effective training implementation. We have seen how learning has individual and social aspects, providing a way to develop skills and link people together in a community of practice. By understanding the ways individuals learn, we can start to develop organizations that integrate individual into collective learning.

 ## Practice Insights: Paul Walsh

Paul Walsh is a Learning and Development Specialist at Manchester Metropolitan University, whose job involves delivering training for individuals and teams, providing coaching and mentoring, and working on organizational development projects. In the video he talks about the rewards and challenges in this work and how to make the move into this career, as well as giving some tips on how to maximize learning transfer in organizational training.

Go online to www.macmillanihe.com/sutton-people to access the interview with Paul.

# FURTHER READING

- Grete Netteland reports on an interesting case study of a large telecom company that introduced e-learning to support a move of 6,000 employees to new, state-of-the-art headquarters and attempt to develop into a learning organization: Netteland, G. (2009) 'Implementation of e-learning in a large organization: the critical role of relevance to work', *International Journal of Advanced Corporate Learning*, 2(3), pp. 58–65.

- For a detailed discussion of the influence of background music on differences between introverts and extraverts in learning, see Furnham, A. and Allass, K. (1999) 'The influence of musical distraction of varying complexity on the cognitive performance of extraverts and introverts', *European Journal of Personality*, 13(1), pp. 27–38.

# REVIEW QUESTIONS

1. Outline the different ways individuals learn and consider their relevance for learning at work.

2. Why is it important to evaluate the training and development activities an organization carries out and what is the best way to do this?

3. How does 'organizational learning' differ from a 'learning organization'?

# ONLINE RESOURCES

Go online to www.macmillanihe.com/sutton-people to access a MCQ quiz for this chapter and for further resources to support your learning.

# REFERENCES

Argyris, C. (1977) 'Double loop learning in organizations', *Harvard Business Review*, 55(5), pp. 115–25. Available at: www.westernsnowandice.com/09-Presos/DoubleLoop.pdf.

Arthur Jr, W., Bennett Jr, W., Edens, P. S. and Bell, S. T. (2003) 'Effectiveness of training in organizations: a meta-analysis of design and evaluation features', *Journal of Applied Psychology*, 88(2), pp. 234–45. doi: 10.1037/0021-9010.88.2.234.

Bandura, A. (1977) *Social Learning Theory*. Englewood Cliffs, NJ: Prentice Hall.

Barash, D. (2016) 'Tele-mentoring is creating global communities of practice in health care', *Harvard Business Review*, November.

Barnett, S. M. and Ceci, S. J. (2002) 'When and where do we apply what we learn?: A taxonomy for far transfer', *Psychological Bulletin*, 128(4), pp. 612–37.

Blackler, F. (1995) 'Knowledge, knowledge work and organizations: an overview and interpretation', *Organization Studies*, 16(6), pp. 1021–46.

Blume, B. D., Ford, J. K., Baldwin, T. T. and Huang, J. L. (2010) 'Transfer of training: a meta-analytic review', *Journal of Management*, 36(4), pp. 1065–105. doi: 10.1177/0149206309352880.

Caldwell, R. (2012) 'Leadership and learning: a critical reexamination of Senge's learning organization', *Systemic Practice and Action Research*, 25(1), pp. 39–55. doi: 10.1007/s11213-011-9201-0.

CIPD (2016) 'Continuing professional development policy'. Available at: www.cipd.co.uk/learn/cpd/policy (Accessed 8 December 2016).

Clegg, S. R., Kornberger, M. and Pitsis, T. (2015) *Managing and Organizations: An Introduction to Theory and Practice*, 3rd edn. London: Sage.

Coffield, F., Moseley, D., Hall, E. and Ecclestone, K. (2004) 'Learning styles and pedagogy in post-16 learning: a systematic and critical review', Learning and Skills Research Centre, p. 84. doi: 10.1016/S0022-5371(81)90483-7.

Conlon, T. J. (2004) 'A review of informal learning literature, theory and implications for practice in developing global professional competence', *Journal of European Industrial Training*, 28(2), pp. 283–95. doi: 10.1108/03090590410527663.

Coradi, A., Heinzen, M. and Boutellier, R. (2015) 'A longitudinal study of workspace design for knowledge exploration and exploitation in the research and development process', *Creativity & Innovation Management*, 24(1), pp. 55–71.

Cunningham, J. and Hillier, E. (2013) 'Informal learning in the workplace: key activities and processes', *Education + Training*, 55(1), pp. 37–51. doi: 10.1108/00400911311294960.

Dale, M. and Bell, J. (1999) *Informal Learning in the Workplace*, DfEE Research Report No. 134. London: Department for Education and Employment. Available at: http://webarchive.nationalarchives.gov.uk/20130402134131/https://www.education.gov.uk/publications/eOrderingDownload/RB134.pdfhttp.

Department of Employment (2017) *Skill Shortage List: Australia*.

Department of Higher Education and Training (2016) *Department of Higher Education and Training Republic of South Africa List of Occupations in High Demand: 2015*. Pretoria.

DeRouin, R. E., Fritzsche, B. A. and Salas, E. (2004) 'Optimizing e-learning: research-based guidelines for learner-controlled training', *Human Resource Management*, 43(2–3), pp. 147–62. doi: 10.1002/hrm.20012.

Donovan, J. J. and Radosevich, D. J. (1999) 'A meta-analytic review of the distribution of practice effect: now you see it, now you don't', *Journal of Applied Psychology*, 84(5), pp. 795–805. doi: 10.1037/0021-9010.84.5.795.

Easterby-Smith, M., Snell, R. and Gherardi, S. (1998) 'Organizational learning: diverging communities of practice?', *Management Learning*, 29(3), pp. 259–72. doi: 10.1177/1350507698293001.

Furnham, A. and Allass, K. (1999) 'The influence of musical distraction of varying complexity on the cognitive performance of extraverts and introverts', *European Journal of Personality*, 13(1), pp. 27–38. doi: 10.1002/(SICI)1099-0984(199901/02)13:1<27::AID-PER318>3.0.CO;2-R.

Garavan, T. (1997) 'The learning organization: a review and evaluation', *The Learning Organization*, 4(1), pp. 18–29. doi: 10.1108/09696479710156442.

Garavan, T. N., Carbery, R., O'Malley, G. and O'Donnell, D. (2010) 'Understanding participation in e-learning in organizations: a large-scale empirical study of employees', *International Journal of Training and Development*, 14(3), pp. 155–68. doi: 10.1111/j.1468-2419.2010.00349.x.

Garvin, D. (1993) 'Building a learning organization', *Harvard Business Review*, July-August, pp. 78–91.

Harvey, F. (2016) 'Africa's shortage of engineering skills "will stunt its growth"', *The Guardian*, 14 September.

Hodges, T. D. and Clifton, D. O. (2004) 'Strengths-based development in practice', in P. A. Linley and S. Joseph (eds) *International Handbook of Positive Psychology in Practice: From Research to Application*. Hobken, NJ: John Wiley and Sons, pp. 256–68.

Howarth, E. (1969) 'Personality differences in serial learning under distraction.', *Perceptual and Motor Skills*, pp. 379–82.

Keevy, J. and Chakroun, B. (2015) *Level-setting and Recognition of Learning Outcomes*. Paris: UNESCO. Available at: http://unesdoc.unesco.org/images/0024/002428/242887e.pdf.

Kirkpatrick, D. and Kirkpatrick, J. (2006) *Evaluating Training Programs: The Four Levels*, 3rd edn. San Francisco: Berrett-Koehler.

Kolb, D. A. (1984) *Experiential Learning: Experience as the Source of Learning and Development*. Englewood Cliffs, NJ: Prentice Hall.

Kolb, A. Y. and Kolb, D. A. (2005) 'Learning styles and learning spaces: enhancing experiential learning in higher education', *Academy of Management Learning & Education*, 4(2), pp. 193–212. doi: 10.5465/AMLE.2005.17268566.

Lawless, A. and McQue, L. (2008) 'Becoming a community of critically reflective HR practitioners: challenges and opportunities within an MA partnership programme', *Journal of European Industrial Training*, 32(5), pp. 323–35. doi: 10.1108/03090590810877058.

Levitt, B. and March, J. G. (1988) 'Organizational learning', *Annual Review of Sociology*, 14, pp. 319–40. doi: 10.1146/annurev.so.14.080188.001535.

Linstead, S., Fulop, L. and Lilley, S. (2009) *Management and Organization: A Critical Text*. Basingstoke: Palgrave Macmillan.

Macpherson, A., Elliot, M., Harris, I. and Homan, G. (2004) 'E-learning: reflections and evaluation of corporate programmes', *Human Resource Development International*, 7(3), pp. 295–313. doi: 10.1080/13678860310001630638.

March, J. (1991) 'Exploration and exploitation in organizational learning', *Organization Science*, 2(1), pp. 71–87. doi: 10.1287/orsc.2.1.71.

Marsick, V. J. (2009) 'Toward a unifying framework to support informal learning theory, research and practice', *Journal of Workplace Learning*, 21(4), pp. 265–75. doi: 10.1108/13665620910954184.

Morgenstern, F. S., Hodgson, R. J. and Law, J. (1974) 'Work efficiency and personality: a comparison of introverted and extraverted subjects exposed to conditions of distraction and distortion of stimulus in a learning task.', *Ergonomics*, 17, pp. 211–20.

Netteland, G. (2009) 'Implementation of e-learning in a large organization: the critical role of relevance to work', *International Journal of Advanced Corporate Learning*, 2(3), pp. 58–65. doi: 10.3991/ijac.v2i3.1002.

Nonaka, I. (1994) 'A dynamic theory of organization knowledge creation', *Organization Science*, 5(1), pp. 14–37. doi: 10.1287/orsc.5.1.14.

Nonaka, I. and von Krogh, G. (2009) 'Tacit knowledge and knowledge conversion: controversy and advancement in organizational knowledge creation theory', *Organization Science*, 20(3), pp. 635–52. doi: 10.1287/orsc.1080.0412.

Pashler, H., McDaniel, M., Rohrer, D. and Bjork, R. (2009) 'Learning styles: concepts and evidence', *Psychological Science in the Public Interest*, 9(3), pp. 105–19. doi: 10.1111/j.1539-6053.2009.01038.x.

Polanyi, M. (1967) *The Tacit Dimension*. New York: Anchor Books.

Project ECHO (2016) *Project ECHO: Changing the World, Fast!* Available at: http://echo.unm.edu/ (Accessed 23 December 2016).

Rigg, C. and Trehan, K. (2008) 'Critical reflection in the workplace: Is it just too difficult?', *Journal of European Industrial Training*, 32(5), pp. 374–84. doi: 10.1108/03090590810877094.

Robert Wood Johnson Partners (2017) 'Project ECHO is launched', *MyCentralJersey*, 7 May. Available at: http://mycj.co/2qPVsOX.

Santa, M. (2015) 'Learning organisation review: a "good " theory perspective', *The Learning Organization*, 22(5), pp. 242–70. doi: 10.1108/TLO-12-2014-0067.

Senge, P. M. (1990) *The Fifth Discipline: The Art and Practice of the Learning Organization*. London: Currency Doubleday.

Sonnentag, S., Niessen, C. and Ohly, S. (2008) 'Learning and training at work', in N. Chmiel (ed.) *An Introduction to Work and Organizational Psychology: A European Perspective*. Oxford: Blackwell, pp. 56–75.

Sorgenfrei, C. and Smolnik, S. (2016) 'The effectiveness of e-learning systems : a review of the empirical literature on learner control', *Decision Sciences Journal of Innovative Education*, 14(2), pp. 154–84.

Sutton, A. (2016) 'Measuring the effects of self-awareness: construction of the self-awareness outcomes questionnaire', *Europe's Journal of Psychology*, 12(4), pp. 645–58. doi: 10.5964/ejop.v12i4.1178.

Svensson, L., Ellström, P.-E. and Åberg, C. (2004) 'Integrating formal and informal learning at work', *Journal of Workplace Learning*, 16(8), pp. 479–91. doi: 10.1108/13665620410566441.

Taylor, P. J., Russ-Eft, D. F. and Chan, D. W. L. (2005) 'A meta-analytic review of behavior modeling training', *Journal of Applied Psychology*, 90(4), pp. 692–709. doi: 10.1037/0021-9010.90.4.692.

Tosey, P. (2005) 'The hunting of the learning organization: a paradoxical journey', *Management Learning* , 36(3), pp. 335–52. doi: 10.1177/1350507605055350.

UK Commission for Employment and Skills (2015) *UK Employer Skills Survey 2015*.

UNESCO (2014) *Teaching and Learning: Achieving Quality for All*, EFA Global Monitoring Report 2013/14. Paris: UNESCO.

Upadhyaya, K. T. and Mallik, D. (2013) 'E-learning as a socio-technical system : an insight into factors influencing its effectiveness', *Business Perspectives and Research*, 1(7), pp. 1–13.

Wang, C. L. and Ahmed, P. K. (2003) 'Organisational learning: a critical review', *The Learning Organization*, 10(1), pp. 8–17. doi: 10.1108/09696470310457469.

Wenger, E. (1998) 'Communities of practice: learning as a social system', *Systems Thinker*, 9(5), pp. 1–10. doi: 10.2277/0521663636.

Winter, S. (1987) 'Knowledge and competence as strategic assets', in D. Teece (ed.) *The Competitive Challenge: Strategies for Industrial Innovation and Renewal*. Cambridge, MA: Ballinger, pp. 159–84.

# 11 WELL-BEING AND ENGAGEMENT

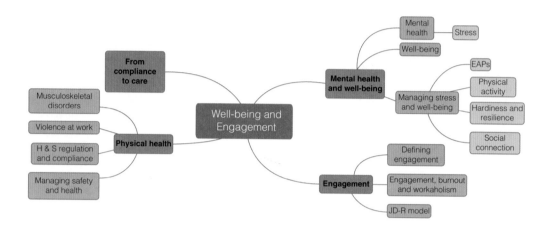

## INTRODUCTION

In this chapter, we will be looking at the role of employee health at work. This is covered in several different ways in HRM and OB, from legislation concerned with reducing accidents at work to considerations of the impact of stress on employees to the promotion of holistic well-being at work programmes. We will discuss physical and mental/emotional health in this chapter as well as the more all-inclusive concept of well-being at work. Of course, some work is inherently dangerous and we will take a special look at what can be done to protect people working in these kinds of difficult and risky occupations.

In considering physical and mental health, we will discuss practical approaches to managing health

and well-being at work. Here, we give considerable attention to issues around stress at work as well as the importance of creating safe workplaces. We will look at the substantial economic impact that stress has and some of the approaches that organizations take to try to minimize stress or help employees to cope with the negative impact.

We complete the chapter by discussing the concept of engagement at work. Engagement and the related concept of 'burnout' are closely related to health and well-being, but make a more overt link to performance and so have become important areas of study for HRM and OB researchers and practitioners.

*Getty Images/Caiaimage/Sam Edwards*

## LEARNING FEATURES

Applications: Preventing workplace violence

Applications: International H&S

Applications: Work friends

Weighing the Evidence: Well-being is good for business

Web Explorer: EAPs

In the News: Technology and workaholism

Transferrable Skills: Enhancing engagement

Practice Insights: Ginger Chen

 Video overview

Julian Perkins

Go online to www.macmillanihe.com/sutton-people to access a video of Anna Sutton introducing the chapter's main themes.

# FROM COMPLIANCE TO CARE

Safety, health and well-being are interrelated concepts and Gilmore and Williams (2009) suggest that health and safety (H&S) policies and practices can be seen as a *mechanism* for improving individual well-being at work. Different organizations have differing approaches to dealing with these issues, from simply fulfilling legal H&S requirements through to a genuine concern for overall employee well-being. One way of picturing the relationship between the three concepts is to see them as lying on a continuum from 'compliance' with regulations to 'care' for employees, shown in Figure 11.1.

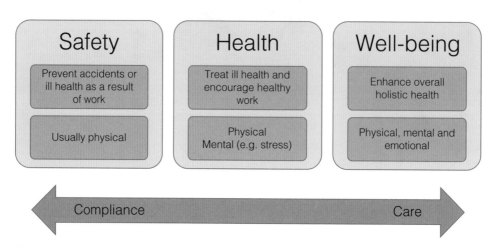

*Figure 11.1 The well-being continuum*

At one end of the continuum, HR policies and practices are concerned with compliance with legal requirements and regulations to assure the physical safety of staff. As we progress to the opposite end of the continuum, there is an increasing emphasis on care for employees: there is less regulation involved and organizations have greater freedom in how (or even if) they choose to address the issues. This continuum is reflected in the historical development of the focus on H&S/well-being over the past decades: from a concern with identifying risks so that the workforce could be protected and accidents prevented, there has been an evolution to a more comprehensive approach to health promotion and quality of working life (Schulte and Vainio, 2010).

At the compliance end of the spectrum, the emphasis is on safety and tends to be focused primarily on the physical aspects of work. It is chiefly concerned with preventing accidents in the workplace or ill health that is a direct result of working conditions. Legislation around accident prevention is a good example of this approach and many practices that are fairly common today, such as wearing high-visibility clothing, have their origins in this kind of approach.

A focus on health takes this concern a step further. As heavy industry and dangerous work has decreased in many developed countries, there has been a corresponding increase in service industries. This has led to a change in focus from preventing physical harm to include a consideration of mental issues, especially where these result in physical symptoms. Probably the most well-known example here is the issue of workplace stress and how this can damage employees' health.

More recently, there has been a development of focus on well-being. This sees employee health as a holistic concept, which takes into account not just physical or the more obvious mental health issues but includes an overall concern with employees' subjective experiences. It recognizes that work may be affected by non-work experiences and vice versa and is an expression of a concern for the employee as a 'whole person'. At this end of the scale, much of HR policy will be directed by beliefs about the right way to treat employees and, often, how different practices can enhance employee engagement. The Weighing the Evidence activity considers the debate over whether concern for well-being makes good business sense.

## Weighing the Evidence: **Well-being is good for business**

One thing that the diverse approaches to health, safety and well-being at work have in common is the claim that they are 'good for business'. The business case for taking care of employees' health often includes the following, seemingly reasonable statements:

- healthy workers take less time off sick and therefore cost the company less

- healthy workers are able to perform at higher levels than unhealthy workers, thereby boosting productivity

- ensuring that employees do not have accidents at work and are not exposed to health risks ensures that employers do not lose valuable workers and will not face potentially costly law suits.

But is this business case justified? Certainly, there is evidence that workers' ill health (physical and mental) does bring substantial costs to the organization: work-related illness is estimated to cost the EU €200 billion a year, of which about 10% is stress related, while work-related depression has been estimated to cost Europe a staggering €600 billion annually, mainly through loss of productivity or absenteeism rather than healthcare costs (EU-OSHA et al., 2014).

Despite this, we do need to be aware that not all organizations will be concerned about these costs or potential damage to their employees. For some, it can actually be cheaper to replace workers than to invest in ensuring their health or safety. In other organizations, 'survival' of particularly unhealthy, demanding or dangerous work can be seen as a rite of passage. An example of this is found in investment banking, where junior bankers are expected to do basic, routine tasks for 15–16 hours a day, and effectively be 'on-call' in any free time they have left (Luyendijk, 2013). There is also a strong driver in many organizations to focus on short-term performance rather than considering the longer term implications of ill health.

Yet, there is also an ethical dimension to health and well-being at work. This was recognized during the Industrial Revolution by some notable industry figures who were also Quakers – a Christian group that historically had a great focus on philanthropy – for example the Rowntree and Cadbury families in the UK. These employers were distinguished by their concern for their workers, providing housing, education and medical facilities. Cadbury was, in fact, the first company to have a five-day working week (Quakers in the World, 2016). For these employers, it was important not just to treat their workers fairly but to actively try to improve their lives. In the same way, an organizational concern for well-being can often go beyond simply trying to ensure that employees are not harmed by their work to attempting to provide employees with work and benefits that will enhance their lives.

More recently, further reasons for investing in well-being at work have emerged. With the increase in employee mobility, organizations need to work hard to attract the best workers. They often now want to present themselves to potential job applicants as employers who care for their employees. In addition, there has been a rise in the interest in employee engagement, and concern for well-being is often seen as going hand in hand with promoting engagement. This image of a caring, engaging employer can also benefit the wider brand of the organization and be attractive to potential customers. So, while there may well be a business case for some organizations, the wider focus on well-being is about more than just increasing productivity.

---

Whether from a belief that it makes 'good business sense' or in order to comply with H&S legislation or from a genuine belief that caring for employees is a moral duty, organizations will make some efforts to manage the health and well-being of their staff. HR practitioners often have a key role in developing and implementing the policies and interventions that are designed to do this. In the following sections, we will review several different approaches, starting with health and safety compliance and then moving on to ways of promoting holistic well-being. Although we structure our discussion by distinguishing between physical health and mental health/well-being, bear in mind that this is something of an imprecise distinction and the concepts are interrelated: our physical health and safety can impact on our mental health and mental health (and particularly stress) can affect physical health.

# PHYSICAL HEALTH

In this section we will discuss the different elements of physical health at work, from how the work itself might cause injury – in musculoskeletal disorders – to the experience of violence at work. This latter issue serves to highlight the integration of physical and mental health, as violence can be limited to threats and has physical and mental effects. We also consider health and safety regulations and the practical approaches organizations take to managing physical health at work.

## Musculoskeletal disorders

One of the key issues in physical health at work is **musculoskeletal disorders (MSDs)**. MSDs include a range of different disorders, such as upper and lower back pain and repetitive strain injuries. These latter are the result of using the same muscles frequently during the course of the day and are particularly common where the same movement is required for long periods in the job, for example in typing.

In fact, work-related MSDs account for nearly half (44%) of all work-related ill health and 40% of all working days lost in the UK (Buckley, 2015). The rates are highest in industries that entail active physical work, such as construction, and the most common cause of back injuries, accounting for 48% of cases is, perhaps unsurprisingly, lifting and carrying. Similar patterns are found in other countries. For example, a survey of Chinese workers found a high prevalence of MSDs in many occupational groups, particularly assembly and construction workers, with up to 76% of workers in these groups reporting lower back complaints (Bao et al., 2000). But over one in ten cases of back injury and 14% of upper limb disorders are reported to be due to keyboard work (Buckley, 2015), so dealing with MSDs is certainly not an issue only for more physically demanding work.

We should not, however, view physical demands at work solely as a hazard. Physical movement and exercise are essential to long-term health and the physical demands of work can contribute to people's health. In fact, for many people, it is a lack of activity or physical movement that can have negative health impacts. Lee et al. (2012) estimated that inactivity accounts for about 9% of premature deaths worldwide. Of course, this inactivity is not limited to the workplace, but to a generally sedentary lifestyle in which inactivity at work is a contributor. Merely sitting a lot, whether at work or in leisure time, is not in itself a predictor of mortality risk (Pulsford et al., 2015). Instead, it is the overall energy expenditure that is key in protecting against the potential negative health impact of the number of hours spent sitting. Some organizations try to encourage their employees to be more active at work, for example by providing standing desks or encouraging employees to walk in their lunch breaks, in order to combat the health problems that can be caused by inactivity.

## Violence at work

Violence at work can be defined as 'any incident in which a person is abused, threatened or assaulted in circumstances relating to their work' (Health and Safety Executive, 2016). In this definition, violence is not necessarily physical: it can also include verbal threats or abuse. Just over 1% of workers in the UK experience a violent incident at work but a substantial number of these (20%) experience three or more violent incidents in a year (Health and Safety Executive, 2015). In Europe as a whole, 6% of workers report that they have experienced threats of physical violence from co-workers and others (European Agency for Safety and Health at Work, 2010).

The UK's Health and Safety Executive (HSE) makes several good practice recommendations for organizations attempting to manage the violence that their employees are exposed to, including:

- improving the security of the working environment (e.g. CCTV, visibility)

- improving working practices (ensuring there are enough staff available, reducing cash handling)

- providing training (in how to prevent and deal with violence).

Work through the Applications activity to see how these recommendations can be put into practice.

## Health and safety regulation and compliance

The legal framework governing health and safety at work varies in each country. However, there is a move towards developing a universal expectation that people should be able to work safely. *Occupational*

## Applications: Preventing workplace violence

The definition of workplace violence provided by the HSE includes verbal abuse. In these examples we will consider the context of the work and the implications this has for how violence is perceived and responded to by employees and the organization.

Police officers are exposed to potentially violent situations and people as a normal part of their job. But that does not mean that police forces ignore it. Some of the steps they have taken to try and reduce the number of violent incidents include personal safety training and careful design of the work environment (Health and Safety Executive, 2017a). In addition, the police force encourages officers to report every violent incident that results in injury. However, they do not record verbal abuse 'as it is too prevalent'.

Compare this with a call centre such as the Student Loans Company, where the risk of verbal abuse is the primary focus of the employer's efforts. In this case, employees are given training in managing their own well-being in order to complete a call, dealing with 'phone rage' from upset or frustrated customers and not taking a customer's abusive behaviour personally (Health and Safety Executive, 2017b).

» To what extent do you agree with the police's approach to not recording verbal abuse?

» Why do you think the Student Loans Company has invested so much in trying to help employees deal with verbal abuse? Should they bother or should employees be expected to 'toughen up'?

» Having considered these two examples, do you think it's possible to create a violence-free workplace? And how prepared would you be to work somewhere you were exposed to verbal or physical violence?

Getty Images/iStockphoto/BartekSzewczyk

*Violence at work is not necessarily physical but can include verbal abuse.*

**health and safety (OHS)** is defined by the International Labour Office (Alli, 2008, p. vii) as:

> the science of the anticipation, recognition, evaluation and control of hazards arising in or from the workplace that could impair the health and well-being of workers, taking into account the possible impact on the surrounding communities and the general environment.

Protecting workers was one of the foundational issues for the ILO and nearly 100 years later, it remains central to much of its work.

Alli's definition helps to highlight the impact that OHS has on individuals, societies and the wider environment. It also notes that there are four elements in the effective management of OHS:

- **Anticipation:** OHS management should be proactive, it should be aware of potential hazards and make efforts to reduce or remove them before they cause an incident.

- **Recognition:** Some hazards or risks may be hidden, especially where the effect might be longer term. Part of the proactive approach involves recognizing these hidden risks.

- **Evaluation:** There are risks inherent in much of human activity and work, and no OHS management will be able to remove them all. But it should evaluate their potential impact and make informed decisions about the extent to which a hazard is acceptable or how it will be dealt with.

- **Control:** Good OHS management should ensure that hazards and risks are controlled as much as possible. This is only possible if the previous three steps have been undertaken well.

Worldwide, about 2.3 million people are estimated to die annually because of work-related reasons (Nenonen et al., 2010). Of these, 300,000 deaths are due to occupational injuries but by far the greater proportion (2 million) is due to work-related illness. Two-thirds of these illnesses are cardiovascular or cancer. There are also significant differences in the safety of workers in different countries. For example, a transport worker in Kenya is ten times more likely to die at work than a transport worker in Denmark (Alli, 2008). Nenonen et al. (2010) called for a new standard of 'zero harm' to be practised in working life. This ideal is what the ILO and similar national H&S bodies are working towards: eliminating the negative effects of work and promoting sustainable working practices.

Three key areas need to be integrated in promoting H&S at work: worker's rights, employer's responsibilities and the government's duties (Alli, 2008):

- **Workers:** have a right to decent (safe) work, but also a responsibility for their own and others' safety. In order to fulfil this responsibility well, they need to have knowledge of the potential risks and the training to carry out their work safely.

- **Employers:** have a responsibility to ensure that the workplace is safe, by, as far as possible, preventing risks and protecting workers from those risks. In addition, they should promote H&S and take these issues into account when making decisions about new technology or working conditions. Finally, employers should provide training, first aid facilities and adequate compensation for work-related injuries or illnesses.

- **Governments:** should develop, implement and monitor the legal framework that ensures that organizations and individuals work in a safe way. While they are unlikely to specify the details of 'safe working' in a particular industry, there should be clear general guidelines for acceptable standards.

The Applications activity explores the challenges in improving H&S faced by employees and governments when dealing with powerful multinational companies.

## Applications: International H&S

On 24 April 2013, over 1,100 workers died when the factory they were working in collapsed. It was the worst occupational accident in the world in decades (Burke, 2013). Rana Plaza, in Bangladesh, housed several different companies making garments for high-street brands in the UK and elsewhere in the world, and the low wages for workers here made it a popular supplier for these fashion chains.

Following the disaster, there were calls for the brands supplied by this factory to contribute to compensation for injured workers and the families of the victims. A year later, Primark had contributed $10 million but other companies had still not agreed to do so (Butler, 2014). The disaster also prompted action to improve the working conditions and safety of workers in Bangladesh and other countries, but, so far, little progress has been made. For example, despite H&M, a global clothing retailer, signing up to a legally enforceable code on fire safety for its factories, progress has been so slow that three years later less than 0.5% of its factories have met the required standards (Kasperkevic, 2016). Other chains, including Walmart and Gap, have refused to sign up to the code.

» The ILO suggests that creating safe work is a joint responsibility between employees, employers and governments. How much do you think large organizations should be responsible for the treatment of workers in their supply chain even if they do not directly employ them?

» This case highlights some of the complexities that can arise when powerful multinationals come into conflict with national attempts to improve health and safety. What can be done to encourage governments and large organizations to make employee safety a priority?

## Managing safety and health

There are a variety of means that organizations use to create safer and healthier workplaces, and these fall into three broad categories: management, workers and training.

In delineating management responsibilities, Alli (2008) notes that an organization's strategy and mission demonstrate the value that is placed on employees' health. The system for managing H&S needs to be integrated with the organization's culture and processes in order to be effective. For example, if there is a safety requirement that workers should take breaks from their computer screens throughout the day, but the culture of the organization places great emphasis on being seen to be working at the computer constantly, then employees will be less likely to follow the safety processes. A commitment to H&S needs to be made at the highest levels and demonstrated in words and actions for it to have a positive impact on workers. This commitment can be demonstrated by delegating the responsibility for safety throughout the organizational hierarchy and allocating sufficient resources for tasks to be completed safely as well as for the H&S programme to function effectively.

Workers also have a responsibility to engage with H&S initiatives and processes. While they have a right to a safe workplace, they also have a responsibility to cooperate and participate in the safety programmes. Those who are closest to the tasks have a key role to play in developing safe working practices.

Finally, there is the importance of training to OHS. Training should include technical skills so that tasks can be carried out correctly but also raise awareness of the importance of safety and guide employees on adapting to their work in a healthy manner.

# MENTAL HEALTH AND WELL-BEING

We have already seen how physical health and safety can impact on mental health and well-being, so in this section we are moving on to consider these interrelated issues in greater detail. We start by defining each of the concepts before looking at the different ways we can build mental health and encourage well-being at work.

## Mental health

There is fairly minimal research on the impact of work on common or severe mental health problems, so although there is evidence that work can be indirectly beneficial to overall well-being, it is hard to say for certain what effect work has on the range of different mental illnesses. A substantial number of people with severe mental health problems actually do want to work (EU-OSHA et al., 2014), and it is likely that the effect of work will depend very much on the individual's situation as well as the specific illness they are dealing with. However, while there is a lack of significant evidence on the wider mental health issues, there has been a large amount of research on stress and work and it is worth considering this in more detail.

### Stress

The reaction we call 'stress' is essentially the process our bodies go through when we are faced with a potential threat, or 'stressor', in order to prepare us for action. In response to a stressor, our heart rate and blood to our muscles increases, digestion slows down and our pupils dilate. This physical response to a physical stressor is usually very helpful, and developed from the evolutionary need to survive. Known as the 'fight or flight' response (Cannon, 1929), it enables us to either fight the threat or flee from it. Either way, the stressor is then gone and our bodies can return to their normal state. But this is also the reason that stress at work can be so dangerous. We have the same physical response whether the stressor is physical, emotional or mental. In many cases, stressors at work, such as working to deadlines or work overload, are continuous and the physical response does not actually help us to deal with them. This means that the stress response – this constant state of tension and 'preparedness' – becomes continuous or chronic. If we cannot adapt to the stressors, we eventually reach a state of exhaustion (Selye, 1956), where the immune response is lowered and we feel burned out. Chronic stress can even result in heart attacks and other severe physical symptoms.

Estimates of the costs of stress to organizations and society are wide-ranging but generally agree that the cost is significant. For example, the European Agency for Safety and Health at Work (EU-OSHA et al., 2014) estimates that stress costs *billions* a year and that in the UK, stress, anxiety and depression cost organizations about £1,000 *per employee per year*. In addition, there is good evidence that investing in reducing stress is worthwhile: it can reduce the costs associated with absenteeism and turnover or even presenteeism – where employees are at work but not performing well due to health problems. For example, one study found that for every €1 spent on mental health promotion and disorder prevention in the workplace, there was a benefit of €14 in the first year (EU-OSHA et al., 2014).

There are, of course, significant challenges associated with estimating these costs, not least the fact that stress is not recognized as a clinical condition in itself and so estimates have to use proxies such as depression, anxiety, musculoskeletal disorders and cardiovascular disease. There are even further 'hidden' costs, such as increases in workplace conflict, reduction in quality of products or services, and even damage to the employer's reputation or brand. In addition, there is the conceptual confusion around defining 'stress' and 'stressors'. Sometimes, this is done circularly: stressors are defined as demands that cause a stress response and a stress response is defined as an adverse health impact associated with a stressor. One of the difficulties in understanding stress at work is the fact that it is so subjective.

A key factor in determining our response to stressors is the extent to which we evaluate them as threats or not. This is known as **cognitive appraisal** and consists of two steps (Folkman and Lazarus, 1988). First, we evaluate the potential harm or benefit of an experience and, second, we evaluate our **coping** options. If we evaluate an experience as having no impact on us or those we are close to, there is no need to respond to it. If, however, we evaluate it as having a particular impact, we will then need to choose what to do about it in order to reduce the potential harm or increase the chances of the benefit occurring (Folkman et al., 1986). These coping mechanisms can be problem-focused, where we attempt to change the situation, or emotion-focused if we believe we cannot affect the outcome and need to adjust our emotional reaction in order to cope with it. As an example, consider what you could do if you felt your manager had given you too tight a deadline to complete a project. A problem-focused coping mechanism could be to approach your manager to renegotiate the deadline or reorganize your workload to prioritize the project. If you felt there was no way to change the situation, an emotion-focused approach would be to try and remain calm under the pressure or to view the project as an exciting challenge rather than an impossible problem.

Besides the individual appraisals of stressors and the coping strategies that different people utilize, there are other aspects of work that influence our response to stress. These include the balance between the demands work places on us and the control we have over our work and the support we receive from our colleagues (Johnson and Hall, 1988). The balance of these elements can determine whether the stressor has a negative or positive impact on health and performance at work.

It is worth remembering that the stress response is defined as 'non-specific', that is, it is a demand for activity but the body does not specify what that activity should be. So, although the reviews on the 'costs of stress' invariably focus on the negative impact of stress on workers, we also need to bear in mind that some stress is actually good for us. In fact, Selye (1973, p. 693), who first described our general adaptation response to stress, said that 'complete freedom from stress is death'. He distinguished between eustress (positive stress) and distress. Eustress helps us to perform better, while distress can cause some of the negative results we saw above.

This review of the interaction between stress and work brings us back to a consideration of the effect of work on mental health generally. As we have seen, it is a complex relationship. Work can provide a sense of meaning to individuals, social contact and a sense of achievement, all of which enhance mental well-being, but work can also be a contributor to mental ill-health. Perhaps this is why there has been a move to considering well-being as a broader concept rather than just physical health.

## Well-being

Well-being can be difficult to define exactly. Partly this is because it is inherently a holistic concept: it is meant to convey the subjective experience that we have of our whole life and how well we feel we are functioning, or, as the New Economics Foundation puts it, 'feeling good and functioning well' (Aked et al., 2008, p. 1). This aspect of 'functioning well' is particularly important for organizational applications, because it is there that we can see why well-being might be of interest and use in the workplace. Employees who are functioning well are expected to be more productive than those who are not.

The focus on well-being at work is matched by a shift in focus in the medical and psychological arenas from 'illness' to 'health'. While reducing the number of workplace accidents or prevalence of illnesses associated with work remain important elements, promotion of well-being at work considers the wider context of employees and has a central place for employees' subjective feelings of satisfaction or happiness at work. Well-being at work can sometimes be conceptualized rather narrowly as job satisfaction (Sousa-Poza and Sousa-Poza, 2000) or as including our contentment with and enthusiasm for our work (Warr, 1990), but is more often described as a comprehensive concept capturing our perceptions of the *quality* of our working lives (Schulte and Vainio, 2010). Waddell and Burton (2006, p. 4) provide just such a comprehensive definition of well-being as:

> the subjective state of being healthy, happy, contented, comfortable and satisfied with one's quality of life. It includes physical, material, social, emotional ('happiness'), and development and activity dimensions.

From these definitions, we can see that we need to consider a range of different factors in trying to understand and improve well-being at work. But an interesting side note is that the relationship between work and well-being is two way. Our well-being affects our work, but there is also good evidence that work affects our well-being (Waddell and Burton, 2006): it helps us to meet psychosocial needs, provides us with the economic resources we need, is a key part of our identity and status, and, on average, promotes physical and mental health. Remaining in or re-entering work also has beneficial effects for sick and disabled people, while unemployment is detrimental to physical and mental health. We therefore move on now from our discussions of the concepts of mental health and well-being to the practical issues of how best to manage them at work.

## Managing stress and well-being

Much of the work on understanding how to manage stress and well-being grew out of efforts to reduce stress or help employees to cope with stressful work situations, and interventions can be divided into five broad groups depending on which stage of the stress process they aim to affect (Quick et al., 1997; Le Blanc et al., 2008):

1. **Identification:** focuses on the early *detection of possible stressors* in the workplace and noticing potential stress reactions in the workforce. For example, HR departments may monitor sickness and absence levels for unexpected increases that might indicate increased stress.

2. **Primary interventions:** attempt to reduce or remove the *sources of stress*, for example by redesigning jobs or encouraging participative management.

3. **Secondary interventions:** focus on helping employees to *modify their responses* to the stressors that primary interventions cannot reduce, thereby attempting to decrease the severity of stress symptoms and subsequent progression into health problems. For example, some organizations provide resilience training to employees to help them build resilience to everyday stressors.

4. **Tertiary interventions:** involve *treating the health problem* and come into play when employees are suffering the effects of stress. They can include providing counselling to employees.

5. **Rehabilitation:** this needs to be considered for employees who have experienced ill health, including a planned return to work.

Most organizational interventions tend to be aimed at the secondary level, helping employees to manage their stress and training them in better coping strategies (Giga et al., 2003). Cartwright and Cooper (1997) have suggested that many organizations have an assumption that the 'problem' in stress and well-being lies in the individual, and so interventions are focused on helping employees adapt to the organizational demands rather than removing sources of stress.

Because these stress interventions come in so many different shapes and sizes, it can be useful to gain an overview of them by categorizing their approaches. A meta-analysis of stress intervention studies did this and demonstrated that they had a medium to large effect size in reducing the negative effects of stress (Richardson and Rothstein, 2008), with the first in the list being most effective:

- **Cognitive behavioural:** helps employees learn about the role of their thoughts and emotions in appraising stressful events and how to modify their thoughts and feelings in order to cope better. Examples include assertiveness training and collaborative problem-solving approaches, as well as cognitive behavioural therapy (CBT) in general.

- **Relaxation:** this can include meditation or deep breathing exercises and the aim is to help employees to change their physiological state. This kind of intervention increases people's ability to feel relaxed in the face of pressure, rather than allowing the stress response to build up.

- **Organizational:** focused around management techniques or job redesign to reduce the stressors themselves or their impact on employees. Examples include introducing an 'innovation promotion' programme, which involves participatory action and goal-setting, or a social support group to enhance coping abilities.

- **Multimodal:** many real-life interventions actually draw on more than one of the categories above. For example, they may combine CBT with relaxation techniques and time management training.

- **Alternative or other:** this category was for interventions that did not fit into the other groups because they were new or unique. As an example, providing employees with electromyographic biofeedback – feedback on the tension in their muscles or hand temperature – enables them to become more aware of how their bodies are responding to different events.

For the rest of this section, we will consider in more detail some of the practical interventions that organizations adopt for improving well-being at work.

## Employee assistance programme

**'Employee assistance programme' (EAP)** is an umbrella term for a collection of assistance programmes and well-being initiatives that an organization can introduce. From an organizational perspective, an EAP is seen as a way of improving productivity and attendance by providing support and assistance to employees on a reasonably individualized basis. The individual employee can contact the EAP with an assurance of confidentiality and can access the services or help that they need at that time. EAPs also take a holistic approach to stress, recognizing that stressors in our personal life often have an impact on our work, and offering support for employee needs to cover all the areas that people might struggle with.

Many EAPs are subcontracted to professional companies specializing in providing a range of services, including (UK EAPA, 2011):

*For employees:*

- Short-term psychological services, such as counselling.

- Information and advice, for example money advice and debt management, legal guidance, elder and childcare information, and information on emotional, work–life and workplace issues.

*For organizations:*

- A means for management to refer staff who need support.

- Anonymized reports on utilization, that is, how many staff have accessed different types of support or advice.

People who use EAP services report a reduction in their symptoms as well as satisfaction with and appreciation for the service (Arthur, 2000), although there is less evidence for organizational-level improvements. The Web Explorer activity looks at how EAPs differ around the world.

**Web Explorer: EAPS**

The employee assistance programmes that organizations provide differ widely in what they offer. Do a web search to find some EAP organizations in your country and compare their offerings. If you were tasked with identifying an EAP provider for your organization, which one would you choose and why? Which elements of an EAP are essential, which would be desirable, and which ones do you think might be simply a waste of money?

After this, choose another country and compare the offerings of EAPs in that country with your own. What differences are there? Do the programmes in different countries represent differing health and well-being concerns or do they offer the same general approaches? If the latter, to

what extent might there be a niche in the market for a more tailored approach?

Here are some EAP providers to get you started:

- UK: P&MM www.pmmemployeebenefits.co.uk/default.asp and Health Assured www.health assured.org

- Denmark: Falck www.falck.com/en/services/employee-assistance-programmes/

- Australia: DTC www.davcorp.com.au and Access EAP www.accesseap.com.au

- South Africa: Icon Health www.inconhealth.co.za and Kaelo www.kaelo.co.za/

- New Zealand: EAP Services www.eapservices.co.nz.

## Physical activity

Many organizations promote well-being at the individual level by encouraging employees to be more physically active. They may negotiate reduced cost gym membership for their employees, have company sports teams or even invest in an onsite fitness centre. The general health benefits of exercise are well known, but there is also good evidence that physical activity can promote mental health and help people to deal with stress (see for example Hamer et al., 2006). A large-scale study of 40,000 people in Norway (Harvey et al., 2010) confirmed this but also highlighted the importance of distinguishing between work and leisure activity, as well as the role of social interaction. The study found that those who did more hours of leisure time exercise a week had lower levels of depression, but that physical activity which was part of the job, such as heavy lifting or walking a lot, was unrelated to mental health symptoms. This may be partly explained by the finding that it was the social benefits of exercise (rather than physical) that seemed to be more important at reducing depression.

## Hardiness and resilience

In the late 1970s, psychologist Suzanne Kobasa (1979) studied how executives coped with stressful life events. She found that, although their levels of stress were similar, some of the executives suffered

significant ill health while others remained healthy. Those who remained healthy were characterized as having higher levels of hardiness. 'Hardiness' was later defined in more detail as consisting of three attitudes or orientations towards stressful events (Maddi and Kobasa, 1984):

1. **Commitment:** believing that a meaningful purpose can be found in life and staying involved in events rather than becoming isolated.

2. **Control:** the determination to try and influence events rather than giving up and feeling powerless.

3. **Challenge:** seeing change as a positive challenge rather than a threat and a stressful situation as an opportunity to learn.

The idea that our hardiness is rooted in the perceptions we have of potentially stressful events relates back to our discussion of the role of cognitive appraisal in the stress response. There is good evidence that people who are more hardy are less susceptible to the negative outcomes of stress (Beasley et al., 2003).

Hardiness is also closely related to 'resilience' – our ability to maintain our equilibrium in the face of stressful events (Bonanno et al., 2001). A resilient response to stress involves lower levels of disruption to normal functioning following the event, which is maintained over time. Bonanno (2004) suggests that hardiness is one of the 'paths to resilience', that is, one of the ways that people naturally deal successfully with stressful events. Bonanno also points out that resilience is far more common than we might think if we looked at the literature around stress and coping, because most studies have focused on when things go wrong. Many employers and consultancies offer resilience training to help employees develop this skill.

## Social connection

An important aspect of the studies of hardiness and resilience, as well as the models of stress we have looked at, is the central place they give to social support. We have seen throughout this chapter how important social connection is to our sense of well-being and this has been confirmed in meta-analyses of how people cope with and recover from stress and traumatic events (Ozer et al., 2003). In fact, social connection is one of the five actions that the New Economics Foundation recommends to enhance well-being (Aked et al., 2008), listed in Table 11.1.

The important thing to remember about well-being is that it locates the individual within the social world: no one can experience a good life or

### Table 11.1 Actions to improve well-being

| Action | How and why |
| --- | --- |
| Connect | Build relationships with the people around you, at work, home and the community. These relationships will be a source of support for you when you face difficult times |
| Be active | Exercise improves mood and helps us to cope with the physical responses to stress |
| Take notice | Be aware of the world around you and take time to appreciate beauty and reflect on your experiences |
| Keep learning | Learning helps us to feel good about ourselves and our achievements and improves our sense of competency |
| Give | We get a sense of reward when we help others, but it also builds reciprocity and trust in the community |

cope with stress successfully if they are in isolation. Consequently, organizational efforts to reduce the impact of stress or enhance well-being will never succeed if they simply try to reduce an individual's negative response to stress and do not address the social issues of support, connection and relationships at work. The Applications activity considers the role of work friends in our support networks.

 Applications: **Work friends**

*Getty Images/Geber86*

The research on well-being provides solid evidence for the importance of social relationships, and a study by Riordan and Griffeth (1995) showed that the opportunity to develop friendships at work was associated with higher job satisfaction and involvement, as well as increased organizational commitment. However, there are downsides to having friendships at work, including distraction and difficulties with issues related to organizational hierarchies, such as having to discipline a friend (Morrison and Nolan, 2007).

» What is your experience of friendships in the workplace? Are your 'work friendships' different from other friendships?

» How have you benefited from having friends at work? Have there been any incidents where a friendship has led to difficulty at work?

» To what extent should organizations encourage work friendships? Should they make any attempts to limit friendships or to promote a more 'objective/professional' approach? Why?

# ENGAGEMENT

The close interrelationship of engagement, health and well-being was highlighted in a recent survey of nearly 10,000 US workers (Witter and Agrawal, 2015), which showed that, compared to employees who were engaged in their work but otherwise had low levels of well-being, those with high engagement and well-being reported:

- having higher levels of individual and organizational performance

- having lower levels of absenteeism and turnover intention

- being more likely to recover from illness or hardship

- being more able to adapt to change

- being more likely to volunteer their time and effort.

This relationship between engagement and well-being is theoretical and practical. As we will see in this section, engagement is often conceptualized as the high end of employee well-being in theoretical models, with burnout and workaholism representing different kinds of low well-being at work (Schaufeli et al., 2008). In addition to this, well-being and engagement are seen as closely interconnected by HR practitioners: a survey of HR and benefits leaders revealed that 97% of them believed that employee well-being influenced engagement and 87% invest (or plan to invest) in well-being initiatives as a part of their strategy for employee engagement (Virgin Pulse, 2016).

## Defining engagement

Employee engagement is important to managers and HR professionals alike because it is seen as a way of eliciting 'discretionary effort' from workers. That is, people who are engaged in their work and jobs will go beyond the bare minimum they are expected to do in that job and will voluntarily work harder or to a higher standard, leading to greater productivity for the organization. However, this claim cannot simply be accepted on face value. Although it seems sensible that engaged employees will be more productive, there are many other factors that affect performance and the causal relationship between engagement and performance is not yet certain.

In HR literature and practice, 'engagement' is a term used for what Robertson and Cooper (2010) describe as a 'commitment/citizenship' model. Engagement is seen as a positive attitude that employees have towards their organizations and their work, which consists of:

- **Organizational commitment:** sense of attachment to the organization

- **Citizenship behaviour:** behaviour that goes beyond the job requirements and contributes to the organization's effectiveness (Organ, 1988).

Armstrong and Taylor (2014) expand on this by suggesting that engagement includes intrinsic motivation as well, although they recognize that commitment, citizenship and motivation are also seen as antecedents or even outcomes of engagement by other authors. Some of the difficulty with defining what 'engagement' actually is likely comes from the fact that it is often measured by organizations by using employee questionnaires, which include questions measuring all kinds of different concepts, including enthusiasm, participation in decision-making and resilience (Robertson and Cooper, 2010). Robertson and Cooper suggest that we should use a concept of 'full engagement', which not only recognizes the organizationally beneficial aspects of commitment and citizenship but also the benefits to the individual, namely better well-being. This would correspond with how the term is used in practice when organizations attempt to measure and improve employee engagement as well as providing an organization/individual balance.

The Gallup organization is generally credited with popularizing the notion of 'engagement' and has provided some convincing evidence of its benefits to organizations. Gallup defines engagement as 'the individual's involvement and satisfaction with as well as enthusiasm for work' (Harter et al., 2002a, p. 269), and the Gallup Workplace Audit was developed to measure this by asking employees about their perceptions of the people-related management practices in the organization. In its analyses of engagement and outcomes at the business unit level, it found positive relationships between engagement and customer satisfaction, productivity and profit, and negative relationships with turnover and accidents. And these relationships were strong enough to have real practical significance – millions of dollars for large organizations. It is no wonder, then, that engagement is such a popular concept in HR practice. This work on the link between engagement and practice has led some researchers to suggest that engagement could be the 'mechanism' for how HR practices influence performance (Truss et al., 2013). Others suggest that engagement produces a greater level of positive emotions and this then influences work efficiency and creativity as well as employee retention (Harter et al., 2002b).

Three key aspects of engagement can be drawn out from all these different definitions:

1. Engagement is a positive attitude that employees have towards their work.

2. Engaged employees are involved in their work, not simply going through the motions.

3. Engagement is closely related to well-being: sometimes it is considered an antecedent of well-being, and sometimes an integral part of well-being by virtue of its relationship with providing a 'sense of meaning' in work.

But we can gain a clearer understanding of what engagement is all about by comparing it to two related states, namely burnout and workaholism.

## Engagement, burnout and workaholism

Engagement and burnout are generally seen as opposite poles of workers' well-being, described as the extent to which work 'activates' them and how much they identify with their work (Schaufeli et al., 2002). In addition, there is the element of professional efficacy: engaged employees feel absorbed in their work, while those suffering from burnout tend to feel ineffective. Table 11.2 illustrates how engagement and burnout differ.

### Table 11.2 Engagement and burnout compared

| Dimension | Engagement (Schaufeli et al., 2002) | Burnout (Schutte et al., 2000) |
|---|---|---|
| Activation | Vigour: high levels of energy and resilience, invests effort in work and persists when faced with difficulties | Exhaustion: feelings of being overextended and drained |
| Identification | Dedication: a sense of the significance of one's work, enthusiasm and pride in work | Cynicism: indifference and a distant attitude to work |
| Efficacy | Absorption: fully concentrated on work and happily engrossed in it, finding that time passes quickly and being unable to detach from the job | Low professional efficacy: a sense of being less competent than others, reduced confidence in own abilities at work |

While activation and identification seem to be the essential elements of burnout, low professional efficacy may develop as part of decreased engagement in work (Schaufeli et al., 2008). Work engagement, therefore, can be defined as a 'positive, fulfilling work-related state of mind', which characterizes employees who are active, take the initiative and seek out new challenges. Rather than being limited to a specific task or time, it is a persistent state of mind, overarching and pervasive through work experience.

If engagement involves such dedication to work, how can it be distinguished from workaholism, or the compulsion that some people feel to work all the time? Engagement and workaholism are both associated with long working hours and commitment to the organization, but are, of course, different in terms of their longer term outcomes and health impacts. While engagement is associated with good physical health and positive job satisfaction, burnout and workaholism are associated with poor health and low job satisfaction (Schaufeli et al., 2008). The In the News feature explores the influence of technology on workaholism.

Although we might all be familiar with the idea of 'burnout' – a feeling of being exhausted by work and generally dissatisfied with the work and our efforts – there is sometimes a misconception that burnout only affects 'high-flyers' or people who work all the time. In fact, burnout was first identified in the early 1980s by researchers working with human services professionals, people whose jobs required intense involvement with other people, dealing with their problems and emotions (Maslach and Jackson, 1981). These types of jobs included teachers, social workers and nurses. Workers who were experiencing burnout provided poorer care, had lower morale and were more likely to be absent or leave the job – serious problems for the employer to deal with. In addition, they reported distress in their personal lives, including insomnia and problems in the family. Since then, further research has demonstrated that people can experience burnout in a wide range of different occupations (Schutte et al., 2000).

In addition, Schaufeli et al. (2008) have shown that one of the main differences between burnout/workaholism and engagement is the relative importance given to non-work life and the quality of social relations. While workaholics focus all their energies on work to the exclusion of family, friends and the rest of life, engaged employees are engaged in *all* of life. Engagement, burnout and workaholism can be seen as related *kinds* of employee well-being, with workaholism perhaps being a root cause of burnout. Both are associated with high job demands and low job resources, meaning that it is likely that workaholics use up all their resources until they are exhausted and 'burned out'. Engaged employees, on the other hand, can draw on a wide range of resources to meet the demands of their jobs. Job resources seem to be particularly important for engagement (Le Blanc et al., 2008) and we move on to consider this in more detail now.

## In the News: Technology and workaholism

Because technology such as smartphones and laptops means that people can increasingly take their work home with them, the lines between 'work' and 'home' are increasingly blurring. For some people, that can be a good thing. Traci Fiatte, group president at Randstad US, for example, likes to check her emails on a Sunday evening to prepare for the coming week, while others enjoy the sense of importance they get from having the boss email them late at night (Rayasam, 2016).

For other people, though, the sense of being 'always on' can be a real strain, especially where it is seen as an obligation rather than a way to take personal control of the work. In fact, some research indicates that workaholism may be related to mental illnesses, including attention deficit hyperactivity disorder, obsessive-compulsive disorder, anxiety and depression (Andreassen et al., 2016). For these people, working is a way to combat feelings of guilt or anxiety rather than a source of enjoyment or sense of accomplishment.

Fiatte noticed this and realized that not everyone in her company was viewing the flexibility provided by technology as a positive thing. Instead, many felt that leaving the company would be the only way to have a personal life, because Fiatte's example made them think this would be impossible if they stayed. So Fiatte has changed how she works so that she and the other managers now make it clear when things are urgent and when not (Rayasam, 2016). They still work when they want but there is no implicit assumption that emails must be answered immediately.

ComStock

## For discussion

» Do you think that technology has increased people's workaholic tendencies?

» What practical steps could managers take to enhance the positive benefits of technology while avoiding the pressures of increased workaholism?

## Job demands-resources model

*The job demands-resources (JD-R) model* (see Figure 11.2) was first put forward by Demerouti et al. (2001) and has since gathered substantial research support. It captures the positive and negative aspects of stress and shows how they are related to job demands (such as workload and pressure) and job resources (such as feedback and participation). Job demands are those things that are challenging to us at work, while the resources are those things we can draw on to help deal with challenges. The model proposes two processes:

- **Health impairment:** high job demands deplete our energy and lead to burnout

- **Motivational:** high job resources enhance our motivation and increase engagement.

These processes do not simply add together, but interact in such a way that high demands combined with low resources lead to much *more* exhaustion than we would expect from the main effects alone.

Bakker and Demerouti (2007, p. 312) define job demands as the aspects of a job that 'require sustained physical and/or psychological effort or skills'. Remember that demands are not necessarily negative in themselves, but they can become stressors if we are not able to recover adequately from them. Resources are the aspects of a job that help us to achieve work goals, reduce the demands experienced (or reduce the cost of those demands on the individual) and/or stimulate our personal growth and development. Job resources can be present at many different levels:

- **Organizational:** career opportunities or job security

- **Interpersonal and social relations:** support from co-workers or supervisor, good team climate

- **Job role:** clarity on role, involvement in decision-making

- **Task:** skill variety, task identity, significance.

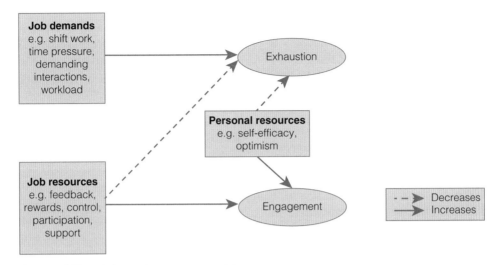

*Figure 11.2 The job demands-resources model*

Source: Adapted from Xanthopoulou, D., Bakker, A. B., Demerouti, E. and Schaufeli, W. B. (2007) 'The role of personal resources in the job demands-resources model', *International Journal of Stress Management*, 14(2), pp. 121–41 Copyright © 2007 by the American Psychological Association.

There is also a place for our 'personal resources' in mitigating the negative effects of job demands and enhancing the effects of job resources. Personal resources include individual differences in our levels of resilience and the sense of control we have over our environment. The role of personal resources is fairly complex. Not only do they mediate the relationship between job resources and engagement or exhaustion, but they also influence our perceptions of the job resources themselves (Xanthopoulou et al., 2007). Employees with greater personal resources tend to be able to identify more job resources.

Finally, the model also shows how having plentiful resources can buffer the effects of high job demands. The JD-R model provides us with an integrative understanding of stress, well-being and engagement at work. It recognizes that the demands and resources will vary across different occupations and industries but shows how the specifics of different situations can still be brought together in a coherent explanation of how positive and negative well-being results from the interaction between the job context and the individual worker. The Transferrable Skills activity uses this model to help you develop your skills in enhancing your own and others' engagement.

 ## Transferrable Skills: Enhancing engagement

We have seen in this chapter how the concepts of well-being and engagement are closely intertwined, and this is reflected in HRM practice too. Many well-being programmes are developed with the specific aim of enhancing employee engagement (Sutton et al., 2016). But too often, these programmes use a scattergun approach, that is, the people tasked with developing the well-being programmes just pick a random assortment of benefits or training and development that they think will help to improve employee well-being. However, if we choose elements of a well-being programme based on a model that is supported by research, we can be more confident of gaining the results we want. In this activity, we are going to

use the JD-R model as a basis for developing your own personal well-being programme. If you are not currently in work, you can do this activity while thinking about your 'job' as a student.

1. Develop a list of all the demands you currently experience. These can be mental, emotional or physical and remember that they are not necessarily negative in and of themselves. Instead, they are aspects of the work that require you to make a sustained effort and that you may need to recover from.

2. Write a list of all the resources you can currently draw on. You will probably find that many of these are motivational aspects of your work:

good relationships with colleagues or opportunities for learning and development. These aspects of work can either buffer the effects of the demands or help you to recover from them.

3. Make a note of the personal resources available to you. This could include your self-efficacy beliefs (how much you believe you can succeed in specific tasks or challenges), optimism or resilience. Because personal resources can influence the extent to which we even feel able to identify job resources, it may be worth considering whether you could start by developing your own personal resources. Many organizations take this approach, for example offering training and development activities to increase resilience.

Bring together your analysis of your demands and resources by drawing up a plan to reduce job demands and develop job resources. You can draw on the evidence on interventions to manage stress and well-being provided in this chapter for ideas. This will work best if you choose just one or two demands or resources to focus on at a time. For example, if you find that you are low on social connection or support, you can start to develop a support network. Make sure that you identify clear and specific steps in the plan rather than vague or general outlines. Developing a support network takes time, so could be broken down into specific steps such as: identifying people's key skills so that you know where to go for advice or help, identifying your own strengths and being willing to offer help should a colleague need it, spending time with colleagues even when not specifically related to the job, and thanking people and showing appreciation.

After a month, take some time to re-evaluate your position. As part of this, make sure that you recognize the progress you have made: this will help to develop your own feelings of self-efficacy and enhance your personal resources. This kind of activity can help you to deal with the demands of work as well as increase your motivation by identifying the positive resources of your job. It can also be 'scaled up' to develop a well-being or engagement programme for a whole organization.

 ## Practice Insights: Ginger Chen

Ginger Chen is a Senior Manager in the Human Resources Department at Cigna, a life and health insurance company in Taipei, Taiwan. In the video, Ginger talks about the key role of employee engagement in promoting performance and motivation, giving examples of how she and her team work to improve engagement at the corporate and team level.

Go online to www.macmillanihe.com/sutton-people to access the interview with Ginger.

# SUMMARY

By understanding the role of physical health and safety and the more holistic concept of well-being at work, we can work towards building safer and more fulfilling workplaces. We have seen in this chapter that managers and organizations take a range of approaches in addressing these issues, ranging from basic compliance with legal requirements through to complex and detailed programmes to build well-being and engagement at work. Differentiating between engagement and burnout helps us to recognize the contributions of work demands and resources to workplace performance. Managers who can increase the work resources can potentially enhance employees' engagement and thereby their efficacy and performance.

# FURTHER READING

- For a case study evaluation of a well-being programme developed to try and improve employee engagement, see Sutton, A., Evans, M., Davies, C. and Lawson, C. (2016) 'The development and longitudinal evaluation of a wellbeing programme: an organisation case study', *International Journal of Wellbeing*, 6(1), pp. 180–95.

- The discussion of the Gallup studies on engagement and business outcomes is a good read: Harter, J. K., Schmidt, F. L. and Keyes, C. L. M. (2002) 'Well-being in the workplace and its relationship to business outcomes: a review of the Gallup studies', in C. L. Keyes and J. Haidt (eds) *Flourishing: The Positive Person and the Good Life.*

# REVIEW QUESTIONS

1. To what extent do you think organizations should take responsibility for their employees' health and well-being?

2. What practical steps can managers take to manage stress at work?

3. Why do you think so many organizations are trying to develop employee engagement?

# ONLINE RESOURCES

Go online to www.macmillanihe.com/sutton-people to access a MCQ quiz for this chapter and for further resources to support your learning.

# REFERENCES

Aked, J., Marks, N., Cordon, C. and Thompson, S. (2008) *Five Ways to Wellbeing*. London: The New Economics Foundation. Available at: www.neweconomics.org/publications/entry/five-ways-to-well-being-the-evidence.

Alli, B. O. (2008) *Fundamental Principles of Occupational Health and Safety*, 2nd edn. Geneva: International Labour Office.

Andreassen, C. S., Griffiths, M. D., Sinha, R. et al. (2016) 'The relationships between workaholism and symptoms of psychiatric disorders: a large-scale cross-sectional study', *PLoS ONE*, 11(5), pp. 1–19. doi: 10.1371/journal.pone.0152978.

Armstrong, M. and Taylor, S. (2014) *Handbook of Human Resource Management*. 13th edn. London: Kogan Page.

Arthur, A. R. (2000) 'Employee assistance programmes: The emperor's new clothes of stress management?', *British Journal of Guidance and Counselling*, 28(4), pp. 549–59. doi: 10.1080/03069880020004749.

Bakker, A. B. and Demerouti, E. (2007) 'The job demands-resources model: state of the art', *Journal of Managerial Psychology*, 22(3), pp. 309–28.

Bao, S., Winkel, J. and Shahnavaz, H. (2000) 'Prevalence of musculoskeletal disorders at workplaces in the People's Republic of China.', *International Journal of Occupational Safety and Ergonomics*, 6(4), pp. 557–74. doi: 10.1080/10803548.2000.11076472.

Beasley, M., Thompson, T. and Davidson, J. (2003) 'Resilience in response to life stress: the effects of coping style and cognitive hardiness', *Personality and Individual Differences*, 34(1), 77–95.

Bonanno, G. A. (2004) 'Loss, truama, and human resilience: Have we underestimated the human capacity to thrive after extremely adverse events?', *American Psychologist*, 59(1), 20–8. https://doi.org/10.1037/0003-066X.59.1.20.

Bonanno, G. A., Papa, A. and O'Neill, K. (2001) 'Loss and human resilience', *Applied and Preventive Psychology*, 10(3), 193–206.

Buckley, P. (2015) *Work-related Musculoskeletal Disorder (WRMSDs) Statistics, Great Britain, 2015*. Available at: www.hse.gov.uk/statistics/index.htm.

Burke, J. (2013) 'Bangladeshi workers still missing eight months after Rana Plaza collapse', *The Guardian*, 25 December. Available at: www.theguardian.com/world/2013/dec/25/bangladesh-workers-missing-rana-plaza.

Butler, S. (2014) 'Primark to pay £6m more to victims of Rana Plaza factory in Bangladesh', *The Guardian*, 16 March. Available at: www.theguardian.com/world/2014/mar/16/primark-payout-victims-rana-plaza-bangladesh.

Cannon, W. B. (1929) *Bodily Changes in Pain, Hunger, Fear and Rage*. London: Appleton.

Cartwright, S. and Cooper, C. L. (1997) *Managing Workplace Stress*. London: Sage.

Demerouti, E., Bakker, A. B., Nachreiner, F. and Schaufeli, W. B. (2001) 'The job demands-resources model of burnout', *Journal of Applied Psychology*, 86(3), 499–512. https://doi.org/10.1108/02683940710733115.

EU-OSHA, Hassard, J., Teoh, K. et al. (2014) *Calculating the Cost of Work-related Stress and Psychosocial Risks*. EU-OSHA European Agency for Safety and Health at Work. doi: 10.2802/20493.

European Agency for Safety and Health at Work (2010) *Workplace Violence and Harassment: A European Picture*. Luxembourg: Publications Office of the European Union. doi: 10.2802/12198.

Folkman, S. and Lazarus, R. S. (1988) 'The relationship between coping and emotion: implications for theory and research', *Social Science & Medicine*, 26(3), pp. 309–17.

Folkman, S., Lazarus, R. S., Dunkel-Schetter, C. et al. (1986) 'Dynamics of a stressful encounter: cognitive appraisal, coping, and encounter outcomes', *Journal of Personality and Social Psychology*, 50(5), pp. 992–1003.

Giga, S. I., Cooper, C. L. and Faragher, B. (2003) 'The development of a framework for a comprehensive approach to stress management interventions at work', *International Journal of Stress Management*, 10(4), pp. 280–96.

Gilmore, S. and Williams, S. (2009) *Human Resource Management*. Oxford: Oxford University Press.

Hamer, M., Taylor, A. and Steptoe, A. (2006) 'The effect of acute aerobic exercise on stress related blood pressure responses: a systematic review and meta-analysis', *Biological Psychology*, 71(2), 183–90.

Harter, J. K., Schmidt, F. L. and Hayes, T. L. (2002a) 'Business-unit-level relationship between employee satisfaction, employee engagement, and business outcomes: a meta-analysis', *Journal of Applied Psychology*, 87(2), pp. 268–79.

Harter, J. K., Schmidt, F. L. and Keyes, C. L. M. (2002b) 'Well-being in the workplace and its relationship to business outcomes: a review of the Gallup studies', in C. L. Keyes and J. Haidt (eds) *Flourishing: The Positive Person and the Good Life*. Washington, DC: American Psychological Association, pp. 205–24.

Harvey, S. B., Hotopf, M., Øverland, S. and Mykletun, A. (2010) 'Physical activity and common mental disorders', *British Journal of Psychiatry*, 197(5), pp. 357–364. doi: 10.1192/bjp.bp.109.075176.

Health and Safety Executive (2015) *Violence at Work Statistics*. Available at: www.hse.gov.uk/statistics/causinj/violence/index.htm (Accessed 24 October 2016).

Health and Safety Executive (2016) *Work-related Violence*. Available at: www.hse.gov.uk/violence/ (Accessed 24 October 2016).

Health and Safety Executive (2017a) *Security and Protective Services: Police Officers*. Available at: www.hse.gov.uk/violence/hslcasestudies/police.htm (Accessed 11 May 2017).

Health and Safety Executive (2017b) *Case Study 1: Student Loans Company (SLC)*. Available at: www.hse.gov.uk/violence/verbal-abuse/slc.htm (Accessed 11 May 2017).

Johnson, J. V. and Hall, E. M. (1988) 'Job strain, work place social support, and cardiovascular disease: a cross-sectional study of a random sample of the Swedish working population', *American Journal of Public Health*, 78(10), pp. 1336–42.

Kasperkevic, J. (2016) 'Rana Plaza collapse: workplace dangers persist three years later, reports find', *The Guardian*, 31 May. Available at: www.theguardian.com/business/2016/may/31/rana-plaza-bangladesh-collapse-fashion-working-conditions.

Kobasa, S. C. (1979) 'Stressful life events, personality, and health: an inquiry into hardiness', *Journal of Personality and Social Psychology*, 37(1), pp. 1–11.

Le Blanc, P., de Jonge, J. and Schaufeli, W. B. (2008) 'Job stress and occupational health', in N. Chmiel (ed.) *An Introduction to Work and Organizational Psychology: A European Perspective*. Oxford: Blackwell, pp. 119–48.

Lee, I.-M., Shiroma, E. J., Lobelo, F. et al. (2012) 'Effect of physical inactivity on major non-communicable diseases worldwide: an analysis of burden of disease and life expectancy', *Lancet*, 380(9838), pp. 219–29. doi: 10.1016/S0140-6736(12)61031-9.

Luyendijk, J. (2013) 'Former M&A banker: "A lot of them just need a hug"', *The Guardian*, 2 May. Available at: www.theguardian.com/commentisfree/joris-luyendijk-banking-blog/2013/may/02/former-banker-hug-woman-global-bank.

Maddi, S. R. and Kobasa, S. C. (1984) *The Hardy Executive: Health under Stress*. Homewood, IL: Dow Jones-Irwin.

Maslach, C. and Jackson, S. E. (1981) 'The measurement of experienced burnout', *Journal of Occupational Behaviour*, 2(2), pp. 99–113. doi: 10.2307/3000281.

Morrison, R. and Nolan, T. (2007) 'Too much of a good thing? Difficulties with workplace friendships', *University of Auckland Business Review*, 9(2), pp. 33–41. doi: 10.1038/nbt0901-811a.

Nenonen, N., Saarela, K. L., Takala, J. et al. (2010) *Global Estimates of Occupational Accidents and Fatal Work-Related Diseases in 2014*. Singapore: Workplace Safety & Health Institute. Available at: www.wshi.gov.sg/ObservatoryWSH-Landscape/Research-Report.html.

Organ, D. W. (1988) *Organizational Citizenship Behavior: The Good Soldier Syndrome*. Lexington, MA: Lexington Books.

Ozer, E. J., Best, S. R., Lipsey, T. L. and Weiss, D. S. (2003) 'Predictors of posttraumatic stress disorder and symptoms in adults: a meta-analysis', *Psychological Bulletin*, 129(1), 52–73.

Pulsford, R. M., Stamatakis, E., Britton, A. R. et al. (2015) 'Associations of sitting behaviours with all-cause mortality over a 16-year follow-up: the Whitehall II study', *International Journal of Epidemiology*, 44(6), pp. 1909–16. doi: 10.1093/ije/dyv191.

Quakers in the World (2016) *Quakers in Action*. Available at: www.quakersintheworld.org/quakers-in-action/263 (Accessed 23 October 2016).

Quick, J. C., Quick, J. D., Nelson, D. L. and Hurrell Jr, J. J. (1997) *Preventive Stress Management in Organizations*. Washington, DC: American Psychological Association.

Rayasam, R. (2016) 'The upside to being always-on for work'. Available at: www.bbc.com/capital/story/20161006-the-upside-to-being-always-on-for-work (Accessed 23 December 2016).

Richardson, K. M. and Rothstein, H. R. (2008) 'Effects of occupational stress management intervention programs: a meta-analysis', *Journal of Occupational Health Psychology*, 13(1), pp. 69–93.

Riordan, C. M. and Griffeth, R. W. (1995) 'The opportunity for friendship in the workplace: an underexplored construct', *Journal of Business and Psychology*, 10(2), pp. 141–54. Available at: www.jstor.org/stable/25092498.

Robertson, I. T. and Cooper, C. L. (2010) 'Full engagement: the integration of employee engagement and psychological well-being', *Leadership and Organization Development Journal*, 31(4), pp. 324–36. doi: 10.1108/01437731011043348.

Schaufeli, W. B., Taris, T. W. and van Rhenen, W. (2008) 'Workaholism, burnout, and work engagement: Three of a kind or three different kinds of employee well-being?', *Applied Psychology*, 57(2), pp. 173–203.

Schaufeli, W. B., Salanova, M., González-Romá, V. and Bakker, A. B. (2002) 'The measurement of engagement and burnout: a two sample confirmatory factor analytic approach', *Journal of Happiness Studies*, 3(1), pp. 71–92.

Schulte, P. and Vainio, H. (2010) 'Well-being at work: overview and perspective', *Scandinavian Journal of Work, Environment & Health*, 36(5), pp. 422–9. doi: 10.5271/sjweh.3076.

Schutte, N., Toppinen, S., Kalimo, R. and Schaufeli, W. (2000) 'The factorial validity of the Maslach Burnout Inventory-General Survey (MBI-GS) across occupational groups and nations', *Journal of Occupational and Organizational Psychology*, 73(1), pp. 53–66. doi: 10.1348/096317900166877.

Selye, H. (1956) *The Stress of Life*. New York: McGraw-Hill.

Selye, H. (1973) 'The evolution of the stress concept', *American Scientist*, 61(6), pp. 692–99. Available at: www.jstor.org/stable/27844072.

Sousa-Poza, A. and Sousa-Poza, A. A. (2000) 'Well-being at work: a cross-national analysis of the levels and determinants of job satisfaction', *Journal of Socio-Economics*, 29(6), pp. 517–38.

Sutton, A., Evans, M., Davies, C. and Lawson, C. (2016) 'The development and longitudinal evaluation of a wellbeing programme: an organisation case study', *International Journal of Wellbeing*, 6(1), pp. 180–95. doi: 10.5502/ijw.v6i1.487.

Truss, C., Shantz, A., Soane, E. et al. (2013) 'Employee engagement, organisational performance and individual well-being: exploring the evidence, developing the theory', *International Journal of Human Resource Management*, 24(14), pp. 2657–69. doi: 10.1080/09585192.2013.798921.

UK EAPA (2011) *Employee Assistance Programmes: A Buyer's Guide*. Available at: www.eapa.org.uk/wp-content/uploads/2014/02/UK-EAPA-BUYERS-GUIDE.pdf.

Virgin Pulse (2016) *State of the Industry: Employee Well-Being, Culture and Engagement in 2017*. Available at: http://community.virginpulse.com/state-of-the-industry-2017-es.

Waddell, G. and Burton, A. K. (2006) *Is Work Good for your Health and Well-being?* London: TSO.

Warr, P. (1990) 'The measurement of well-being and other aspects of mental health', *Journal of Occupational Psychology*, 63, pp. 193–210.

Witter, D. and Agrawal, S. (2015) 'Well-being enhances benefits of employee engagement', *Gallup Business Journal*. Available at: www.gallup.com/businessjournal/186386/enhances-benefits-employee-engagement.aspx.

Xanthopoulou, D., Bakker, A. B., Demerouti, E. and Schaufeli, W. B. (2007) 'The role of personal resources in the job demands-resources model', *International Journal of Stress Management*, 14(2), pp. 121–41. doi: 10.1037/1072-5245.14.2.121.

# 12 FUTURE-PROOF WORKPLACES

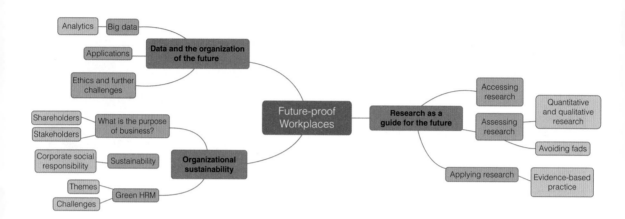

## INTRODUCTION

We have regularly come across the notion of organizational survival in this book and it seems that it is becoming increasingly difficult to build long-lasting companies. Foster (2012) found that the average 'lifespan' of large companies decreased from 61 years in 1958 to 25 years in 1980 and 18 years in 2012. He suggested that the main reason for this is that companies stick to the patterns and course that brought success in the first place and fail to evolve.

In this chapter, we will discuss how we can build and sustain organizations into the future. We look at this from two different directions. The first factor contributing to future-proofing our organizations is making use of data analytics and research to guide decisions about future directions. Effective management and utilization of 'big data' is increasingly important for organizations wishing to improve their decision-making while cutting-edge research provides new knowledge, ideas

and practical recommendations for managerial practice and processes. We will see how the ability to understand and apply analytics and research findings is an essential component of evidence-based management and professional practice, and helps to ensure that the organization is developing in appropriate directions and not repeating the mistakes of the past.

Second, we consider what it means to have a sustainable organization, that is, one that can sustain its activities over the long term. The basic question we need to answer here is what the organization exists for. This determines our measures of success and, ultimately, whether the organization will continue to survive. We will see how 'green' HRM emphasizes the organization and its people as an integral part of the natural environment and can guide the organization towards a sustainable future.

*Getty Images/iStockphoto/Thinkstock/Jacob Wackerhausen*

## LEARNING FEATURES

Applications: HR information systems

Applications: Research implications

Applications: Greening HRM

Weighing the Evidence: A shareholder view in the public sector?

Web Explorer: Inspirational management talks

In the News: Paid parental leave

Transferrable Skills: Reading original research

Practice Insights: Lara Montefiori

 Video overview

*Julian Perkins*

Go online to www.macmillanihe.com/sutton-people to access a video of Anna Sutton introducing the chapter's main themes.

# DATA AND THE ORGANIZATION OF THE FUTURE

In Chapter 10 we discussed the importance of knowledge management and organizational learning. Closely allied with regard to future-proofing the organization is the key challenge of how the organization manages, analyses and utilizes all its data. Modern technology has resulted in an exponential increase in the scope of the challenge and the opportunity here: first, in making more and more data available and, second, in providing sophisticated ways to analyse that data. In this section we will explore these two elements in turn, as well as consider some of the applications and ethical issues that need to be addressed.

## Big data

Diebold (2003) defined **big data** as the increase in the availability and quantity of data that resulted from technological advances in data storage and recording, and Church and Dutta (2013, p. 24) widened this definition to consider big data as a 'concept, approach, or way of thinking about massive amounts of information and the outcomes that can be achieved by integrating that data'. One of the first interventions to establish the practical effectiveness of using big data to link employee, customer and financial outcomes was at the US department store chain Sears. Analysts here developed a model that demonstrated how a 4% increase in employee satisfaction would increase customer satisfaction by a similar amount, and predicted that this would result in an increase of $200 million in revenue (Rucci et al., 1998).

Big data gives the organization access to whole areas of information that were previously unavailable to it, for example the time someone spends on social media and how they interact on the various platforms, the type of language they use when talking about the organization, or how frequently they conduct job searches. The potential of big data is that it more closely approaches and represents the real world we live in, and therefore gives managers the opportunity to analyse the complexities of our interactions, attitudes and so on in predicting organizationally relevant outcomes, such as job turnover, engagement and performance.

Church and Dutta (2013) describe a four-level model for how big data can provide a more integrated and data-driven basis for organizational change initiatives:

- **Level 1:** The individual level consists of information drawn from, for example, employee engagement surveys.

- **Level 2:** Combines individual-level data with operational metrics, such as team performance, telling us whether a more engaged team provides better customer service.

- **Level 3:** Integrates this data even further with organization-level metrics and trends, such as organizational change impacts.

- **Level 4:** All this data is combined with a huge variety of other forms of data from national labour force participation rates to individual browsing trends.

Ultimately, the strategic aim of using big data is simply to make better informed, data-driven organizational decisions (McAbee et al., 2017).

## Analytics

Analysing and making sense of big data is often referred to as the discipline of **'analytics'**, which is described as an essential capability in the modern business world (CIPD and Oracle, 2013). There are several issues that can reduce the HR function's ability to use analytics effectively, including structural barriers that prevent timely sharing and use of data and information, lack of appropriate skills in IT and analysis, personal scepticism about its usefulness when dealing with people decisions, or concern that it may reduce people to numbers. This latter concern is echoed by Angrave et al. (2016), who note that the current trend towards using big data analytics in HR-related decisions serves to bolster engineering or finance perspectives on people management, which tend to reduce people issues to numbers. Rather than strengthening the role of HR professionals at board level, this could, in fact, undermine their efforts to introduce a more nuanced view of human issues. Angrave et al. go further and suggest that analytics could even have a negative impact on employee well-being if it focuses exclusively on short-term financial gains.

For HR professionals to make good use of big data and analytics (Angrave et al., 2016), they need to ensure that they:

1. Have a strategic understanding of how their human capital contributes to success in their specific organization, rather than relying on general models or generic strategies.

2. Understand the context within which the data was gathered so that meaningful metrics can be developed.

3. Use the data to identify key groups of employees who have a significant impact on the organization, that is, talent segments.

4. Use careful analysis to determine how the people inputs influence organizational performance.

A 'Human Resource Information System' (HRIS), a specialist software package, can help the HR function to achieve these ends. A HRIS is the integration of HRM with IT: it not only collects data on employees and manages policies and procedures but also distributes the information to relevant stakeholders. The Applications box explores some of the considerations and implications of implementing these kinds of packages.

 Applications: **HR information systems**

Devan is an HR director in a large manufacturing company, who is keen to demonstrate the value that HR brings to the business, and to find a more integrated way of managing all the HR data around selection, **workforce planning**, performance management and so on. She knows that given her organization's focus on engineering and production, data-driven decisions are more convincing than those based on intuition or subjective impressions, so she thinks that an integrated software solution may be the way to provide the kind of detailed data and analytics to convince her fellow directors in making people decisions. She has tasked you, as a member of the HR team, to evaluate the various HR information systems that are available with a view to recommending one for the company to invest in. Ideally, she would like a solution that can integrate with the rest of the organization's data and is prepared to make a strong case to the board if there is a solution that would benefit the whole organization and not just the HR department.

» Do some research to explore the different options of software packages available in your country. What are the advantages and disadvantages to each option?

» Which is your preferred option? Why?

» If your recommendation was accepted by the board, what would be the implications for HR? For example, would employees need training on the system, how would it be rolled out, and would experts need to be recruited in order to utilize and maintain the system properly?

The effective analysis of big data can help organizations in a number of ways. Organizations can identify past trends and predict future changes, find patterns among different variables, and increase the objectivity of decision-making (Lipkin, 2015). When it comes to manipulating the data and drawing conclusions, there are three main analytical methods, which provide different kinds of information for decision-makers, illustrated in Figure 12.1 overleaf.

Because these skills, previously often the domain of researchers, are now so essential to management and HR practice, McAbee et al. (2017) have called for all students of HRM and OB to be trained in statistical techniques.

## Applications

One of the advantages of big data is that it can help organizations and practitioners to make connections between pieces of data that may previously have seemed unrelated. For example, people who used a web browser that had to be specially installed rather than the default pre-installed browser on their computer performed better in their jobs and changed jobs less often, perhaps because they took the time to make more informed decisions (*The Economist*, 2013).

Selection is an emerging area of big data application and many different approaches are

| Descriptive | Provide information |
|---|---|
| | • Help understand the business as it is now or has been in the past<br>• Skills needed: ability to understand and utilize basic statistics, and knowledge of which questions are particularly relevant to the organization, e.g. how do current workforce demographics compare to 20 years ago? |
| Predictive | Provide insights |
| | • Help the business to anticipate the future by using statistical models to forecast and predict future possibilities<br>• Skills needed: ability to understand and utilize complex statistical modelling, skills in interpreting statistical results, and understanding what they mean in the context of the organization and wider society, e.g. how might workforce demographics change, given current trends in wider society, and what kind of effect might this have on organization-level training needs? |
| Prescriptive | Provide evaluation |
| | • Help the business to test decisions in order to determine their impact<br>• Skills needed: ability to construct well-designed pieces of research, collect and analyse appropriate data, and then draw conclusions and evaluations from the results, e.g. how does increasing the diversity of a customer service team impact on customer satisfaction? |

Figure 12.1 Basic analytical methods and the skills needed to engage effectively with them

being trialled. For example, information from social networking sites is being used for targeted recruitment drives or to screen applicants (McAbee et al., 2017). Analysis of information from email or social networks can help to build a picture of an individual's or group's communication networks; this kind of social network analysis has been used in studies of diversity and inclusion at work as well as leadership emergence (McAbee et al., 2017). Some of the insights that big data can generate provide a useful balance to the normal, stereotyped decisions often used in selection. For example, people with a criminal background, who are often filtered out at the early stages of the selection process, were found to perform better in customer service roles than those without (*The Economist*, 2013).

Another burgeoning area in the use of big data in selection is adopting 'gamification' in the selection process. Gamification uses elements from game design in non-game contexts, making the service or product feel more like a game and eliciting similar psychological responses to those we have when playing a game, such as motivation (Hamari et al., 2014). A specially developed game can provide

hundreds if not thousands of pieces of data, which can be used to measure anything from problem-solving ability through to personality traits such as competitiveness and team focus. The Practice Insights video interview for this chapter explores this exciting new area in more detail.

Big data can also be used for training and development applications. For example, analysis could identify which types of instruction or training design were most effective for different individuals and use a collection of individual, contextual and organizational variables to predict the best ways to develop each employee's skills and abilities (McAbee et al., 2017). The inclusion of social media in an organization's analytics also provides the opportunity to increase engagement and provide opportunities for peer-to-peer learning (James, 2014).

Other sources of data the organization might use in developing models to improve productivity or other important outcomes can include location data from company-provided mobile phones or information from wearable tech that tracks employee movements. Some companies are even using sensors in ID badges or on office furniture to indicate how long an employee spends at their desk or in particular buildings. This level of monitoring raises the important issue of privacy and the ethical approach to using big data, which we move on to consider in more detail now.

## Ethics and further challenges

While having so much data available certainly provides organizations with substantial potential to gain insights and new knowledge, there are also challenges, which Laney (2001) referred to as the three Vs:

1.  **Volume:** the depth and breadth of data available to the organization has increased. For example, analysing thousands of comments on a blog by the CEO could provide valuable insights about the company's culture (Church and Dutta, 2013). In addition, all this data is considered an asset and organizations therefore wish to retain and store that information.

2.  **Velocity:** the speed with which information is exchanged (or transactions completed) has also increased, so that now it is not unusual for data speeds to be real time. Making use of this data requires dynamic analytical tools and systems.

3.  **Variety:** the types of data have also increased and they are often in incompatible formats, so that it becomes difficult for the organization to integrate and use them appropriately. For example, an organization may have data on internal employee databases, social network interactions and video blogs.

Church and Dutta (2013) add a fourth challenge: the *veracity* of the data. Especially where big data is used for critical business decisions, it is essential to evaluate the accuracy and reliability of the data that is gathered. Considered as a whole, Church and Dutta suggest that the main challenge facing organizations and practitioners is how to make use of all that data. The organization not only needs good systems to analyse the data but also people with the skills to make sense of the insights it generates.

In a review of the literature, Sivarajah et al. (2017) note three main challenges to the use of big data in organizations:

1.  **Data challenges:** characteristics of the data itself that can prevent effective use (e.g. the three Vs discussed above).

2.  **Process challenges:** how to utilize the data, for example how to store the data, integrate various forms of data and how to analyse and interpret them appropriately.

3.  **Management challenges:** includes issues such as privacy and security, data governance, information-sharing and costs.

Effectively navigating these challenges requires a substantial level of effort and expertise, so while big data has much potential, just like other knowledge management activities, its true effectiveness is only achieved with significant investment.

In all the excitement about big data, there is a risk that the individual employee may be reduced to a 'data point' and the human connection lost. For HR to utilize big data effectively, it needs to remain aware of this human element and balance the data-driven decision with people-centric considerations (Lipkin, 2015). As an example, allowing selection decisions to be purely data driven without a good understanding of the context of the data could introduce adverse impacts. A company might find a link between speed of promotion and ethnic origin and conclude that people from a certain ethnicity are more successful and should therefore be prioritized in recruitment. But this would not take account of other factors that might underlie this association, such as organizational cultural factors, embedded bias in promotion decisions, or simply a lack of a significant proportion of employees from other ethnic groups.

A second issue, perhaps particularly important to employee-relevant data is that the legal structures governing privacy of data vary significantly across different countries. This means that multinational corporations (MNCs) in particular need to be careful about transborder data flow (Harris, 2015), but smaller companies also need to be careful about where their data is stored especially if they use cloud services. The impact of changes in these legal requirements was illustrated in dramatic fashion in 2015 when, following revelations from Edward Snowden about the level of access US authorities had to individual data, the European Court of Justice determined that the USA no longer complied with EU regulations about the privacy rights of European citizens. This meant that the 'safe harbour' scheme, which had allowed US–EU data transfer, was invalidated and US companies were no longer allowed to import personal data from

Europe. Instead, individual companies now have to demonstrate that they are complying with EU regulations.

Finally, a repeated theme in the discussions of big data analytics is that no matter how extensive the data collected, it is the *interpretation* that provides the narrative and the basis for decision-making. While it can be tempting to see big data as the answer to everything, it does not, in and of itself, provide an answer to the question of *why*. Real-time analysis of employee interactions and language use may flag up a drop in morale and an increase in internet job searches, but the interpretation of causal factors still takes significant skills in analysis and interpretation. We therefore turn now to consider the wider role of research in HRM and OB.

on the context and application of the findings. Three main competencies are important in ensuring the effective utilization of research in organizations, which can be summarized as the three As: accessing, assessing and applying research, as shown in Figure 12.2.

## Accessing research

There are two main elements to accessing research: first, finding relevant research reports and, second, understanding them.

Traditionally, research has been published in specialist peer reviewed journals and access provided to individuals or institutions who pay for subscriptions. 'Peer reviewed' means that the article has been evaluated and reviewed by other experts in the field – usually two or more anonymous reviewers.

Figure 12.2 The three As of utilizing research

# RESEARCH AS A GUIDE FOR THE FUTURE

Having looked at the use of big data in enabling data-driven decisions, we now turn to consider how to integrate research findings effectively to ensure that the organization, and our own professional practice, is as future-proof as possible. In order to use research well, we need to have an understanding of how it is conducted and the choices that researchers have made when designing a study so that we can be clear

The aim of these reviews is to ensure that the theory, method, analysis and conclusions of the study meet basic scientific requirements. The advantage of a peer reviewed article is that it has gone through one stage of verification and checking before you read it, so you can have more confidence in the reliability of the findings. One of the drawbacks of original research articles, however, is that they can often use jargon-heavy, complex writing styles. The Transferrable Skills activity can help you develop your skills in understanding original research papers.

 Transferrable Skills: **Reading original research**

A key skill in developing your professional practice is understanding and interpreting original research appropriately. It is important to read original research for several reasons, including keeping up to date with the latest developments in your field, assessing the evidence base for the latest new ideas, ensuring that you are not promoting outdated or

even harmful practices, and to ensure that you are managing and developing people in the most effective ways possible.

To carry out this exercise, find a peer reviewed paper on a topic that interests you by using your library's journal databases. As a first step, make sure that your chosen paper reports on an original research study, as some may also be theoretical discussions or debates, which do not follow the same structure. Then work through the following steps, which will help you to develop your skills in reading and understanding original research.

1. Read the abstract a couple of times to get an overview of the study. Don't worry if you don't understand everything at this stage because abstracts often use jargon and dense language to get as much information as possible into a small number of words.

2. Now skim over the whole paper. At this stage, you do not need to know the details, but highlight or make notes of sections that seem particularly important.

3. Read the paper again, this time in detail. Original research papers tend to have a standard layout with four main sections, each of which addresses different questions. As you read, see if you can find the answers to these questions.

| Abstract | Provides a very concise summary of the research |
|---|---|
| Introduction or literature review | Why was this study done? What is the background to this research? What has been found before? Why is this topic considered interesting or important? |
| Methodology | How was the research carried out? Why did the authors choose to do it like this? |
| Findings | What did the authors find out? |
| Discussion/conclusions | How does this study add to our understanding of HRM or OB? Very often, this section also considers some of the implications of the findings for practice |

4. Write a summary of the paper in your own words, making sure you address the main issues of each section.

5. Building on the paper's discussion section, think of three or four ways you might be able to use the findings of this study in your own work, being aware of the limitations of the research.

As you gain practice in doing this, you may well find that a different method works better for you, so feel free to adapt the process to suit your own style.

Professional magazines are another good source of up-to-date research. Most professional bodies produce their own magazines, which are generally written in a more easily accessible style than peer reviewed journals, and often with a clear explanation of the practical implications of new research findings. Finally, direct contact with researchers working in relevant areas can also be a good source and has the added advantage that researcher-practitioner collaboration can result in more relevant, immediately applicable findings.

## Assessing research

One of the important questions we need to ask when reading research findings is: How reliable is this evidence? It can be tempting to think that anything published in an academic journal is true and that the authors' conclusions can be taken at face value. Unfortunately, this is not always the case. A recent study of academics in top AACSB-accredited US business schools found that the majority of them knew of members of the faculty who had engaged in research misconduct within the past year (Bedeian et al., 2010). Two types of misconduct were investigated:

1. **Fabrication, falsification and plagiarism:** such as selecting or withholding data to strengthen the findings, using another person's ideas without giving credit, and making up results

2. **Questionable research practices:** such as publishing the same data in more than one article, making up hypotheses after the data

is known, developing relationships with editors to help publication, and circumventing ethical requirements.

The second category of misconduct was more widespread than the first, but it is still disturbing that the majority of academic staff know of at least one person in their faculty who has engaged in these behaviours. This means that we have to develop our own critical awareness of the strengths and limitations of published research. We cannot ignore evidence because it 'might' be unreliable or incomplete, instead we need to use it in a 'conscientious, explicit and judicious way' (Briner, 2013, p. 14).

Briner (2013) suggests that we bear three things in mind when evaluating published research:

1. Journals have a bias towards publishing positive results because they are seen as advancing our knowledge, so negative relationships or null findings are less likely to be reported. This means, for example, that you may find plenty of evidence of a positive relationship between job satisfaction and performance simply because the studies finding the opposite do not get published.

2. Related to this, journals want to publish new and exciting studies and are therefore less likely to publish straightforward replications. This means that it can be difficult to tell if a finding is generalizable to other situations.

3. Although many research studies use statistics to tell us how significant a finding is, that does not tell us its *practical* significance: that is something practitioners are best placed to evaluate.

Evidence-based practitioners will make their own informed decisions based on the evidence collected from several sources and their judgements about its quality and reliability. And it is only by knowing how research is conducted that we can make those informed decisions, which is why we now move on to consider research design.

## Quantitative and qualitative research

The criteria we use to evaluate the quality of a piece of research will vary depending on the kind of data the research has collected. Quantitative data is anything that can be expressed in numbers, while qualitative data uses text or speech, or sometimes even images and more abstract data such as movement or interaction. Both are useful in different ways. For example, if we want to find out how engagement and performance are related, each approach will give us different information. A quantitative approach could measure engagement and performance in numbers by asking participants to complete questionnaires where they rate the frequency of certain behaviours or the strength of certain feelings on a scale. We could then compare whether greater engagement was related to higher performance. A qualitative approach, on the other hand, might involve interviewing employees and asking them about their own understandings and experiences of engagement and performance. We could then draw out themes from the interviews to make suggestions for how the two concepts are related.

*Getty Images/PhotoAlto/Vincent Hazat*

*Questionnaires are a popular method of data collection.*

Quantitative research should aim to meet three quality criteria:

1. **Reliability:** determines how replicable the research is. Another researcher should be able to repeat the study using the same measures and procedures and gain similar results. It is important that researcher and participant bias is removed as much as possible.

2. **Validity:** the extent to which the research actually measured the concepts or relationships it claimed to. Partly this is down to having valid ways to measure the variables and partly how the results are analysed and interpreted. If the

research only showed an association, we should not assume causality.

3. **Generalizability:** the extent to which the findings can be applied in settings other than the one the research was conducted in. For example, can a study that took place in a small, family-run business be generalized to an MNC?

A quantitative approach can be useful because it helps us to make some fairly abstract concepts more concrete and applicable as well as enabling us to compare the differential effects of several variables. We could tell, for example, whether good working relationships with colleagues or level of pay is more important to employee job satisfaction. But many people would argue that to really understand what is happening in the complex, dynamic world of work, we need to use detailed, in-depth data that cannot be reduced to a number. Qualitative research focuses on our *socially constructed* reality, meaning that 'reality' is not some objective thing out there in the world that we can measure accurately, but is made up of our perceptions and interpretations. For example, it may not so much be the fact that we have lost our job that is important, but how each of us makes sense of that change that determines the outcomes. Qualitative research takes the individual's point of view seriously (Alvesson and Deetz, 2000) rather than trying to average out responses and find general laws of behaviour that fit everyone.

While quantitative research focuses on reliability, validity and generalizability as key criteria for assessing the quality of the work, there is some debate about how to evaluate qualitative research. This is partly because of the diversity of qualitative methods and analyses, which makes it difficult to develop a definitive list of criteria that every study could be evaluated against (Symon and Cassell, 2012). Tracy (2010), however, identified eight key markers of quality. Several of these can be applied equally well to quantitative research, including choosing a relevant and timely topic, or conducting research that encourages application by the audience and makes a significant contribution to our knowledge and practice. Research should also be conducted in an ethical manner and have a sense of coherence so that appropriate methods are used to address the goals. But three of Tracy's markers of quality are more exclusive to qualitative research:

1. **Rich rigour:** 'Rich' means that the data and the concepts are of the requisite variety and not oversimplified, that is, they are *at least as complex* as the phenomena being studied. But they must also be rigorous: using enough data to support the claims, ensuring that the study was conducted carefully and methodically, and that it meets the goals of the research.

2. **Sincerity:** The researcher should be self-reflexive, that is, able to articulate how their own values or approach to the topic may have influenced the findings. Sincerity can also be assured by having transparency in methodology.

3. **Credibility:** 'Show' rather than 'tell' the reader: provide enough detail and explanation about the findings that readers can come to their own conclusions. Part of credibility also involves gaining feedback from participants themselves on the results of the research.

Judging the quality of research, whether it uses a quantitative, qualitative or mixed approach is an essential element in understanding the extent to which the findings are relevant to our own organizational context, as well as the extent to which the findings should be incorporated into our decision-making. It is also a key skill in avoiding management fads, which we turn to consider now.

## Avoiding fads

Linstead et al. (2009) point out that, unlike other professions like doctors or lawyers, becoming a manager does not require any formal qualifications or expertise in 'management'. This often means that managers are looking for advice on how to deal with incredibly complex challenges but without applying a critical or reflective lens. Despite the complexity of management challenges, many people are attracted to the idea that there is a simple solution endorsed by a clearly successful manager. This gives rise to 'fads', that is, management ideas that have little evidence to back them up but become very popular, very quickly. Management consultants provide managers with techniques and tools that will supposedly help, while 'gurus' make millions a year from inspirational and motivational books and talks.

Fads can be defined by their life-cycles: ideas that quickly become popular stay popular for a short space of time (a few years in management circles) and then disappear quickly (Miller et al., 2004). In a study of management publications over a 15-year period, Miller et al. identified eight common properties of fads that managers can use to critically assess the new ideas they come across:

1. **Simple, straightforward:** the ideas are easy to communicate and make clear distinctions or describe ideal types and recommend simple solutions.

2. **Promising results:** they promise great results without any consideration of potential limitations or complexities.

3. **Universal:** the solutions will work for everyone, regardless of culture, type of organization or task, or individual differences.

4. **Step-down capability:** they can be implemented quickly and easily (and superficially), and do not require any great expenditure or changes.

5. **In tune with the zeitgeist:** fads are suited to current problems or trends and are in line with currently held values.

6. **Novel, not radical:** they look new and suggest novel ways of doing things but do not require any radical reassessment of underlying assumptions or practices. If you explore them further, you often find they are a repacking of old ideas.

7. **Legitimacy via gurus and star examples:** the evidence base is stories about 'successful' companies, supported by reference to role models and celebrity businesspeople. There is little or any empirical evidence.

8. **Lively, entertaining:** ideas are presented in a memorable and motivational way.

Having just one of these properties does not make an idea a fad, of course. It is more a matter of extent. Miller et al. (2004) found that fads had about 75% of these signs, whereas enduring management theories and models had only 25% of the signs. Miller et al. also note that fads are not without merit: they often have insightful and useful elements, but their quick decline indicates they were found to be less useful than hoped. The Web Explorer box contains an exercise to help you practise evaluating TED talks to determine the extent to which they might represent fads or valuable insights that you could apply in your own organization.

## Applying research

Although research results are often presented as objective, any scientific study involves some level of interpretation by the researcher. Just as we saw in our discussion of big data, this expert interpretation

---

 ## Web Explorer: Inspirational management talks

TED developed from an annual conference in California to a non-profit organization devoted to spreading ideas. The TED Talks website (www.ted.com/talks) hosts over 2,400 talks covering a huge range of subjects and describes itself as 'building a clearinghouse of free knowledge from the world's most inspired thinkers' (www.ted.com/about/our-organization). It is certainly the source of many of today's most popular and inspirational ideas about business. But do these talks present good advice or just another management fad?

Go to the TED Talks website and choose the 'Business' topic, then sort by 'most viewed' and watch a couple of the most popular talks. Use the following questions to evaluate what you are watching:

» How inspiring and interesting did you find the talk? What is your immediate response to it?

» What recommendations or advice is the person giving? How specific are the suggestions?

» What evidence does the speaker provide that this advice will work? How convincing do you find it?

» Would the recommendations work in any organization? What kind of contextual factors might be important to take account of?

» What kind of investment of time or money is required?

» Would you recommend this talk? Why?

Overall, this kind of evaluation can help you to think about whether the talk is about a fad that may soon disappear or a source of business advice that could genuinely improve your own and others' working lives.

is what turns raw data into something that can be used by other researchers or practitioners. That link between theory and practice is one of the biggest challenges faced by researchers and practitioners alike. For practitioners, it can be difficult to know how to apply the results of research: if it is very generalized, how do we know it will work for this specific situation? If it is a very specific case study, how can we apply the results to a different organization? For researchers, it can be challenging to know how to turn the research findings into practical recommendations that can be used by people from a range of different backgrounds and situations. These challenges do need to be met, however, because *evidence-based practice* is an essential component of professional practice. The Applications activity illustrates how research can be applied in practice in more detail.

## Applications: **Research implications**

Many research studies aim to identify causal relationships between different **variables** of interest in the workplace. If we are testing a causal relationship, the *independent variable* is the cause or predictor and the *dependent variable* is the effect or the outcome. Two other types of variables are moderators and mediators. *Moderators* increase or decrease the strength of the relationship, while *mediators* are the variables through which the independent variable has its effect.

Figure 12.3 illustrates the interaction of different variables in a study on HRM, engagement and organizational citizenship behaviour: certain HRM practices decreased employees' turnover intention and this relationship was stronger where there was positive organizational support (the moderator). HRM practices also improved engagement (the mediator), which in turn reduced turnover intention.

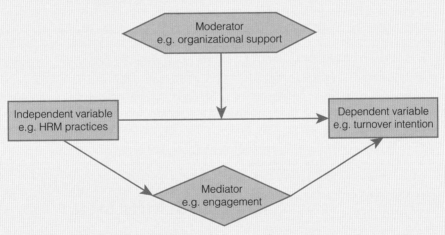

*Figure 12.3 The relationship between HRM, engagement and organizational citizenship behaviour*
Source: Based on findings in Alfes et al. (2013).

» Read Alfes et al.'s (2013) paper and identify further variables that they tested. Draw up a model similar to the example given above for the full set of variables, identifying independent, dependent, mediator and moderator variables. Note that you do not need to understand all the details of the statistical tests they conducted in order to do this. Simply identify the stated hypotheses and find out whether they were supported or not.

» What are the implications of these findings for HRM practice? Draw up a list of recommendations you could make for an HR department based on these findings.

## Evidence-based practice

What sets the professional practitioner apart from the layperson or the con artist is not simply that they claim to have evidence to support their claims or practices, but the *quality* of that evidence (Briner and Rousseau, 2011). **Evidence-based practice** involves drawing on personal experience and up-to-date knowledge of theory and interventions in order to develop a context-specific solution that has the highest possible chance of success. There are four sources of information that the evidence-based practitioner needs to integrate when making these decisions (Briner et al., 2009), as depicted in Figure 12.4.

Practitioner's own expertise and judgement

- Have I faced a similar situation before? What happened and what did I learn from it? Can I use that experience here?

Evidence from local context

- Seeking out information from the specific situation to help refine understanding and gain insight, e.g. What are the current strategies? What are the costs/benefits of intervention? What about the wider environment?

Critical evaluation of research evidence

- Using **systematic reviews** and evaluating different interventions. Using industry-level comparison data

Perspective of those affected

- How will employees feel about the intervention? What impact might it have on people at different levels or in different roles? Can they suggest alternatives?

*Figure 12.4 Sources of information for evidence-based practice*
Source: Based on Briner et al. (2009).

There are advantages for researchers who are also actively engaged in management practice (Saunders et al., 2009). They will have easier access to the data they need, whether research participants or organizational metrics. They also know the organization better than an outsider, which can help give them insights into the topic they are studying. But they also face particular challenges, such as having to overcome their own assumptions about a situation they are familiar with and negotiating the dual role of 'researcher' and 'management practitioner'.

We saw in the introduction to this chapter how difficult it is to sustain organizational performance in the long term. Big data and research findings can provide organizations with an evidence base to improve decision-making and help them to take advantage of emerging trends to ensure they stay competitive. But the other essential element is considering the wider context of the organization: what it exists for and how it can continue to meet its goals, as well as a deeper consideration of the organization's place in the wider environment.

These issues of organizational sustainability are part of the context we need to take account of when interpreting and applying data and research findings, but they also echo some of the debates we discussed in Part 1 around the reasons for and meaning of work.

# ORGANIZATIONAL SUSTAINABILITY

**Organizational sustainability** is all about seeing the organization in relationship with the whole environment. From the time of the Industrial Revolution in the West, if not earlier, the common approach to business and building organizations was to see them as having to fight 'against' nature for survival. Businesses had to overcome natural obstacles and work hard to extract as many natural resources from the world as possible. But recently, in line with the wider movement towards environmental sustainability, people have started to change the way they view their work organizations. A sustainable approach recognizes that the natural world is not simply something to be exploited for profit, but is our home and needs nurturing and protecting. An organization that wants long-term survival needs to ensure that it is contributing to that wider environment rather than just taking from it.

## Sustainability and the purpose of business

Discussions around sustainability and environmental/social responsibility are challenging because they strike at the root of our assumptions of what the purpose of our work organizations and businesses is. In this section we consider two alternative views of the purpose of business: the shareholder and stakeholder perspectives.

### *Shareholders*

We saw in Chapter 11 that some of the famous industrialists in the 18th and 19th centuries were actively trying to improve the lives of their employees and wider society by doing things such as providing housing, schooling and healthcare. The economist Milton Friedman, however, famously proclaimed that the only social responsibility that a business has is to maximize its profits, dismissing any claims that businesses should be considered to have any wider responsibilities to society, such as providing employment, eliminating discrimination or reducing pollution. Those who believed this were, in his words, 'unwitting puppets of the intellectual forces that have been undermining ... a free society' (Friedman, 1970). He felt that if people wanted social change, they should pay for it themselves, not expect businesses to invest in it. This shareholder or *profit maximization* view of business has been and continues to be influential (Carson, 1993).

However, this extreme individualist view, which sees only individual people (not corporations) as having responsibilities and then only to their shareholders, has been heavily critiqued. Chakraborty et al. (2004) note that wealth maximization has had devastating consequences, particularly in countries where the legal framework and governance structures are less powerful than the businesses operating there. Aiming for maximum profit has led to exploitation of workers, a disregard for health and safety at work, bribing of officials, and lethal pollution of the environment, as in the Deepwater Horizon oil spill in the Gulf of Mexico in 2010, for

example. This view values nothing at work unless it increases profits, and we can see its continuing influence in much of the HRM and OB literature, where researchers and practitioners feel the need to justify 'humane' management by showing how it contributes to the bottom line. A focus on employee well-being, for example, is only valid if it has a link with performance: 'if yoga reduces tension and high blood pressure, then human resources will "yield" more work and output' (Chakraborty et al., 2004, p. 101). The shareholder perspective also leads to a narrowly focused evaluation of performance that has knock-on effects on HR: performance is measured solely in terms of contributions to profit rather than a broader value proposition including customer service, engagement and longer term sustainability (Collings, 2014).

### *Stakeholders*

The **stakeholder view** provides a sharp contrast to the **shareholder view**. Instead of seeing the business as solely responsible to its shareholders, it recognizes that any organization has relationships with many constituent groups, which both affect and are affected by its decisions, and that the organization creates value of some kind for all of them. The stakeholder approach is drawn from an ecological framework, recognizing that the organization's survival is intimately bound up with its environment. All those stakeholders have valid interests, and organizational decision-making or strategy should not be dominated by the needs or desires of one group (Jones and Wicks, 1999). Primary stakeholders include people or groups such as employees, suppliers, financiers, customers and communities, while secondary stakeholders include the government, competitors, the media and so on (Freeman, 2007). Pursuing profit for shareholders at the expense of employee health or pollution of the natural environment is seen as unjustifiable. Instead of profit being an end in itself, it can become the means for the organization to achieve other ends. The debate around the stakeholder and shareholder perspectives as applied in public organizations is explored further in the Weighing the Evidence box.

The stakeholder perspective is particularly important for HRM because it changes the way we measure 'success' and can give a broader understanding of the contribution of HRM to the organization. HRM is often viewed as needing to

**A shareholder view in the public sector?**

While the stakeholder and shareholder views were developed in the context of privately owned companies, the basic ideas have sometimes also been applied to public organizations. For example, the **new public management (NPM) movement**, which emerged in the 1980s, claimed that management techniques from the private sector can (and should) be transferred to the public sector to improve quality and efficiency (Hood, 2001). Somewhat ironically, just as the private sector started to expand its understanding of value and success to include a variety of stakeholder interests, the public sector in countries such as the UK, the USA and Australia seemed to undergo 'reforms' based in a limited profit maximization perspective.

The evidence seems to indicate that NPM is not as effective as was originally expected. A meta-analysis of the impact of NPM in 10 European countries concluded that the evidence base for NPM reforms is 'fragile', with a substantial proportion reporting no or even negative effects of NPM adoption on performance (Pollitt and Dan, 2011). In addition, even for the positive impacts there was wide variability dependent on contextual factors. A review of the impact of NPM practices in local government in England found that there were negative relationships with customer satisfaction with local services, particularly in more deprived areas (Andrews and van de Walle, 2012).

For many policy makers and politicians, the underlying assumptions of this perspective go largely unquestioned and it becomes a moot point that the priority for public health services and government departments, for example, should be to operate *cost-effectively* rather than integrate the needs of different stakeholders. Public sector organizations, however, do not 'make a profit' for shareholders – or at least not in the way that Milton envisaged – and rarely operate in the free-market environment he considered necessary.

Instead, they exist to provide services and goods to the public. The range of these public services and goods varies from country to country, with, for example, some countries providing healthcare publically and others funding it through private insurance companies.

Traditionally, public sector organizations have focused on public accountability, becoming a model employer and valuing the public good. Public sector organizations differ from private sector in three key ways (Christensen et al., 2007):

1. **Leaders:** public sector leaders and the people who make decisions about how they should function are publically elected (at least in democratic countries).

2. **Multifunctional:** they do not exist to meet a single purpose (e.g. making profit) but inherently balance the needs of different groups, for example political steering versus a desire for impartiality and neutrality in service delivery.

3. **Do not operate in a free market:** although there has certainly been an attempt in recent years to make the public sector operate in a more 'market-like' way, these organizations often deal with problems that cannot be solved by a supposedly free market. Some services, for example police protection, benefit everyone in society but some individuals may be unwilling to pay for them directly. They therefore need to be funded through taxation. In addition, some public sector organizations are actually set up to deal with problems caused by private companies, for example regulation of air pollution.

Because of these differences, Christensen et al. (2007) suggest that a stakeholder perspective is more appropriate to the public sector than a variation of the shareholder perspective.

---

justify itself, and in a shareholder perspective, this justification has to be limited to how HR practices increase efficiency and financial performance. But a stakeholder perspective also gives weight to the other types of value that HRM adds, for example in its effect on customer satisfaction, organizational climate or individual employee experience (Colakoglu et al., 2006).

## Sustainability

Sustainability is a concept that has developed out of environmental concerns that the earth's natural resources were being exhausted and businesses were seen as dominating the natural environment. It is based on the principles of equity, consideration of the future, global environmentalism and biodiversity

(Basiago, 1995). In effect, sustainability is an ethical framework, one that recognizes the natural world as a legitimate stakeholder in work organizations and emphasizes a balanced approach – a balance between taking and giving, current and future needs.

Although based in ecology – the study of how biological organisms interact with each other and their environment – the concept of sustainability has become a broader framework for evaluating the effects of human actions on the social and natural world. Managing sustainably usually refers to ensuring that the organization actively works to integrate environmental issues into its strategy, but is also sometimes used to accentuate the organization's internally focused long-term strategy. HRM can make two distinct contributions to an organization pursuing sustainability. First, it can help to embed sustainability practices throughout the organization and, second, it can ensure HRM processes are themselves sustainable (Cohen et al., 2012). For example, sustainable HRM would need to consider how the organization can continue to develop or recruit people with the skill sets needed in the future, would have clear succession plans in place to ensure the organization could continue to flourish

even if key positions became vacant, and would also need to consider the longer term well-being of employees and the communities in which they live.

Sustainable organizations tend to adopt a 'triple bottom line' method of measuring performance, rather than relying solely on the financial bottom line (Elkington, 1997). This method evaluates economic, social and environmental performance, looking at the organization's practices in terms of how bearable, viable and equitable they are, as illustrated in Figure 12.5. Bearable practices are those which do not negatively impact on the people or the planet – or even have a positive impact; viable practices are of economic benefit to the organization and society as well as the environment; and equitable practices provide economic benefits as well as contributing to fairness and well-being among workers and the wider society. The In the News box (overleaf) explores parental leave policies using this triple bottom line model.

## Corporate social responsibility

Corporate social responsibility (CSR) emerged as a response to Friedman's profit maximization view, and an attempt to put the triple bottom

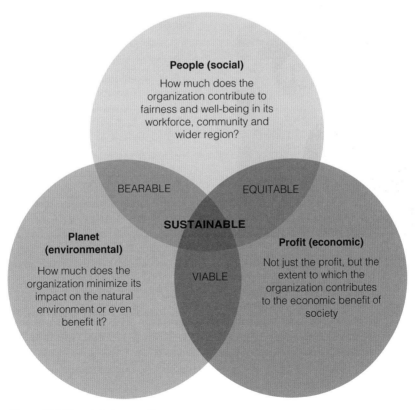

*Figure 12.5 The triple bottom line*

## In the News: **Paid parental leave**

The USA is the only developed country in the world with no national laws requiring paid parental leave (OECD Social Policy Division, 2016). While some individual states have started introducing basic parental leave, mostly it is left up to organizations themselves to decide if and how much leave they will offer. Tech companies seem to be leading the way here, with Etsy, for example, offering six months paid leave for all new parents, whether through birth or adoption (O'Connor, 2016). But 100 million employees in the USA are not offered paid parental leave and a quarter of new mothers go back to work within two weeks of giving birth (Dishman, 2016).

Getty Images

Heading the table of paid maternity leave in OECD countries is Bulgaria, with up to 60 weeks of paid maternity leave; the average across all countries is about 18 weeks (OECD Social Policy Division, 2016). The picture is very different for fathers, with nine countries offering no paid paternity leave and the average being less than a week. Rules in the UK changed in 2015 so that parental leave could be shared: mothers could effectively share their maternity leave with their partners, although take-up in the first year after it became law was still fairly low (Calnan, 2016).

In 2016, Meghann Foye released a novel called *Meternity* about a woman who fakes a pregnancy in order to get the 'perks' that her co-workers who are parents seem to get. It was based on her observations that mothers coming back from maternity leave were more sure of themselves and had a whole new perspective on work, which Foye thought might be due to the time 'detached from their desks' (Davies, 2016). She suggested that everyone would benefit from 'meternity' leave after a decade in work to help them rebalance their lives.

### For discussion

» Should different kinds of parents have different rights to parental leave, for example adoptive or birth parents, male or female? What about same-sex partnerships or single parents? Why do you think this? Should non-parents have a right to extended paid leave? Why or why not? (Consider how the stakeholder and shareholder perspectives might influence our assumptions about parental leave rights.)

» Evaluate the parental leave policy of your organization or country using the triple bottom line model. What kind of impact do you think an increase or decrease in the current arrangements would have?

line into practice. It holds that corporations do indeed have a social responsibility beyond making profit. Instead of assuming that profits would automatically benefit society, CSR dealt with the question of how firms could be expected to do good when profit was their only goal. Before the global financial crisis of 2007–8, CSR theorists

suggested that self-regulation and voluntary standards were ways for firms to demonstrate prosocial attitudes and behaviours within a profit-focused business environment. CSR was seen as a route to competitive advantage and justified in terms of its influence on the bottom line. But since the crisis and the recognition that self-regulation often simply does not happen, there has been a move back towards government regulation and calls for greater transparency in how businesses function. CSR is no longer solely discussed in terms of providing competitive advantage but in terms of an end in itself (Kemper and Martin, 2010).

## Green HRM: linking HR with environmental issues

There are increased calls for companies to be more socially and environmentally responsible in how they conduct their business and HRM has a role in supporting this change, particularly in terms of rewarding and measuring performance (Berrone and Gomez-Mejia, 2009). As we saw in Chapter 5, performance management has a great impact on the kinds of behaviours that employees engage in, as well as the values they follow in making their choices at work. *'Green' HRM* is a new field of study, which looks at how HRM can contribute to environmentally responsible change. It is about recognizing that environmental issues such as climate change and pollution need to be addressed by work organizations as well as individual citizens (Renwick et al., 2016).

The focus of many HRM scholars on demonstrating the economic value of HRM is typical of a shareholder perspective, but the emergence of green HRM allows the focus to widen to a stakeholder perspective. A strategic approach to HRM, which emphasizes environmental sustainability, acknowledges that all these stakeholders have a legitimate concern in the organization and that HRM has a central role in supporting learning and aligning everyday practices with environmental policies (Jackson and Seo, 2010). Green HRM can enhance the financial benefits that organizations can gain through a proactive approach to environmental management (O'Donohue and Torugsa, 2016).

Green HRM practices can also be seen as a way for organizations to respond to stakeholder pressures relating to environmental issues (Guerci et al., 2016a). These practices include incorporating environmental responsibilities into job descriptions and performance management systems, as well as providing environmental training and incentives to support green behaviours (Guerci and Carollo, 2016). Green HRM also recognizes the symbolic role of HRM systems. For example, linking executive pay to the achievement of environmentally friendly

targets sends a clear message to employees and external stakeholders that the organization prioritizes environmental impact as an indicator of overall performance (Berrone and Gomez-Mejia, 2009). Another example is a company planting a tree for each 'employee of the month' or funding their attendance at environmental charity events (Guerci and Carollo, 2016).

### Green HRM themes

The 2016 special issue of the *International Journal of Human Resource Management* explored the emergent research in green HRM around the world. Renwick et al. (2016), the editors, identified three general themes that demonstrate the range of practices and issues important in green HRM, shown in Figure 12.6. These themes are explored further in the Applications activity.

We can see how the green HRM approach can impact on the whole organization by considering the example of recruitment and selection. A green HRM approach here is focused on developing the organization's ability to manage in an environmentally conscious manner. This can be done by integrating environmental concerns throughout the attraction, recruitment and selection of candidates. For example, companies with green reputations are more attractive to candidates, and research has shown that this green reputation has an additive effect beyond the reputation of the company as an employer (Guerci et al., 2016b). This means that organizations wishing to be employers of choice should focus not only on building a reputation as a good employer, but also on how environmentally friendly they are. Second, HRM has a role in designing systems that can identify and recruit individuals with so-called 'green competencies' in order to aid the organization in meeting its environmental goals. These green competencies include environmental knowledge, as well as attitude and intention towards green purchasing, that is, preferring products or services that have a reduced impact on the environment or people's health (Subramanian et al., 2016).

Employee participation is a critical component of the effective 'greening' of organizational activities. But a study of the role of participation in emissions reductions showed that this participation needs to be substantive and embedded throughout the organization rather than just in the area of environmental concern (Markey et al., 2016).

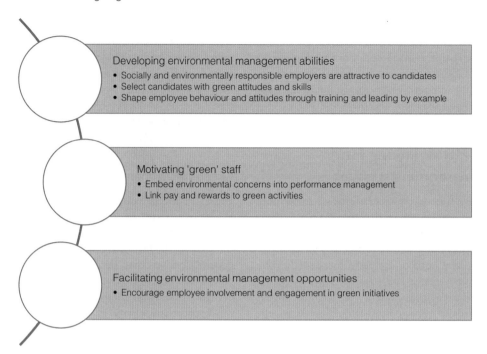

*Figure 12.6 Green HRM issues*

## Applications: **Greening HRM**

Margaret is the HRM director at a large construction company. Based on recent trends, she believes that the company is losing business and high-quality talent because it is not seen as environmentally friendly. She is meeting the rest of the board to present a plan for improving the company's green credentials. Because she is also personally passionate about the importance of being environmentally friendly, Margaret does not want this to become a 'greenwash', where the company tries to have a green image without making real changes. She believes that the HRM department can make a substantial contribution to encouraging the company along the path to greater environmental concern.

» Using the three themes identified by Renwick et al. (2016), what practical recommendations should Margaret take to the board?

## Green HRM challenges

Unfortunately, evidence indicates that organizations are not taking advantage of the possibilities of green HRM, with very few of them using HRM practices to encourage employees to become more environmentally friendly (Zibarras and Coan, 2015). Jackson and Seo (2010) note several barriers to the 'greening' of strategic HRM:

- **Apathy:** the biggest barrier to developing greener HRM. Many people still do not recognize the importance of environmental responsibility or prioritize taking action on it.

- **Complexity:** developing green HRM is not a simple process because of the complexity of knowing how different activities will affect the environment. Understanding these impacts requires detailed knowledge of whole processes within the organization, not simply specific knowledge of HRM systems.

- **Confusing terminology:** 'sustainability' is used to mean many different things, including environmental, social and developmental sustainability. In addition, sustainable HRM often refers only to a narrow set of practices for internal organizational issues such as health and safety.

Another challenge faced by green HRM is the fact that attitudes and practices that are relevant to environmental issues are learnt outside the workplace as well. So HR policies that focus only on employees' work lives are not enough (Jackson et al., 2011). Drawing on the literature around *work–life balance* and the interactions between the two spheres, Jackson et al. recommend a green work–life balance model to enhance the positive influences between work and non-work and reduce the negative ones. Examples of positive work-to-life interventions include:

- **Information-based:** give employees information and suggestions about how to make environmentally friendly decisions and actions, such as newsletters, blogs and so on.

- **Service-based:** provide easy access to green products and services, such as environmentally friendly options in the canteen, centralized ordering of organic fruit and vegetables, car-sharing system.

- **Finance-based:** offer employees financial incentives for green services and choices, such as subsidized public transport tickets, discounts on green services and products, or cycle-to-work schemes.

- **Time-based:** give employees the opportunity to work in a more environmentally friendly way, such as flexible working, which can reduce transport needs.

In addition, green HRM can bring about positive life-to-work spillover by encouraging employees to develop their environmental values at work. This can be done by involving them in designing environmental policies and activities, a suggestion scheme for green ideas, and rewarding green behaviour.

And finally, there are the specific challenges that MNCs face when trying to implement green HRM in various subsidiaries, as a case study of a US restaurant chain operating in three European countries demonstrated (Haddock-Millar et al., 2016). While the MNC and its subsidiaries shared an overall commitment to environmental issues, difficulties arose in terms of defining key objectives that could be embedded in performance management and engage the workforce in the different countries.

HRM faces several paradoxes as it attempts to integrate environmental concerns, and the success of green HRM is dependent on practitioners navigating these paradoxes appropriately within their specific contexts (Guerci and Carollo, 2016). One of these paradoxes is the tension between green and other important social or economic performance indicators. For example, if an organization is pursuing a cost reduction strategy, how can the HR team

*Getty Images/Yellow Dog Productions*

*Employees can get involved in environmental efforts.*

support green initiatives that cost money? A second paradox is how managers balance the professional requirements of the role with their own personal values about sustainability and environmental issues. The role of individual HR managers' competencies, particularly in terms of strategic positioning, has been found to be critical in the process of implementing green HRM (Yong and Mohd-Yusoff, 2016).

## SUMMARY

In this chapter we have looked at the essential elements in the quest to build future-proof organizations: the effective use of big data and research and how to build sustainability. The first element in ensuring organizational survival is making good use of organizational data and up-to-date research findings. Effective utilization of the huge amount of data available to modern organizations is certainly a challenge, but it is one that the organization of the future will need to excel at. In addition, competence in understanding and applying research helps to identify current trends and evaluate different ways of building and maintaining organizations.

We have also seen that a long-term, wider perspective on business (the stakeholder approach) allows us to redefine what is meant by organizational success so that it takes account of the organization's impact on the whole of its environment. The emerging field of green HRM takes these sustainability issues to heart by aiming to develop a workforce and organization that can make a positive impact on the wider environment. Bringing a concern for sustainability together with cutting-edge research will enable us to build organizations that stand the test of time.

 ### Practice Insights: Lara Montefiori

Lara Montefiori is Head of Psychology at Arctic Shores, a company that specializes in game-based assessment. In the video she explains what game-based assessment is all about and talks through some of its advantages and the challenges she faces, as well as how her company integrates scientific research with commercial awareness to create innovative products.

Go online to www.macmillanihe.com/sutton-people to access the interview with Lara.

## FURTHER READING

- For a provocative and thoughtful paper on the challenges of big data and analytics for the HR profession, see Angrave, D., Charlwood, A., Kirkpatrick, I. et al. (2016) 'HR and analytics: why HR is set to fail the big data challenge', *Human Resource Management Journal*, 26(1), pp. 1–11.

- For an excellent critique of the profit maximization paradigm from the point of view of academics, consultants and managers in a developing country, see Chakraborty, S. K., Kurien, V., Singh, J. et al. (2004) 'Management paradigms beyond profit maximization', *Journal for Decision Makers*, 29(3), pp. 97–117.

- For a report on the green practices that UK organsiations are adopting, see Zibarras, L., Judson, H. and Barnes, C. (2012) *Promoting Environmental Behaviour in the Workplace: A Survey of UK Organisations*. Available at: http://greenedge.co.za/files/Downloads-Pro-environmental-behaviour-in-the-workplace-UK-survey-2012.pdf.

## REVIEW QUESTIONS

1. How does the drive towards using big data and analytics differ from traditional (often academic) research efforts?

2. Why is it important for managers and HR practitioners to keep up to date with research?

3. Compare and contrast the shareholder and stakeholder perspectives and consider their implications for organizational sustainability.

## ONLINE RESOURCES

Go online to www.macmillanihe.com/sutton-people to access a MCQ quiz for this chapter and for further resources to support your learning.

## REFERENCES

Alfes, K., Shantz, A. D., Truss, C. and Soane, E. C. (2013) 'The link between perceived human resource management practices, engagement and employee behaviour: a moderated mediation model', *International*

*Journal of Human Resource Management*, 24(2), pp. 330–51. doi: 10.1080/09585192.2012.679950.

Alvesson, M. and Deetz, S. (2000) *Doing Critical Management Research*. London: Sage.

Andrews, R. and van de Walle, S. (2012) *New Public Management and Citizens' Perceptions of Local Service Efficiency, Responsiveness, Equity and Effectiveness, COCOPS Working Paper*. doi: 10.1080/14719037.2012.725757.

Angrave, D., Charlwood, A., Kirkpatrick, I. et al. (2016) 'HR and analytics: why HR is set to fail the big data challenge', *Human Resource Management Journal*, 26(1), pp. 1–11. doi: 10.1111/1748-8583.12090.

Basiago, A. D. (1995) 'Methods of defining "sustainability"', *Sustainable Development*, 3(3), pp. 109–19. doi: 10.1002/sd.3460030302.

Bedeian, A. G., Taylor, S. G. and Miller, A. N. (2010) 'Management science on the credibility bubble: cardinal sins and various misdemeanours', *Academy of Management Learning & Education*, 9(4), 715–25.

Berrone, P. and Gomez-Mejia, L. R. (2009) 'The pros and cons of rewarding social responsibility at the top', *Human Resource Management*, 48(6), pp. 959–71. doi: 10.1002/hrm.20324.

Briner, R. B. (2013) 'Unreliable evidence? Understanding and working with the limitations of the academic literature', *OP Matters*, 19, pp. 11–15.

Briner, R. B. and Rousseau, D. M. (2011) 'Evidence-based I–O psychology: not there yet', *Industrial and Organizational Psychology*, 4(1), pp. 3–22.

Briner, R. B., Denyer, D. and Rousseau, D. M. (2009) 'Evidence-based management: concept cleanup time?', *The Academy of Management Perspectives*, 23(4), pp. 19–32. Available at: http://amp.aom.org/content/23/4/19.abstract.

Calnan, M. (2016) 'Only 5 per cent of new fathers opt for shared parental leave', *People Management*, December. Available at: www2.cipd.co.uk/pm/peoplemanagement/b/weblog/archive/2016/12/15/only-5-per-cent-of-fathers-opt-for-shared-parental-leave.aspx (Accessed 10 January 2017).

Carson, T. (1993) 'Friedman's theory of corporate social responsibility', *Business & Professional Ethics Journal*, 12(1), pp. 3–32. Available at: www.jstor.org/stable/27800897.

Chakraborty, S. K., Kurien, V., Singh, J. et al. (2004) 'Management paradigms beyond profit maximization', *Journal for Decision Makers*, 29(3), pp. 97–117.

Christensen, T., Lægreid, P., Roness, P. G. and Røvik, K. A. (2007) *Organization Theory and the Public Sector: Instrument, Culture and Myth*. London: Routledge.

Church, A. H. and Dutta, S. (2013) 'The promise of big data for OD: Old wine in new bottles or the next generation of data-driven methods for change?', *OD Practitioner*, 45(4), pp. 23–31.

CIPD and Oracle (2013) *Talent Analytics and Big Data: The Challenge for HR*, CIPD Research Report. London. Available at: www.oracle.com/us/products/applications/human-capital-management/talent-analytics-and-big-data-2063584.pdf.

Cohen, E., Taylor, S. and Muller-Camen, M. (2012) *HRM's Role in Corporate Social and Environmental Sustainability, Advances in Developing Human Resources*. SHRM Foundation. Available at: www.shrm.org/hr-today/trends-and-forecasting/special-reports-and-expert-views/Documents/Corporate-Social-Environmental-Sustainability.pdf.

Colakoglu, S., Lepak, D. P. and Hong, Y. (2006) 'Measuring HRM effectiveness: considering multiple stakeholders in a global context', *Human Resource Management Review*, 16(2), pp. 209–18. doi: 10.1016/j.hrmr.2006.03.003.

Collings, D. G. (2014) 'Toward mature talent management: beyond shareholder value', *Human Resource Development Quarterly*, 25(3), pp. 301–19. doi: 10.1002/hrdq.21198.

Davies, A. (2016) 'I want all the perks of maternity leave – without having any kids', *New York Post*, 28 April. Available at: http://nypost.com/2016/04/28/i-want-all-the-perks-of-maternity-leave-without-having-any-kids/ (Accessed 10 January 2017).

Diebold, F. X. (2003) '"Big data" dynamic factor models for macroeconomic measurement and forecasting: a discussion of the papers by Lucrezia Reichlin and by Mark W. Watson', in M. Dewatripont, L. P. Hansen and S. J. Turnovsky (eds) *Advances in Economics and Econometrics*. Cambridge: Cambridge University Press, pp. 115–22.

Dishman, L. (2016) *How Paid Parental Leave Changed in 2016*, Fast Company. Available at: www.fastcompany.com/3066856/the-future-of-work/how-paid-parental-leave-changed-in-2016 (Accessed 10 January 2017).

Elkington, J. (1997) *Cannibals with Forks: The Triple Bottom Line of 21st Century Business*. Oxford: Capstone.

Foster, R. (2012) 'Creative destruction whips through corporate America', *Innosight Executive Briefing*, pp. 1–7.

Freeman, R. E. (2007) 'Managing for stakeholders', *SSRN Electronic Journal*, January, pp. 1–22. doi: 10.2139/ssrn.1186402.

Friedman, M. (1970) 'The social responsibility of business is to increase its profits', *The New York Times Magazine*, 13 September.

Guerci, M. and Carollo, L. (2016) 'A paradox view on green human resource management: insights from the Italian context', *International Journal of Human Resource Management*, 27(2), pp. 212–38. doi: 10.1080/09585192.2015.1033641.

Guerci, M., Longoni, A. and Luzzini, D. (2016a) 'Translating stakeholder pressures into environmental performance: the mediating role of green HRM practices', *International Journal of Human Resource Management*, 27(2), pp. 262–89. doi: 10.1080/09585192.2015.1065431.

Guerci, M., Montanari, F., Scapolan, A. and Epifanio, A. (2016b) 'Green and nongreen recruitment practices for attracting job applicants: exploring independent and interactive effects', *International Journal of Human Resource Management*, 27(2), pp. 129–50. doi: 10.1080/09585192.2015.1062040.

Haddock-Millar, J., Sanyal, C. and Müller-Camen, M. (2016) 'Green human resource management: a comparative qualitative case study of a United States multinational corporation', *International Journal of Human Resource Management*, 27(2), pp. 192–211. doi: 10.1080/09585192.2015.1052087.

Hamari, J., Koivisto, J. and Sarsa, H. (2014) 'Does gamification work? A literature review of empirical studies on gamification', *Proceedings of the Annual Hawaii International Conference on System Sciences*, pp. 3025–34. doi: 10.1109/HICSS.2014.377.

Harris, D. F. (2015) 'HR data privacy in the era of big data', *Workforce Solutions Review*, September, pp. 41–3.

Hood, C. (2001) 'New public management', *International Encyclopedia of the Social & Behavioral Sciences*, pp. 12553–6. doi: 10.1016/B0-08-043076-7/01180-3.

Jackson, S. E. and Seo, J. (2010) 'The greening of strategic HRM scholarship', *Organization Management Journal*, 7(4), pp. 278–90. doi: 10.1057/omj.2010.37.

Jackson, S. E., Renwick, D. W. S., Jabbour, C. J. C. and Muller-Camen, M. (2011) 'State-of-the-art and future directions for green human resource management', *Zeitschrift für Personalforschung*, 25(2), pp. 140–56. doi: 10.1688/1862-0000.

James, H. (2014) 'How the interaction of social and big data influences employee engagement', *Workforce Solutions Review*, 5(2), pp. 35–6.

Jones, T. M. and Wicks, A. C. (1999) 'Convergent stakeholder theory', *Academy of Management Review*, 24(2), pp. 206–21.

Kemper, A. and Martin, R. (2010) 'After the fall: the global financial crisis as a test of corporate social responsibility theories', *European Management Review*, 7(4), pp. 229–39. doi: 10.1057/emr.2010.18.

Laney, D. (2001) '3-D data management: controlling data volume, velocity and variety', *META Group Research Note*, February, p. 4. Available at: http://goo.gl/Bo3GS.

Linstead, S., Fulop, L. and Lilley, S. (2009) *Management and Organization: A Critical Text*. Basingstoke: Palgrave Macmillan.

Lipkin, J. (2015) 'Sieving through the data to find the person: HR's imperative for balancing big data with people centricity', *Cornell HR Review*, pp. 1–5.

McAbee, S. T., Landis, R. S. and Burke, M. I. (2017) 'Inductive reasoning: the promise of big data', *Human Resource Management Review*, 27(2), pp. 277–90. doi: 10.1016/j.hrmr.2016.08.005.

Markey, R., McIvor, J. and Wright, C. F. (2016) 'Employee participation and carbon emissions reduction in Australian workplaces', *International Journal of Human Resource Management*, 27(2), pp. 173–91. doi: 10.1080/09585192.2015.1045009.

Miller, D., Hartwick, J. and Le Breton-Miller, I. (2004) 'How to detect a management fad – and distinguish it from a classic', *Business Horizons*, 47(4), pp. 7–16. doi: 10.1016/S0007-6813(04)00043-6.

O'Connor, C. (2016) 'These companies all boosted paid parental leave in 2016', *Forbes*, December. Available

at: www.forbes.com/sites/clareoconnor/2016/12/30/these-companies-all-boosted-paid-parental-leave-in-2016/#208a3b92678d (Accessed 10 January 2017).

O'Donohue, W. and Torugsa, N. (2016) 'The moderating effect of "green" HRM on the association between proactive environmental management and financial performance in small firms', *International Journal of Human Resource Management*, 27(2), pp. 239–61. doi: 10.1080/09585192.2015.1063078.

OECD Social Policy Division (2016) *Key Characteristics of Parental Leave Systems*. Available at: www.oecd.org/els/soc/PF2_1_Parental_leave_systems.pdf.

Pollitt, C. and Dan, S. (2011) *The Impacts of the New Public Management in Europe: A Meta-analysis*. Available at: www.cocops.eu/wp-content/uploads/2012/03/WP1_Deliverable1_Meta-analysis_Final.pdf.

Renwick, D. W. S., Jabbour, C. J. C., Muller-Camen, M. et al. (2016) 'Contemporary developments in Green (environmental) HRM scholarship', *International Journal of Human Resource Management*, 27(2), pp. 114–28. doi: 10.1080/09585192.2015.1105844.

Rucci, A. J., Kirn, S. P. and Quinn, R. T. (1998) 'The employee-customer-profit chain at SEARS', *Harvard Business Review*, 76(1), pp. 82–97.

Saunders, M., Lewis, P. and Thornhill, A. (2009) *Research Methods for Business Students*. Harlow: Financial Times/Prentice Hall.

Sivarajah, U., Kamal, M. M., Irani, Z. and Weerakkody, V. (2017) 'Critical analysis of big data challenges and analytical methods', *Journal of Business Research*, 70, pp. 263–86. doi: 10.1016/j.jbusres.2016.08.001.

Subramanian, N., Abdulrahman, M. D., Wu, L. and Nath, P. (2016) 'Green competence framework: evidence from China', *International Journal of Human Resource Management*, 27(2), pp. 151–72. doi: 10.1080/09585192.2015.1047394.

Symon, G. and Cassell, C. (2012) 'Assessing qualitative research', in G. Symon and C. Cassell (eds) *Qualitative Organizational Research: Core Methods and Current Challenges*. London: Sage.

*The Economist* (2013) 'Robot recruiters; big data and hiring', *The Economist*, 407(8830), p. 78.

Tracy, S. J. (2010) 'Qualitative quality: eight "big-tent" criteria for excellent qualitative research', *Qualitative Inquiry*, 16(10), pp. 837–51. doi: 10.1177/1077800410383121.

Yong, J. Y. and Mohd-Yusoff, Y. (2016) 'Studying the influence of strategic human resource competencies on the adoption of green human resource management practices', *Industrial and Commercial Training*, 48(8), pp. 416–22. doi: 10.1108/ICT-03-2016-0017.

Zibarras, L. D. and Coan, P. (2015) 'HRM practices used to promote pro-environmental behavior: a UK survey', *International Journal of Human Resource Management*, 26(16), pp. 2121–42. doi: 10.1080/09585192.2014.972429.

# PART 4 CASE STUDY: THE END OF THE CIRCUS?

The Ringling Bros and Barnum & Bailey Circus had a history stretching back nearly 150 years in the USA when the decision was taken in 2017 that it would close. It meant over 400 employees losing their jobs and 60 performing animals needing to be rehomed. How did a circus that had survived the Great Depression, two world wars and dramatic changes in societal tastes and expectations from entertainment lose its momentum?

The history of this circus shows an organization that was able to undergo dramatic changes and face significant challenges while remaining profitable. The Ringling Bros circus began in the 1880s, the same decade that P.T. Barnum partnered with James Bailey to form the circus that would eventually become Barnum & Bailey (Associated Press & wltx, 2017). These two circuses were both touring entertainment shows with human and animal performers and for a while they split the USA between them rather than competing directly with each other. When James Bailey died in 1907, the Ringling brothers bought Barnum & Bailey and merged the two shows. In 1967, the circus was bought by Feld Entertainment. The parent company now produces several other live touring entertainment shows around the world, including Disney on Ice, and presents about 5,000 shows a year (Marketline, 2015).

Circus life is sometimes viewed as having quite a romantic appeal and Megan O'Malley (2015), a musician who worked for Ringling Bros, lists several positive points about working for the circus. She enjoyed travelling and meeting new people, living on the circus train, working with passionate and gifted performers, and doing what she loves as a job. She also notes that the circus has a guiding premise that 'the show must go on', no matter what. This was highlighted in dramatic fashion in 2004 when acrobat Dessi España fell to the ground during her performance. Clowns came out to distract the audience while she was being treated and although she died later that night from her injuries, the later show that same day continued as normal (Asis, 2014).

The circus has faced many challenges in its history, including several tragedies, such as a fire in 1944 that killed 167 people and led to several executives going to jail for negligence. Ringling Bros and Barnum & Bailey made many changes to its programme over the years to stay in tune with changing tastes and customer desires. When it was acquired by Irving Feld in the late 1960s, for example, the 'freak show' element, which involved displaying people with physical deformities, was removed. Most recently, increasing pressure

from animal rights groups led to the circus retiring its elephants from the live shows. The US organization People for the Ethical Treatment of Animals (PETA, 2017) had campaigned for the retirement of all live animal acts from Ringling Bros for 36 years. PETA claimed that circus animals were treated cruelly during training and that the transportation involved harsh conditions, although lawsuits brought against the company failed (Neuhaus, 2017). When the announcement of the closure came, PETA released a statement saying that society has changed to such an extent that people are now unwilling to go and see shows that capture and exploit wild animals.

Despite the many changes and evolutions the circus went through in its nearly 150-year history, by 2016 ticket sales were declining and costs increasing to the point where it was no longer feasible to keep it running. The decline in sales had been continuous over eight or nine years but dropped dramatically when the elephants were retired (Neuhaus, 2017). The circus was also facing high costs, including such unsustainable components as moving the whole show by rail and providing a school for performers' children (Ellis-Petersen, 2017). While entertainment shows based on human acrobatics, such as Cirque de Soleil, remain very popular (Ellis-Petersen, 2017), the end of Ringling Bros and Barnum & Bailey in 2017 may signal the end of traditional circus acts.

- What were the main challenges Ringling Bros faced? Why do you think it failed in 2017 when it had survived dramatic changes and challenges over the previous century and a half?

- Ringling Bros employed a wide variety of highly skilled people, yet in its later years did not seem able to continue its development. To what extent could it have adopted the principles of a learning organization and how might that have impacted on its long-term sustainability?

- Can organizations such as circuses, where the work inherently involves physical risk, ever really promote the well-being of their staff? Do you think that Ringling Bros could have developed a better response to concerns over animal welfare that would have enhanced rather than undermined its future?

- What changes do you think the circus should have made to build a sustainable future? Would adopting a stakeholder perspective have helped here or has society changed so much that any kind of circus will fail?

# REFERENCES

Asis, A. (2014) 'The most horrifying circus accidents in history'. Available at: www.therichest.com/rich-list/most-shocking/the-most-horrifying-circus-accidents-in-history/ (Accessed 17 January 2017).

Associated Press & wltx (2017) 'The history of Ringling Bros and Barnum & Bailey Circus'. Available at: www.wltx.com/news/the-history-of-ringling-bros-and-barnum-bailey-circus/386169905 (Accessed 17 January 2017).

Ellis-Petersen, H. (2017) 'The big stop: Ringling Bros circus closes after 146 years'. *The Guardian*, 17 January.

Marketline (2015) *Feld Entertainment, Inc.: Company Profile*.

Neuhaus, L. (2017) 'Without elephants, the circus couldn't go on, Ringling Bros. officials say'. *Los Angeles Times*, 16 January.

O'Malley, M. (2015) 'What's it like to work at Ringling Brothers and Barnum & Bailey Circus?' Available at: www.quora.com/Whats-it-like-to-work-at-Ringling-Brothers-and-Barnum-Bailey-Circus (Accessed 17 January 2017).

PETA (2017) 'It's over for Ringling Bros. Circus'. Available at: www.peta.org/blog/ringling-bros-its-over/ (Accessed 17 January 2017).

# GLOSSARY

| Term | Definition |
|---|---|
| 360-degree appraisal | Measures an employee's performance; draws on the evaluations of superiors, peers, subordinates and sometimes even customers or clients; also known as 'multisource appraisal' |
| Action research | Applied research process; involves a thorough analysis and understanding of the situation followed by taking action to achieve a desired outcome and reflection on the process |
| Adhocracy | Type of organizational structure with specialized but informal jobs; uses collaboration and decentralized decision-making. Associated with complex, dynamic environments |
| Adverse impact | Sometimes, groups of people, e.g. men and women, score differently on a selection measure. If this difference means that one group is less successful in gaining the job, the measure has an *adverse impact* on that group |
| Analytics | Ways of analysing and making sense of big data |
| Assessment centre | In selection, combination of several selection methods to distinguish between job candidates, usually based on a competency framework |
| Attitude | Evaluative judgement of an object |
| Attributions | Processes we use to make sense of other people's behaviour; the reason we think they did something. When explaining people's behaviour, we tend to overestimate the effect of personality or internal qualities and underestimate the effect of the situation |
| Authentic leadership | Based on the leader's personal values; involves a high degree of self-awareness. Authentic leaders are set apart from other leaders by their high moral character |
| Autonomy | Amount of freedom you have to make your own decisions at work |
| Balanced scorecard | Method for evaluating the individual or organization's performance using non-financial as well as financial measurements |
| Behaviourally anchored rating scales (BARS) | Used to measure employee performance; a numerical scale 'anchored' by specific behaviours. Less effective behaviours are given a low score, while more effective behaviours are given a higher score |
| Behavioural theory of leadership | Attempts to identify the behaviours that leaders exhibit rather than their personal traits. Often grouped into people-focused or task-focused behaviours |
| Behaviour modelling training (BMT) | Training based on social learning theory; defines the behaviours to be learnt, provides clear models of those behaviours and gives feedback as people practise them |
| Bias | In selection, bias occurs when a measure systematically overestimates or underestimates the performance of people from different groups |
| Big data | Increased availability and quantity of data resulting from technological advances in data storage and recording |
| Big Five | Comprehensive, universal model of personality that recognizes five broad traits:<br><br>• Extraversion: outgoing and confident vs reserved and quiet<br>• Agreeableness: friendly and considerate vs forthright and argumentative<br>• Emotional stability: calm and unemotional vs sensitive and easily upset<br>• Conscientiousness: organized and dependable vs flexible and disorganized<br>• Openness to experience: creative and imaginative vs down-to-earth and conventional |
| Biodata | Collection of information about a person's life and work experience, e.g. qualifications or job history |
| Bureaucracy | 'Ideal' organizational structure, based on clear hierarchy and rules, job specialization and division of labour, and objective criteria for appointments and evaluations |
| Burnout | End result of prolonged stress at work: emotional exhaustion, cynical attitude towards clients, and dissatisfaction with oneself and one's work efforts |

| Career path | Routes through the organization for people who wish to develop their careers. Traditionally, paths were hierarchical but, in flatter organizations, they increasingly include horizontal moves |
|---|---|
| Centralization | Extent to which authority and decision-making power are located at the top of the organizational hierarchy |
| Chain of command | Chain of reporting relationships through the organization; a way of describing the hierarchical structure. Clear chain of command helps workers to know who they report to |
| Classical conditioning | Simple associative learning: we learn to associate a new stimulus with a certain response |
| Climate | Another term for organizational or team culture, although there is some debate (see Chapter 7) |
| Coaching | Guiding employees in their development at work and career direction, usually in a one-to-one relationship |
| Cognitive appraisal | Process by which we determine whether a particular encounter or experience is relevant to our well-being or how stressful it is |
| Cognitive bias | Shortcuts our minds make, to try and save us time when dealing with a complex world, can become the source of biases in decision-making, e.g. when making decisions in interviewing |
| Collective representation | Employees may form groups in order to negotiate the terms of the employment relationship |
| Communication | Active process of transmitting and understanding information |
| Communities of practice | Networks of people that help each other to develop the knowledge they need in order to complete their tasks |
| Competency | Meaningful workplace behaviours or outcomes associated with effective performance in a job. Often used as the basis for selection decisions |
| Competency framework | Detailed description of all the competencies required for a particular job; can be used as a basis for selection, development and performance appraisal. An organization-wide competency framework outlines the competencies required by workers across the whole organization |
| Construct validity | Extent to which a test accurately measures the construct it claims to measure |
| Content validity | Extent to which a measure is representative of the *whole* of the ability or attribute it claims to measure |
| Contingency theory | Recognizes there is no 'one best way' but that the best course of action is dependent (contingent) on the situation. Contingency theories attempt to define the characteristics of a situation that determine which approach will work best |
| Contingency theory of leadership (Fiedler) | Defines aspects of the situation that interact with leader styles to determine effectiveness |
| Continuing (or continuous) professional development (CPD) | Ongoing development of skills and knowledge to ensure that professionals stay up to date with current practice |
| Coping | Mechanisms or strategies for reducing stress; can be emotional or cognitive |
| Corporate social responsibility (CSR) | Strategic approach to setting out the ethical principles that guide the organization's actions, including taking responsibility for the effect of those actions on all potential stakeholders |
| Criterion validity | How well a measure predicts something important in the real world of work. This link can be established *concurrently* or *predictively*:<br><br>• Concurrent criterion validity: the test and criterion measure are taken at the same time, indicating whether the test predicts current employees' performance<br>• Predictive criterion validity: there is a time gap between the two, indicating whether the test predicts future performance |
| Culture | A group's shared understanding of the customary ways of thinking and doing things (their 'norms'); helps to distinguish one group of people from another |

| Decentralization | Extent to which people at the lower levels of the organization have control over decisions |
|---|---|
| Declarative knowledge | Knowledge you can express, e.g. in a written test |
| Departmentalization | Individual jobs are grouped together dependent on their function or their market |
| Development | Personal and professional growth relevant to employees' future career |
| Divisional structure | Groups of departments that operate as separate business units, with head office providing overall strategic planning control |
| Division of labour | Dividing work into smaller components based on the skills that are needed. Each employee completes a part of the overall task and can become more efficient at it |
| Double-loop learning | Process of questioning and adjusting underlying objectives or policies, rather than simply trying to meet them |
| Ecological fallacy | A fault in reasoning made when we assume something about an individual based on something we know about a group |
| E-learning | Training method involving delivering training by electronic means |
| Emergent change | Made up of ongoing adaptations and alterations that ultimately produce fundamental changes that were not planned for or perhaps even expected |
| Emotional labour | Workers are expected to follow rules about how and when they display emotion, managing or working with their own or others' emotions |
| Employee assistance programme (EAP) | Umbrella term for a collection of assistance programmes and well-being initiatives an organization can introduce to help employees deal with potential stressors |
| Employee voice | Contribution or 'say' employees have in the organization |
| Employer branding | Idea that an organization can build up a brand (or reputation) for itself as an employer: a good employer brand can help the organization attract and retain the best calibre and best suited employees |
| Engagement | Feeling positive towards work and actively involved in it |
| Equity theory | Suggests we want fairness and are motivated by how equitable we think our efforts and rewards are in comparison with other people's |
| ERG theory (Alderfer) | Suggests we are motivated by the needs for existence, relatedness and growth |
| Evidence-based practice | Drawing on personal experience and up-to-date knowledge of theory and interventions in order to develop a context-specific solution with the highest possible chance of success |
| Expectancy theory (Vroom) | Motivation theory suggesting our level of motivation is based on our expectations of the outcome or end result of our efforts |
| Experiential learning | 'Learning by doing'; involves reflecting on experiences in order to learn from them |
| Face validity | The measure *appears* to assess what it claims to assess |
| Fairness | In selection, ensures that candidates are treated equally and the decision is made based on fair and balanced procedures |
| Five forces | The five basic forces in the environment that influence an organization's strategic positioning |
| Flexible benefits | Organization offers employees a range of different benefits of varying value and employees can choose the ones they prefer |
| Formalization | Extent to which the organization has clearly defined rules and procedures |
| Gig economy | Describes the increasing prevalence of on-demand, short-term work that is replacing traditional secure employment |
| Globalization | Increasing global, economic interdependence of countries |

| Goal-setting theory (Locke and Latham) | Theory of motivation and performance that emphasizes how conscious goals can affect performance |
|---|---|
| Green HRM | Contributes to environmentally responsible change, based on a recognition that environmental issues need to be addressed by work organizations as well as individual citizens |
| Groupthink | Tendency some groups have towards seeking agreement, to the exclusion of a realistic appraisal of the situation or consideration of alternative courses of action |
| Hard HRM | Quantitative approach to HRM; managing 'human resources' in the same way as other factors and emphasizing the business strategy |
| Hawthorne effect | Changes in performance due to employees feeling observed or knowing that someone is paying attention to them. Named after a series of experiments conducted by Elton Mayo and associates at the Hawthorne factory |
| Horizontal fit | Emphasis in SHRM on the integration of different HR practices into a coherent system |
| HR bundles | SHRM approach that recommends bundling together mutually reinforcing sets of HR practices |
| Human Resource Management (HRM) | Management of work and employees towards the organization's goals. Gives a central place to the employment relationship and ideally should consider the strategic integration of HR activities with organizational strategy |
| Implicit leadership theory | Suggests that a leader's effectiveness is largely determined by followers' perceptions; followers have an unconscious set of expectations about what a leader will be like. Leaders who conform better to the expectations are seen as more effective |
| Implicit needs (McClelland) | Motivation is based on our individual levels of three main (unconscious) needs:<br><br>• Affiliation (nAff): desire to build friendly, cooperative relationships<br>• Achievement (nAch): drive to do well, to succeed<br>• Power (nPow): desire to have influence over others |
| Informal learning | Relevant to job performance but not organized by the employing organization |
| Internal consistency (reliability) | Checks that different parts of the test are measuring the same thing; e.g., in a questionnaire measuring cognitive ability, are a person's scores on one half of the questionnaire similar to their scores on the other? |
| Inter-rater reliability | Measure of how well two or more different raters, e.g. interviewers, agree on the ratings they give to an individual |
| Intrinsic rewards | Suggestion that some activities are inherently rewarding to us |
| Job analysis | Identifies the knowledge, skills and behaviours that contribute to good job performance for a specific role |
| Job characteristics model (Hackman and Oldham) | Emphasizes how particular job characteristics, e.g. skill or task variety, influence our internal motivation |
| Job crafting | Process of redesigning our own job by changing the task or relational boundaries of the work |
| Job demands-resources (JD-R) model of stress | Captures the positive and negative aspects of stress; shows how they are related to job demands, e.g. workload and pressure, and job resources, e.g. feedback and participation |
| Job design | How the organization can redesign work in order to try and motivate employees or reap other positive outcomes of enriched jobs |
| Job enrichment | Process of increasing the autonomy and responsibility in a job |
| Job satisfaction | Evaluation of how happy or content we are with our jobs |
| Knowledge | Resources, e.g. facts, information, skills, that the organization has |
| Knowledge management | How the organization manages its knowledge resources to meet its current and future needs |
| Knowledge society | Where knowledge is the primary resource for individuals and organizations |

| Knowledge work | Involves employees generating value for the organization by using their minds rather than physical efforts |
|---|---|
| Knowledge, skills and abilities (KSAs) | Knowledge, skills and abilities required to perform effectively in a particular job |
| Labour market power | Power an organization has to attract and retain workers; can be created through good remuneration packages, e.g. salary, benefits, working conditions etc., or because there are few viable employment alternatives |
| Labour mobility | Extent to which workers are able to move around for work |
| Leader | Someone who is able to influence others to work towards a goal |
| Leader–member exchange theory (LMX) | Recognizes that leaders have different relationships with different followers: high quality of exchange with an ingroup and low quality of exchange with an outgroup |
| Learning | Acquisition of new knowledge or skills |
| Learning organization | Proactive in its approach to change, encourages and facilitates learning by all its members and engages in continual transformation and development |
| Learning style | Suggestion that different people learn things in different ways |
| Management by objectives | Performance goals are agreed between the employee and the manager; later performance appraisals are based on the extent to which these goals are achieved |
| Mechanistic structure | Rigid organizational structure; usually consisting of centralization, high level of job specialization and strict hierarchies |
| Meta-analysis | Research study that evaluates the relationships between variables across a large number of studies |
| Motivation theory | Explanation of the intensity, direction and persistence of the effort we put into work |
| Musculoskeletal disorders | Range of disorders that can develop at work, such as upper and lower back pain and repetitive strain injuries |
| New public management | Approach to public sector management, which emerged in the 1980s, claiming that management techniques from the private sector can (and should) be transferred to the public sector to improve quality and efficiency |
| Occupational health and safety (OHS) | Anticipating and controlling hazards at work |
| Operant conditioning | Explanation of how the *consequences* of a response or action influence our learning |
| Organic structure | Flexible organizational structure with little hierarchy, decentralized decision-making and high levels of interaction between members |
| Organizational Behaviour (OB) | Study of how people behave in organizations and how organizations themselves behave |
| Organizational commitment | A person's psychological bond to an organization: how attached they feel and how much effort they will put into supporting it |
| Organizational learning | Integration and embedding of individual learning into and through the whole organization |
| Organizational sustainability | Recognizing that work organizations are in relationship with the whole environment; long-term survival needs to be based on contributing to that wider environment rather than just taking from it |
| Organization Development (OD) | Approach to organizational change that emphasizes organization-wide interventions to ensure continual organizational survival |
| Path–goal theory of leadership (House) | Leadership is essentially motivational; that is, an effective leader motivates followers by clarifying the path they need to take to achieve a goal |
| Performance-based pay | Pay based on employees' job performance |
| Performance management | Systems for managing employee performance by clarifying expectations and goals and providing feedback on progress |
| Personality | An individual's stable patterns of thinking, feeling and behaving |
| Personality theory of leadership | Centres around identifying the personality traits associated with leadership |

| | |
|---|---|
| Personal transitions | Psychological processes we go through when dealing with change |
| Piece-rate pay | Employees are paid per item they produce or amount they sell |
| Pluralist | View of organizations which recognizes that different groups of employees will have different interests and will actively pursue them, and that power is not limited to those with formal authority but comes from a range of sources in an organization |
| Preferential selection | Approach to dealing with equality at work; standards for selection are lowered in order to increase the success of an underrepresented group |
| Procedural knowledge | Knowledge of how to do things, also known as 'skills' |
| Psychological contract | Perceptions that individual workers and the organization have of the respective obligations implied in the employment relationship |
| Psychometrics | Literally, a 'measure of the mind'; systematic ways of trying to measure psychological phenomena, e.g. intelligence or personality traits |
| Punctuated equilibrium model of change | Proposes that sudden large changes are interspersed with longer periods of relative stability |
| Radical | View of organizations which holds that management and workers will always be in conflict, because elite groups maintain control and engage in manipulation and suppression of the interests of conflicting groups |
| Recruitment channels | Routes for attracting and recruiting job candidates, e.g. job boards, adverts |
| Reference | Common part of the selection process; involves asking a potential employee's previous employer for relevant job performance information |
| Reliability | A reliable measure is one that gives consistent results |
| Resilience | Our ability to maintain our equilibrium in the face of stressful events |
| Resource-based view | Strategic approach that analyses the organization's current resource profile and from there develops a strategy for its optimal activities |
| Scientific management | Attempt to use the scientific method to study management techniques; aimed to find the most efficient ways of doing a job to improve productivity |
| Scientific method | Five-stage process for explaining why things are the way they are:<br>1. Observe patterns or regularities in the world<br>2. Develop a possible explanation (theory)<br>3. From that explanation, develop a specific prediction<br>4. Test the prediction<br>5. Evaluate the explanation and refine it if necessary |
| Shareholder view | View that business exists purely to create value for shareholders; also known as 'profit maximization' |
| Single-loop learning | Enables the organization to meet its current objectives: it can take in and evaluate information in order to take action within a certain set of parameters |
| Social learning theory | Suggests we learn complex behaviours by copying other people |
| Soft HRM | Emphasizes human interactions, focusing on communication, leadership and motivation |
| Span of control | Number of people whose work the manager is responsible for coordinating |
| Stakeholder view | View of business that recognizes that any organization has relationships with many constituent groups, which affect and are affected by its decisions, and that the organization creates value of some kind for all of them |
| Strategic HRM | Emphasizes a strategic approach to managing human resources within the organization; targeted focus on how HRM is critical to organizational success |
| Strategy | Organization's understanding of the business it is, or should be, in and its plan for future success |
| Strengths-based development | Approach to personal and professional development; builds on our strengths and finds new ways of applying them, rather than focusing on weaknesses |
| Stress | Process our bodies go through when we are faced with a potential threat, or 'stressor', in order to prepare us for action |

| Stress (types) | General term for the sense that we are under pressure; usually used to mean negative pressure or levels we cannot comfortably cope with: eustress – positive stress, distress – negative stress |
|---|---|
| Sustainability | Ethical framework that recognizes the natural world as a legitimate stakeholder in work organizations and emphasizes a balanced approach: a balance between taking and giving, current and future needs |
| SWOT analysis | Analysis of the organization's current strengths and weaknesses as well as an understanding of environmental opportunities and challenges |
| Systematic review | Research study that systematically draws together and evaluates a wide range of evidence to address a practice-based question |
| Talent acquisition strategy | HR strategy and practices for attracting the best talent to the organization from external sources |
| Talent improvement strategy | HR strategy that aims to provide continuous training, development and guidance for existing employees in order to maximize their talents and contributions |
| Talent management | Attracting, developing and retaining the people the business needs to meet its current and future goals |
| Test-retest reliability | Test must give us consistent results if given to the same people on different occasions |
| Total reward | Provides employees with a clearer understanding of the value of their total reward package, including salary and other benefits |
| Trade unions | Membership-based organizations that usually exist independently of the employer; represent the views and interests of their members as well as providing some protection to them when needed |
| Training | Process of helping employees to develop the knowledge, skills and abilities needed for their current roles or jobs in the near future |
| Training transfer | Extent to which what we learn in one situation is 'transferred' to a new situation |
| Transactional leadership | Based on a transaction between the leader and the follower; good performance is rewarded and poor performance is punished |
| Transfer of learning | The content of what we learn is often reliant on the context in which we learn it, so an important part of training is helping people to transfer or apply their learning from one context to another |
| Transferrable skills | Skills that are needed in a variety of contexts within and outside employment, e.g. communication or teamworking |
| Transformational leadership | Based on engaging followers' emotions and inspiring them to achieve certain goals |
| Unitarist | Approach or underlying assumption that assumes that organizations and employees have a single goal. Views conflict in the organization as dysfunctional and sees managers as the legitimate (and only) source of power |
| Validity | A valid measure is one that is actually measuring what it claims to measure |
| Values | The things we believe are important in life |
| Variable | Concept or characteristic we want to know more about in research:<br><br>• Independent variable: the cause or predictor<br>• Dependent variable: the effect or the outcome<br>• Moderating variable: increases or decreases the *strength* of the relationship<br>• Mediating variable: the variable through which the independent variable has its effect |
| Vertical fit | An emphasis in SHRM on aligning HR practices with organizational context and strategy |
| Voluntary work | Commonly thought of as work that is given freely rather than in exchange for pay, but there is debate over the definition (see Chapter 2) |
| Well-being | General term for psychological, social and physical health and contentment |
| Work councils | Elected employees make up a formal, independent representation of workers' interests within the organization |

| Workforce planning | Clarifies how the business strategy will be operationalized through the organization's human resources |
|---|---|
| Work orientation | Purpose that paid work serves in an individual's life; the meaning an individual finds in work |
| Work–life balance | How we balance the time and resources we invest in work and home or leisure activities; sometimes referred to as work–non-work balance to emphasize that work is part of our lives |
| Work sample | In selection, exercise designed to be as close as possible to the work done in a particular job; provides evidence of how a job applicant performs in a realistic job situation |

# INDEX